*Modern and
Classical Essayists*

Modern and Classical Essayists

Twelve Masters

PAUL MARX

University of New Haven

Mayfield Publishing Company
Mountain View, California
London • Toronto

Library of Congress Cataloging-in-Publication Data
Modern and classical essayists: twelve masters / [edited by] Paul
  Marx.
       p.   cm.
    Includes index.
    ISBN 1-55934-451-2
    1. College readers.   2. English language—Rhetoric.   3. Essays.
  I. Marx, Paul
  PE1417.M573   1995
  808′ .0427—dc20   95-17608
                                                        CIP

Manufactured in the United States of America
10   9   8   7   6   5   4   3   2   1

Mayfield Publishing Company
1280 Villa Street
Mountain View, CA 94041

Sponsoring editor, Thomas V. Broadbent; production
editor, Julianna Scott Fein; manuscript editor, Barney
Hamby; art director, Jeanne M. Schreiber, text and cover
designer, Donna Davis; manufacturing manager, Randy
Hurst. The text was set in 11/12 Bembo by Graphic
World and printed on 50# Text White Opaque by The
Maple-Vail Book Manufacturing Group.

Letter to the Instructor

With the publication since the 1960s of hundreds of college readers, do we need still another one? Well, let me explain what motivated me to put this book together. First, there was the recurring disappointment of opening a newly arrived essay collection and discovering that the book's earliest writer was Virginia Woolf; I was disappointed because some of the most rewarding essayists wrote long before Woolf. As a result of recent fashions in essay collections, perhaps ninety percent of American students would go through college without ever reading an essay by Emerson or Hazlitt or Lamb! But I not only wanted a book that included older, classical writers; I also wanted the writers to be represented in some depth—with at least three essays. Finally, I wanted a book that, in addition to good reading, would offer some practical instruction in writing.

Tom Broadbent, Mayfield Publishing's veteran English editor, was very quick to see the need for and the logic of the book I proposed to him. So here we have a book that offers earlier writers along with moderns—to the depth of three or four essays each. The book also offers, in the twelve Nuts and Bolts sections, discussions expressly intended to help students become better writers. With this kind of book, we are going against the trend among composition instructors of relying on anthologies organized around the "patterns" of exposition. It is my firm conviction that books with rhetorical patterns as their organizing principle are of only minimal value in helping students become better writers. In the real world, writers just don't think much about patterns of exposition. And if they do, such thinking occurs only when they are well into a piece, not at the outset. The composition assignment in which a student is asked to write in one dominant pattern is artificial and creates the false impression that in a good piece of writing there is always one dominant pattern. Too often, having given such assignments, instructors feel compelled to grade compositions on the basis of how well instructions have been followed rather than on the overall merits of the writing.

To find examples of writing in one dominant pattern, editors of anthologies organized around patterns frequently stretch the meaning of the term *essay* to include chapters or sections of chapters from books. In my opinion, to do that is to misrepresent what an essay is. Essay writers know they have a more or less limited scope; writers of books do not feel the same constraint. Writing a chapter for a book is not the same as writing an essay.

There are no chapters or fragments of chapters in this collection of essays.

Since the *New York Times* began publishing its op-ed page in the 1960s, op-eds have become a favorite form of contemporary essay writers. Many excellent essays have been written at the op-ed length of 600–750 words (I've written a good number of op-eds myself). But too many essay books are overloaded with op-eds. An op-ed does not demand of a reader the patience and concentration that a longer essay does, nor does it offer the satisfaction that comes with having stayed with a writer throughout his or her treatment of a subject. Although there are some shorter essays in this book, most of the essays are longer; in contrast to the few minutes required to read an op-ed, some of the essays here may require an hour or more. To some students, bearing with a longer essay will be burdensome. But if a student is to succeed as a white-collar professional or become more than a surface intellectual, he or she must be capable of sustained reading.

Normally, the inclusion of older, classical essayists would dictate a chronological ordering. But a chronological ordering would put the most difficult reading for students at the beginning. To avoid making students struggle at the outset, I decided to use reverse chronological order. That way, instructors who choose to follow the order of the book will begin with the most recent writers, whose vocabulary and style should pose the least difficulty for students. Furthermore, as students' vocabularies grow (as they will even through reading relatively easy essays), students will become better prepared to tackle the older writers.

To be consistent, I have used reverse chronological order for the essays by each writer: For each essayist, the most recent essay appears first and the oldest essay last; an essay written in the latter part of a career appears first and an early essay last. The year given at the beginning of each essay is the year the essay was written, unless otherwise indicated.

Without inconvenience, however, the instructor may take up the essays in any desired order. The reverse chronological order of the essayists can itself be reversed, as can that of the individual essays. The parts of the book do not build on each other. None of the suggestions for writing presupposes a knowledge of any essay except the one immediately preceding the suggestions. The same is true for the Nuts and Bolts sections. So feel free to proceed in whatever way you find most convenient and productive.

In making abundant use of published essays in teaching writing, I have always felt that, as an instructor of *writing,* I should point out some principles or techniques the authors use that students also can use. That is what I attempt to do in each of the Nuts and Bolts sections. Among those techniques might be such matters as the use of examples, or comparison and contrast, or parallelism. Such techniques, however, merely contribute to the making of the whole essay, the presence of any one technique is not *the* reason for the essay's inclusion in the book. Each essay has been included because of its overall quality and interest.

The discussions in the Nuts and Bolts sections focus on some principle or technique in the preceding essay that students too can use. What I decided to focus on is certainly not the only thing that could have been discussed. The principle or technique discussed in any of the Nuts and Bolts sections can be shown in numerous other essays, and it would be a good idea for instructors to point it out in other essays. For example, I have chosen to discuss Orwell's use of parallelism in some of the sentences in "Shooting an Elephant." Effective use of parallelism, of course, can be found in many other essays. Once attention has been called to a technique, though, the important thing is to encourage students to try it in their own work.

The Suggestions for Writing following each essay are spin-offs of themes in the essay, asking the student to consider the presence or the role of a particular theme in his or her own life. The new awareness that results from this thinking through is usually quite enlightening. Most of the suggestions ask the student to "discuss" something. *Discuss* is used generically. When students discuss, they use whatever patterns turn out to be appropriate for their material and their particular slant. "Discuss" is an invitation to deal with the topic: to think it through, to examine both their own experience and what they have read and heard, to consider what it all adds up to, to formulate a point of view or thesis—and then to plan the paper and write.

Some of the writing suggestions may require research. Individual instructors will have to set the ground rules for research assignments. The readiness of students to do research varies widely. Some students have done a significant amount of research in high school, some none. Instructors will have to decide how much research instruction is needed. Similarly, the required length of the papers to be written in response to the writing suggestions will have to be decided. For some students, a five-paragraph composition will be a significant accomplishment; other students will be capable of more comprehensive discussions. I feel confident that many of the writing suggestions will evoke especially interesting pieces of writing. I would appreciate it if instructors would send me, at the University of New Haven, copies of final versions of first-rate papers that were prompted by one of the writing suggestions. I would like to include such student work in the next edition. The student, the instructor, and the institution will be acknowledged.

The book contains the work of twelve essayists. Study of the essayists naturally breaks down into twelve units. I think it would be a worthy goal to have students read all twelve writers, even in courses that are only twelve weeks long; although it might not be possible to discuss every essay or essayist, there is no need to discuss everything students are asked to do. In the more typical fifteen-week course, discussions of particular essayists' range, voice, and development, of usage and style issues in the essays, of student papers, and of research techniques, as well as in-class writing can all be worked in quite comfortably. In any case, passing up a writer or two certainly will not affect the coherence of a course, and some students may be interested enough to read the unassigned selections on their own.

I would like to thank Gary Carlson for his help in getting permissions. The book has benefited greatly from the superb copyediting of Barney Hamby, up there in Vermont. Whenever I had a question, Yamil Lara returned home with books and books.

Julianna Scott Fein, Mayfield production editor, has been a pleasure to work with. Every writer or editor should be as fortunate as I was in having someone at the business end as experienced, knowledgeable, and sympathetic as Tom Broadbent. We discussed the project, and then we shook hands over the phone.

Letter to the Student

Let me say right off the bat that first-year college English courses can be very frustrating. Students are asked to read and write, they do what they are asked to do, and many still end up getting a grade they are unhappy with. That happened to me years ago. When I entered the University of Michigan, I thought I was a pretty good writer. But for most of that first English course I struggled with a D average on my compositions. Although I managed to come out of the course with a C, that course was very disheartening. For a long time afterwards, when I thought back to my freshman year, I still could not understand why all the time and effort I put into my compositions didn't get them returned with A's or at least B's. Eventually, though, I realized there probably was quite a gap between what I considered good writing and what Mr. E. S. Moon, my instructor, considered good. He had read a lot more good writing than I had, and as a result he had a much clearer idea of the qualities that made a piece of writing good. I realized that discussing a familiar subject with understanding and feeling did not by itself make a composition good.

Well, lives take strange turns and twists: after a series of events I could not have anticipated, there I was teaching composition courses myself. For one thing, if there had not been a GI Bill, which provided me with enough money so that I could go to graduate school, I definitely would not be writing this letter. The world turns, and I ended up enjoying teaching the course I least enjoyed taking as a freshman.

One of the things I try to do as an instructor of writing is to be clear about what constitutes good writing. It often happens that a student who put in relatively little time and effort gets a better grade on a composition than a student who was far more diligent. The paper that was worked on less turns out to be the truly better paper. Why? Here is an explanation that generally holds true. Students who write better compositions with less effort usually have *read* more good writing than students who put in more effort but get lower grades. This wider reading has led to a kind of unconscious absorption of the practices of good writers. In short, the most natural way to learn to write well is to read a lot of good writing. But the techniques of good writers also can be learned in a more deliberate and direct way. In the Nuts and Bolts sections of this book, I point out and describe some of those techniques. Students who endeavor to understand them and then to work them into their own writing will find their writing much improved.

Regular reading of good writing remains the basic source of good writing. Although creative writing is limited in what it can transfer to the student in the way of principles of effective nonfiction prose writing, essays of various kinds offer models for the practical, utilitarian writing that most students will have to do in college and thereafter. But that does not mean essays are dull. In fact, the distinguishing characteristic of the essay as a form is the presence of a unique personality, a compelling voice. And these can find their way into a piece of writing only when what is being written about has some special importance to the writer, when the subject has gripped the writer and engaged his or her whole emotional and intellectual being.

The essays in this book range from those by Shelby Steele, who was born in 1946, to those by Michel de Montaigne, who was born more than four hundred years earlier. Montaigne was the first essayist; Steele is one of thousands of essayists writing in English today. Between them in this book are some of the most highly praised of essayists. It is my hope that all twelve writers here, the older as well as the more recent, will be entertaining and enlightening to you. Earlier writers such as Emerson, Hazlitt, and Lamb will require more effort, but if you make that effort you will reap a considerable reward in amusement and wisdom. Reading Montaigne and Bacon, the oldest of essayists, will give you the satisfaction of knowing where the trail begins. Wandering through the National Air and Space Museum, in Washington, D.C., and seeing the progression from the earliest flying machines to the latest can provide a very special appreciation of ingenuity. A similar feeling of satisfaction can be had in grasping the evolution of the essay.

To make sure you are getting all you can out of the essays, you should read with a college-level dictionary beside you, and you should put it to frequent use. When you read the older writers, you'll need to use the dictionary more frequently. But you'll find that even Shelby Steele uses words you won't know the meaning of. If you want to get the most out of your college education, try to abide by this rule: check out every word whose meaning you are not sure of (okay, maybe not *every* word, but don't give yourself more than a little bit of slack), and read through the entire entry for the word. I promise you, on the basis of my many years of experience, that if you do that, within a year your competence as a reader and as a writer will be greatly increased.

The world turns, unanticipated events occur, plans change—and although you may not be able to see it happening now, what you learn in this English course can end up being of great benefit to you. That is true even if, as you look years ahead, you see yourself as an accountant, an engineer, a software wizard, an interior designer, a surgeon. Some of the essays you're going to read will stick with you and, at times throughout your life, will provoke you to think. Some of the things you're going to learn about writing will have a dramatic effect on the quality of your writing. As someone who writes well, you'll be much more successful in your college work than you would have been otherwise. And when you leave college, if you can back up a description of yourself as "a good writer," you'll find a surprising number of doors opening for you.

Contents

story by White

Boxing essay

CHARLES LAMB 278

FRANCIS BACON 310

MICHEL DE MONTAIGNE 332

Shelby Steele

[1946–   ]

Shelby Steele, along with his twin brother and two sisters, is a child of a black Chicago truck driver and a white social worker. A generation later, the mother of Steele's two children is a white clinical psychologist. Steele's childhood was spent mainly in Phoenix, Illinois, a Chicago suburb. In Phoenix there were two elementary schools, one for white children and one for black; Steele attended the latter. The black school had a faculty that was, in Steele's words, a "menagerie of misfits." Steele's sixth grade teacher was a white ex-marine who "ran the class like a gang leader, picking favorites one day and banishing them the next." On the very first day of that class, Steele misread a sentence, and his fate was set. In that class, he was "Stupid Steele."

For his mistakes, Steele's punishments grew more and more cruel. One day the teacher ordered him to pick up all the broken glass on the playground. Steele began to comply, but after an hour he quit. The ex-marine then told an eighth-grader with a bicycle to run Steele around the school grounds until he dropped. The boy was given a baseball bat to use in case the runner slowed down. Steele ran for a bit and then pretended to pass out. The sympathetic older boy biked away.

When they learned about the incident, Steele's parents organized a boycott of the school, and the teacher was fired. When Steele's confidence was restored, he went on to excel in school, and as a senior in high school he was the student council president. In 1964 he enrolled at Coe College in Cedar Rapids, Iowa, where he became a campus civil rights leader, wore African-style clothing, and led protests against the college administration. One of the favorite pastimes of Steele and his black friends was "nap matching"—contests, in which they would try to top each other with stories of nastiness by whites.

In the late sixties, Steele says, he was "caught up in the new spirit of black power and pride that swept over black America like one of those storms that change the landscape. . . . What I gained from it was the power to be racially unapologetic, no mean benefit considering the long trial of patience that blacks were subjected to during the civil rights movement." But the black power movement did not offer individual blacks much guidance about what to do with their lives besides opposing white power: "'Blackness' . . . cut so deeply into one's individual space that it seemed also to *be* an individual identity." But the two were not the same: "Being black in no way spared me the necessity of being myself."

So Steele struck a bargain with himself. He would continue to be angry with and mistrustful of white America, and he would remember that "a tight racial unity was necessary for survival and advancement." But he also would set goals for himself and pursue them. Upon graduating from Coe, he enrolled at the Edwardsville branch of Southern Illinois University in a master's program in sociology. While there, he taught African-American literature to poor blacks enrolled in an experimental college program in nearby East St. Louis. With the master's degree completed, he continued to follow the career path he had chosen and moved on to the University of Utah, from which he earned a Ph.D. in English.

In 1974, with that credential in hand, Steele took a position in the English Department at San Jose State University, where he quickly rose through the ranks to full professor. In addition to fulfilling his duties at San Jose State, Steele has become a prolific writer on race relations in America. *The Content of Our Character* (1990) contains the more important of those essays, including "On Being Black and Middle Class" and "The Recoloring of Campus Life."

MALCOLM LITTLE

1992

When asked recently what he thought of Malcolm X, Thurgood   1
Marshall is reported to have said, "All he did was talk." And yet there is a kind
of talk that constitutes action, a catalytic speech that changes things as
irrevocably as do events or great movements. Malcolm X was an event, and
his talk transformed American culture as surely, if not as thoroughly, as the
civil rights movement, which might not have found the moderation
necessary for its success had Malcolm not planted in the American
consciousness so uncompromised a vision of the underdog's rage.

Malcolm staked out this territory against his great contemporary and
foil, Martin Luther King Jr. Sneering at King's turn-the-other-cheek
Christianity, he told blacks, "Don't ask God to have mercy on him [the white
man]; ask God to judge him. Ask God to do onto him what he did onto you.
Ask God that he suffer as you suffered." To use the old Christian categories,
Malcolm was the Old Testament to King's New Testament. Against the moral
nobility of the civil rights movement, he wanted whites to know that he was
not different from them; that he, too, would kill or die for freedom. "The
price of freedom is death," he often said.

Like all true revolutionaries, Malcolm had an intimate relationship with
his own death. By being less afraid of it than other men, he took on power.
And this was not so much a death wish as it was the refusal of a compromised
life. These seemed to be his terms, and for many blacks like myself who came
of age during his era, there was nothing to do but love him, since he, foolishly
or not, seemed to love us more than we loved ourselves.

It is always context that makes a revolutionary figure like Malcolm X a
hero or a destroyer. Even when he first emerged in the late '50s and early '60s,
the real debate was not so much about him (he was clear enough) as about
whether or not the context of black oppression was severe enough to justify
him. And now that Malcolm has explosively re-emerged on the American
scene, those old questions about context are with us once again.

Spike Lee has brought Malcolm's autobiography to the screen in one of   5
the most thoroughly hyped films in American history. Malcolm's life is
available in airport bookstalls. Compact discs and videotapes of his "blue-
eyed devil" speeches can be picked up at Tower Records. His "X" is
ubiquitous to the point of gracing automobile air fresheners. Twenty-seven
years after his death, in sum, he is more visible to Americans than he was
during his life. Of course Americans will commercialize anything; but that
is a slightly redundant point. The really pressing matter is what this says about
the context of race relations in America today. How can a new generation of
blacks—after pervasive civil rights legislation, Great Society programs, school
busing, open housing, and more than two decades of affirmative action—be
drawn to a figure of such seething racial alienation?

The life of Malcolm X touched so many human archetypes that his story itself seems to supersede any racial context, which is to say that it meshes with virtually every context. Malcolm X is a story. And so he meets people, particularly young people, in a deeply personal way. To assess whether or not he is a good story for these times, I think we have to consider first the nature of his appeal.

Let me say—without, I hope, too many violins—that when I was growing up in the 1950s, I was very often the victim of old-fashioned racism and discrimination. These experiences were very much like the literal experience of being burned. Not only did they hurt, they also caused me to doubt myself in some fundamental way. There was shame in these experiences as well, the suspicion that by some measure of human worth I deserved them. This, of course, is precisely what they were designed to make me feel. So right away there was an odd necessity to fight and to struggle for both personal and racial dignity.

Those were the experiences that enabled me to hear Malcolm. The very soul of his legend was the heroic struggle that he was waging against racial doubt and shame. After a tortuous childhood and an early life of crime that left him shattered, he reconstructed himself—against the injuries of racial oppression—by embracing an ideology of black nationalism. Black nationalism offered something very important to Malcolm, and this quickly became his magnificently articulated offering to other blacks. What it offered was a perfectly cathartic distribution of love and hate. Blacks were innocent victims, whites were evil oppressors, and blacks had to distribute their love and hate accordingly. But if one focuses on the called-for hatred of whites, the point of Malcolm's redistribution of emotion will be missed. If Malcolm was screaming his hatred of whites, his deeper purpose was to grant blacks a license to give themselves what they needed most: self-love.

This license to love and to hate in a way that soothed my unconscious doubts was nothing less than compelling by the time I reached college. Late at night in the dorm, my black friends and I would turn off the lights for effect and listen to his album of speeches, *The Ballot or the Bullet,* over and over again. He couldn't have all that anger and all that hate unless he really loved black people, and, therefore, us. And so he massaged the injured part of ourselves with an utterly self-gratifying and unconditional love.

With Martin Luther King, by contrast, there were conditions. King asked blacks—despised and unloved—to spread their meager stock of love to all people, even to those who despised us. What a lot to ask, and of a victim. With King, we were once again in second place, loving others before ourselves. But Malcolm told us to love ourselves first and to project all of our hurt into a hatred of the "blue-eyed devil" who had hurt us in the first place.

In Malcolm's deployment of love and hate there was an intrinsic logic of dignity that was very different from King's. For King, racial dignity was established by enlarging the self into a love of others. For Malcolm, dignity came from constriction, from shrinking to the enemy's size, and showing him not that you could be higher than he was, but that you could go as low. If King rose up, Malcolm dropped down. And here is where he used the hatred side of his formula to lay down his two essential principles of black dignity: the dehumanization of the white man and the threat of violence.

What made those principles essential to the dignity of blacks for Malcolm was that they followed a tit-for-tat logic—the logic by which, in his mind, any collective established its dignity against another collective. And both these principles could be powerfully articulated by Malcolm because they were precisely the same principles by which whites had oppressed blacks for centuries. Malcolm dehumanized whites by playing back, in white-face, the stereotypes that blacks had endured. He made them animals—if they like their meat rare, "that's the dog in 'em." In the iconography of his Black Muslim period, whites were heathen, violent, drooling beasts who lynched and raped. But he often let his humor get the best of him in this, and most blacks took it with a grain of salt.

What made Malcolm one of the most controversial Americans of this century was the second principle of his logic of dignity: the threat of violence. "If we have a funeral in Harlem, make sure they have one downtown, too." "If he puts his hand on you, send him to the cemetery." Tit-for-tat logic taken to its logical conclusion. In fact, Malcolm's focus on violence against whites was essentially rhetorical. Like today's black street gangs, his Black Muslims were far more likely to kill each other than go after whites. Yet no one has ever played the white hysteria over black violence better than Malcolm.

He played this card very effectively to achieve two things. The first was to breach the horrible invisibility that blacks have endured in America. White racism has always been sustained by the white refusal or reluctance to see blacks, to think about them as people, to grant them the kind of place in the imagination that one would grant, say, to the English or even the Russians. Blacks might be servile or troublesome, but never worthy of serious, competitive consideration. Against this Malcolm sent a concrete message: we are human enough to want to kill you for what you have done to us. How does it feel to have people you never paid much attention to want to kill you? (This was the terror Richard Wright captured so powerfully in *Native Son*: your humble chauffeur may kill your daughter. And that novel, too, got attention.) Violence was a means to black visibility for Malcolm, and later for many other militants.

Today this idea of violence as black visibility means that part of Malcolm's renewed popularity comes from his power as an attention-getting figure. If today's "X" is an assertion of self-love, it is also a demand to be seen. This points to the second purpose of Malcolm's violent rhetoric: to restore dignity to blacks in an almost Hegelian sense. Those unwilling to kill and to die for dignity would forever be a slave class. Here he used whites as the model. They would go to war to meet any threat, even when it was far removed. Many times he told his black audiences that whites would not respect them unless they used "any means necessary" to seize freedom. For a minority outnumbered 10-to-1, this was not rational. But it was a point that needed to be made in the name of dignity. It was something that many blacks needed to feel about themselves, that there was a line that no one could cross.

Yet this logic of dignity only partly explains Malcolm's return as an icon in our own day. I believe that the larger reason for his perdurability and popularity is one that is almost never mentioned: that Malcolm X was a deeply conservative man. In times when the collective identity is besieged and confused, groups usually turn to their conservatives, not to their liberals; to their extreme partisans, not to their open-minded representatives. The last twenty-five years have seen huge class and cultural differences open up in black America. The current bromide is that we are not a monolith, and this is profoundly true. We now have a black governor and a black woman senator and millions of black college graduates and so on, but also hundreds of thousands of young blacks in prison. Black identity no longer has a centrifugal force in a racial sense. And in the accompanying confusion we look to the most conservative identity figure.

Malcolm was a conservative through and through. As a black nationalist, he was a hard-line militarist who believed in the principle of self-mastery through force. His language and thinking in this regard were oddly in line with Henry Kissinger's description of the world as a brutal place in which safety and a balance of power is maintained through realpolitik. He was Reaganesque in his insistence on negotiating with whites from a position of strength—meaning the threat of violence. And his commitment (until the last year of his life) to racial purity and separatism would have made him the natural ally of David Duke.

In his personal life, moreover, Malcolm scrupulously followed all the Islamic strictures against alcohol, tobacco, drugs, fornication, and adultery, and his attitude toward women was decidedly patriarchal: as a Black Muslin minister he counseled that women could never be completely trusted because of their vanity, and he forbade dancing in his mosque. In his speeches he reserved a special contempt for white liberals, and he once praised Barry Goldwater as a racial realist. Believing entirely in black self-help, he had no use for government programs to uplift blacks, and sneered at the 1964 Civil Rights Bill as nothing more than white expedience.

Malcolm X was one of the most unabashed and unqualified conservatives of his time. And yet today he is forgiven his sexism by black feminists, his political conservatism by black and white liberals, his Islamic faith by black Christians, his violent rhetoric by non-violent veterans of the civil rights struggle, his anti-Semitism by blacks and whites who are repulsed by it, his separatism by blacks who live integrated lives, and even the apparent fabrication of events in his childhood by those who would bring his story to the screen. Malcolm enjoys one of the best Teflon-coatings of all time.

I think one of the reasons for this is that he was such an extreme *20* conservative, that is, such an extreme partisan of his group. All we really ask of such people is that they love the group more than anything else, even themselves. If this is evident, all else is secondary. In fact, we demand conservatism from such people, because it is a testament of their love. Malcolm sneered at government programs because he believed so much in black people: they could do it on their own. He gave up all his vices to intensify his love. He was a father figure who distributed love and hate in our favor. Reagan did something like this when he called the Soviet Union an "evil empire," and he, too, was rewarded with Teflon.

The point is that all groups take their extreme partisans more figuratively than literally. Their offer of unconditional love bribes us into loving them back rather unconditionally, so that our will to be literal with them weakens. We will not see other important black leaders of the 1960s—James Farmer, Whitney Young, Andrew Young, Medgar Evers (a genuine martyr), Roy Wilkins, John Lewis—gracing the T-shirts of young blacks who are today benefiting more from their efforts than from Malcolm's. They were too literal, too much of the actual world, for iconography, for the needs of an unsure psyche. But Malcolm, the hater and the lover, the father figure of romantic blackness, is the perfect icon.

It helps, too, that he is dead, and therefore unable to be literal in our own time. We can't know, for example, if he would now be supporting affirmative action as the reparation that is due to blacks, or condemning it as more white patronization and black dependency. In a way, the revival of Malcolm X is one of the best arguments I know of for the validity of the deconstructionist view of things: Malcolm is now a text. Today we *read* Malcolm. And this—dare I say—is one quality he shares with Christ, who also died young and became a text. He was also an Odyssean figure who journeyed toward self-knowledge. He was a priest and a heretic. For many whites he was a devil and for many blacks a martyr. Even those of my generation who grew up with him really came to know him through the autobiography that he wrote with Alex Haley. Even in his time, then, he was a text, and it is reasonable to wonder if he would have the prominence he has today without that book.

How will the new epic movie of his life—yet another refracting text—add to his prominence? Clearly it will add rather than subtract. It is a film that enhances the legend, that tries to solidify Malcolm's standing as a symbol of identity. To this end, the film marches uncritically through the well-known episodes of the life. It is beautifully shot and superbly acted by a cast that seemed especially inspired by the significance of the project. And yet it is still, finally, a march. Spike Lee, normally filled with bravado, works here like a T.V. docudramatist with a big budget, for whom loyalty to a received version of events is more important than insight, irony, or vision. Bruce Perry's recent study of Malcolm's life, *Malcolm: A Life of the Man Who Changed Black America,* which contradicts much of the autobiography, is completely and indefensibly ignored.

Against Lee's portrayal of Malcolm's father as a stalwart Garveyite killed by the Klan, Perry reveals a man with a reputation for skirt-chasing who moved from job to job and was often violent with his children. Lee shows the

Klan burning down Malcolm's childhood home, while Perry offers considerable evidence to indicate that Malcolm's father likely burned it down himself after he received an eviction notice. Lee offers a dramatic scene of the Klan running Earl Little and his family out of Nebraska, yet Malcolm's mother told Perry that the event never happened. The rather heroic cast that Malcolm (and Lee) gave to his childhood is contradicted by Perry's extensive interviews with childhood friends, who portray Malcolm as rather fearful and erratic. Lee's only response to Perry's work was simply, "I don't believe it."

25

It was Spike Lee's unthinking loyalty to the going racial orthodoxy, I believe, that led him to miss more than he saw, and to produce a film that is finally part fact, part fiction, and entirely middlebrow. That racial orthodoxy is a problem for many black artists working today, since its goal is to make the individual artist responsible for the collective political vision. This orthodoxy arbitrates the artist's standing within the group: the artist can be as individual as he or she likes as long as the group view of things is upheld. The problem here for black artists is that their racial identity will be held hostage to the practice of their art. The effect of this is to pressure the work of art, no matter what inspired it, into a gesture of identification that reunites the artist and the group.

In this sense Lee's *Malcolm X* might be called a reunion film, or a gesture of identification on his part toward the group. Thus his loyalist, unquestioning march through Malcolm's mythology. It is certainly ironic, given the debate over whether a white man could direct this film, that Spike Lee sees his hero as only a black man with no more than black motivations. Human motivations like doubt, fear, insecurity, jealousy, and love, or human themes like the search for the father, betrayal, and tragedy, are present in the film because they were present in Malcolm's story, but Lee seems unaware of them as the real stuff of his subject's life. The film expresses its identification with much racial drama, but in a human monotone.

Thus many of the obvious ironies of Malcolm's life are left hanging. If black nationalism resurrected Malcolm in prison, it also killed him in the end. This was a man who put all his faith in the concept of a black nation, in the idea that blackness, in itself, carried moral significance, and yet it was black nationalist fingers pulling the triggers that killed him. Even on its surface this glaring irony points to the futility of cultish racial ideologies, to the collective insecurities that inspire them, and to the frightened personalities that adhere to them as single-mindedly as Malcolm did. But doesn't this irony also underscore the much more common human experience of falling when we grip our illusions too tightly, when we need them too much? It should not embarrass Lee to draw out the irony of Malcolm being killed by blacks. He was. And there is a lesson in it for everyone, since we are all hurt by our illusions. To make his gesture of identification, however, Lee prefers to sacrifice the deeper identification that his entire audience might have with his subject.

He also fails to perform the biographer's critical function. Clearly Malcolm had something of the true believer's compulsion to believe blindly and singularly, to eradicate all complexity as hypocrisy. All his life he seemed to have no solid internal compass of his own to rely on in the place of ideology—which is not to say that he didn't have brilliance once centered by a faith. But in this important way he was very unlike King, who, lacking Malcolm's wounds, was so well centered that he projected serenity and composure even as storms raged around him. Out of some underlying agitation Malcolm searched for authorities, for systems of belief, for father figures, for revelations: West Indian Archie, Elijah Muhammad, the Black Muslim faith, Pan Africanism, and finally the humanism of traditional Islam. All this in thirty-nine years! What else might have followed? How many more fathers? How many more isms?

Moreover, once Malcolm learned from these people, faiths, ideologies—or had taken what he could from them—he betrayed them all, one after another. There was always this pattern of complete, true-believing submission to authority and then the abrupt betrayal of it. There was something a little narcissistic in this, as though his submissions were really set-ups for the victories that he would later seize. And with each betrayal-victory there was something of a gloat—his visit to West Indian Archie when he was broken, his telling Mike Wallace on national television about Elijah Muhammad's infidelities. Betrayal was triumph for Malcolm, a moving beyond some smallness, some corruption, some realm that was beneath him.

The corruption at the heart of Malcolm's legend is that he looked   *30* bigger than life because he always lived in small, cultish worlds, and always stood next to small people. He screamed at whites, but he had no idea of how to work with them to get things done. King was the man who had to get things done. I don't think that it is farfetched to suggest that finally Malcolm was afraid of white people. While King stared down every white from Bull Connor to the Kennedys, Malcolm made a big deal out of facing off with Elijah Muhammad, whom he had likely propped up for the purpose. His proclivity for little people who made him look big suggests that his black nationalism covered his fear of hard, ordinary work in the American crucible. Up against larger realities and bigger people, he might have felt inadequate.

Lee's film, as beautifully executed as it is, refuses to ask questions about Malcolm's legend. A quick look behind the legend, however, shows that Malcolm's real story was, in truth, tragedy. And the understanding of this grim truth would have helped the film better achieve the racial protest it is obviously after. Malcolm was hurt badly by oppression early in his childhood. If his family was not shattered in the way he claimed, it was shattered nevertheless. And this shattering had much to do with America's brutal racial history. He was, in his pain, a product of America. But his compensations for the hurt only extended the hurt. And the tragedy was the life that this extraordinary man felt that he needed to live, that Malcolm Little had to become Malcolm X, had to be a criminal, then a racial ideologue, and finally a martyr for an indefinable cause. Black nationalism is a tragedy of white racism, and can sometimes be as ruinous as the racism itself.

And so it is saddening to witness the re-emergence of this hyped-up, legendary Mr. X, this seller of wolf tickets and excuses not to engage American society. This Malcolm is back to conceal rather than to reveal. He is here to hide our fears as he once hid his own, to keep us separated from any helpful illumination. Had the real Malcolm, the tragic Malcolm, returned, however, it would have represented a remarkable racial advancement. That Malcolm might have given both blacks and whites a way to comprehend our racial past and present. In him we all could have seen the damage done, the frustrations borne, and the fruitless heroism of the American insistence on race.

Questions for Understanding

1. What role did Malcolm X play in Steele's youth?
2. What was Malcolm X's attitude toward Martin Luther King?
3. Does Steele believe that the 1990s provide an appropriate context for reviving Malcolm's "seething racial alienation"?
4. What does Steele mean when he says that for Malcolm "violence was a means to black visibility"?
5. What does Steele believe are the shortcomings of Spike Lee's film about the life of Malcolm X?

Suggestions for Writing

1. Write an essay in which you describe a leader, either real or fictional, whose weaknesses limited what he or she was able to accomplish. Be sure to discuss how the weaknesses had the effect of preventing the person from accomplishing more.
2. Write an essay in which you describe a person who had a profound effect on you during your elementary school years. Be sure you show the causal relationship—that is, exactly what it was that caused the effect.
3. Write an essay in which you discuss your reactions to threats of violence made against someone you know because of his or her ethnic or racial group.
4. Does it matter that the facts about the life of Malcolm X—or some other legendary hero—have been distorted? Is it necessary that everything told about the person be one hundred percent accurate?
5. Write an essay in which you discuss why a film you looked forward to with great anticipation turned out to be a disappointment.

NUTS AND BOLTS 1: PLANNING THE ESSAY AS A WHOLE

It was one of the most eagerly awaited movies ever made. Spike Lee, the most successful and best-known African-American filmmaker, was making a movie about Malcolm X, the black leader who, newly rediscovered more than twenty-five years after his death, was becoming a cult hero. "X" baseball caps and jackets were the things to wear in America's cities. And when the movie was released, the critics almost unanimously loved it.

Yet to Shelby Steele, who had been aware of Malcolm since boyhood, the movie was very disappointing. As he thought back, he considered Malcolm's life tragic, not heroic. As he pondered what Spike Lee had done with the facts of Malcolm's life, he concluded that Lee had missed an opportunity to make a truly great film. The movie stirred up a lot of feeling and thinking in Shelby Steele, and it all led to sorrow and anger about Malcolm X and Spike Lee. But to express what he felt would mean swimming against the rising tide of adulation for Malcolm and Lee. So Steele had to find a way to write about the movie that would keep him from sounding like a crank, a killjoy, a betrayer of his own people, someone who for his own strange reasons was throwing mud at two African-American heroes. As a writer, Steele faced two difficult but not uncommon problems: how to get his readers to open their minds to ideas they would not like and how to persuade them that those ideas were correct.

In his essay, Steele makes use of three effective strategies. First, he delays coming straight out with a clear-cut statement of his thesis until the essay's final paragraph. By doing so, he keeps the hostility and resentment he anticipates at bay until after he has said everything he can to persuade readers of the justness of his position. Second, for the same reason, early on he concedes as much as he possibly can to the opposing point of view, giving personal testimony to what a powerful force Malcolm had been. Third, he brings into the essay someone against whom he can set Malcolm, in order to bring out Malcolm's weaknesses on the one hand and real strengths on the other. Although Steele refers to Martin Luther King in only five of his thirty-two paragraphs, King nevertheless looms large throughout the essay. As Steele portrays first the real Malcolm and then the Malcolm of Lee's movie, the comparison and contrast with King becomes a powerful tool for persuading readers that Malcolm is unworthy of the adulation he is receiving.

It is very revealing to juxtapose what Steele says in his final paragraph with some of the things he says earlier. Considering his concluding assertion: "It is saddening to witness the re-emergence of this hyped-up legendary Mr. X, this seller of wolf tickets and excuses not to engage American society. This Malcolm is back to conceal rather than to reveal. He is here to hide our fears as he once hid his own, to keep us separated from any helpful illumination." Consider that final judgment alongside Steele's assertions that Malcolm's speeches "transformed American culture," that his power lay in his "refusal of a compromised life," that his life "touched so many human archetypes that his story itself seems to supersede any racial context, which is to say that it meshes with virtually every context."

Shelby Steele's "Malcolm Little" is a powerful essay on a very controversial figure. As a result of his strategies in the essay as a whole, Steele comes through as sympathetic, respectful, measured, forceful, courageous, and—ultimately—correct.

ON BEING BLACK AND MIDDLE CLASS

1989

Not long ago, a friend of mine, black like myself, said to me that the   *1*
term *black middle class* was actually a contradiction in terms. Race, he insisted,
blurred class distinctions among blacks. If you were black, you were just black
and that was that. When I argued, he let his eyes roll at my naïveté. Then he
went on. For us, as black professionals, it was an exercise in self-flattery, a
pathetic pretension, to give meaning to such a distraction. Worse, the very
idea of class threatened the unity that was vital to the black community as a
whole. After all, since when had white America taken note of anything but
color when it came to blacks? He then reminded me of an old Malcolm X
line that had been popular in the sixties. Question: What is a black man with
a Ph.D.? Answer: A nigger.

For many years I had been on my friend's side of this argument. Much
of my conscious thinking on the old conundrum of race and class was shaped
during my high school and college years in the race-charged sixties, when the
fact of my race took on an almost religious significance. Progressively, from
the mid-sixties on, more and more aspects of my life found their explanation,
their justification, and their motivation in my race. My youthful concerns
about career, romance, money, values, and even styles of dress became subject
to consultation with various oracular sources of racial wisdom. And these
ranged from a figure as ennobling as Martin Luther King, Jr., to the
underworld elegance of dress I found in jazz clubs on the South Side of
Chicago. Everywhere there were signals, and in those days I considered
myself so blessed with clarity and direction that I pitied my white classmates
who found more embarrassment than guidance in the fact of *their* race. In
1968, inflated by new power, I took a mischievous delight in calling them
culturally disadvantaged.

But now, hearing my friend's comment was like hearing a priest from
a church I'd grown disenchanted with. I understood him, but my faith was
weak. What had sustained me in the sixties sounded monotonous and
off-the-mark in the eighties. For me, race had lost much of its juju, its singular
capacity to conjure meaning. And today, when I honestly look at my life and
the lives of many other middle-class blacks I know, I can see that race never
fully explained our situation in American society. Black though I may be, it
is impossible for me to sit in my single-family house with two cars in the
driveway and a swing set in the backyard and *not* see the role class has played
in my life. And how can my friend, similarly raised and similarly situated, not
see it?

Yet despite my certainty I felt a sharp tug of guilt as I tried to explain
myself over my friend's skepticism. He is a man of many comedic facial
expressions and, as I spoke, his brow lifted in extreme moral alarm as if I were

uttering the unspeakable. His clear implication was that I was being elitist and possibly (dare we suggest?) anti-black—crimes for which there might well be no redemption. He pretended to fear for me. I chuckled along with him, but inwardly I did wonder at myself. Though I never doubted the validity of what I was saying. I felt guilty saying it. Why?

After he left (to retrieve his daughter from a dance lesson) I realized that   5 the trap I felt myself in had a tiresome familiarity and, in a sort of slow motion epiphany, I began to see its outline. It was like the suddenly sharp vision one has at the end of a burdensome marriage when all the long-repressed incompatibilities come undeniably to light.

What became clear to me is that people like myself, my friend, and middle-class blacks in general are caught in a very specific double bind that keeps two equally powerful elements of our identity at odds with each other. The middle-class values by which we were raised—the work ethic, the importance of education, the value of property ownership, of respectability, of "getting ahead," of stable family life, of initiative, of self-reliance, et cetera—are, in themselves, raceless and even assimilationist. They urge us toward participation in the American mainstream, toward integration, toward a strong identification with the society, and toward the entire constellation of qualities that are implied in the word individualism. These values are almost rules for how to prosper in a democratic, free enterprise society that admires and rewards individual effort. They tell us to work hard for ourselves and our families and to seek our opportunities whenever they appear, inside or outside the confines of whatever ethnic group we may belong to.

But the particular pattern of racial identification that emerged in the sixties and that still prevails today urges middle-class blacks (and all blacks) in the opposite direction. This pattern asks us to see ourselves as an embattled minority, and it urges an adversarial stance toward the mainstream and an emphasis on ethnic consciousness over individualism. It is organized around an implied separatism.

The opposing theme of these two parts of our identity results in the double bind of middle-class blacks. There is no forward movement on either plane that does not constitute backward movement on the other. This was the familiar trap I felt myself in while talking with my friend. As I spoke about class, his eyes reminded me that I was betraying race. Clearly, the two indispensable parts of my identity were a threat to one another.

Of course when you think about it, class and race are both similar in some ways and also naturally opposed. They are two forms of collective identity with boundaries that intersect. But whether they clash or peacefully coexist has much to do with how they are defined. Being both black and middle-class becomes a double bind when class and race are defined in sharply antagonistic terms, so that one must be repressed to appease the other.

But what is the "substance" of these two identities, and how does each   10 establish itself in an individual's overall identity?

It seems to me that when we identify with any collective we are basically identifying with images that tell us what it means to be a member of that collective. Identity is not the same thing as the fact of membership in a collective; it is, rather, a form of self-definition, facilitated by images of what we wish our membership in the collective to mean. In this sense, the images we identify with may reflect the aspirations of the collective more than they reflect reality, and their content can vary with shifts in those aspirations.

But the process of identification is usually dialectical. It is just as necessary to say what we are *not* as it is to say what we are—so that, finally, identification comes about by embracing a polarity of positive and negative images. To identify as middle-class, for example, I must have both positive and negative images of what being middle-class entails; then I will know what I should and should not be doing in order to be middle-class. The same goes for racial identity. In the racially turbulent sixties the polarity of images that came to define racial identification was very antagonistic to the polarity that defined middle-class identification. One might say that the positive images of one lined up with the negative images of the other, so that to identify with both required either a contortionist's flexibility or a dangerous splitting of the self. The double bind of the black middle class was in place.

The black middle class has always defined its class identity by means of positive images gleaned from middle- and upper-class white society and by means of negative images of lower-class blacks. This habit goes back to the institution of slavery itself, when "house" slaves both mimicked the whites they served and held themselves above the "field" slaves. But, in the sixties, the old bourgeois impulse to dissociate from the lower classes (the we/they distinction) backfired when racial identity suddenly called for the celebration of this same black lower class. One of the qualities of a double bind is that one feels it more than sees it, and I distinctly remember the tension and strange sense of dishonesty I felt in those days as I moved back and forth like a bigamist between the demands of class and race.

Though my father was born poor, he achieved middle-class standing through much hard work and sacrifice (one of his favorite words) and by identifying fully with solid middle-class values—mainly hard work, family life, property ownership, and education for his children (all four of whom have advanced degrees). In his mind these were not so much values as laws of nature. People who embodied them made up the positive images in his class polarity. The negative images came largely from the blacks he had left behind because they were "going nowhere."

No one in my family remembers how it happened, but as time went on, the negative images congealed into an imaginary character named Sam who, from the extensive service we put him to, quickly grew to mythic proportions. In our family lore he was sometimes a trickster, sometimes a boob, but always possessed of a catalogue of sly faults that gave up graphic images of everything we should not be. On sacrifice: "Sam never thinks about tomorrow. He wants it now or he doesn't care about it." On work: "Sam doesn't favor it too much." On children: "Sam likes to have them but not to raise them." On money: "Sam drinks it up and pisses it out."

15

On fidelity: "Sam has to have two or three women." On clothes: "Sam features loud clothes. He likes to see and be seen." And so on. Sam's persona amounted to a negative instruction manual in class identity.

I don't think that any of us believed Sam's faults were accurate representations of lower-class black life. He was an instrument of self-definition, not of sociological accuracy. It never occurred to us that he looked very much like the white racist stereotype of blacks, or that he might have been a manifestation of our own racial self-hatred. He simply gave us a counterpoint against which to express our aspirations. If self-hatred was a factor, it was not, for us, a matter of hating lower-class blacks but of hating what we did not want to be.

Still, hate or love aside, it is fundamentally true that my middle-class identity involved a dissociation from images of lower-class black life and a corresponding identification with values and patterns of responsibility that are common to the middle class everywhere. These values sent me a clear message: Be both an individual and a responsible citizen, understand that the quality of your life will approximately reflect the quality of effort you put into it, know that individual responsibility is the basis of freedom, and that the limitations imposed by fate (whether fair or unfair) are no excuse for passivity.

Whether I live up to these values or not, I know that my acceptance of them is the result of lifelong conditioning. I know also that I share this conditioning with middle-class people of all races and that I can no more easily be free of it than I can be free of my race. Whether all this got started because the black middle class modeled itself on the white middle class is no longer relevant. For the middle-class black, conditioned by these values from birth, the sense of meaning they provide is as immutable as the color of his skin.

I started the sixties in high school feeling that my class-conditioning was the surest way to overcome racial barriers. My racial identity was pretty much taken for granted. After all, it was obvious to the world that I was black. Yet I ended the sixties in graduate school a little embarrassed by my class background and with an almost desperate need to be "black." The tables had turned. I knew very clearly (though I struggled to repress it) that my aspirations and my sense of how to operate in the world came from my class background, yet "being black" required certain attitudes and stances that made me feel, secretly, a little duplicitous. The inner compatibility of class and race I had known in 1960 was gone.

For blacks, the decade between 1960 and 1969 saw racial identification undergo the same sort of transformation that national identity undergoes in times of war. It became more self-conscious, more narrowly focused, more prescribed, less tolerant of opposition. It spawned an implicit party line that tended to disallow competing forms of identity. Race-as-identity was lifted from the relative slumber it knew in the fifties and pressed into service in a social and political war against oppression. It was redefined along sharp adversarial lines and directed toward the goal of mobilizing the great mass of black Americans in this warlike effort. It was imbued with strong moral authority, useful for denouncing those who opposed it and for celebrating those who honored it as a positive achievement rather than a mere birthright.

The form of racial identification that quickly evolved to meet this challenge presented blacks as a racial monolith, a singular people with a common experience of oppression. Differences within the race, no matter how ineradicable, had to be minimized. Class distinctions were one of the first such differences to be sacrificed, since they not only threatened racial unity but also seemed to stand in contradiction to the principle of equality, which was the announced goal of the movement for racial progress. The discomfort I felt in 1969, the vague but relentless sense of duplicity, was the result of a historical necessity that put my class and race at odds, that was asking me to cast aside the distinction of my class and identify with a monolithic view of my race.

If the form of this racial identity was the monolith, its substance was victimization. The civil rights movement and the more radical splinter groups of the late sixties were all dedicated to ending racial victimization, and the form of black identity that emerged to facilitate this goal made blackness and victimization virtually synonymous. Since it was our victimization more than any other variable that identified and unified us, it followed logically that the purest black was the poor black. It was images of him that clustered around the positive pole of the race polarity; all other blacks were, in effect, required to identify with him in order to confirm their own blackness.

Certainly, there were more dimensions to the black experience than victimization, but no other had the same capacity to fire the indignation needed for war. So, again out of historical necessity, victimization became the overriding focus of racial identity. But this only deepened the double bind for middle-class blacks like me. When it came to class we were accustomed to defining ourselves against lower-class blacks and identifying with at least the values of middle-class whites; when it came to race we were now being asked to identify with images of lower-class blacks and to see whites, middle-class or otherwise, as victimizers. Negative lining up with positive, we were called upon to reject what we had previously embraced and to embrace what we had previously rejected. To put it still more personally, the Sam figure I had been raised to define myself against had now become the "real" black I was expected to identify with.

The fact that the poor black's new status was only passively earned by the condition of his victimization, not by assertive, positive action, made little difference. Status was status apart from the means by which it was achieved, and along with it came a certain power—the power to define the terms of access to that status, to say who was black and who was not. If a lower-class black said you were not really "black"—a sellout, an Uncle Tom—the judgment was all the more devastating because it carried the authority of his status. And this judgment soon enough came to be accepted by many whites as well.

In graduate school I was once told by a white professor, "Well,   *25*
but . . . you're not really black. I mean, you're not disadvantaged." In his
mind my lack of victim status disqualified me from the race itself.

To overcome marginal status, the middle-class black had to identify
with a degree of victimization that was beyond his actual experience. In
college (and well beyond) we used to play a game called "nap matching." It
was a game of one-upmanship, in which we sat around outdoing each other
with stories of racial victimization, symbolically measured by the naps of our
hair. Most of us were middle-class, and so had few personal stories to relate,
but if we could not match naps with our own biographies, we would move
on to those legendary tales of victimization that came to us from the public
domain.

The single story that sat atop the pinnacle of racial victimization for us
was that of Emmett Till, the Northern black teenager who, on a visit to the
South in 1955, was killed and grotesquely mutilated for supposedly looking
at or whistling at (we were never sure which, though we argued the point
endlessly) a white woman. Oh, how we probed his story, finding in his youth
and Northern upbringing the quintessential embodiment of black innocence
brought down by a white evil so portentous and apocalyptic, so gnarled and
hideous, that it left us with a feeling not far from awe. By telling his story and
others like it, we came to *feel* the immutability of our victimization, its utter
indigenousness, as a thing on this earth like dirt or sand or water.

Of course, these sessions were a ritual of group identification, a means
by which we, as middle-class blacks, could be at one with our race. But why
were we, who had only a moderate experience of victimization (and that
offset by opportunities our parents never had), so intent on assimilating or
appropriating an identity that in so many ways contradicted our own?
Because, I think, the sense of innocence that is always entailed in feeling
victimized filled us with a corresponding feeling of entitlement, or even
license, that helped us endure our vulnerability on a largely white college
campus.

In my junior year in college I rode to a debate tournament with three
white students and our faculty coach, an elderly English professor. The
experience of being the lone black in a group of whites was so familiar to me
that I thought nothing of it as our trip began. But then, halfway through the
trip, the professor casually turned to me and, in an isn't-the-world-funny sort
of tone, said that he had just refused to rent an apartment in a house he owned
to a "very nice" black couple because their color would "offend" the white
couple who lived downstairs. His eyebrows lifted helplessly over his hawkish
nose, suggesting that he too, like me, was a victim of America's racial farce.
His look assumed a kind of comradeship: he and I were above this grimy
business of race, though for expediency we had occasionally to concede the
world its madness.

My vulnerability in this situation came not so much from the professor's   *30*
blindness to his own racism as from his assumption that I would participate

in it, that I would conspire with him against my own race so that he might remain comfortably blind. Why did he think I would be amenable to this? I can only guess that he assumed my middle-class identity was so complete and all-encompassing that I would see his action as nothing more than a trifling concession to the folkways of our land; that I would in fact applaud his decision not to disturb propriety. Blind to both his own racism and to me—one blindness serving the other—he could not recognize that he was asking me to betray my race in the name of my class.

His blindness made me feel vulnerable because it threatened to expose my own repressed ambivalence. His comment pressured me to choose between my class identification, which had contributed to my being a college student and a member of the debating team, and my desperate desire to be "black." I could have one but not both; I was double-bound.

Because double binds are repressed, there is always an element of terror in them: the terror of bringing to the conscious mind the buried duplicity, self-deception, and pretense involved in serving two masters. This terror is the stuff of vulnerability, and since vulnerability is one of the least tolerable of all human feelings, we usually transform it into an emotion that seems to restore the control of which it has robbed us; most often, that emotion is anger. And so, before the professor had even finished his little story, I had become a furnace of rage. The year was 1967, and I had been primed by endless hours of nap-matching to feel, at least consciously, completely at one with the victim-focused black identity. This identity gave me the license, and the impunity, to unleash upon this professor one of those volcanic eruptions of racial indignation familiar to us from the novels of Richard Wright. Like Cross Damon in *The Outsider,* who kills in perfectly righteous anger, I tried to annihilate the man. I punished him, not according to the measure of his crime, but according to the measure of my vulnerability, a measure set by the cumulative tension of years of repressed terror. Soon, I saw that terror in *his* face as he stared black-eyed at the road ahead. My white friends in the backseat, knowing no conflict between their own class and race, were astonished that someone they had taken to be so much like themselves could harbor a rage that for all the world looked murderous.

Though my rage was triggered by the professor's comment, it was deepened and sustained by a complex of need, conflict, and repression in myself of which I had been wholly unaware. Out of my racial vulnerability I had developed the strong need of an identity with which to defend myself. The only such identity available was that of me as victim, him as victimizer. Once in the grip of this paradigm, I began to do far more damage to myself than he had done.

Seeing myself as a victim meant that I clung all the harder to my racial identity, which, in turn, meant that I suppressed my class identity. This cut me off from all the resources my class values might have offered me. In those values, for instance, I might have found the means to a more dispassionate response, the response less of a victim attacked by a victimizer than of an individual offended by a foolish old man. As an individual, I might have reported this professor to the college dean. Or, I might have calmly tried to reveal his blindness to him, and possibly won a convert. (The flagrancy of his remark suggested a hidden guilt and even a self-recognition on which I might have capitalized. Doesn't confession usually signal a willingness to face oneself?) Or I might have simply chuckled and then let my silence serve as an answer to his provocation. Would not my composure, in any form it might take, deflect into his own heart the arrow he'd shot at me?

Instead, my anger, itself the hair-trigger expression of a long-repressed   35
double bind, not only cut me off from the best of my own resources, it also distorted the nature of my true racial problem. The righteousness of this anger and the easy catharsis it brought buoyed the delusion of my victimization and left me as blind as the professor himself.

As a middle-class black I have often felt myself *contriving* to be "black." And I have noticed this same contrivance in others—a certain stretching away from the natural flow of one's life to align oneself with a victim-focused black identity. Our particular needs are out of sync with the form of identity available to meet those needs. Middle-class blacks need to identify racially; it is better to think of ourselves as black and victimized than not black at all; so we contrive (more unconsciously than consciously) to fit ourselves into an identity that denies our class and fails to address the true source of our vulnerabilty.

For me, this once meant spending inordinate amounts of time at black faculty meetings, though these meetings had little to do with my real racial anxieties or my professional life. I was new to the university, one of two blacks in an English department of over seventy, and I felt a little isolated and vulnerable, though I did not admit it to myself. But at these meetings we discussed the problems of black faculty and students within a framework of victimization. The real vulnerability we felt was covered over by all the adversarial drama the victim/victimizer polarity inspired, and hence went unseen and unassuaged. And this, I think, explains our rather chronic ineffectiveness as a group. Since victimization was not our primary problem—the university had long ago opened its doors to us—we had to contrive to make it so, and there is not much energy in contrivance. What I got at these meetings was ultimately an object lesson in how fruitless struggle can be when it is not grounded in actual need.

At our black faculty meetings, the old equation of blackness with victimization was ever present—to be black was to be a victim; therefore, not to be a victim was not to be black. As we contrived to meet the terms of this formula, there was an inevitable distortion of both ourselves and the larger university. Through the prism of victimization, the university seemed more impenetrable than it actually was, and we more limited in our powers. We fell prey to the victim's myopia, making the university an institution from which we could seek redress, but which we could never fully join. This mind-set often led us to look for more compensations for our supposed victimization than for opportunities we could pursue as individuals.

The discomfort and vulnerability felt by middle-class blacks in the sixties, it could be argued, was a worthwhile price to pay considering the progress achieved during that time of racial confrontation. But what might have been tolerable then is intolerable now. Though changes in American society have made it an anachronism, the monolithic form of racial identification that came out of the sixties is still very much with us. It may be more loosely held, and its power to punish heretics has probably diminished, but it continues to catch middle-class blacks in a double bind, thus impeding not only their own advancement but even, I would contend, that of blacks as a group.

The victim-focused black identity encourages the individual to feel that his advancement depends almost entirely on that of the group. Thus he loses sight not only of his own possibilities but of the inextricable connection between individual effort and individual advancement. This is a profound encumbrance today, when there is more opportunity for blacks than ever before, for it reimposes limitations that can have the same oppressive effect as those the society has only recently begun to remove.

It was the emphasis on mass action in the sixties that made the victim-focused black identity a necessity. But in the nineties and beyond, when racial advancement will come only through a multitude of individual advancements, this form of identity inadvertently adds itself to the forces that hold us back. Hard work, education, individual initiative, stable family life, property ownership—these have always been the means by which ethnic groups have moved ahead in America. Regardless of past or present victimization, these "laws" of advancement apply absolutely to black Americans also. There is no getting around this. What we need is a form of racial identity that energizes the individual by putting him in touch with both his possibilities and his responsibilities.

It has always annoyed me to hear from the mouths of certain arbiters of blackness that middle-class blacks should "reach back" and pull up those blacks less fortunate than they—as though middle-class status was an unearned and essentially passive condition in which one needed a large measure of noblesse oblige to occupy one's time. My own image is of reaching back from a moving train to lift on board those who have no tickets. A noble enough sentiment—but might it not be wiser to show them the entire structure of principles, effort, and sacrifice that puts one in a position to buy a ticket anytime one likes? This, I think, is something members of the black middle class can realistically offer to other blacks. Their example is not only a testament to possibility but also a lesson in method. But they cannot lead by example until they are released from a black identity that regards that example as suspect, that sees them as "marginally" black; indeed that holds *them* back by catching them in a double bind.

To move beyond the victim-focused black identity, we must learn to make a difficult but crucial distinction: between actual victimization, which we must resist with every resource, and identification with the victim's status.

Until we do this, we will continue to wrestle more with ourselves than with the new opportunities that so many paid so dearly to win.

Questions for Understanding

1. What does Steele mean when he says there was a time in his life when he regarded his white classmates as "culturally disadvantaged"?
2. What does Steele mean when he says that one of the qualities of the double bind for a member of the black middle class is that he or she "feels it more than sees it"?
3. Steele says he shares a lifelong conditioning with middle-class people of all races. What are the effects of that conditioning?
4. Why did "Sam" become the kind of black a middle-class black was expected to identify with?
5. Why does the story of the white professor illustrate well Steele's point about being "double bound"?

Suggestions for Writing

1. Do you perceive your racial or ethnic identity somewhat differently now from the way you did five or ten years ago? If so, write an essay in which you describe the process that has led to your present perception of that identity.
2. Write an essay in which you describe the characteristics that people who don't really know your racial or ethnic group attribute to it. To what extent are those characteristics imaginary?
3. Write an essay in which you discuss the advantages and disadvantages of being a member of your particular racial or ethnic group.
4. Write an essay in which you discuss the extent to which you feel the kind of double bind Steele describes.
5. Is it possible to be purely "an American," someone who does not feel the pull of an ethnic or racial heritage? Discuss.

THE RECOLORING OF
CAMPUS LIFE

1989

In the past few years, we have witnessed what the National Institute   1
Against Prejudice and Violence calls a "proliferation" of racial incidents on
college campuses around the country. Incidents of on-campus "intergroup
conflict" have occurred at more than 160 colleges in the last two years,
according to the institute. The nature of these incidents has ranged from open
racial violence—most notoriously, the October 1986 beating of a black
student at the University of Massachusetts at Amherst after an argument
about the World Series turned into a racial bashing, with a crowd of up to
three thousand whites chasing twenty blacks—to the harassment of minority
students and acts of racial or ethnic insensitivity, with by far the greatest
number of episodes falling in the last two categories. At Yale last year, a
swastika and the words "white power" were painted on the university's
Afro-American cultural center. Racist jokes were aired not long ago on a
campus radio station at the University of Michigan. And at the University of
Wisconsin at Madison, members of the Zeta Beta Tau fraternity held a mock
slave auction in which pledges painted their faces black and wore Afro wigs.
Two weeks after the president of Stanford University informed the incoming
freshmen class last fall that "bigotry is out, and I mean it," two freshmen
defaced a poster of Beethoven—gave the image thick lips—and hung it on
a black student's door.

In response, black students around the country have rediscovered the
militant protest strategies of the sixties. At the University of Massachusetts at
Amherst, Williams College, Penn State University, University of California–
Berkeley, UCLA, Stanford University, and countless other campuses, black
students have sat in, marched, and rallied. But much of what they were
marching and rallying about seemed less a response to specific racial incidents
than a call for broader action on the part of the colleges and universities they
were attending. Black students have demanded everything from more black
faculty members and new courses on racism to the addition of "ethnic" foods
in the cafeteria. There is the sense in these demands that racism runs deep. Is
the campus becoming the battleground for a renewed war between the races?
I don't think so, not really. But if it is not a war, the problem of campus racism
does represent a new and surprising hardening of racial lines within the most
traditionally liberal and tolerant of America's institutions—its universities.

As a black who has spent his entire adult life on predominantly white
campuses, I found it hard to believe that the problem of campus racism was
as dramatic as some of the incidents seemed to make it. The incidents I read
or heard about often seemed prankish and adolescent, though not necessarily
harmless. There is a meanness in them but not much menace; no one is

proposing to reinstitute Jim Crow on campus. On the California campus where I now teach, there have been few signs of racial tension.

And, of course, universities are not where racial problems tend to arise. When I went to college in the mid-sixties, colleges were oases of calm and understanding in a racially tense society; campus life—with its traditions of tolerance and fairness, its very distance from the "real" world—imposed a degree of broad-mindedness on even the most provincial students. If I met whites who were not anxious to be friends with blacks, most were at least vaguely friendly to the cause of our freedom. In any case, there was no guerrilla activity against our presence, no "mine field of racism" (as one black student at Berkeley recently put it to me) to negotiate. I wouldn't say that the phrase "campus racism" is a contradiction in terms, but until recently it certainly seemed an incongruence.

But a greater incongruence is the generational timing of this new   5 problem on the campuses. Today's undergraduates were born after the passage of the 1964 Civil Rights Act. They grew up in an age when racial equality was for the first time enforceable by law. This too was a time when blacks suddenly appeared on television, as mayors of big cities, as icons of popular culture, as teachers, and in some cases even as neighbors. Today's black and white college students, veterans of "Sesame Street" and often of integrated grammar and high schools, have had more opportunities to know each other than any previous generation in American history. Not enough opportunities, perhaps, but enough to make the notion of racial tension on campus something of a mystery, at least to me.

To look at this mystery, I left my own campus with its burden of familiarity and talked with black and white students at California schools where racial incidents had occurred: Stanford, UCLA, and Berkeley. I spoke with black and white students—not with Asians and Hispanics—because, as always, blacks and whites represent the deepest lines of division, and because I hesitate to wander onto the complex territory of other minority groups. A phrase by William H. Gass—"the hidden internality of things"—describes, with maybe a little too much grandeur, what I hoped to find. But it is what I wanted to find, for this is the kind of problem that makes a black person nervous, which is not to say that it doesn't unnerve whites as well. Once every six months or so someone yells "nigger" at me from a passing car. I don't like to think that these solo artists might soon make up a chorus, or worse, that this chorus might one day soon sing to me from the paths of my own campus.

I have long believed that the trouble between the races is seldom what it appears to be. It was not hard to see after my first talks with students that racial tension on campus is a problem that misrepresents itself. It has the same look, the archetypal pattern, of America's timeless racial conflict—white racism and black protest. And I think part of our concern over it comes from the fact that it has the feel of a relapse, illness gone and come again. But if we are seeing the same symptoms, I don't believe we are dealing with the same illness. For one thing, I think racial tension on campus is more the result of racial equality than inequality.

How to live with racial difference has been America's profound social problem. For the first hundred years or so following emancipation it was controlled by a legally sanctioned inequality that kept the races from each other. No longer is this the case. On campuses today, as throughout society, blacks enjoy equality under the law—a profound social advancement. No student may be kept out of a class or a dormitory or an extracurricular activity because of his or her race. But there is a paradox here: on a campus where members of all races are gathered, mixed together in the classroom as well as socially, differences are more exposed than ever. And this is where the trouble starts. For members of each race—young adults coming into their own, often away from home for the first time—bring to this site of freedom, exploration, and (now, today) equality, very deep fears, anxieties, inchoate feelings of racial shame, anger, and guilt. These feelings could lie dormant in the home, in familiar neighborhoods, in simpler days of childhood. But the college campus, with its structures of interaction and adult-level competition—the big exam, the dorm, the mixer—is another matter. I think campus racism is born of the rub between racial difference and a setting, the campus itself, devoted to interaction and equality. On our campuses, such concentrated micro-societies, all that remains unresolved between blacks and whites, all the old wounds and shames that have never been addressed, present themselves for attention—and present our youth with pressures they cannot always handle.

I have mentioned one paradox: racial fears and anxieties among blacks and whites, bubbling up in an era of racial equality under the law, in settings that are among the freest and fairest in society. But there is another, related paradox, stemming from the notion of—and practice of—affirmative action. Under the provisions of the Equal Employment Opportunity Act of 1972, all state governments and institutions (including universities) were forced to initiate plans to increase the proportion of minority and women employees and, in the case of universities, of students too. Affirmative action plans that establish racial quotas were ruled unconstitutional more than ten years ago in *University of California* v. *Bakke,* but such plans are still thought by some to secretly exist, and lawsuits having to do with alleged quotas are still very much with us. But quotas are only the most controversial aspect of affirmative action: the principle of affirmative action is reflected in various university programs aimed at redressing and overcoming past patterns of discrimination. Of course, to be conscious of past patterns of discriminations—the fact, say, that public schools in the black inner cities are more crowded and employ fewer top-notch teachers than a white suburban public school, and that this is a factor in student performance—is only reasonable. But in doing this we also call attention quite obviously to difference: in the case of blacks and whites, racial difference. What has emerged on campus in recent years—as a result of the new equality and of affirmative action and, in a sense, as a result of progress—is a *politics of difference,* a troubling, volatile politics in which each group justifies itself, its sense of worth and its pursuit of power, through difference alone.

In this context, racial, ethnic, and gender differences become forms of sovereignty, campuses become balkanized, and each group fights with whatever means are available. No doubt there are many factors that have contributed to the rise of racial tension on campus: What has been the role of fraternities, which have returned to campus with their inclusions and exclusions? What role has the heightened notion of college as some first step to personal, financial success played in increasing competition, and thus tension? But mostly, what I sense is that in interactive settings, fighting the fights of "difference," old ghosts are stirred and haunt again. Black and white Americans simply have the power to make each other feel shame and guilt. In most situations, we may be able to deny these feelings, keep them at bay. But these feelings are likely to surface on college campuses, where young people are groping for identity and power, and where difference is made to matter so greatly. In a way, racial tension on campus in the eighties might have been inevitable.

I would like, first, to discuss black students, their anxieties and vulnerabilities. The accusation black Americans have always lived with is that they are inferior—inferior simply because they are black. And this accusation has been too uniform, too ingrained in cultural imagery, too enforced by law, custom, and every form of power not to have left a mark. Black inferiority was a precept accepted by the founders of this nation; it was a principle of social organization that relegated blacks to the sidelines of American life. So when young black students find themselves on white campuses surrounded by those who have historically claimed superiority, they are also surrounded by the myth of their inferiority.

Of course, it is true that many young people come to college with some anxiety about not being good enough. But only blacks come wearing a color that is still, in the minds of some, a sign of inferiority. Poles, Jews, Hispanics, and other groups also endure degrading stereotypes. But two things make the myth of black inferiority a far heavier burden—the broadness of its scope and its incarnation in color. There are not only more stereotypes of blacks than of other groups, but these stereotypes are also more dehumanizing, more focused on the most despised human traits: stupidity, laziness, sexual immorality, dirtiness, and so on. In America's racial and ethnic hierarchy, blacks have clearly been relegated to the lowest level—have been burdened with an ambiguous, animalistic humanity. Moreover, this is made unavoidable for blacks by sheer visibility of black skin, a skin that evokes the myth of inferiority on sight. Today this myth is sadly reinforced for many black students by affirmative action programs, under which blacks may often enter college with lower test scores and high school grade point averages than whites. "They see me as an affirmative action case," one black student told me at UCLA. This reinforces the myth of inferiority by implying that blacks are not good enough to make it into college on their own.

So when a black student enters college, the myth of inferiority compounds the normal anxiousness over whether he or she will be good enough. This anxiety is not only personal but also racial. The families of these students will have pounded into them the fact that blacks are not inferior. And probably more than anything it is this pounding that finally leaves the mark. If I am not inferior, why the need to say so?

This myth of inferiority constitutes a very sharp and ongoing anxiety for young blacks, the nature of which is very precise: it is the terror that somehow, through one's actions or by virtue of some "proof" (a poor grade, a flubbed response in class), one's fear of inferiority—inculcated in ways large and small by society—will be confirmed as real. On a university campus where intelligence itself is the ultimate measure, this anxiety is bound to be triggered.

A black student I met at UCLA was disturbed a little when I asked him if he ever felt vulnerable—anxious about "black inferiority"—as a black student. But after a long pause, he finally said, "I think I do." The example he gave was of a large lecture class he'd taken with over three hundred students. Fifty or so black students sat in the back of the lecture hall and "acted out every stereotype in the book." They were loud, ate food, came in late—and generally got lower grades than whites in the class. "I knew I would be seen like them, and I didn't like it. I never sat by them." Seen like what, I asked, though we both knew the answer. "As lazy, ignorant, and stupid," he said sadly.

Had the group at the back been white fraternity brothers, they would not have been seen as dumb whites, of course. And a frat brother who worried about his grades would not worry that he would be seen "like them." The terror in this situation for the black student I spoke with was that his own deeply buried anxiety would be given credence, that the myth would be verified, and that he would feel shame and humiliation not because of who he was but simply because he was black. In this lecture hall his race, quite apart from his performance, might subject him to four unendurable feelings— diminishment, accountability to the preconceptions of whites, a powerlessness to change those preconceptions, and finally, shame. These are the feelings that make up his racial anxiety, and that of all blacks on any campus. On a white campus a black is never far from these feelings, and even his unconscious knowledge that he is subject to them can undermine his self-esteem. There are blacks on any campus who are not up to doing good college-level work. Certain black students may not be happy or motivated or in the appropriate field of study—*just like whites.* (Let us not forget that many white students get poor grades, fail, drop out.) Moreover, many more blacks than whites are not quite prepared for college, may have to catch up, owing to factors beyond their control: poor previous schooling, for example. But the white who has to catch up will not be anxious that his being behind is a matter of his whiteness, of his being racially inferior. The black student may well have such a fear.

This, I believe, is one reason why black colleges in America turn out 37 percent of all black college graduates though they enroll only 16 percent of black college students. Without whites around on campus, the myth of inferiority is in abeyance and, along with it, a great reservoir of culturally imposed self-doubt. On black campuses, feelings of inferiority are personal; on campuses with a white majority, a black's problems have a way of becoming a "black" problem.

But this feeling of vulnerability a black may feel, in itself, is not as serious a problem as what he or she does with it. To admit that one is made anxious in integrated situations about the myth of racial inferiority is difficult for young blacks. It seems like admitting that one is racially inferior. And so, most often, the student will deny harboring the feelings. This is where some of the pangs of racial tension begin, because denial always involves distortion.

In order to deny a problem we must tell ourselves that the problem is something different from what it really is. A black student at Berkeley told me that he felt defensive every time he walked into a classroom of white faces. When I asked why, he said, "Because I know they're all racists. They think blacks are stupid." Of course it may be true that some whites feel this way, but the singular focus on white racism allows this student to obscure his own underlying racial anxiety. He can now say that his problem—facing a classroom of white faces, *fearing* that they think he is dumb—is entirely the result of certifiable white racism and has nothing to do with his own anxieties, or even that this particular academic subject may not be his best. Now all the terror of his anxiety, its powerful energy, is devoted to simply *seeing* racism. Whatever evidence of racism he finds—and looking this hard, he will no doubt find some—can be brought in to buttress his distorted view of the problem while his actual deep-seated anxiety goes unseen.

Denial, and the distortion that results, places the problem *outside* the self and in the world. It is not that I have any inferiority anxiety because of my race; it is that I am going to school with people who don't like blacks. This is the shift in thinking that allows black students to reenact the protest pattern of the sixties. *Denied racial anxiety—distortion—reenactment* is the process by which feelings of inferiority are transformed into an exaggerated white menace—which is then protested against with the techniques of the past. Under the sway of this process, black students believe that history is repeating itself, that it's just like the sixties, or fifties. In fact, it is not-yet-healed wounds from the past, rather than the inequality that created the wounds, that is the real problem.

This process generates an unconscious need to exaggerate the level of racism on campus—to make it a matter of the system, not just a handful of students. Racism is the avenue away from the true inner anxiety. How many students demonstrating for black theme dorms—demonstrating in the style of the sixties, when the battle was to win for blacks a place on campus—might be better off spending their time reading and studying? Black students have the highest dropout rate and the lowest grade point average of any group in

20

American universities. This need not be so. And it is not the result of not having black theme dorms.

It was my very good fortune to go to college in 1964, when the question of black "inferiority" was openly talked about among blacks. The summer before I left for college, I heard Martin Luther King speak in Chicago, and he laid it on the line for black students everywhere: "When you are behind in a footrace, the only way to get ahead is to run faster than the man in front of you. So when your white roommate says he's tired and goes to sleep, you stay up and burn the midnight oil." His statement that we were "behind in a footrace" acknowledged that, because of history, of few opportunities, of racism, we were, in a sense, "inferior." But this had to do with what had been done to our parents and their parents, not with inherent inferiority. And because it was acknowledged, it was presented to us as a challenge rather than a mark of shame.

Of the eighteen black students (in a student body of one thousand) who were on campus in my freshman year, all graduated, though a number of us were not from the middle class. At the university where I currently teach, the dropout rate for black students is 72 percent, despite the presence of several academic support programs, a counseling center with black counselors, an Afro-American studies department, black faculty, administrators, and staff, a general education curriculum that emphasizes "cultural pluralism," an Educational Opportunities Program, a mentor program, a black faculty and staff association, and an administration and faculty that often announce the need to do more for black students.

It may be unfair to compare my generation with the current one. Parents do this compulsively and to little end but self-congratulation. But I don't congratulate my generation. I think we were advantaged. We came along at a time when racial integration was held in high esteem. And integration was a very challenging social concept for both blacks and whites. We were remaking ourselves—that's what one did at college—and making history. We had something to prove. This was a profound advantage; it gave us clarity and a challenge. Achievement in the American mainstream was the goal of integration, and the best thing about this challenge was its secondary message—that we *could* achieve.

There is much irony in the fact that black power would come along in the late sixties and change all this. Black power was a movement of uplift and pride, and yet it also delivered the weight of pride—a weight that would burden black students from then on. Black power "nationalized" the black identity, made blackness itself an object of celebration, an allegiance. But if it transformed a mark of shame into a mark of pride, it also, in the name of pride, required the denial of racial anxiety. Without a frank account of one's anxieties, there is no clear direction, no concrete challenge. Black students today do not get as clear a message from their racial identity as my generation got. They are not filled with the same urgency to prove themselves because black pride has said, *You're already proven, already equal, as good as anybody.*

The "black identity" shaped by black power most forcefully contributes to racial tensions on campuses by basing entitlement more on race than on constitutional rights and standards of merit. With integration, black entitlement derived from constitutional principles of fairness. Black power changed this by skewing the formula from rights to color—if you were black, you were entitled. Thus the United Coalition Against Racism (UCAR) at the University of Michigan could "demand" two years ago that all black professors be given immediate tenure, that there is a special pay incentive for black professors, and that money be provided for an all-black student union. In this formula, black becomes the very color of entitlement, an extra right in itself, and a very dangerous grandiosity is promoted in which blackness amounts to specialness.

Race is, by any standard, an unprincipled source of power. And on campuses the use of racial power by one group makes racial, ethnic, or gender difference a currency of power for all groups. When I make my *difference* into power, other groups must seize upon their difference to contain my power and maintain their position relative to me. Very quickly a kind of politics of difference emerges in which racial, ethnic, and gender groups are forced to assert their entitlement and vie for power based on the single quality that makes them different from one another.

On many campuses today academic departments and programs are established on the basis of difference—black studies, women's studies, Asian studies, and so on—despite the fact that there is nothing in these "difference" departments that cannot be studied within traditional academic disciplines. If their rationale is truly past exclusion from the mainstream curriculum, shouldn't the goal now be complete inclusion rather than separateness? I think this logic is overlooked because these groups are too interested in the power their difference can bring, and they insist on separate departments and programs as tribute to that power.

This politics of difference makes everyone on campus a member of a minority group. It also makes racial tension inevitable. To highlight one's difference as a source of advantage is also, indirectly, to inspire the enemies of that difference. When blackness (and femaleness) become power, then white maleness is also sanctioned as power. A white male student I spoke with at Stanford said, "One of my friends said the other day that we should get together and start up a white student union and come up with a list of demands."

It is certainly true that white maleness has long been an unfair source of power. But the sin of white male power is precisely its use of race and gender as a source of entitlement. When minorities and women use their race, ethnicity, and gender in the same way, they not only commit the same sin but also, indirectly, sanction the very form of power that oppressed them in the first place. The politics of difference is based on a tit-for-tat sort of logic in which every victory only calls one's enemies to arms.

This elevation of difference undermines the communal impulse by making each group foreign and inaccessible to others. When difference is celebrated rather than remarked, people must think in terms of difference, they must find meaning in difference, and this meaning comes from an endless process of contrasting one's group with other groups. Blacks use whites to define themselves as different, women use men, Hispanics use whites and blacks, and on it goes. And in the process each group mythologizes and mystifies its difference, puts it beyond the full comprehension of outsiders. Difference becomes inaccessible preciousness toward which outsiders are expected to be simply and uncomprehendingly reverential. But beware: in this world, even the insulated world of the college campus, preciousness is a balloon asking for a needle. At Smith College graffiti appears: "Niggers, spics, and chinks. Quit complaining or get out."

I think that those who run our colleges and universities are every bit as responsible for the politics of difference as are minority students. To correct the exclusions once caused by race and gender, universities—under the banner of affirmative action—have relied too heavily on race and gender as criteria. So rather than break the link between difference and power, they have reinforced it. On most campuses today, a well-to-do black student with two professional parents is qualified by his race for scholarship monies that are not available to a lower-middle-class white student. A white female with a private school education and every form of cultural advantage comes under the affirmative action umbrella. This kind of inequity is an invitation to backlash.

What universities are quite rightly trying to do is compensate people for past discrimination and the deprivations that followed from it. But race and gender alone offer only the grossest measure of this. And the failure of universities has been their backing away from the challenge of identifying principles of fairness and merit that make finer and more equitable distinctions. The real challenge is not simply to include a certain number of blacks, but to end discrimination against all blacks and to offer special help to those with talent who have also been economically deprived.

With regard to black students, affirmative action has led universities to correlate color with poverty and disadvantage in so absolute a way as to encourage the politics of difference. But why have they gone along with this? My belief is that it is due to the specific form of racial anxiety to which whites are most subject.

Most of the white students I talked with spoke as if from under a faint cloud of accusation. There was always a ring of defensiveness in their complaints about blacks. A white student I spoke to at UCLA told me: "Most white students on this campus think the black student leadership here is made up of oversensitive crybabies who spend all their time looking for things to kick up a ruckus about." A white student at Stanford said, "Blacks do nothing but complain and ask for sympathy when everyone really knows that they don't do well because they don't try. If they worked harder, they could do as well as everyone else."

That these students felt accused was most obvious in their compulsion to assure me that they were not racist. Oblique versions of some-of-my-best-friends-are stories came ritualistically before or after critiques of black students. Some said flatly, "I am not a racist, but. . . ." Of course, we all deny being racist, but we only do this compulsively, I think, when we are working against an accusation of bias. I think it was the color of my skin itself that accused them.

This was the meta-message that surrounded these conversations like an aura, and it is, I believe, the core of white American racial anxiety. My skin not only accused them; it judged them. And this judgment was a sad gift of history that brought them to account whether they deserved such accountability or not. It said that wherever and whenever blacks were concerned, they had reason to feel guilt. And whether it was earned or unearned, I think it was guilt that set off the compulsion in these students to disclaim. I believe it is true that, in America, black people make white people feel guilty.

Guilt is the essence of white anxiety just as inferiority is the essence of black anxiety. And the terror that it carries for whites is the terror of discovering that one has reason to feel guilt where blacks are concerned—not so much because of what blacks might think but because of what guilt can say about oneself. If the darkest fear of blacks is inferiority, the darkest fear of whites is that their better lot in life is at least partially the result of their capacity for evil—their capacity to dehumanize an entire people for their own benefit and then to be indifferent to the devastation their dehumanization has wrought on successive generations of their victims. This is the terror that whites are vulnerable to regarding blacks. And the mere fact of being white is sufficient to feel it, since even whites with hearts clean of racism benefit from being white—benefit at the expense of blacks. This is a conditional guilt having nothing to do with individual intentions or actions. And it makes for a very powerful anxiety because it threatens whites with a view of themselves as inhuman, just as inferiority threatens blacks with a similar view of themselves. At the dark core of both anxieties is a suspicion of incomplete humanity.

So, the white students I met were not just meeting me; they were also meeting the possibility of their own inhumanity. And this, I think, is what explains how some young white college students in the late eighties could so frankly take part in racially insensitive and outright racist acts. They were expected to be cleaner of racism than any previous generation—they were born into the Great Society. But this expectation overlooks the fact that, for them, color is still an accusation and judgment. In black faces there is a discomforting reflection of white collective shame. Blacks remind them that their racial innocence is questionable, that they are the beneficiaries of past and present racism, and the sins of the father may well have been visited on the children.

And yet young whites tell themselves that they had nothing to do with the oppression of black people. They have a stronger belief in their racial innocence than any previous generation of whites and a natural hostility toward anyone who would challenge that innocence. So (with a great deal of individual variation) they can end up in the paradoxical position of being hostile to blacks as a way of defending their own racial innocence.

I think this is what the young white editors of the *Dartmouth Review* were doing when they harassed black music professor William Cole. Weren't they saying, in effect, I am so free of racial guilt that I can afford to attack blacks ruthlessly and still be racially innocent? The ruthlessness of these attacks was a form of denial, a badge of innocence. The more they were charged with racism, the more ugly and confrontational their harassment became (an escalation unexplained even by the serious charges against Professor Cole). Racism became a means of rejecting racial guilt, a way of showing that they were not, ultimately, racists.

The politics of difference sets up a struggle for innocence among all groups. When difference is the currency of power, each group must fight for the innocence that entitles it to power. To gain this innocence, blacks sting whites with guilt, remind them of their racial past, accuse them of new and more subtle forms of racism. One way whites retrieve their innocence is to discredit blacks and deny their difficulties, for in this denial is the denial of their own guilt. To blacks this denial looks like racism, a racism that feeds black innocence and encourages them to throw more guilt at whites. And so the cycle continues. The politics of difference leads each group to pick at the vulnerabilities of the other.

Men and women who run universities—whites, mostly—participate in the politics of difference because they handle their guilt differently than do many of their students. They don't deny it, but still they don't want to *feel* it. And to avoid this feeling of guilt they have tended to go along with whatever blacks put on the table rather than work with them to assess their real needs. University administrators have too often been afraid of guilt and have relied on negotiation and capitulation more to appease their own guilt than to help blacks and other minorities. Administrators would never give white students a racial theme dorm where they could be "more comfortable with people of their own kind," yet more and more universities are doing this for black students, thus fostering a kind of voluntary segregation. To avoid the anxieties of integrated situations blacks ask for theme dorms; to avoid guilt, white administrators give theme dorms.

When everyone is on the run from their anxieties about race, race relations on campus can be reduced to the negotiation of avoidances. A pattern of demand and concession develops in which both sides use the other to escape themselves. Black studies departments, black deans of student affairs, black counseling programs, Afro houses, black theme dorms, black homecoming dances and graduation ceremonies—black students and white administrators have slowly engineered a machinery of separatism that, in the name of sacred difference, redraws the ugly lines of segregation.

Black students have not sufficiently helped themselves, and universities, despite all their concessions, have not really done much for blacks. If both faced their anxieties, I think they would see the same thing: academic parity with all other groups should be the overriding mission of black students, and it should also be the first goal that universities have for their black students. Blacks can only *know* they are as good as others when they are, in fact, as good—when their grades are higher and their dropout rate lower. Nothing under the sun will substitute for this, and no amount of concessions will bring it about.

Universities can never be free of guilt until they truly help black students, which means leading and challenging them rather than negotiating and capitulating. It means inspiring them to achieve academic parity, nothing less, and helping them to see their own weaknesses as their greatest challenge. It also means dismantling the machinery of separatism, breaking the link between difference and power, and skewing the formula for entitlement away from race and gender and back to constitutional rights.

As for the young white students who have rediscovered swastikas and the word "nigger," I think that they suffer from an exaggerated sense of their own innocence, as if they were incapable of evil and beyond the reach of guilt. But it is also true that the politics of difference creates an environment that threatens their innocence and makes them defensive. White students are not invited to the negotiating table from which they see blacks and others walk away with concessions. The presumption is that they do not deserve to be there because they are white. So they can only be defensive, and the less mature among them will be aggressive. Guerrilla activity will ensue. Of course this is wrong, but it is also a reflection of an environment where difference carries power and where whites have the wrong "difference."

I think the universities should emphasize commonality as a higher value than "diversity" and "pluralism"—buzzwords for the politics of difference. Difference that does not rest on a clearly delineated foundation of commonality is not only inaccessible to those who are not part of the ethnic or racial group, but also antagonistic to them. Difference can enrich only the common ground.

Integration has become an abstract term today, having to do with little more than numbers and racial balances. But it once stood for a high and admirable set of values. It made difference second to commonality, and it asked members of all races to face whatever fears they inspired in each other. I doubt the word will have a new vogue, but the values, under whatever name, are worth working for.

Questions for Understanding

1. Why does Steele think racial tension on America's campuses "is more the result of racial equality than inequality"?
2. According to Steele, what have been the consequences of the rise of the "politics of difference"?
3. What does Steele believe is the effect on blacks of college affirmative action policies?

4. According to Steele, what are the feelings that make up the racial anxiety felt by blacks on college campuses? What are the feelings that contribute to white anxiety?
5. What does Steele believe are the effects when black students deny they feel anxiety in situations in which blacks and whites are together?

Suggestions for Writing

1. "Difference can enrich only the common ground." The emphasis in Steele's statement is on *common*. Do you agree or disagree? Write an essay in which you argue for the truth of your position.
2. Write an essay in which you discuss the extent to which your college or university emphasizes commonality over diversity.
3. Write an essay in which you discuss what it would take to bring true integration to your campus. Or discuss why you think an attempt to attain true integration would be a mistake.
4. Was the politics of difference more or less apparent in your high school than in your college? Discuss.
5. Write an essay in which you compare the racial anxieties you feel now with those you felt when you entered high school.

Barbara Ehrenreich

[1941–]

The daughter of Ben Howes and Isabelle Oxley Alexander, Barbara Ehrenreich was born and raised in Butte, Montana, a copper-mining and railroad town with a reputation for being wide open. Growing up in a place with the diversity of population and the relative tolerance of Butte helped shape Ehrenreich's attitudes and beliefs.

Just as some people inherit the religion of their parents and ancestors, Ehrenreich inherited atheism, in which, she says, her father believed with all the conviction of a devoutly religious person. Her father's ideas profoundly influenced Ehrenreich, and the greatest influence on her father was the renowned nineteenth-century orator Robert Ingersoll, whose lectures had been published in a twelve-volume edition.

Ben Howes had all twelve volumes, which included such lectures as "Some Mistakes of Moses," "Why I Am an Agnostic," and "Superstition." In an interview published in 1992, Ehrenreich recalls her father reading to his children from Ingersoll on Sunday mornings. She says that her father's incipient atheism was reinforced when he asked the high school librarian in Butte about Ingersoll and was told that Ingersoll's books were kept in a locked cabinet. Her father claimed that freethinking was widespread in Butte because among the miners there was a lot of class resentment. The miners, Ehrenreich says, "equated the clergy with lawyers and doctors and bosses—guys who sat around and didn't do anything while other men broke their backs and risked their lives."

There were no locked cabinets in the Howes household. "We had over seventy Bibles lying around where anyone could browse through them—Gideons my dad had removed from the motel rooms he stayed in. And I remember how he gloried in every Gideon he lifted, thinking of all the traveling salesmen whose minds he'd probably saved from dry rot." And her mother, Ehrenreich recalls, consistently responded to her children's questions with "Think for yourself! Think for yourself!" On religion, Ehrenreich sees herself as a bit mellower than her parents, from whom, she says, she heard many things "which I now think of as fairly intolerant: that religion was nothing but superstition, that anybody who'd be hookwinked by it was a fool. . . ."

Given this background, it is not surprising that Ehrenreich is an astute observer of social class, a strong supporter of working-class causes, and an officer of the Democratic Socialists of America. Indeed, Ehrenreich's second husband is a director of organizing for the Teamsters union. At twenty-nine, she wrote a book with her first husband, John Ehrenreich, that attacked the American health-care industry—*The American Health Empire: Power, Profits, and Politics* (1970). Also with John Ehrenreich, she wrote *Long March, Short Spring* (1969). Having earned a Ph.D. in biology from Rockefeller University, Ehrenreich was well equipped to write about health and medical issues. With Deirdre English, she wrote three books on such issues: *Witches, Midwives, and Nurses* (1972); *Complaints and Disorders: The Sexual Politics of Sickness* (1973); and *For Her Own*

Good: One Hundred Fifty Years of the Experts' Advice to Women (1978). Ehrenreich's other books are *The Hearts of Men: American Dreams and the Flight from Commitment* (1983); *Re-Making Love; The Feminization of Sex* (1986), with Elizabeth Hess and Gloria Jacobs; *Fear of Falling: The Inner Life of the Middle Class* (1989); *The Worst Years of Our Lives* (1991); and *Kipper's Game,* a novel (1993).

CULTURAL BAGGAGE

1992

An acquaintance was telling me about the joys of rediscovering her   1
ethnic and religious heritage. "I know exactly what my ancestors were doing
2,000 years ago," she said, eyes gleaming with enthusiasm, "and *I can do the
same things now.*" Then she leaned forward and inquired politely, "And what
is your ethnic background, if I may ask?"

"None," I said, that being the first word in line to get out of my mouth.
Well, not "none," I backtracked. Scottish, English, Irish—that was something, I supposed. Too much Irish to qualify as a WASP; too much of the
hated English to warrant a "Kiss Me, I'm Irish" button; plus there are a
number of dead ends in the family tree due to adoptions, missing records,
failing memories and the like. I was blushing by this time. Did "none" mean
I was rejecting my heritage out of Anglo-Celtic self-hate? Or was I revealing
a hidden ethnic chauvinism in which the Brittanically derived serve as a kind
of neutral standard compared with the ethnic "others"?

Throughout the 60's and 70's, I watched one group after another—
African-Americans, Latinos, Native Americans—stand up and proudly
reclaim their roots while I just sank back ever deeper into my seat. All this
excitement over ethnicity stemmed, I uneasily sensed, from a past in which
their ancestors had been trampled upon by *my* ancestors, or at least by people
who looked very much like them. In addition, it had begun to seem almost
un–American not to have some sort of hyphen at hand, linking one to more
venerable times and locales.

But the truth is, I was raised with none. We'd eaten ethnic foods in my
childhood home, but these were all borrowed, like the pasties, or Cornish
meat pies, my father had picked up from his fellow miners in Butte, Mont.
If my mother had one rule, it was militant ecumenism in all matters of food
and experience. "Try new things," she would say, meaning anything from
sweetbreads to clams, with an emphasis on the "new."

As a child, I briefly nourished a craving for tradition and roots. I   5
immersed myself in the works of Sir Walter Scott. I pretended to believe that
the bagpipe was a musical instrument. I was fascinated to learn from a
grandmother that we were descended from certain Highland clans and
longed for a pleated skirt in one of their distinctive tartans.

But in "Ivanhoe," it was the dark-eyed "Jewess" Rebecca I identified
with, not the flaxen-haired bimbo Rowena. As for clans: Why not call them
"tribes," those bands of half-clad peasants and warriors whose idea of cuisine
was stuffed sheep gut washed down with whiskey? And then there was the
sting of Disraeli's remark—which I came across in my early teens—to the
effect that his ancestors had been leading orderly, literate lives when my
ancestors were still rampaging through the Highlands daubing themselves
with blue paint.

Motherhood put the screws on me, ethnicity-wise. I had hoped that by marrying a man of Eastern European-Jewish ancestry I would acquire for my descendants the ethnic genes that my own forebears so sadly lacked. At one point, I even subjected the children to a seder of my own design, including a little talk about the flight from Egypt and its relevance to modern social issues. But the kids insisted on buttering their matzohs and snickering through my talk. "Give me a break, Mom," the older one said. "You don't even believe in God."

After the tiny pagans had been put to bed, I sat down to brood over Elijah's wine. What had I been thinking? The kids knew that their Jewish grandparents were secular folks who didn't hold seders themselves. And if ethnicity eluded me, how could I expect it to take root in my children, who are not only Scottish-English-Irish, but Hungarian-Polish-Russian to boot?

But, then, on the fumes of Manischewitz, a great insight took form in my mind. It was true, as the kids said, that I didn't "believe in God." But this could be taken as something very different from an accusation—a reminder of a genuine heritage. My parents had not believed in God either, nor had my grandparents or any other progenitors going back to the great-great level. They had become disillusioned with Christianity generations ago—just as, on the in-law side, my children's other ancestors had shaken off their Orthodox Judaism. This insight did not exactly furnish me with an "identity," but it was at least something to work with: we are the kind of people, I realized—whatever our distant ancestors' religions—who do *not* believe, who do not carry on traditions, who do not do things just because someone has done them before.

The epiphany went on: I recalled that my mother never introduced a procedure for cooking or cleaning by telling me, "Grandma did it this way." What did Grandma know, living in the days before vacuum cleaners and disposable toilet mops? In my parents' general view, new things were better than old, and the very fact that some ritual had been performed in the past was a good reason for abandoning it now. Because what was the past, as our forebears knew it? Nothing but poverty, superstition and grief. "Think for yourself," Dad used to say. "Always ask why."

In fact, this may have been the ideal cultural heritage for my particular ethnic strain—bounced as it was from the Highlands of Scotland across the sea, out to the Rockies, down into the mines and finally spewed out into high-tech, suburban America. What better philosophy, for a race of migrants, than "Think for yourself"? What better maxim, for a people whose whole world was rudely inverted every 30 years or so, than "Try new things"?

The more tradition-minded, the newly enthusiastic celebrants of Purim and Kwanzaa and Solstice, may see little point to survival if the survivors carry no cultural freight—religion, for example, or ethnic tradition. To which I would say that skepticism, curiosity and wide-eyed ecumenical tolerance are also worthy elements of the human tradition and are at least as old as such notions as "Serbian" or "Croatian," "Scottish" or "Jewish." I make no claims for my personal line of progenitors except that they remained loyal to the values that may have induced all of our ancestors, long, long ago, to climb down from the trees and make their way into the open plains.

A few weeks ago, I cleared my throat and asked the children, now mostly grown and fearsomely smart, whether they felt any stirrings of ethnic or religious identity, etc., which might have been, ahem, insufficiently nourished at home. "None," they said, adding firmly, "and the world would be a better place if nobody else did, either." My chest swelled with pride, as would my mother's, to know that the race of "none" marches on.

Questions for Understanding

1. What does Ehrenreich mean when she asks rhetorically, "Or was I revealing a hidden ethnic chauvinism in which the Britannically derived serve as a kind of neutral standard compared with the ethnic 'others'"?
2. What does Ehrenreich mean when she says her mother had a rule of "militant ecumenism in all matters of food and experience"?
3. What is Ehrenreich's attitude toward her mother?
4. Ehrenreich, who was not raised Jewish, married a Jewish man. What attitude did she take toward her husband's Jewishness?
5. Whereas others take pride in their ethnic and religious heritage, what does Ehrenreich believe is more important?

Suggestions for Writing

1. Write an essay in which you describe the main characteristics of the ethnic or religious group to which you belong.
2. Write an essay in which you compare and contrast two typical members of the group to which you belong.
3. Select one interesting belief of the group to which you belong, and point out how it is similar to, yet different from, a parallel belief of some other ethnic or religious group.
4. Discuss the pressures you have felt to be a "good" representative of your group.
5. As far as Ehrenreich is concerned, "skepticism, curiosity, and wide-eyed ecumenical tolerance" are the elements of the human tradition that are most worthy of her allegiance. Write an essay in which you discuss the particular elements of the human tradition with which you like to ally yourself.

NUTS AND BOLTS 2: INTRODUCTIONS

Writing instructors expect introductions to accomplish two basic objectives: to grab the reader's attention and to reveal clearly what the writer's intention is. In student writing, getting the reader's attention is not nearly as important as making the intention clear. Instructors want to be told up front, in the very first paragraph, where the writer intends to take them—that is, what point the writer plans to prove, explain, or illustrate. They want to know what the writer plans to do—what the paper's *thesis* is. Most instructors assume that the first step in becoming a successful writer is to be able to write an introduction that effectively states a thesis.

The thesis is sometimes called the *controlling idea* because it controls—determines—what should be in the rest of the paper. Writing instructors usually expect everything in the body of the paper to contribute to the development of the thesis. If there is no thesis, or if the thesis is unclear, it is unlikely that the paper will be logically developed and coherent. The ability to write an essay in which a clearly stated thesis is developed logically and coherently is like a sports team's ability to run its basic offense effectively—in practices. I say "in practices" because no real-world editor will think much of a piece of writing that adheres rigidly to this basic formula, just as no real-world sports opponent is likely to have much difficulty coping with an offense that is nothing more than a basic pattern.

Experienced writers usually do not organize their essays the way instructors expect students to; this can be readily seen in the essays in this book or in any other essay anthology. Experienced writers certainly recognize the need to communicate their purpose and to organize effectively, but they like to fulfill that requirement in ways that are less formal and more interesting. In reading the work of an experienced writer, therefore, a reader may have to *infer* the thesis; for instead of stating it clearly and unambiguously, the writer may have chosen to *imply* it. Implying rather than stating the thesis enables the words that are actually used to do the job of getting the reader's attention.

One effective way of arousing interest is to begin an essay with an *anecdote,* a brief story that is particularly dramatic, ironic, or amusing. The anecdote packs a punch, and the punch gets the reader's attention. At the beginning of "Cultural Baggage," Barbara Ehrenreich uses an anecdote. She tells about an encounter with an acquaintance who was rejoicing in rediscovering her ethnic and religious heritage. As Ehrenreich continues, she arranges her information so that she can conclude the first paragraph with the question she was asked about her own background—and thereby succeed in creating some suspense.

Ehrenreich then begins her second paragraph with the blunt, abrupt, word "none." As an answer, "none" is such a surprise, both to the acquaintance and to the speaker herself, that Ehrenreich is forced to do some hard thinking about what that answer means. By the end of the second paragraph, Ehrenreich has provided the thrust for the rest of the essay. She is going to explore the meaning of her unusual ethnic background.

Beginning with an anecdote, then, is one alternative to the formal statement of a thesis. Some writers may use a significantly longer narrative or a descriptive passage. Others may pose a series of rhetorical questions or cite a series of startling facts. However, before you settle on an introduction that is primarily designed to arouse interest and gain attention, try to find out what your instructor's expectations are. How "basic" does he or she expect students' writing to be?

THE WARRIOR CULTURE

1990

In what we like to think of as "primitive" warrior cultures, the passage   *1*
to manhood requires the blooding of a spear, the taking of a scalp or head.
Among the Masai of eastern Africa, the North American Plains Indians and
dozens of other pretechnological peoples, a man could not marry until he had
demonstrated his capacity to kill in battle. Leadership too in a warrior culture
is typically contingent on military prowess and wrapped in the mystique of
death. In the Solomon Islands a chief's importance could be reckoned by the
number of skulls posted around his door, and it was the duty of the Aztec
kings to nourish the gods with the hearts of human captives.

All warrior peoples have fought for the same high-sounding reasons:
honor, glory or revenge. The nature of their real and perhaps not conscious
motivations is a subject of much debate. Some anthropologists postulate a
murderous instinct, almost unique among living species, in human males.
Others discern a materialistic motive behind every fray: a need for slaves,
grazing land or even human flesh to eat. Still others point to the similarities
between war and other male pastimes—the hunt and outdoor sports—and
suggest that it is boredom, ultimately, that stirs men to fight.

But in a warrior culture it hardly matters which motive is most basic.
Aggressive behavior is rewarded whether or not it is innate to the human
psyche. Shortages of resources are habitually taken as occasions for armed
offensives, rather than for hard thought and innovation. And war, to a warrior
people, is of course the highest adventure, the surest antidote to malaise, the
endlessly repeated theme of legend, song, religious myth and personal quest
for meaning. It is how men die and what they find to live for.

"You must understand that Americans are a warrior nation," Senator
Daniel Patrick Moynihan told a group of Arab leaders in early September,
one month into the Middle East crisis. He said this proudly, and he may,
without thinking through the ugly implications, have told the truth. In many
ways, in outlook and behavior the U.S. has begun to act like a primitive
warrior culture.

We seem to believe that leadership is expressed, in no small part, by a   *5*
willingness to cause the deaths of others. After the U.S. invasion of Panama,
President Bush exulted that no one could call him "timid"; he was at last a
"macho man." The press, in even more primal language, hailed him for
succeeding in an "initiation rite" by demonstrating his "willingness to shed
blood."

For lesser offices too we apply the standards of a warrior culture. Female
candidates are routinely advised to overcome the handicap of their gender by
talking "tough." Thus, for example, Dianne Feinstein has embraced capital
punishment, while Colorado senatorial candidate Josie Heath has found it
necessary to announce that although she is the mother of an 18-year-old

son, she is prepared to vote for war. Male candidates in some of the fall contests are finding their military records under scrutiny. No one expects them, as elected officials in a civilian government, to pick up a spear or a sling and fight. But they must state, at least, their willingness to have another human killed.

More tellingly, we are unnerved by peace and seem to find it boring. When the cold war ended, we found no reason to celebrate. Instead we heated up the "war on drugs." What should have been a public-health campaign, focused on the persistent shame of poverty, became a new occasion for marital rhetoric and muscle flexing. Months later, when the Berlin Wall fell and communism collapsed throughout Europe, we Americans did not dance in the streets. What we did, according to the networks, was change the channel to avoid the news. Nonviolent revolutions do not uplift us, and the loss of mortal enemies only seems to leave us empty and bereft.

Our collective fantasies center on mayhem, cruelty and violent death. Loving images of the human body—especially of bodies seeking pleasure or expressing love—inspire us with the urge to censor. Our preference is for warrior themes: the lone fighting man, bandoliers across his naked chest, mowing down lesser men in gusts of automatic-weapon fire. Only a real war seems to revive our interest in real events. With the Iraqi crisis, the networks report, ratings for news shows rose again—even higher than they were for Panama.

And as in any primitive warrior culture, our warrior élite takes pride of place. Social crises multiply numbingly—homelessness, illiteracy, epidemic disease—and our leaders tell us solemnly that nothing can be done. There is no money. We are poor, not rich, a debtor nation. Meanwhile, nearly a third of the federal budget flows, even in moments of peace, to the warriors and their weaponmakers. When those priorities are questioned, some new "crisis" dutifully arises to serve as another occasion for armed and often unilateral intervention.

Now, with Operation Desert Shield, our leaders are reduced to begging   *10*
foreign powers for the means to support our warrior class. It does not seem to occur to us that the other great northern powers—Japan, Germany, the Soviet Union—might not have found the stakes so high or the crisis quite so threatening. It has not penetrated our imagination that in a world where the powerful, industrialized nation-states are at last at peace, there might be other ways to face down a pint-size Third World warrior state than with massive force of arms. Nor have we begun to see what an anachronism we are in danger of becoming: a warrior nation in a world that pines for peace, a high-tech state with the values of a warrior band.

A leftist might blame "imperialism"; a right-winger would call our problem "internationalism." But an anthropologist, taking the long view, might say this is just what warriors do. Intoxicated by their own drumbeats and war songs, fascinated by the glint of steel and the prospect of blood, they will go forth, time and again, to war.

Questions for Discussion

1. Why does Ehrenreich think the United States is driven by a warrior culture?
2. Does Ehrenreich imply that being a warrior nation is inevitable for the United States?
3. Why does Ehrenreich object to the United States' being a warrior nation?
4. What does Ehrenreich mean when she says that, as a warrior nation, the United States is in danger of becoming an anachronism?
5. Does Ehrenreich imply that, if there were more women leaders, the warrior culture of the United States would fade away?

Suggestions for Writing

1. Write an essay in which you discuss the pressures you, as an American, have felt to be a warrior.
2. Write an essay in which you discuss the question of whether aggressive behavior is more common in American males than in American females.
3. What aspects of their social conditioning contribute to Americans' aggressiveness? Discuss.
4. Write an essay in which you discuss the question of whether Operation Desert Storm was the result of American aggressiveness or of other causes.
5. Discuss whether the kind of aggressive behavior Ehrenreich describes is basically desirable or undesirable. If you argue that it is undesirable, explain what you think can be done to make Americans less aggressive.

MARGINAL MEN

1989

Crime seems to change character when it crosses a bridge or a tunnel.   *1*
In the city, crime is taken as emblematic of the vast injustices of class and race.
In the suburbs, though, it's intimate and psychological—resistant to gener-
alization, a mystery of the individual soul. Recall the roar of commentary that
followed the murderous assault on a twenty-eight-year-old woman jogging
in Central Park. Every detail of the assailants' lives was sifted for sociological
significance. Were they poor? How poor? Students or dropouts? From
families with two parents or one? And so on, until the awful singularity of the
event was lost behind the impersonal grid of Class, Race, and Sex.

Now take the Midtown Tunnel east to the Long Island Expressway, out
past the clutter of Queens to deepest suburbia, where almost every neighborhood is "good" and "social pathology" is something you learn about in
school. Weeks before the East Harlem youths attacked a jogger, Long
Islanders were shaken by two murders which were, if anything, even more
inexplicably vicious than the assault in Central Park. In early March, the body
of thirteen-year-old Kelly Tinyes was found in the basement of a house just
down the block from her own. She had been stabbed, strangled, and hit with
a blunt instrument before being mutilated with a bayonet. A few weeks later,
fourteen-year-old Jessica Manners was discovered along the side of a road in
East Setauket, strangled to death, apparently with her own bra, and raped.

Suspects have been apprehended. Their high-school friends, parents,
and relatives have been interviewed. Their homes and cars have been
searched; their photos published. We know who they hung out with and
what they did in their spare time. But on the scale of large social meanings,
these crimes don't rate. No one is demanding that we understand—or
condemn—the white communities that nourished the killers. No one is
debating the roots of violence in the land of malls and tract homes. Only in
the city, apparently, is crime construed as something "socioeconomic." Out
here it's merely "sick."

But East Setauket is not really all that far from East Harlem. If something
is festering in the ghetto, something very similar is gnawing away at
Levittown and East Meadow. A "way of life," as the cliché goes, is coming to
an end, and in its place a mean streak is opening up and swallowing everything
in its path. Economists talk about "deindustrialization" and "class polariza-
tion." I think of it as the problem of *marginal men:* they are black and white,
Catholic and Pentecostal, rap fans and admirers of technopop. What they
have in common is that they are going nowhere—nowhere legal, that is.

Consider the suspects in the Long Island murders. Twenty-one-year-   *5*
old Robert Golub, in whose basement Kelly Tinyes was killed, is described
in *Newsday* as an "unemployed bodybuilder." When his high-school friends
went off to college, he stayed behind in his parents' home in Valley Stream.

For a while, he drove a truck for a cosmetics firm, but he lost that job, in part because of his driving record: his license has been suspended twelve times since 1985. At the time of the murder, he had been out of work for several months, constructing a life around his weight-lifting routine and his dream of becoming an entrepreneur.

Christopher Loliscio, the suspect in the Manners case, is nineteen, and, like Golub, lives with his parents. He has been in trouble before, and is charged with third-degree assault and "menacing" in an altercation that took place on the campus of the State University at Stony Brook last December. Loliscio does not attend college himself. He is employed as a landscaper.

The suburbs are full of young white men like Golub and Loliscio. If they had been born twenty years earlier, they might have found steady work in decent-paying union jobs, married early, joined the volunteer fire department, and devoted their leisure to lawn maintenance. But the good blue-collar jobs are getting sparser, thanks to "deindustrialization"—which takes the form, in Long Island, of cutbacks in the defense and aerospace industries. Much of what's left is likely to be marginal, low-paid work. Nationwide, the earnings of young white men dropped 18 percent between 1973 and 1986, according to the Census Bureau, and the earnings of male high-school dropouts plunged 42 percent.

Landscaping, for example—a glamorous term for raking and mowing—pays four to five dollars an hour; truck driving for a small firm is in the same range: not enough to pay for a house, a college education, or even a mid-size wedding reception at the VFW hall.

And even those modest perquisites of life in the subyuppie class have become, in some sense, "not enough." On Long Island, the culture that once sustained men in blue-collar occupations is crumbling as more affluent settlers move in, filling the vacant lots with their new, schooner-shaped, $750,000 homes. In my town, for example, the last five years saw the bowling alley close and the blue-collar bar turn into a pricey dining spot. Even the volunteer fire department is having trouble recruiting. The prestigious thing to join is a $500-a-year racquetball club; there's just not much respect anymore for putting out fires.

So the marginal man lives between two worlds—one that he aspires to and one that is dying, and neither of which he can afford. Take "Rick," the twenty-two-year-old son of family friends. His father is a machinist in an aerospace plant which hasn't been hiring anyone above the floor-sweeping level for years now. Not that Rick has ever shown any interest in his father's trade. For one thing, he takes too much pride in his appearance to put on the dark green company-supplied work clothes his father has worn for the past twenty years. Rick has his kind of uniform: pleated slacks, high-tops, Italian knit cardigans, and a $300 leather jacket, accessorized with a gold chain and earring stud.

To his parents, Rick is a hard-working boy for whom things just don't seem to work out. For almost a year after high school, he worked behind a counter at Crazy Eddie's, where the pay is low but at least you can listen to rock and roll all day. Now he has a gig doing valet parking at a country club. The tips are good and he loves racing around the lot in the Porsches and Lamborghinis of the stockbroker class. But the linchpin of his economic strategy is living at home, with his parents and sisters, in the same room he's occupied since third grade. Rick is a long way from being able to afford even a cramped, three-bedroom house like his family home; and, given the choice, he'd rather have a new Camaro anyway.

If this were the seventies, Rick might have taken up marijuana, the Grateful Dead, and vague visions of a better world. But like so many of his contemporaries in the eighties, Rick has no problem with "the system," which, in his mind, embraces every conceivable hustle, legal or illegal. Two years ago, he made a tidy bundle dealing coke in a local dance club, bought a $20,000 car, and smashed it up. Now he spends his evenings as a bouncer in an illegal gambling joint—his parents still think he's out "dancing"—and is proud of the handgun he's got stowed in his glove compartment.

Someday Rick will use that gun, and I'll probably be the first to say—like Robert Golub's friends—"but he isn't the kind of person who would hurt *anyone*." Except that even now I can sense the danger in him. He's smart enough to know he's only a cut-rate copy of the upscale young men in GQ ads and MTV commercials. Viewed from Wall Street or Southampton, he's a peon, a member of the invisible underclass that parks cars, waits on tables, and is satisfied with a five-dollar tip and a remark about the weather.

He's also proud. And there's nowhere for him to put that pride except into the politics of gesture: the macho stance, the seventy-five-mile-per-hour takeoff down the expressway, and eventually maybe, the drawn gun. Jobs are the liberal solution; conservatives would throw in "traditional values." But what the marginal men—from Valley Stream to Bedford-Stuyvesant—need most of all is *respect*. If they can't find that in work, or in a working-class life-style that is no longer honored, they'll extract it from someone weaker—a girlfriend, a random jogger, a neighbor, perhaps just any girl. They'll find a victim.

Questions for Understanding

1. According to Ehrenreich, what different characteristics are usually associated with city crime on the one hand and suburban crime on the other?
2. What does Ehrenreich believe young, urban, male criminals have in common with their suburban counterparts?
3. What does Ehrenreich believe was the major change in suburban life—or at least Long Island suburban life—between the 1960s and the 1980s?
4. What is the kind of world that the marginal man aspires to but cannot afford?
5. Why does Ehrenreich believe that "someday Rick will use that gun"?

Suggestions for Writing

1. Write an essay in which you describe the lifestyle of the young city man who verges on becoming a criminal.
2. Write an essay in which you describe the lifestyle of the young suburban man who verges on becoming a criminal.
3. Discuss the changes in America's economy that have had important effects on your life. In discussing a change, be sure to describe what the situation was like before the change as well as after it.
4. Write an essay in which you describe the different ways two of your friends seek respect.
5. Write an essay in which you discuss aspects of suburban life or city life that you believe Ehrenreich is unaware of or fails to understand.

James Baldwin

[1924–1987]

James Baldwin's mother never told him who his real father was, but when James was three, she married David Baldwin, whose surname became James's. David Baldwin had recently arrived in Harlem from New Orleans with his aged mother and twelve-year-old son, Samuel. James's mother and David had eight more children, three boys and five girls. Getting by in the Baldwin family was no easy matter.

Emma Jones Baldwin, James's mother, earned money working as a domestic in the homes of whites. David Baldwin was a preacher, which, for one thing, meant an irregular income. As the second oldest child, James had to work at whatever odd jobs he could find, and he also had to look after the younger children when his mother and stepfather were away. When he was at home, however, he frequently immersed himself in reading, for which he had acquired a taste at the local public school.

James was a good student. By the time he left his sixth-grade school at eleven, he had already written a history of Harlem and had won a prize for a short story. In junior high, the wrote stories and editorials for the school paper. At De Witt Clinton High School, one of New York's best schools at the time, he not only continued his writing but also became editor of the school's literary magazine. Baldwin has claimed that by the time he was thirteen he had read almost all the books in Harlem's two public libraries.

But Baldwin lived in a neighborhood in which crime and drugs were rampant, and he was afraid he might get caught up in the life of the streets. To prevent this, he embraced the Christianity of the storefront churches, even though he had been turned off by his stepfather's preaching at home. At fourteen he joined the Pentecostals. By that time he had achieved fluency in the language of the King James Bible and in English generally, and he was a great success as a boy preacher. As he entered adolescence, his developing sexuality made it hard for him to uphold the ideals he preached, and so he stopped.

Because of his family's poverty, college never seemed to be an option. Furthermore, he had set his sights on becoming a professional writer, and college hardly seemed necessary. He would go out into the world, find work, lap up experience, and write. He began to execute his plan and set to work on his first novel, *Go Tell It on the Mountain*. Then, because of the death of his stepfather and his family's desperate need for money, he had to leave his job laying railroad track in New Jersey and return home.

When he left home for the second time, he headed downtown to Greenwich Village, then the center of New York's artistic community and a neighborhood where homosexuals could feel relatively at ease. In the mid-1940s, James Baldwin was one of the very few black homosexuals living in the Village. While there, he experienced one of the turning points in his life: meeting the black writer Richard Wright. Wright, a dozen years older than Baldwin, already had published three important books, *Uncle Tom's Children* (1938), *Native Son* (1940), and *Black Boy* (1945). Being Richard Wright's protegé helped Baldwin land a fellowship and meet many influential people in New York's literary world. As a result, he was able to earn some money as a book reviewer. He also published the essay "Harlem Ghetto," which says some harsh things about Jews, in *Commentary* magazine, a publication of the American Jewish Committee.

Richard Wright moved to Paris in 1946, and in 1948 so did Baldwin. Taken under Wright's wing, Baldwin quickly became part of the community of American writers in Paris. He lived in France and Switzerland for eight years. During that period, Baldwin finished his first novel and completed *Giovanni's Room,* in which homosexuality is an important motif. He also wrote the essays that were collected in the volume called *Notes of a Native Son* (1955), which includes "Stranger in the Village."

Baldwin went on to produce two more collections of essays, *Nobody Knows My Name: More Notes of a Native Son* (1961) and *The Fire Next Time* (1963). He also wrote the long essay *No Name in the Street* (1972), a book in itself. All of Baldwin's essays appear in *The Price of the Ticket: Collected Nonfiction* (1985). Upon Baldwin's death in 1987, the novelist and essayist Norman Mailer said, "Nobody has more elegance than Baldwin as an essayist; not one of us hasn't learned something about the art of the essay from him." An outstanding example of Baldwin's elegance as an essayist is "Stranger in the Village."

NEGROES ARE ANTI-SEMITIC
BECAUSE THEY'RE ANTI-WHITE

1967

When we were growing up in Harlem our demoralizing series of   *1*
landlords were Jewish, and we hated them. We hated them because they
were terrible landlords, and did not take care of the building. A coat of
paint, a broken window, a stopped sink, a stopped toilet, a sagging floor,
a broken ceiling, a dangerous stairwell, the question of garbage disposal,
the question of heat and cold, of roaches and rats—all questions of life and
death for the poor, and especially for those with children—we had to cope
with all of these as best we could. Our parents were lashed down to
futureless jobs, in order to pay the outrageous rent. We knew that the
landlord treated us this way only because we were colored, and he knew
that we could not move out.

The grocer was a Jew, and being in debt to him was very much like
being in debt to the company store. The butcher was a Jew and, yes, we
certainly paid more for bad cuts of meat than other New York citizens, and
we very often carried insults home, along with the meat. We bought our
clothes from a Jew and, sometimes, our secondhand shoes, and the
pawnbroker was a Jew—perhaps we hated him most of all. The merchants
along 125th Street were Jewish—at least many of them were; I don't know
if Grant's or Woolworth's are Jewish names—and I well remember that it was
only after the Harlem riot of 1935 that Negroes were allowed to earn a little
money in some of the stores where they spent so much.

Not all of these white people were cruel—on the contrary, I remember
some who were certainly as thoughtful as the bleak circumstances allowed—
but all of them were exploiting us, and that was why we hated them.

But we also hated the welfare workers, of whom some were white,
some colored, some Jewish, and some not. We hated the policemen, not all
of whom were Jewish, and some of whom were black. The poor, of whatever
color, do not trust the law and certainly have no reason to, and God knows
we don't. "If you *must* call a cop," we said in those days, "for God's sake, make
sure it's a white one." We did not feel that the cops were protecting us, for
we knew too much about the reasons for the kinds of crimes committed in
the ghetto; but we feared black cops even more than white cops, because the
black cop had to work so much harder—on *your* head—to prove to himself
and his colleagues that he was not like all the other niggers.

We hated many of our teachers at school because they so clearly   *5*
despised us and treated us like dirty, ignorant savages. Not all of these teachers
were Jewish. Some of them, alas, were black. I used to carry my father's union
dues downtown for him sometimes. I hated everyone in that den of thieves,

especially the man who took the envelope from me, the envelope which contained my father's hard-earned money, that envelope which contained bread for his children. "Thieves," I thought, "everyone of you!" And I know I was right about that, and I have not changed my mind. But whether or not all these people were Jewish, I really do not know.

The Army may or may not be controlled by Jews; I don't know and I don't care. I know that when I worked for the Army I hated all my bosses because of the way they treated me. I don't know if the post office is Jewish but I would certainly dread working for it again. I don't know if Wanamaker's was Jewish, but I didn't like running their elevator, and I didn't like any of their customers. I don't know if Nabisco is Jewish, but I didn't like cleaning their basement. I don't know if Riker's is Jewish, but I didn't like scrubbing their floors. I don't know if the big, white bruiser who thought it was fun to call me "Shine" was Jewish, but I know I tried to kill him—and he stopped calling me "Shine." I don't know if the last taxi driver who refused to stop for me was Jewish, but I know I hoped he'd break his neck before he got home. And I don't think that General Electric or General Motors or R.C.A. or Con Edison or Mobiloil or Coca-Cola or Pepsi-Cola or Firestone or the Board of Education or the textbook industry or Hollywood or Broadway or television—or Wall Street, Sacramento, Dallas, Atlanta, Albany, or Washington—are controlled by Jews. I think they are controlled by Americans, and the American Negro situation is a direct result of this control. And anti-Semitism among Negroes, inevitable as it may be, and understandable, alas, as it is, does not operate to menace this control, but only to confirm it. It is not the Jew who controls the American drama. It is the Christian.

The root of anti-Semitism among Negroes is, ironically, the relationship of colored peoples—all over the globe—to the Christian world. This is a fact which may be difficult to grasp, not only for the ghetto's most blasted and embittered inhabitants, but also for many Jews, to say nothing of many Christians. But it is a fact, and it will not be ameliorated—in fact, it can only be aggravated—by the adoption, on the part of colored people now, of the most devastating of the Christian vices.

Of course, it is true, and I am not so naive as not to know it, that many Jews despise Negroes, even as their Aryan brothers do. (There are also Jews who despise Jews, even as their Aryan brothers do.) It is true that many Jews use, shamelessly, the slaughter of the 6,000,000 by the Third Reich as proof that they cannot be bigots—or in the hope of not being held responsible for their bigotry. It is galling to be told by a Jew whom you know to be exploiting you that he cannot possibly be doing what you know he is doing because he is a Jew. It is bitter to watch the Jewish storekeeper locking up his store for the night, and going home. Going, with your money in his pocket, to a clean neighborhood, miles from you, which you will not be allowed to enter. Nor can it help the relationship between most Negroes and most Jews when part of this money is donated to civil rights. In the light of what is now known as the white backlash, this money can be looked on as conscience money merely, as money given to keep the Negro happy, in his place, and out of white neighborhoods.

One does not wish, in short, to be told by an American Jew that his suffering is as great as the American Negro's suffering. It isn't, and one knows that it isn't from the very tone in which he assures you that it is.

For one thing, the American Jew's endeavor, whatever it is, has managed to purchase a relatively safety for his children, and a relative future for them. This is more than your father's endeavor was able to do for you, and more than your endeavor has been able to do for your children. There are days when it can be exceedingly trying to deal with certain white musical or theatrical celebrities who may or may not be Jewish—what, in show business, is a name?—but whose preposterous incomes cause one to think bitterly of the fates of such people as Bessie Smith or King Oliver or Ethel Waters. Furthermore, the Jew can be proud of his suffering, or at least not ashamed of it. His history and his suffering do not begin in America, where black men have been taught to be ashamed of everything, especially their suffering.

The Jew's suffering is recognized as part of the moral history of the world and the Jew is recognized as a contributor to the world's history: this is not true for the blacks. Jewish history, whether or not one can say it is honored, is certainly known: the black history has been blasted, maligned, and despised. The Jew is a white man, and when white men rise up against oppression, they are heroes: when black men rise, they have reverted to their native savagery. The uprising in the Warsaw ghetto was not described as a riot, nor were the participants maligned as hoodlums: the boys and girls in Watts and Harlem are thoroughly aware of this, and it certainly contributes to their attitude toward the Jews.

But, of course, my comparison of Watts and Harlem with the Warsaw ghetto will be immediately dismissed as outrageous. There are many reasons for this, and one of them is that while America loves white heroes, armed to the teeth, it cannot abide bad niggers. But the bottom reason is that it contradicts the American dream to suggest that any gratuitous, unregenerate horror can happen here. We make our mistakes, we like to think, but we are getting better all the time.

Well, to state it mildly, this is a point of view which any sane or honest Negro will have some difficulty holding. Very few Americans, and this includes very few Jews, wish to believe that the American Negro situation is as desperate and dangerous as it is. Very few Americans, and very few Jews, have the courage to recognize that the America of which they dream and boast is not the America in which the Negro lives. It is a country which the Negro has never seen. And this is not merely a matter of bad faith on the part of Americans. Bad faith, God knows, abounds, but there is something in the American dream sadder and more wistful than that.

No one, I suppose, would dream of accusing the late Moss Hart of bad faith. Near the end of his autobiography, *Act One,* just after he has become a successful playwright, and is riding home to Brooklyn for the first time in a cab, he reflects:

> I stared through the taxi window at a pinch-faced ten-year-old hur-   *15*
> rying down the steps on some morning errand before school, and
> I thought of myself hurrying down the streets on so many gray
> mornings out of a doorway and a house much the same as this one.
> My mind jumped backward in time and then whirled forward, like a
> many-faceted prism—flashing our old neighborhood in front of
> me, the house, the steps, the candy store—and then shifted to the
> skyline I had just passed by, the opening last night, and the notices I
> still hugged tightly under my arm. It was possible in this wonder-
> ful city for that nameless little boy—for any of its millions—to have a
> decent chance to scale the walls and achieve what they wished.
> Wealth, rank, or an imposing name counted for nothing. The only
> credential the city asked was the boldness to dream.

But this is not true for the Negro, and not even the most successful or fatuous Negro can really feel this way. His journey will have cost him too much, and the price will be revealed in his estrangement—unless he is very rare and lucky—from other colored people, and in his continuing isolation from whites. Furthermore, for every Negro boy who achieves such a taxi ride, hundreds, at least, will have perished around him, and not because they lacked the boldness to dream, but because the Republic despises their dreams.

Perhaps one must be in such a situation in order really to understand what it is. But if one is a Negro in Watts or Harlem, and knows why one is there, and knows that one has been sentenced to remain there for life, one can't but look on the American state and the American people as one's oppressors. For that, after all, is exactly what they are. They have corralled you where you are for their ease and their profit, and are doing all in their power to prevent you from finding out enough about yourself to be able to rejoice in the only life you have.

One does not wish to believe that the American Negro can feel this way, but that is because the Christian world has been misled by its own rhetoric and narcoicized by its own power.

For many generations the natives of the Belgian Congo, for example, endured the most unspeakable atrocities at the hands of the Belgians, at the hands of Europe. Their suffering occurred in silence. This suffering was not indignantly reported in the western press, as the suffering of white men would have been. The suffering of this native was considered necessary, alas, for European, Christian dominance. And, since the world at large knew virtually nothing concerning the suffering of this native, when he rose he was not hailed as a hero fighting for his land, but condemned as a savage, hungry for white flesh. The Christian world considered Belgium to be a civilized country; but there was not only no reason for the Congolese to feel that way about Belgium; there was no possibility that they could.

What will the Christian world, which is so uneasily silent now, say on   20
that day which is coming when the black native of South Africa begins to massacre the masters who have massacred him so long? It is true that two wrongs don't make a right, as we love to point out to the people we have wronged. But one wrong doesn't make a right, either. People who have been wronged will attempt to right the wrong; they would not be people if they didn't. They can rarely afford to be scrupulous about the means they will use. They will use such means as come to hand. Neither, in the main, will they distinguish one oppressor from another, nor see through to the root principle of their oppression.

In the American context, the most ironical thing about Negro anti-Semitism is that the Negro is really condemning the Jew for having become an American white man—for having become, in effect, a Christian. The Jew profits from his status in America, and he must expect Negroes to distrust him for it. The Jew does not realize that the credential he offers, the fact that he has been despised and slaughtered, does not increase the Negro's understanding. It increases the Negro's rage.

For it is not here, and not now, that the Jew is being slaughtered, and he is never despised, here, as the Negro is, because he is an American. The Jewish travail occurred across the sea and America rescued him from the house of bondage. But America is the house of bondage for the Negro, and no country can rescue him. What happens to the Negro here happens to him because he is an American.

When an African is mistreated here, for example, he has recourse to his embassy. The American Negro who is, let us say, falsely arrested, will find it nearly impossible to bring his case to court. And this means that because he is a native of this country—"one of our niggers"—he has, effectively, no recourse and no place to go, either within the country or without. He is a parish in his own country and a stranger in the world. This is what it means to have one's history and one's ties to one's ancestral homeland totally destroyed.

This is not what happened to the Jew and, therefore, he has allies in the world. That is one of the reasons no one has ever seriously suggested that the Jew be nonviolent. There was no need for him to be nonviolent. On the contrary, the Jewish battle for Israel was saluted as the most tremendous heroism. How can the Negro fail to suspect that the Jew is really saying that the Negro deserves his situation because he has not been heroic enough? It is doubtful that the Jews could have won their battle had the western powers been opposed to them. But such allies as the Negroes may have are themselves struggling for their freedom against tenacious and tremendous western opposition.

This leaves the American Negro, who technically represents the   25
western nations, in a cruelly ambiguous position. In this situation, it is not the American Jew who can either instruct him or console him. On the contrary,

the American Jew knows just enough about this situation to be unwilling to imagine it again.

Finally, what the American Negro interprets the Jew as saying is that one must take the historical, the impersonal point of view concerning one's life and concerning the lives of one's kinsmen and children. "We suffered, too," one is told, "but we came through, and so will you. In time."

In whose time? One has only one life. One may become reconciled to the ruin of one's own life, but to become reconciled to the ruin of one's children's lives is not reconciliation. It is the sickness unto death. And one knows that such counselors are not present on these shores by following this advice. They arrived here out of the same effort the American Negro is making: they wanted to live, and not tomorrow, but today. Now, since the Jew is living here, like all the other white men living here, he wants the Negro to wait. And the Jew sometimes—often—does this in the name of his Jewishness, which is a terrible mistake. He has absolutely no relevance in this context as a Jew. His only relevance is that he is white and values his color and uses it.

He is singled out by Negroes not because he acts differently from other white men, but because he doesn't. His major distinction is given him by that history of Christendom, which has so successfully victimized both Negroes and Jews. And he is playing in Harlem the role assigned him by Christians long ago: he is doing their dirty work.

No more than the good white people of the South, who are really responsible for the bombings and lynchings, are ever present at these events, do the people who really own Harlem ever appear at the door to collect the rent. One risks libel by trying to spell this out too precisely, but Harlem is really owned by a curious coalition which includes some churches, some universities, some Christians, some Jews, and some Negroes. The capital of New York, which is not a Jewish state, is Albany, and the Moses they sent us, whatever his ancestry, certainly failed to get the captive children free.

A genuinely candid confrontation between American Negroes and   *30* American Jews would certainly prove of inestimable value. But the aspirations of the country are wretchedly middle-class and the middle class can never afford candor.

What is really at question is the American way of life. What is really at question is whether Americans already have an identity or are still sufficiently flexible to achieve one. This is a painfully complicated question, for what now appears to be the American identity is really a bewildering and sometimes demoralizing blend of nostalgia and opportunism. For example, the Irish who march on St. Patrick's Day, do not, after all, have any desire to go back to Ireland. They do not intend to go back to live there, though they may dream of going back there to die. Their lives, in the meanwhile, are here, but they cling, at the same time, to those credentials forged in the Old World, credentials which cannot be duplicated here, credentials which the American

Negro does not have. These credentials are the abandoned history of Europe—the abandoned and romanticized history of Europe. The Russian Jews here have no desire to return to Russia either, and they have not departed in great clouds for Israel. But they have the authority of knowing it is there. The Americans are no longer Europeans, but they are still living, at least as they imagine, on that capital.

That capital also belongs, however, to the slaves who created it for Europe and who created it here; and in that sense, the Jew must see that he is part of the history of Europe, and will always be so considered by the descendant of the slave. Always, that is, unless he himself is willing to prove that this judgment is inadequate and unjust. This is precisely what is demanded of all the other white men in this country, and the Jew will not find it easier than anybody else to be hated. I learned this from Christians, and I ceased to practice what the Christians practiced.

The crisis taking place in the world, and in the minds and hearts of black people everywhere, is not produced by the Star of David, but by the old, rugged Roman cross on which Christendom's most celebrated Jew was murdered. And not by Jews.

Questions for Understanding

1. When James Baldwin, who was born in 1924, was growing up, in what ways did he and other people in Harlem usually encounter Jews?
2. What was the main reason for the young Baldwin's attitude toward Jews?
3. Why is Baldwin unsympathetic to American Jews who talk about the sufferings of the Holocaust?
4. In Baldwin's view, what is the main difference between Jewish history and black history?
5. What does Baldwin mean when he says, at the conclusion of the essay, that what is stirring in the "minds and hearts of black people everywhere is not produced by the Star of David but by the old, rugged Roman cross on which Christendom's most celebrated Jew was murdered"?

Suggestions for Writing

1. Have you ever been involved with a group of people who made you feel despised? If so, write an essay in which you describe three bad experiences and their effects on you.
2. Write an essay in which you describe a relationship with a person of another ethnic group that left you feeling badly misunderstood. Focus on three specific events.
3. Are you aware of any neighborhood, organization, or business that has made deliberate attempts to exclude certain people? Describe how the policy is carried out.
4. Baldwin doesn't think the statement Moss Hart makes near the end of his

autobiography is true for blacks. "Wealth, rank, or an imposing name counted for nothing," Hart says. "The only credential the city asked was the boldness to dream." Discuss the extent to which you think Hart or Baldwin is right.

5. To Baldwin in 1967, Jews in Harlem were playing the role assigned to them by Christians long ago: Jews were doing Christians' dirty work. Discuss the extent to which you agree with Baldwin's perception of the relationships among Jews, Christians, and blacks.

STRANGER IN THE VILLAGE

1955

From all available evidence no black man had ever set foot in this tiny   *1*
Swiss village before I came. I was told before arriving that I would probably
be a "sight" for the village; I took this to mean that people of my complexion
were rarely seen in Switzerland, and also that city people are always something
of a "sight" outside of the city. It did not occur to me—possibly because I am
an American—that there could be people anywhere who had never seen a
Negro.

It is a fact that cannot be explained on the basis of inaccessibility of the
village. The village is very high, but it is only four hours from Milan and three
hours from Lausanne. It is true that it is virtually unknown. Few people
making plans for a holiday would elect to come here. On the other hand, the
villagers are able, presumably, to come and go as they please—which they do:
to another town at the foot of the mountain, with a population of
approximately five thousand, the nearest place to see a movie or go to the
bank. In the village there is no movie house, no bank, no library, no theater;
very few radios, one jeep, one station wagon; and, at the moment, one
typewriter, mine, an invention which the woman next door to me here had
never seen. There are about six hundred people living here, all Catholic—I
conclude this from the fact that the Catholic church is open all year round,
whereas the Protestant chapel, set off on a hill a little removed from the
village, is open only in the summertime when the tourists arrive. There are
four or five hotels, all closed now, and four or five *bistros*, of which, however,
only two do any business during the winter. These two do not do a great deal,
for life in the village seems to end around nine or ten o'clock. There are a few
stores, butcher, baker, *épicerie*, a hardware store, and a money-changer—who
cannot change travelers' checks, but must send them down to the bank, an
operation which takes two or three days. There is something called the *Ballet
Haus*, closed in the winter and used for God knows what, certainly not ballet,
during the summer. There seems to be only one schoolhouse in the village,
and this for the quite young children; I suppose this to mean that their older
brothers and sisters at some point descend from these mountains in order to
complete their education—possibly, again, to the town just below. The
landscape is absolutely forbidding, mountains towering on all four sides, ice
and snow as far as the eye can reach. In this white wilderness, men and women
and children move all day, carrying washing, wood, buckets of milk or water,
sometimes skiing on Sunday afternoons. All week long boys and young men
are to be seen shoveling snow off the rooftops, or dragging wood down from
the forest in sleds.

The village's only real attraction, which explains the tourist season, is
the hot spring water. A disquietingly high proportion of these tourists are
cripples, or semi-cripples, who come year after year—from other parts of

Switzerland, usually—to take the waters. This lends the village, at the height of the season, a rather terrifying air of sanctity, as though it were a lesser Lourdes. There is often something beautiful, there is always something awful, in the spectacle of a person who has lost one of his faculties, a faculty he never questioned until it was gone, and who struggles to recover it. Yet people remain people, on crutches or indeed on deathbeds; and wherever I passed, the first summer I was here, among the native villagers or among the lame, a wind passed with me—of astonishment, curiosity, amusement, and outrage. That first summer I stayed two weeks and never intended to return. But I did return in the winter, to work; the village offers, obviously, no distractions whatever and has the further advantage of being extremely cheap. Now it is winter again, a year later, and I am here again. Everyone in the village knows my name, though they scarcely ever use it, knows that I come from America—though, this, apparently, they will never really believe: black men come from Africa—and everyone knows that I am the friend of the son of a woman who was born here, and that I am staying in their chalet. But I remain as much a stranger today as I was the first day I arrived, and the children shout *Neger! Neger!* as I walk along the streets.

It must be admitted that in the beginning I was far too shocked to have any real reaction. In so far as I reacted at all, I reacted by trying to be pleasant—it being a great part of the American Negro's education (long before he goes to school) that he must make people "like" him. This smile-and-the-world-smiles-with-you routine worked about as well in this situation as it had in the situation for which it was designed, which is to say that it did not work at all. No one, after all, can be liked whose human weight and complexity cannot be, or has not been, admitted. My smile was simply another unheard-of phenomenon which allowed them to see my teeth—they did not, really, see my smile and I began to think that, should I take to snarling, no one would notice any difference. All of the physical characteristics of the Negro which had caused me, in America, a very different and almost forgotten pain were nothing less than miraculous—or infernal—in the eyes of the village people. Some thought my hair was the color of tar, that it had the texture of wire, or the texture of cotton. It was jocularly suggested that I might let it all grow long and make myself a winter coat. If I sat in the sun for more than five minutes some daring creature was certain to come along and gingerly put his fingers on my hair, as though he were afraid of an electric shock, or put his hand on my hand, astonished that the color did not rub off. In all of this, in which it must be conceded there was the charm of genuine wonder and in which there was certainly no element of intentional unkindness, there was yet no suggestion that I was human: I was simply a living wonder.

I knew that they did not mean to be unkind, and I know it now; it is   *5* necessary, nevertheless, for me to repeat this to myself each time that I walk out of the chalet. The children who shout *Neger!* have no way of knowing the echoes this sound raises in me. They are brimming with good humor and the more daring swell with pride when I stop to speak with them. Just the same, there are days when I cannot pause and smile, when I have no heart to play with them; when, indeed, I mutter sourly to myself, exactly as I muttered on the streets of a city these children have never seen, when I was no bigger than these children are now: *Your* mother *was a nigger.* Joyce is right about history being a nightmare—but it may be the nightmare from which no one *can* awaken. People are trapped in history and history is trapped in them.

There is a custom in the village—I am told it is repeated in many villages—of "buying" African natives for the purpose of converting them to Christianity. There stands in the church all year round a small box with a slot for money, decorated with a black figurine, and into this box the villagers drop their francs. During the *carnaval* which precedes Lent, two village children have their faces blackened—out of which bloodless darkness their blue eyes shine like ice—and fantastic horsehair wigs are placed on their blond heads; thus disguised, they solicit among the villagers for money for the missionaries in Africa. Between the box in the church and the blackened children, the village "bought" last year six or eight African natives. This was reported to me with pride by the wife of one of the *bistro* owners and I was careful to express astonishment and pleasure at the solicitude shown by the village for the souls of black folks. The *bistro* owner's wife beamed with a pleasure far more genuine than my own and seemed to feel that I might now breathe more easily concerning the souls of at least six of my kinsmen.

I tried not to think of these so lately baptized kinsmen, of the price paid for them, or the peculiar price they themselves would pay, and said nothing about my father, who having taken his own conversion too literally never, at bottom, forgave the white world (which he described as heathen) for having saddled him with a Christ in whom, to judge at least from their treatment of him, they themselves no longer believed. I thought of white men arriving for the first time in an African village, strangers there, as I am a stranger here, and tried to imagine the astounded populace touching their hair and marveling at the color of their skin. But there is a great difference between being the first white man to be seen by Africans and being the first black man to be seen by whites. The white man takes the astonishment as tribute, for he arrives to conquer and to convert the natives, whose inferiority in relation to himself is not even to be questioned; whereas I, without a thought of conquest, find myself among a people whose culture controls me, has even, in a sense, created me, people who have cost me more in anguish and rage than they will ever know, who yet do not even know of my existence. The astonishment with which I might have greeted them, should they have stumbled into my African village a few hundred years ago, might have rejoiced their hearts. But the astonishment with which they greet me today can only poison mine.

And this is so despite everything I may do to feel differently, despite my friendly conversations with the *bistro* owner's wife, despite their three-year-old son who has at last become my friend, despite the *saluts* and *bonsoirs* which I exchange with people as I walk, despite the fact that I know that no individual can be taken to task for what history is doing, or has done. I say that the culture of these people controls me—but they can scarcely be held responsible for European culture. America comes out of Europe, but these people have never seen America, nor have most of them seen more of Europe than the hamlet at the foot of their mountain. Yet they move with an authority which I shall never have; and they regard me, quite rightly, not only as a stranger in their village but as a suspect latecomer, bearing no credentials, to everything they have—however unconsciously—inherited.

For this village, even were it incomparably more remote and incredibly more primitive, is the West, the West onto which I have been so strangely grafted. These people cannot be, from the point of view of power, strangers anywhere in the world; they have made the modern world, in effect, even if they do not know it. The most illiterate among them is related, in a way that I am not, to Dante, Shakespeare, Michelangelo, Aeschylus, Da Vinci, Rembrandt, and Racine; the cathedral at Chartres says something to them which it cannot say to me, as indeed would New York's Empire State Building, should anyone here ever see it. Out of their hymns and dances come Beethoven and Bach. Go back a few centuries and they are in their full glory—but I am in Africa, watching the conquerors arrive.

The rage of the disesteemed is personally fruitless, but it is also *10*
absolutely inevitable; this rage, so generally discounted, so little understood even among the people whose daily bread it is, is one of the things that makes history. Rage can only with difficulty, and never entirely, be brought under the domination of the intelligence and is therefore not susceptible to any arguments whatever. This is a fact which ordinary representatives of the *Herrenvolk,* having never felt this rage and being unable to imagine it, quite fail to understand. Also, rage cannot be hidden, it can only be dissembled. This dissembling deludes the thoughtless, and strengthens rage and adds, to rage, contempt. There are, no doubt, as many ways of coping with the resulting complex of tensions as there are black men in the world, but no black man can hope ever to be entirely liberated from this internal warfare—rage, dissembling, and contempt having inevitably accompanied his first realization of the power of white men. What is crucial here is that, since white men represent in the black man's world so heavy a weight, white men have for black men a reality which is far from being reciprocal; and hence all black men have toward all white men an attitude which is designed, really, either to rob the white man of the jewel of his naïveté, or else to make it cost him dear.

The black man insists, by whatever means he finds at his disposal, that the white man cease to regard him as an exotic rarity and recognize him as a human being. This is a very charged and difficult moment, for there is a great deal of will power involved in the white man's naïveté. Most people are not naturally reflective any more than they are naturally malicious, and the white man prefers to keep the black man at a certain human remove because it is easier for him thus to preserve his simplicity and avoid being called to account for crimes committed by his forefathers, or his neighbors. He is inescapably aware, nevertheless, that he is in a better position in the world than black men are, nor can he quite put to death the suspicion that he is hated by black men therefore. He does not wish to be hated, neither does he wish to change places, and at this point in his uneasiness he can scarcely avoid having recourse to those legends which white men have created about black men, the most usual effect of which is that the white man finds himself enmeshed, so to speak, in his own language which describes hell, as well as the attributes which lead one to hell, as being as black as night.

Every legend, moreover, contains its residuum of truth, and the root function of language is to control the universe by describing it. It is of quite considerable significance that black men remain, in the imagination, and in overwhelming numbers in fact, beyond the disciplines of salvation; and this despite the fact that the West has been "buying" African natives for centuries. There is, I should hazard, an instantaneous necessity to be divorced from this so visibly unsaved stranger, in whose heart, moreover, one cannot guess what dreams of vengeance are being nourished; and, at the same time, there are few things on earth more attractive than the idea of the unspeakable liberty which is allowed the unredeemed. When, beneath the black mask, a human being begins to make himself felt one cannot escape a certain awful wonder as to what kind of human being it is. What one's imagination makes of other people is dictated, of course, by the laws of one's own personality and it is one of the ironies of black-white relations that, by means of what the white man imagines the black man to be, the black man is enabled to know who the white man is.

I have said, for example, that I am as much a stranger in this village today as I was the first summer I arrived, but this is not quite true. The villagers wonder less about the texture of my hair than they did then, and wonder rather more about me. And the fact that their wonder now exists on another level is reflected in their attitudes and in their eyes. There are the children who make those delightful, hilarious, sometimes astonishingly grave overtures of friendship in the unpredictable fashion of children; other children, having been taught that the devil is a black man, scream in genuine anguish as I approach. Some of the older women never pass without a friendly greeting, never pass, indeed, if it seems that they will be able to engage me in conversation; other women look down or look away or rather contemptuously smirk. Some of the men drink with me and suggest that I learn how to ski—partly, I gather, because they cannot imagine what I would look like on skis—and want to know if I am married, and ask questions about my *métier*. But some of the men have accused *le sale nègre*—behind my back—of stealing wood and there is already in the eyes of some of them that peculiar, intent, paranoiac malevolence which one sometimes surprises in the eyes of American white men when, out walking with their Sunday girl, they see a Negro male approach.

There is a dreadful abyss between the streets of this village and the streets of the city in which I was born, between the children who shout *Neger!* today and those who shouted *Nigger!* yesterday—the abyss is experience, the American experience. The syllable hurled behind me today expresses, above all, wonder: I am a stranger here. But I am not a stranger in America and the same syllable riding on the American air expresses the war my presence has occasioned in the American soul.

For this village brings home to me this fact: that there was a day, and not really a very distant day, when Americans were scarcely Americans at all but discontented Europeans, facing a great unconquered continent and strolling, say, into a marketplace and seeing black men for the first time. The shock this spectacle afforded is suggested, surely, by the promptness with which they decided that these black men were not really men but cattle. It is true that the necessity on the part of the settlers of the New World of reconciling their moral assumptions with the fact—and the necessity—of slavery enhanced immensely the charm of this idea, and it is also true that this idea expresses, with a truly American bluntness, the attitude which to varying extents all masters have had toward all slaves.

But between all former slaves and slave-owners and the drama which begins for Americans over three hundred years ago at Jamestown, there are at least two differences to be observed. The American Negro slave could not suppose, for one thing, as slaves in past epochs had supposed and often done, that he would ever be able to wrest the power from his master's hands. This was a supposition which the modern era, which was to bring about such vast changes in the aims and dimensions of power, put to death; it only begins, in unprecedented fashion, and with dreadful implications, to be resurrected today. But even had this supposition persisted with undiminished force, the American Negro slave could not have used it to lend his condition dignity, for the reason that this supposition rests on another: that the slave in exile yet remains related to his past, has some means—if only in memory—of revering and sustaining the forms of his former life, is able, in short, to maintain his identity.

This was not the case with the American Negro slave. He is unique among the black men of the world in that his past was taken from him, almost literally, at one blow. One wonders what on earth the first slave found to say to the first dark child he bore. I am told that there are Haitians able to trace their ancestry back to African kings, but any American Negro wishing to go back so far will find his journey through time abruptly arrested by the signature on the bill of sale which served as the entrance paper for his ancestor. At the time—to say nothing of the circumstances—of the enslavement of the captive black man who was to become the American Negro, there was not the remotest possibility that he would ever take power from his master's hands. There was no reason to suppose that his situation would ever change, nor was there, shortly, anything to indicate that his situation had ever been different. It was his necessity, in the words of E. Franklin Frazier, to find a "motive for living under American culture or die." The identity of the American Negro comes out of this extreme situation, and the evolution of this identity was a source of the most intolerable anxiety in the minds and the lives of his masters.

For the history of the American Negro is unique also in this: that the question of his humanity, and of his rights therefore as a human being, became a burning one for several generations of Americans, so burning a question that it ultimately became one of those used to divide the nation. It is out of this argument that the venom of the epithet *Nigger!* is derived. It is an argument which Europe has never had, and hence Europe quite sincerely fails to understand how or why the argument arose in the first place, why its effects are so frequently disastrous and always so unpredictable, why it refuses until today to be entirely settled. Europe's black possessions remained—and do remain—in Europe's colonies, at which remove they represented no threat whatever to European identity. If they posed any problem at all for the European conscience, it was a problem which remained comfortingly abstract: in effect, the black man, *as a man,* did not exist for Europe. But in America, even as a slave, he was an inescapable part of the general social fabric and no American could escape having an attitude toward him. Americans attempt until today to make an abstraction of the Negro, but the very nature of these abstractions reveals the tremendous effects the presence of the Negro has had on the American character.

When one considers the history of the Negro in America it is of the greatest importance to recognize that the moral beliefs of a person, or a people, are never really as tenuous as life—which is not moral—very often causes them to appear, these create for them a frame of reference and a necessary hope, the hope being that when life has done its worst they will be enabled to rise above themselves and to triumph over life. Life would scarcely be bearable if this hope did not exist. Again, even when the worst has been said, to betray a belief is not by any means to have put oneself beyond its power; the betrayal of a belief is not the same thing as ceasing to believe. If this were not so there would be no moral standards in the world at all. Yet one must also recognize that morality is based on ideas and that all ideas are dangerous—dangerous because ideas can only lead to action and where the action leads no man can say. And dangerous in this respect: that confronted with the impossibility of remaining faithful to one's beliefs, and the equal impossibility of becoming free of them, one can be driven to the most inhuman excesses. The ideas on which American beliefs are based are not, though Americans often seem to think so, ideas which originated in America. They came out of Europe. And the establishment of democracy on the American continent was scarcely as radical a break with the past as was the necessity, which Americans faced, of broadening this concept to include black men.

This was, literally, a hard necessity. It was impossible, for one thing, 20 for Americans to abandon their beliefs, not only because these beliefs alone seemed able to justify the sacrifices they had endured and the blood that they had spilled, but also because these beliefs afforded them their own bulwark against a moral chaos as absolute as the physical chaos of the continent it was their destiny to conquer. But in the situation in which Americans found themselves, these beliefs threatened an idea which, whether or not one likes to think so, is the very warp and woof of the heritage of the West, the idea of white supremacy.

Americans have made themselves notorious by the shrillness and the brutality with which they have insisted on this idea, but they did not invent it; and it has escaped the world's notice that those very excesses of which Americans have been guilty imply a certain, unprecedented uneasiness over the idea's life and power, if not, indeed, the idea's validity. The idea of white supremacy rests simply on the fact that white men are the creators of civilization (the present civilization, which is the only one that matters; all previous civilizations are simply "contributions" to our own) and are therefore civilization's guardians and defenders. Thus it was impossible for Americans to accept the black man as one of themselves, for to do so was to jeopardize their status as white men. But not so to accept him was to deny his human reality, his human weight and complexity, and the strain of denying the overwhelmingly undeniable forced Americans into rationalizations so fantastic that they approached the pathological.

At the root of the American Negro problem is the necessity of the American white man to find a way of living with the Negro in order to be able to live with himself. And the history of this problem can be reduced to the means used by Americans—lynch law and law, segregation and legal acceptance, terrorization and concession—either to come to terms with this necessity, or to find a way around it, or (most usually) to find a way of doing both these things at once. The resulting spectacle, at once foolish and dreadful, led someone to make the quite accurate observation that "the Negro-in-America is a form of insanity which overtakes white men."

In this long battle, a battle by no means finished, the unforeseeable effects of which will be felt by many future generations, the white man's motive was the protection of his identity; the black man was motivated by the need to establish an identity. And despite the terrorization which the Negro in America endured and endures sporadically until today, despite the cruel and totally inescapable ambivalence of his status in his country, the battle for his identity has long ago been won. He is not a visitor to the West, but a citizen there, an American; as American as the Americans who despise him, the Americans who fear him, the Americans who love him—the Americans who became less than themselves, or rose to be greater than themselves by virtue of the fact that the challenge he represented was inescapable. He is perhaps the only black man in the world whose relationship to white men is more terrible, more subtle, and more meaningful than the relationship of bitter possessed to uncertain possessor. His survival depended, and his development depends, on his ability to turn his peculiar status in the Western world to his own advantage and, it may be, to the very great advantage of that world. It remains for him to fashion out of his experience that which will give him sustenance, and a voice.

The cathedral at Chartres, I have said, says something to the people of this village which it cannot say to me; but it is important to understand that this cathedral says something to me which it cannot say to them. Perhaps they are struck by the power of the spires, the glory of the windows; but they have known God, after all, longer than I have known him, and in a different way, and I am terrified by the slippery bottomless well to be found in the crypt, down which heretics were hurled to death, and by the obscene, inescapable gargoyles jutting out of the stone and seeming to say that God and the devil can never be divorced. I doubt that the villagers think of the devil when they face a cathedral because they have never been identified with the devil. But I must accept the status which myth, if nothing else, gives me in the West before I can hope to change the myth.

Yet, if the American Negro has arrived at his identity by virtue of the absoluteness of his estrangement from his past, American white men still nourish the illusion that there is some means of recovering the European innocence, of returning to a state in which black men do not exist. This is one of the greatest errors Americans can make. The identity they fought so hard to protect has, by virtue of that battle, undergone a change: Americans are as unlike any other white people in the world as it is possible to be. I do not think, for example, that it is too much to suggest that the American vision of the world—which allows so little reality, generally speaking, for any of the darker forces in human life, which tends until today to paint moral issues in glaring black and white—owes a great deal to the battle waged by Americans to maintain between themselves and black men a human separation which could not be bridged. It is only now beginning to be borne in on us—very faintly, it must be admitted, very slowly, and very much against our will—that this vision of the world is dangerously inaccurate, and perfectly useless. For it protects our moral high-mindedness at the terrible expense of weakening our grasp of reality. People who shut their eyes to reality simply invite their own destruction, and anyone who insists on remaining in a state of innocence long after that innocence is dead turns himself into a monster.

The time has come to realize that the interracial drama acted out on the American continent has not only created a new black man, it has created a new white man, too. No road whatever will lead Americans back to the simplicity of this European village where white men still have the luxury of looking on me as a stranger. I am not, really, a stranger any longer for any American alive. One of the things that distinguishes Americans from other people is that no other people has ever been so deeply involved in the lives of black men, and vice versa. This fact faced, with all its implications, it can be seen that the history of the American Negro problem is not merely shameful, it is also something of an achievement. For even when the worst has been said, it must also be added that the perpetual challenge posed by this problem was always, somehow, perpetually met. It is precisely this black-white experience which may prove of indispensable value to us in the world we face today. This world is white no longer, and it will never be white again.

Questions for Understanding

1. What does Baldwin mean when he says that no one "can be liked whose human weight and complexity cannot be, or has not been, admitted"?

2. When Baldwin talks about the warfare within blacks, what does he imagine is contending with what?
3. What does Baldwin mean when he says that "by means of what the white man imagines the black man to be, the black man is enabled to know who the white man is"?
4. What is Baldwin's attitude toward Western civilization?
5. Why does Baldwin say that it is necessary for American whites "to find a way of living with the Negro" to be able to live with themselves?

Suggestions for Writing

1. Write an essay in which you discuss what it was like to be the only one of your religious or ethnic group in a particular situation.
2. Write an essay in which you discuss the advantages and disadvantages of going to an unfamiliar place to get a lot of work done.
3. After doing some well-focused research, write an essay in which you discuss the differences between America's and Europe's experiences with black people.
4. After reviewing the first ten amendments to the United States Constitution (the Bill of Rights), write an essay in which you discuss one right that strikes you as less a right for blacks than for whites.
5. Write an essay in which you discuss the extent to which Baldwin's analysis of black–white relationships in the United States still holds true.

NUTS AND BOLTS 3: USING THE SEMICOLON

I think I know exactly what Norman Mailer has in mind when he refers to Baldwin's elegance as an essayist. Baldwin's elegance resides in his skill as a maker of sentences, and what makes Baldwin's sentences special, it seems to me, is the way he utilizes the semicolon. Yes, the oft-scorned semicolon can actually make sentences elegant—aesthetically very pleasing. At various times in his writing, Baldwin uses the semicolon to create tension between "opposing clauses"—two clauses whose meanings pull in opposite directions.

To appreciate what Baldwin does—and to try for similar elegance in your own writing—you must understand the two categories of clauses: *dependent clauses* are those that can't stand alone as sentences; *independent clauses* are those that can stand alone as sentences. It is Baldwin's independent clauses to which I am referring: Baldwin's independent opposing clauses. When independent clauses follow one after the other, there are two ways to show the relationship between them: They can be *separated* with a period, or they can be *connected* with a semicolon. Most students automatically separate independent clauses with a period, or, sensing that they really don't want to separate the clauses, they use a comma, which confuses the reader (and causes the instructor to mark a comma-splice error). The more experienced and sophisticated writer does not hesitate to use the semicolon, because he or she knows that to the experienced reader, the semicolon signals a connection in thought between the statements in each of the clauses. On the other hand, the writer who unthinkingly always uses the period gives no signal to the reader that there are such connections. The ideas simply succeed one another; the movement is straight ahead, linear. As red brick is added to red brick, sentence is added to sentence, and there is no looking back to elaborate or reflect on what was just said.

Consider what Baldwin does in paragraph 13. He points out that there was a difference between the way the people of the village reacted to him as someone who had settled in and the way they reacted to him when he first appeared for two weeks during the summer. He then goes on to illustrate the villagers' reactions during the winter, focusing on three groups: children, women, and men. Furthermore, within each group there are two kinds of reactions: friendly and unfriendly. He makes a statement about the friendliness of some of the children, but says that friendliness is offset by the fear and anguish with which other children react. The structure he uses to present these different reactions is a single sentence in which two independent clauses are set side by side and connected by a semicolon: "There are the children who . . . ; other children . . . ." Opposing independent clauses also are used to convey the different attitudes of the women: "Some of the older women . . . ; other women . . . ." What Baldwin wants to say about the differing attitudes of the men is too complex to be contained within a single sentence, so now he uses two sentences. By this point, however, the reader knows that the second sentence will not move on to something new, as is customary, but rather will describe the behavior of the unfriendly men. The very pattern the writer has established is doing some of his work for him.

This paragraph of Baldwin's is among the finest in the essay, largely because the different reactions of members of the same general group have been presented as point-by-point contrasts, for which opposing independent clauses are very useful. Usually such clauses are connected by a semicolon. The semicolon is also useful in connecting independent clauses that have other functions. Present a complex idea; explain it in the independent clause that follows. Present a provocative opinion; comment on it in the second clause. Make a statement that defies belief; in the second clause, cite instances that make the statement credible. In the first clause, state the effect; in the second, state the cause. In the first clause, state the overlooked cause; in the second, reveal the drastic result.

Using the semicolon can lend elegance and sophistication to your prose style, but bear in mind this test for appropriateness. An independent clause should come before the semicolon, and an independent clause should follow the semicolon; you will encounter exceptions in the sentences of professional writers, but ninety-five percent of the time, this rule will hold up. Also, whenever you use the semicolon, be sure the content of the second independent clause is related to that of the first clause.

THE HARLEM GHETTO

1948

Harlem, physically at least, has changed very little in my parents'   1
lifetime or in mine. Now as then the buildings are old and in desperate need
of repair, the streets are crowded and dirty, there are too many human beings
per square block. Rents are 10 to 58 percent higher than anywhere else in the
city; food, expensive everywhere, is more expensive here and of an inferior
quality; and now that the war is over and money is dwindling, clothes are
carefully shopped for and seldom bought. Negroes, traditionally the last to be
hired and the first to be fired, are finding jobs harder to get, and, while prices
are rising implacably, wages are going down. All over Harlem now there is felt
the same bitter expectancy with which, in my childhood, we awaited winter:
it is coming and it will be hard; there is nothing anyone can do about it.

All of Harlem is pervaded by a sense of congestion, rather like the
insistent, maddening, claustrophobic pounding in the skull that comes from
trying to breathe in a very small room with all the windows shut. Yet the
white man walking through Harlem is not at all likely to find it sinister or
more wretched than any other slum.

Harlem wears to the casual observer a casual face; no one remarks
that—considering the history of black men and women and the legends
that have sprung up about them, to say nothing of the ever-present
policemen, wary on the street corners—the face is, indeed, somewhat
excessively casual and may not be as open or as careless as it seems. If an
outbreak of more than usual violence occurs, as in 1935 or in 1943, it is
met with sorrow and surprise and rage; the social hostility of the rest of
the city feeds on this as proof that they were right all along, and the hostility
increases: speeches are made, committees are set up, investigations ensue.
Steps are taken to right the wrong, without, however, expanding or
demolishing the ghetto. The idea is to make it less of a social liability, a
process about as helpful as make-up to a leper. Thus, we have the Boys'
Club on West 134th Street, the playground at West 131st and Fifth Avenue;
and, since Negroes will not be allowed to live in Stuyvesant Town,
Metropolitan Life is thoughtfully erecting a housing project called Riverton
in the center of Harlem; however, it is not likely that any but the
professional class of Negroes—and not all of them—will be able to pay
the rent.

Most of these projects have been stimulated by perpetually embattled
Negro leaders and by the Negro press. Concerning Negro leaders, the best
that one can say is that they are in an impossible position and that the handful
motivated by genuine concern maintain this position with heartbreaking
dignity. It is unlikely that anyone acquainted with Harlem seriously assumes
that the presence of one playground more or less has any profound effect
upon the psychology of the citizens there. And yet it is better to have the

playground; it is better than nothing; and it will, at least, make life somewhat easier for parents who will then know that their children are not in as much danger of being run down in the streets. Similarly, even though the American cult of literacy has chiefly operated only to provide a market for the *Reader's Digest* and the *Daily News,* literacy is still better than illiteracy; so Negro leaders must demand more and better schools for Negroes, though any Negro who takes this schooling at face value will find himself virtually incapacitated for life in this democracy. Possibly the most salutary effect of all this activity is that it assures the Negro that he is not altogether forgotten: people *are* working in his behalf, however hopeless or misguided they may be; and as long as the water is troubled it cannot become stagnant.

The terrible thing about being a Negro leader lies in the term itself. I   5
do not mean merely the somewhat condescending differentiation the term implies, but the nicely refined torture a man can experience from having been created and defeated by the same circumstances. That is, Negro leaders have been created by the American scene, which thereafter works against them at every point; and the best that they can hope for is ultimately to work themselves out of their jobs, to nag contemporary American leaders and the members of their own group until a bad situation becomes so complicated and so bad that it cannot be endured any longer. It is like needling a blister until it bursts. On the other hand, one cannot help observing that some Negro leaders and politicians are far more concerned with their careers than with the welfare of Negroes, and their dramatic and publicized battles are battles with the wind. Again, this phenomenon cannot be changed without a change in the American scene. In a land where, it is said, any citizen can grow up and become president, Negroes can be pardoned for desiring to enter Congress.

The Negro press, which supports any man, provided he is sufficiently dark and well-known—with the exception of certain Negro novelists accused of drawing portraits unflattering to the race—has for years received vastly confusing criticism based on the fact that it is helplessly and always exactly what it calls itself, that is, a press devoted entirely to happenings in or about the Negro world. This preoccupation can probably be forgiven in view of the great indifference and frequent hostility of the American white press. The Negro press has been accused of not helping matters much—as indeed, it has not, nor do I see how it could have. And it has been accused of being sensational, which it is; but this is a criticism difficult to take seriously in a country so devoted to the sensational as ours.

The best-selling Negro newspaper, I believe, is the *Amsterdam Star-News,* which is also the worst, being gleefully devoted to murders, rapes, raids on love-nests, interracial wars, any item—however meaningless—concerning prominent Negroes, and whatever racial gains can be reported for the week—all in just about that order. Apparently, this policy works well; it sells papers—which is, after all, the aim; in my childhood we never missed an edition. The day the paper came out we could hear, far down the street, the news vendor screaming the latest scandal and people rushing to read about it.

The *Amsterdam* has been rivaled, in recent years, by the *People's Voice,*
a journal, modeled on *PM°* and referred to as *PV. PV* is not so wildly
sensational a paper as the *Amsterdam,* though its coverage is much the same
(the news coverage of the Negro press is naturally pretty limited). *PV*'s
politics are less murky, to the left of center (the *Amsterdam* is Republican, a
political affiliation that has led it into some strange doubletalk), and its tone,
since its inception, has been ever more hopelessly militant, full of warnings,
appeals, and open letters to the government—which, to no one's surprise, are
not answered—and the same rather pathetic preoccupation with prominent
Negroes and what they are doing. Columns signed by Lena Horne and Paul
Robeson° appeared in *PV* until several weeks ago, when both severed their
connections with the paper. Miss Horne's column made her sound like an
embittered Eleanor Roosevelt°, and the only column of Robeson's I have
read was concerned with the current witch hunt in Hollywood, discussing
the kind of movies under attack and Hollywood's traditional treatment of
Negroes. It is personally painful to me to realize that so gifted and forceful a
man as Robeson should have been tricked by his own bitterness and by a total
inability to understand the nature of political power in general, or Communist aims in particular, into missing the point of his own critique, which is
worth a great deal of thought: that there are a great many ways of being
un-American, some of them nearly as old as the country itself, and that the
House Un-American Activities Committee might find concepts and
attitudes even more damaging to American life in a picture like *Gone With
the Wind* than in the possibly equally romantic but far less successful *Watch on
the Rhine.*

The only other newspapers in the field with any significant sale in
Harlem are the Pittsburgh *Courier,* which has the reputation of being the
best of the lot, and the *Afro-American,* which resembles the New York
Journal-American in layout and type and seems to make a consistent if
unsuccessful effort to be at once readable, intelligent, and fiery. The *Courier*
is a high-class paper, reaching its peak in the handling of its society news
and in the columns of George S. Schuyler, whose Olympian serenity
infuriates me, but who, as a matter of fact, reflects with great accuracy the
state of mind and the ambitions of the professional, well-to-do Negro who
has managed to find a place to stand. Mr. Schuyler, who is remembered
still for a satirical novel I have not read, called *Black No More,* is aided
enormously in this position by a genteel white wife and a child-prodigy
daughter—who is seriously regarded in some circles as proof of the

---

PM: An innovative New York newspaper published between 1940 and 1948. *PM* had no
advertising.

Lena Horne (1917–   ): the singer and actress.

Paul Robeson (1898–1976): a greatly admired singer and actor who supported many communist
causes and won the Stalin Peace Prize in 1952.

Eleanor Roosevelt (1884–1962): the wife of President Franklin D. Roosevelt. She wrote a
newspaper column and was actively involved in many social causes.

incomprehensible contention that the mating of white and black is more likely to produce genius than any other combination. (The *Afro-American* recently ran a series of articles on this subject, "The Education of a Genius," by Mrs. Amarintha Work, who recorded in detail the development of her mulatto son, Craig.)

Ebony and *Our World* are two big magazines in the field, *Ebony* looking   10 and sounding very much like *Life,* and *Our World* being the black man's *Look.* *Our World* is a very strange, disorganized magazine indeed, sounding sometimes like a college newspaper and sometimes like a call to arms, but principally, like its more skillful brothers, devoted to the proposition that anything a white man can do a Negro can probably do better. *Ebony* digs feature articles out of such things as the "real" Lena Horne and Negro FBI agents, and it travels into the far corners of the earth for any news, however trivial, concerning any Negro or group of Negroes who are in any way unusual and/or newsworthy. The tone of both *Ebony* and *Our World* is affirmative; they cater to the "better class of Negro." *Ebony*'s November 1947 issue carried an editorial entitled "Time To Count Our Blessings," which began by accusing Chester Himes (author of the novel *Lonely Crusade*) of having a color psychosis, and went on to explain that there are Negro racists also who are just as blind and dangerous as Bilbo,° which is incontestably true, and that, compared to the millions of starving Europeans, Negroes are sitting pretty—which comparison, I hazard, cannot possibly mean anything to any Negro who has not seen Europe. The editorial concluded that Negroes had come a long way and that "as patriotic Americans" it was time "we" stopped singing the blues and realized just how bright the future was. These cheering sentiments were flanked—or underscored, if you will—by a photograph on the opposite page of an aging Negro farm woman carrying home a bumper crop of onions. It apparently escaped the editors of *Ebony* that the very existence of their magazine, and its table of contents for any month, gave the lie to this effort to make the best of a bad bargain.

The true *raison d'être* of the Negro press can be found in the letters-to-the-editor sections, where the truth about life among the rejected can be seen in print. It is the terrible dilemma of the Negro press that, having no other model, it models itself on the white press, attempting to emulate the same effortless, sophisticated tone—a tone its subject matter renders utterly unconvincing. It is simply impossible not to sing the blues, audibly or not, when the lives lived by Negroes are so inescapably harsh and stunted. It is not the Negro press that is at fault; whatever contradictions, inanities, and political infantilism can be charged to it can be charged equally to the American press at large. It is a black man's newspaper straining for recognition and a foothold in the white man's world. Matters are not helped in the least by the fact that the white man's world, intellectually, morally, and spiritually, has the meaningless ring of a hollow drum and the odor of slow death. Within

---

Theodore Bilbo: between 1935 and 1947, a racist U.S. Senator from Mississippi.

the body of the Negro press all the wars and falsehoods, all the decay and dislocation and struggle of our society are seen in relief.

The Negro press, like the Negro, becomes the scapegoat for our ills. There is no difference, after all, between the *Amsterdam's* handling of a murder on Lenox Avenue and the *Daily News'* coverage of a murder on Beekman Place,° nor is there any difference between the chauvinism of the two papers, except that the *News* is smug and the *Amsterdam* is desperate. Negroes live violent lives, unavoidably; a Negro press without violence is therefore not possible; and, further, in every act of violence, particularly violence against white men, Negroes feel a certain thrill of identification, a wish to have done it themselves, a feeling that old scores are being settled at last. It is no accident that Joe Louis° is the most idolized man in Harlem. He has succeeded on a level that white America indicates is the only level for which it has any respect. We (Americans in general, that is) like to point to Negroes and to most of their activities with a kind of tolerant scorn; but it is ourselves we are watching, ourselves we are damning, or— condescendingly—bending to save.

I have written at perhaps excessive length about the Negro press, principally because its many critics have always seemed to me to make the irrational demand that the nation's most oppressed minority behave itself at all times with a skill and foresight no one ever expected of the late Joseph Patterson or ever expected of Hearst,° and I have tried to give some idea of its tone because it seems to me that it is here that the innate desperation is betrayed. As for the question of Negro advertising, which has caused so much comment, it seems to me quite logical that any minority identified by the color of its skin and the texture of its hair would eventually grow self-conscious about these attributes and avoid advertising lotions that made the hair kinkier and soaps that darkened the skin. The American ideal, after all, is that everyone should be as much alike as possible.

It is axiomatic that the Negro is religious, which is to say that he stands in fear of the God our ancestors gave us and before whom we all tremble yet. There are probably more churches in Harlem than in any other ghetto in this city and they are going full blast every night and some of them are filled with praying people every day. This, supposedly, exemplifies the Negro's essential simplicity and good-will; but it is actually a fairly desperate emotional business.

These churches range from the august and publicized Abyssinian Baptist Church on West 138th Street to resolutely unclassifiable lofts, basements, storefronts, and even private dwellings. Nightly, Holyroller ministers, spiritualists, self-appointed prophets and Messiahs gather their

15

Beekman Place: An upper-class street in Manhattan.
Joe Louis (1914–1981): heavyweight boxing champion between 1937 and 1949.
Joseph Patterson (1879–1946): founder of *The Daily News* in New York.
William Randolph Hearst (1863–1951): at one time he owned twenty-eight newspapers.

flocks together for worship and for strength through joy. And this is not, as *Cabin in the Sky*° would have us believe, merely a childlike emotional release. Their faith may be described as childlike, but the end it serves is often sinister. It may, indeed, "keep them happy"—a phrase carrying the inescapable inference that the way of life imposed on Negroes makes them quite actively unhappy—but also, and much more significantly, religion operates here as a complete and exquisite fantasy revenge: white people own the earth and commit all manner of abomination and injustice on it; the bad will be punished and the good rewarded, for God is not sleeping, the judgment is not far off. It does not require a spectacular degree of perception to realize that bitterness is here neither dead nor sleeping, and that the white man, believing what he wishes to believe, has misread the symbols. Quite often the Negro preacher descends to levels less abstract and leaves no doubt as to what is on his mind: the pressure of life in Harlem, the conduct of the Italian-Ethiopian war, racial injustice during the recent war, and the terrible possibility of yet another very soon. All these topics provide excellent springboards for sermons thinly coated with spirituality but designed mainly to illustrate the injustice of the white American and anticipate his certain and long overdue punishment.

Here, too, can be seen one aspect of the Negro's ambivalent relation to the Jew. To begin with, though the traditional Christian accusation that the Jews killed Christ is neither questioned nor doubted, the term "Jew" actually operates in this initial context to include all infidels of white skin who have failed to accept the Savior. No real distinction is made: the preacher begins by accusing the Jews of having refused the light and proceeds from there to a catalog of their subsequent sins and the sufferings visited on them by a wrathful God. Though the notion of the suffering is based on the image of the wandering, exiled Jew, the context changes imperceptibly, to become a fairly obvious reminder of the trials of the Negro, while the sins recounted are the sins of the American republic.

At this point, the Negro identifies himself almost wholly with the Jew. The more devout Negro considers that he *is* a Jew, in bondage to a hard taskmaster and waiting for a Moses to lead him out of Egypt. The hymns, the texts, and the most favored legends of the devout Negro are all Old Testament and therefore Jewish in origin: the flight from Egypt, the Hebrew children in the fiery furnace, the terrible jubilee songs of deliverance: *Lord, wasn't that hard trials, great tribulations, I'm bound to leave this land!* The covenant God made in the beginning with Abraham and which was to extend to his children and to his children's children forever is a covenant made with these latter-day exiles also: as Israel was chosen, so are they. The birth and death of Jesus, which adds a non-Judaic element, also implements this identification. It is the covenant made with Abraham again, renewed, signed with his blood.

Cabin in the Sky: A 1943 movie with an all-black cast, starring Lena Horne, Ethel Waters, Duke Ellington, and Louis Armstrong.

("Before Abraham was, I am.")[1] Here the figure of Jesus operates as the intercessor, the bridge from earth to heaven; it was Jesus who made it possible, who made salvation free to all, "to the Jew first and afterwards the Gentile." The images of the suffering Christ and the suffering Jew are wedded with the image of the suffering slave, and they are one: the people that walked in darkness have seen a great light.

But if the Negro has bought his salvation with pain and the New Testament is used to prove, as it were, the validity of the transformation, it is the Old Testament which is clung to and most frequently preached from, which provides the emotional fire and anatomizes the path of bondage; and which promises vengeance and assures the chosen of their place in Zion. The favorite text of my father, among the most earnest of ministers, was not "Father, forgive them, for they know not what they do," but "How can I sing the Lord's song in a strange land?"

This same identification, which Negroes, since slavery, have accepted with their mother's milk, serves, in contemporary actuality, to implement an involved and specific bitterness. Jews in Harlem are small tradesmen, rent collectors, real estate agents, and pawnbrokers; they operate in accordance with the American business tradition of exploiting Negroes, and they are therefore identified with oppression and are hated for it. I remember meeting no Negro in the years of my growing up, in my family or out of it, who would really ever trust a Jew, and few who did not, indeed, exhibit for them the blackest contempt. On the other hand, this did not prevent their working for Jews, being utterly civil and pleasant to them, and, in most cases, contriving to delude their employers into believing that, far from harboring any dislike for Jews, they would rather work for a Jew than for anyone else. It is part of the price the Negro pays for his position in this society that, as Richard Wright points out, he is almost always acting. A Negro learns to gauge precisely what reaction the alien person facing him desires, and he produces it with disarming artlessness. The friends I had, growing up and going to work, grew more bitter every day; and, conversely, they learned to hide this bitterness and to fit into the pattern Gentile and Jew alike had fixed for them.

The tension between Negroes and Jews contains an element not characteristic of Negro-Gentile tension, an element which accounts in some measure for the Negro's tendency to castigate the Jew verbally more often than the Gentile, and which might lead one to the conclusion that, of all white people on the face of the earth, it is the Jew whom the Negro hates most. When the Negro hates the Jew *as a Jew* he does so partly because the nation does and in much the same painful fashion that he hates himself. It is an aspect of his humiliation whittled down to a manageable size and then transferred; it is the best form the Negro has for tabulating vocally his long record of grievances against his native land.

20

---

[1]See John 8:58.

At the same time, there is a subterranean assumption that the Jew should "know better," that he has suffered enough himself to know what suffering means. An understanding is expected of the Jew such as none but the most naïve and visionary Negro has ever expected of the American Gentile. The Jew, by the nature of his own precarious position, has failed to vindicate this faith. Jews, like Negroes, must use every possible weapon in order to be accepted, and must try to cover their vulnerability by a frenzied adoption of the customs of the country; and the nation's treatment of Negroes is unquestionably a custom. The Jew has been taught—and, too often, accepts—the legend of Negro inferiority; and the Negro, on the other hand, has found nothing in his experience with Jews to counteract the legend of Semitic greed. Here the American white Gentile has two legends serving him at once: he has divided these minorities and he rules.

It seems unlikely that within this complicated structure any real and systematic cooperation can be achieved between Negroes and Jews. (This is in terms of the over-all social problem and is not meant to imply that individual friendships are impossible or that they are valueless when they occur.) The structure of the American commonwealth has trapped both these minorities into attitudes of perpetual hostility. They do not dare trust each other—the Jew because he feels he must climb higher on the American social ladder and has, so far as he is concerned, nothing to gain from identification with any minority even more unloved than he; while the Negro is in the even less tenable position of not really daring to trust anyone.

This applies, with qualifications and yet with almost no exceptions, even to those Negroes called progressive and "unusual." Negroes of the professional class (as distinct from professional Negroes) compete actively with the Jew in daily contact; and they wear anti-Semitism as a defiant proof of their citizenship; their positions are too shaky to allow them any real ease or any faith in anyone. They do not trust whites or each other or themselves; and, particularly and vocally, they do not trust Jews. During my brief days as a Socialist I spent more than one meeting arguing against anti-Semitism with a Negro college student, who was trying to get into civil service and was supporting herself meanwhile as a domestic. She was by no means a stupid girl, nor even a particularly narrow-minded one: she was all in favor of the millenium, even to working with Jews to achieve it; but she was not prepared ever to accept a Jew as a friend. It did no good to point out, as I did, that the exploitation of which she accused the Jews was American, not Jewish, that in fact, behind the Jewish face stood the American reality. And *my* Jewish friends in high school were not like that, I said, they had no intention of exploiting *me,* we did not hate each other. (I remember, as I spoke, of being aware of doubt crawling like fog in the back of my mind.) This might all be very well, she told me, we were children now, with no need to earn a living. Wait until later, when your friends go into business and you try to get a job. You'll see!

It is this bitterness—felt alike by the inarticulate, hungry population of Harlem, by the wealthy on Sugar Hill,° and by the brilliant exceptions ensconced in universities—which has defeated and promises to continue to defeat all efforts at interracial understanding. I am not one of the people who believe that oppression imbues a people with wisdom or insight or sweet charity, though the survival of the Negro in this country would simply not have been possible if this bitterness had been all he felt. In America, though, life seems to move faster than anywhere else on the globe and each generation is promised more than it will get: which creates, in each generation, a furious, bewildered rage, the rage of people who cannot find solid ground beneath their feet. Just as a mountain of sociological investigations, committee reports, and plans for recreational centers have failed to change the face of Harlem or prevent Negro boys and girls from growing up and facing, individually and alone, the unendurable frustration of being always, every-where, inferior—until finally the cancer attacks the mind and warps it—so there seems no hope for better Negro-Jewish relations without a change in the American pattern.

Both the Negro and the Jew are helpless; the pressure of living is too   25
immediate and incessant to allow time for understanding. I can conceive of no Negro native to this country who has not, by the age of puberty, been irreparably scarred by the conditions of his life. All over Harlem, Negro boys and girls are growing into stunted maturity, trying desperately to find a place to stand; and the wonder is not that so many are ruined but that so many survive. The Negro's outlets are desperately constricted. In his dilemma he turns first upon himself and then upon whatever most represents to him his own emasculation. Here the Jew is caught in the American crossfire. The Negro, facing a Jew, hates, at bottom, not his Jewishness but the color of his skin. It is not the Jewish tradition by which he has been betrayed but the tradition of his native land. But just as a society must have a scapegoat, so hatred must have a symbol. Georgia has the Negro and Harlem has the Jew.

Questions for Understanding

1. In talking about the black magazine *Ebony,* Baldwin refers to an editorial called "Time to Count Our Blessings" and to a photograph of "an aging Negro farm woman carrying home a bumper crop of onions." Then he says that the very existence of the magazine and the table of contents for any month "gave the lie to this effort to make the best of a bad bargain." What is the truth and what is the lie?
2. What is the main fault Baldwin finds with the black press?
3. Why, in Baldwin's opinion, was Joe Louis the "most idolized man in Harlem"?

Sugar Hill: An upper-class residential neighborhood in Harlem.

4. How does Baldwin explain the depth of religious feeling in Harlem?

5. What does Baldwin mean when he says, "The structure of the American commonwealth has trapped both these minorities [Negroes and Jews] into attitudes of perpetual hostility"? What are the causes of the perpetual hostility?

Suggestions for Writing

1. Write an essay in which you analyze a racial or ethnic neighborhood that you are familiar with. What distinguishes that neighborhood from a typical neighborhood of another racial or ethnic group?

2. Write an essay in which you analyze a newspaper or magazine with which you are familiar and which targets a particular ethnic audience. To what extent does it differ from mainstream newspapers or magazines? To what extent does it try to emulate a mainstream model?

3. Describe the most prominent characteristics of the religion you know best. What particular benefits or rewards does affiliation with that religion offer to its members?

4. Discuss the tension that exists between the religious group you know best and a different religious group that your group is acutely aware of. What are the causes of the tension? How overt has the conflict become?

5. Write an essay in which you tell about an experience in which you were being used as a scapegoat for someone else's frustration. Be sure to make clear why you are convinced the behavior toward you grew out of frustration.

Nadine Gordimer

[1923–   ]

The highest honor a writer can receive is the Nobel Prize for Literature. Nadine Gordimer won a Nobel Prize in 1991, thereby joining the ranks of such writers as Gabriel García Márquez, Isaac Bashevis Singer, Aleksandr Solzhenitsyn, Albert Camus, John Steinbeck, Ernest Hemingway, and William Faulkner. The prize was won primarily for her novels and short stories, but throughout her long career, Gordimer also has been a formidable writer of essays. The overriding concern in almost all of Gordimer's work has been the issue of justice. That is not surprising for a writer who grew up in South Africa, where for three centuries the white minority ruled relentlessly over everyone else. Determined to live in the country of her birth, Gordimer committed herself to the cause of equal rights for all South Africans.

Gordimer spent her childhood in the gold-mining town of Springs, near Johannesburg. Her father, Isidore Gordimer, was a watchmaker, a Jew who had emigrated from a Baltic town to Africa when he was thirteen; her mother came to Africa from England. Although her parents enjoyed their middle-class status, which even allowed them to have black servants, their bookish younger daughter was very uncomfortable in her assigned role. She had little desire to conform to the expectations of the adults around her, and she found their attitude toward black people particularly offensive. In Springs, a middle-class girl was expected to become a clone of her mother. It was assumed that in her early twenties she would be found by a young man from a family similar to her own and shortly thereafter enter upon her "season of glory"—the engagement party, the linen shower, the wedding, and the birth of the first child. There was no point in reading books; reading would only impede the process through which the daughter repeated the life of her mother.

From a young age, however, Gordimer was a rebel. In "The Bolter . . ." she tells how two male friends helped strengthen her refusal to be forced into anyone's mold. The first friend was a young man of her own generation who did her the service of telling her that, despite all her independent thinking and all her reading, she really knew little of life and literature. The second was an older man, Uys Krige. A poet who wrote in Afrikaans, the language of the Afrikaners (the white South Africans descended from the Dutch settlers who came to South Africa in the seventeenth century), Krige gave a hefty push to Gordimer's rebelliousness. After her encounters with him, Gordimer had the strength to live and to write in accordance with values of her own choosing; she would be independent of the values and culture of white South Africa.

After the all-white election of 1948, the victorious National Party formally imposed on South Africa the system of *apartheid,* under which the black population was totally segregated from the white, except for the roles of domineering boss and abject laborer or servant. By the early 1960s, resistance to apartheid had begun. A central figure in that resistance was the black lawyer Nelson Mandela. One of the leaders among whites was the Afrikaner lawyer Abram "Bram" Fischer, a man who hated the social system that bestowed every advantage on people like himself. When the government brought him to trial, Nadine Gordimer was in the courtroom throughout the proceedings. To Gordimer, their bravery, selflessness, and commitment to justice made Bram Fischer and Nelson Mandela great heroes. "Why Did Bram Fischer Choose Jail?" was not published in South Africa but in *The New York Times Magazine* (August 14, 1966). In Gordimer's 1979 novel *Burger's Daughter,* the heroic Lionel Burger is modeled after Bram Fischer.

In the speech she gave upon receiving the Nobel Prize, Gordimer described the paradoxical role of the writer. The writer may support the cause of justice, but he or she must not be blinded by that commitment: "The writer must take the right to explore, warts and all, both the enemy and the beloved comrade in arms. . . ." Human experience is far too complex to lend itself to easy labels such as "good" or "evil." Human experience is like a labyrinth—"the bloody yet beautiful labyrinth of human experience, of being." In the labyrinth of being—the multitude of intricate passages through which a human being must pass—there are many uncertainties and inconsistencies, and there is much confusion. The just writer "uses the word even against his or her own loyalties; trusts the state of being, as it is revealed, to hold somewhere in its complexity filaments of the cord of truth. . . ."

In the Nobel Lecture, Gordimer also asserted her belief that her fiction is more truthful than her nonfiction. For the fiction writer must be able to enter into other lives. As a writer of fiction, Gordimer, indeed, has entered into the lives of an amazing range of people: men as well as women, black villagers as well as urban blacks, Afrikaans-speaking racists as well as English-speaking liberal hypocrites. When a writer of nonfiction has had this kind of experience as a writer of fiction, the nonfiction must be all the more truthful.

SORTING THE IMAGES
FROM THE MAN

1990

I have just come home from the rally that welcomed Nelson Mandela   *1*
back to Soweto.° It was the occasion of a lifetime for everyone there;
including the dot in the crowd that was myself, as one of the whites who have
identified with the African National Congress through the years when it was
a crime to do so. Overwhelmingly, the joyous gyrating mass that filled Soccer
City Stadium, clung to retaining structures like swarming bees, even
somehow hoisted one another up on old gold-mine headgear outside the
fences, had been born and grown to adulthood—young whites as well as
blacks—while Mandela spent nearly 30 years in prison. Yet all that time there
was no black child in whose face, at the mention of his name, there was not
instant recognition. And there were no whites—enemies of the cause of black
freedom as well as its supporters—who did not know who this man was. His
body was hidden behind walls; his presence was never obliterated by them.

When Bishop Desmond Tutu received the Nobel Peace Prize in the
20th year of Mandela's imprisonment, he said he accepted it for Mandela, for
all prisoners of conscience, and for all those ordinary black people whose
employers do not know their workers' surnames. And on the day of
Mandela's release, when Dr. Nthato Motlana, himself a symbolic figure of
resistance, was asked whether he didn't think Mandela should now come to
live in Soweto° "among his people," Motlana said: "He's not a Sowetan, he's
a South African. Wherever he lives in our country he is among his own
people."

That may have sounded like a grandiose put-down but it is strangely
true. Apart from the Afrikaner right wing, whose fringe of Nazi crazies give
the swastika on their flag a new twist and wave "Hang Mandela" posters at
each other, whites have not merely accepted Mandela's return but turn to
him now as the only one who can absolve and resolve: absolve the sin of
apartheid and resolve the problems of reconciliation and integration.
President de Klerk's boldness in freeing Mandela has as its ironic obverse a
fervent submission to this idea. He counts on Mandela: without him, the
legendary bird rising out of the bars, blue winged and with a sprig of olive
held ready for three decades in its beak, the transformation of South Africa
into a place where de Klerk's white electorate can still live can't be realized.
The blacks' personification of the hidden Mandela as the image of their
ultimate liberation is superimposed by the whites' picture of him as their
salvation, forming a single image.

So there were the faded photographs of a tall young man with smiling
eyes and an old-fashioned part in his hair, umpteenth generation reproduc-

---

Soweto: A group of black townships southwest of Johannesburg.

tions that looked like ectoplasmic evidence, and there was the vision of the generic hero who (our Che Guevara° if not messiah) could never be dead even if, as sometimes seemed only too likely, he were to die unseen. On the cover of Time his Identikit portrait° appeared in final apotheosis in the guise of a beaming idol, something between Harry Belafonte and Howard Rollins.°

And then there walked out of prison a man unrecognizable as any of these. The real man, with a face sculpted and drawn by the spirit within himself enduring through 30 years, by the marks of incredible self-discipline, of deep thought, suffering, and the unmistakable confidence of faith in the claims of human dignity. An awesome face.

Now he's here. He confronts us, the man among us. He spoke bluntly, in Soweto, to black and white, sparing us nothing. He cut through the adulation of the crowd to demand from blacks an end to violence between black people. He spelled out to whites their responsibility for the consequences of poverty, homelessness and unemployment caused by the laws they made and must abolish.

By contrast, few care to interpret in equally plain language the staggering responsibility that expectations lay upon Mandela. "Reconciliation" in a "new South Africa" by him ultimately means finding houses for hundreds of thousands of blacks whose needs dating back to World War II have never been met. It means finding the 4,000 skilled personnel the dwindling economy desperately needs, from among a population whose majority has received a hopelessly inadequate, segregated education. It means—turning up only one among monster problems the big buzzwords hide—transforming a police force and Army which have been the brutal enemies of the people of South Africa for generations.

A kind of helplessness among whites—the government—has dumped on Mandela the problems of the moment as well as the long-term: violence, crowd control, black school attendance. The mantra is Mandela; the hum is everywhere, but does it really represent the guru? The man himself is not carried away. He reiterates firmly that "no individual leader" can take on the enormous task of creating unity and remaking South Africa on his own, that any decision by which the bread of negotiation will be broken with the government will be made by the combined leadership of the ANC, of which he is "a loyal and disciplined member." The onus rests on whites; they must accept the policies of the ANC as a standpoint for negotiation as they accept Mandela. And he makes it absolutely clear that whether there will be feast or famine at that symbolic table depends on the whites' and blacks' understanding of what the big words really mean if they are to spell a united, nonracist, democratic and free South Africa. Mandela doesn't want to be worshipped.

Che Guevara: (1928–1967) a leader of the Cuban Revolution.

Identikit portrait: The photograph on the identification card blacks were required to carry under apartheid.

Harry Belafonte and Howard Rollins: very handsome and appealing black entertainers.

He wants the people of South Africa to remake themselves together. That's his greatness.

Questions for Understanding

1. Why did Gordimer attend the rally for Mandela in Soweto?
2. How well known was Mandela among young South Africans?
3. What is the attitude of most whites toward Mandela?
4. According to Gordimer, what were the effects on Mandela of his thirty years in prison?
5. According to Gordimer, what have been the effects on Mandela of all the adulation?

Suggestions for Writing

1. Have you ever been in a crowd of many thousands gathered to celebrate an event, a person, or a group? If so, write an essay in which you discuss the effects the experience had on you.
2. Have you ever found yourself within a few feet of a person you idolized? Write an essay in which you discuss the effects of the experience, especially any changes the experience caused in your attitude toward the person.
3. Do you know anyone who has been in prison? Write an essay in which you discuss what appear to have been the effects of imprisonment on the person. What was the person like before, and what is the person like now?
4. "Mandela doesn't want to be worshipped." Are you aware of any other political leader who doesn't want to be worshipped? Are you aware of any political leader who relishes his or her power? Write an essay in which you discuss the effects of power on a political leader you are familiar with.
5. Do some research to find out how far South Africa has come in dealing with one of the problems Gordimer says the new South Africa must face. How bad was the situation under apartheid? How much change has occurred under the new constitution?

WHY DID BRAM FISCHER CHOOSE JAIL?

1966

In South Africa on May 9, 1966, Abram Fischer, Queen's Counsel, a   *1*
proud Afrikaner and self-affirmed Communist, was sentenced to imprisonment for life. The main counts against him (conspiring to commit sabotage
and being a member of, and furthering the aims of, the Communist Party)
were framed under the Suppression of Communism Act, but anti-
Communists could take no comfort from that: this Act is the much-extended
one under which all extra-parliamentary opposition to apartheid, whether
inspired by socialism, capitalism, religious principles, a sense of justice or just
plain human feeling, is at least under suspicion in South Africa. In his address
to the court a few days before, Fischer himself had pointed out, "The laws
under which I am being prosecuted were enacted by a wholly unrepresen-
tative body . . . in which three-quarters of the people of this country have no
voice whatever." He went on to say, "These laws were enacted not to prevent
the spread of communism, but for the purpose of silencing the opposition of
a large majority of our citizens to a Government intent upon depriving them,
solely on account of their colour, of the most elementary human rights."

All through his trial, Fischer listened and took notes—even when some
erstwhile friends turned state witnesses stood a few feet away, testifying
against him—with the same composed alertness that had been his demeanour
when appearing as counsel in this same Palace of Justice at Pretoria. The
smile, beginning in the brilliant, flecked blue eyes, was his familiar one, as he
turned from the dock to face the public gallery, and sought the faces of family
or friends. The panoply of the court, the shouts drifting up from the cells
below, the press tiptoeing restlessly in and out, his colleagues in their robes,
Mr. Justice Wessel Boshoff on the bench—all this was the everyday scene of
his professional working life as an advocate. But he stood in the prisoner's
dock. Hemmed in by the intimidating presence of plain-clothes security men
and scrutinised by uniformed policemen, the spectators in the gallery stared
into the well of the court as into Fischer's private nightmare, where all
appeared normal except for this one glaring displacement.

Yet it was clear that Abram Fischer recognised the reality of his
position, and knew it to be the climax of the collision course upon which he
and his countrymen were set, nearly thirty years ago, the day he rejected his
student belief in segregation. He told the court:

> All the conduct with which I have been charged has been directed
> towards maintaining contact and understanding between the races of
> this country. If one day it may help to establish a bridge across which
> white leaders and the real leaders of the non-whites can meet to
> settle the destinies of all of us by negotiation and not by force of

arms, I shall be able to bear with fortitude any sentence which this
court may impose on me. It will be a fortitude strengthened by this
knowledge at least, that for twenty-five years I have taken no part,
not even by passive acceptance, in that hideous system of discrimination which we have erected in this country and which has become
a byword in the civilised world today.

Not even those Afrikaners who regard Abram Fischer as the arch-traitor to
Afrikanerdom would deny that if he had been able to stomach white overlord-
ship and the colour bar there would have been no limit to the honours and high
office he might today have attained in the republic his forebears won from British
imperialism. He comes from the right stock, with not only the brains but also the
intellectual *savoir-faire* coveted by a people who sometimes feel, even at the peak
of their political power, some veld-bred disadvantage in their dealings with the
sophistications of the outside world.

He was born in 1908 in the Orange River Colony—formerly the old Boer
republic of the Orange Free State—grandson of its only Prime Minister before
Union in 1910. His father became Judge-President of the Orange Free
State—after Union a province of South Africa. The Boer War defeat at the hands
of the British remained a bitter taste in the mouth of the grandfather; as a school
cadet, it is said that the grandson refused to be seen in the British conqueror's
military uniform.

He was a brilliant scholar, and when he had taken his law degree at   5
Bloemfontein, won a Rhodes scholarship to New College, Oxford. At
twenty-nine he married the daughter of another distinguished Afrikaner
family, Susannah (Molly) Krige, and began a thirty-year career at the bar in
Johannesburg. He reached the top of his profession and was regarded as an
expert on mining law. His services were engaged by the insurance companies,
the newspaper consortiums and the big mining houses.

His success coincided with the growth of Afrikaner political power, but his
recognition of the subjection of the black man on which this power was built
precluded him from taking any part in it. While he saw his people as the first in
Africa to win liberation from colonial domination and therefore well able to
understand and fitted to encourage African aspirations, they were busy codifying
the traditional race prejudice of white South Africans, whether of Boer, British
or any other descent, as an ideology and the "South African way of life."

It was within this situation that Fischer, as a young man, had become a
Communist. The rise of Fascism in the world at that time was turning many of
his contemporaries in other countries to the left. In England, for example, his
counterpart would have gone off to fight with the International Brigade in the
Spanish Civil War. But Fischer's battle was to be fought at home. His instigation
was not youthful idealism, but the injustice and indifference to injustice that he
saw around him every day, and that, indeed, as the first Nationalist prime minister
of a student parliament, and a segregationist, he had been party to. It was Hitler's
sinister theory of race superiority, combined with a "strange revulsion" that
Fischer experienced when, as a formality at a philanthropic meeting he had to

take a black man's hand, that had opened his eyes. Since the days when, as a child, he had made clay oxen with black children on his family's farm, he had been conditioned to develop an antagonism for which he could find no reason. He came to understand colour prejudice as a wholly irrational phenomenon.

At his trial in Pretoria, he told the court why he had been attracted to the Communist Party. There was this

> glaring injustice which exists and has existed for a long time in South African society . . . This is not even a question of the degree of humiliation or poverty or misery imposed by discrimination . . . It is simply and plainly that discrimination should be imposed as a matter of deliberate policy, solely because of the colour which a man's skin happens to be, irrespective of his merits as a man.

Three decades ago there was certainly not much choice for a young man looking for participation in political activity unequivocally aimed to change all this. The Communist Party was then, and for many years, the only political party that observed no colour bar and advocated universal franchise. (Today, more than thirty years later, there is only one other white political party advocating universal franchise—the Liberal Party, founded in 1953.) At his trial Fischer explained:

> My attraction to the Communist Party was a matter of personal observation. By that time the Communist Party had already for two decades stood avowedly and unconditionally for political rights for non-whites, and its white members were, save for a handful of courageous individuals, the only whites who showed complete disregard for the hatred which this attitude attracted from their fellow white South Africans. These members . . . were whites who could have taken full advantage of all the privileges open to them because of their colour . . . They were not prepared to flourish on the deprivations suffered by others.
>
> But apart from the example of white members, it was always *10* the Communists of all races who were prepared to give of their time and their energy and such means as they had, to help . . . with night schools and feeding schemes, who assisted trade unions fighting desperately to preserve standards of living . . . It was African Communists who constantly risked arrest . . . in order to gain or retain some rights . . . This fearless adherence to principle must always exercise a strong appeal to those who wish to take part in politics, not for personal advantage, but in the hope of making some positive contribution.

Fischer's contemporaries among the angry young men in the Western world of the thirties have lived to see a peaceful social revolution in England and the vigorous pursuit of civil-rights legislation against segregation in the United

States. Within the same span, in South Africa, Fischer has seen the deeply felt grievances of the non-white population of his country increasingly ignored, their non-violent campaigns against discriminatory laws in the fifties ruthlessly put down, in the sixties their Congresses banned, responsible leaders jailed and house-arrested, along with white people of many political beliefs who have supported them, and a year-by-year piling up of legislation—Bantustans,° job reservation,° ghetto acts°—increasing restriction by colour in every aspect of human activity.

Those contemporaries who shared what now seems to them a hot-headed youth may sit back in good conscience and ask why Fischer did not leave behind leftist beliefs, as they did, in the disillusion of the Stalinist era. One can only state the facts. Though Fischer never proselytised, he was and remains a doctrinaire Marxist; South Africa, in her political development in relation to the colour problem, has never offered him an acceptable alternative to his socialist beliefs.

At his trial he affirmed in orthodox Marxist terms the theory that political change occurs inevitably when a political form ceases to serve the needs of people who are living under new circumstances created by the development of new economic forces and relations. He obviously sees the colour problem in South Africa as basically an economic one: the white man's fear of losing his job to the overwhelming numbers of Africans, the black man so insecure economically that the numbers of unemployed Africans are never even recorded accurately. Fischer said, "South Africa today is a clear example of a society in which the political forms do not serve the needs of most of the people," and pointed out that ownership of factories, mines and land used for productive purposes is becoming more and more concentrated—in the hands of whites, of course.

Outside the banned Communist Party, there is no group or party open to whites that, however it proposes to go about removing colour discrimina- tion, also visualises radical change in the ownership of the means of produc- tion which underpins the present system of white supremacy. Fischer openly told the court: "I believe that socialism in the long term has an answer to the problem of race relations. But by negotiation, other immediate solutions can be found . . . Immediate dangers [a civil war which he visualized as dwarf- ing the horrors of Algeria] can be avoided by bringing our state at this stage into line with the needs of today by abolishing discrimination, extending political rights, and then allowing our people to settle their own future."

In prison or out, Abram Fischer maintains a dramatic position in South   15 African life. For some years, circumstances surrounding him have been extraordinary. If Afrikaner Nationalist propagandists present him as the anti-Christ, then, curiously moved to lay aside his socialist rationalism, he has

---

Bantustans: Black homelands.

job reservation: Reserving certain categories of work for whites and others, usually menial, for blacks.

ghetto acts: The Group Areas Act of 1950 made it illegal for blacks to live in "white" areas.

taken upon himself some of their sins in an almost Christlike way. In addressing the court he returned again and again to statements like

> What is not appreciated by my fellow Afrikaner, because he has cut himself off from all contact with non-whites, is that . . . he is now blamed as an Afrikaner for all the evils and humiliations of apartheid. Hence today the policeman is known as a 'Dutch'. . . . When I give an African a lift during a bus boycott, he refuses to believe that I am an Afrikaner. . . . All this has bred a deep-rooted hatred for Afrikaners among non-whites. . . . It demands that Afrikaners themselves should protest openly and clearly against discrimination. Surely there was an additional duty cast on me, that at least one Afrikaner should make this protest actively. . . .

Those people, including Afrikaner Nationalists, who know Fischer personally have a special affection and respect for him, no matter how anti-Communist they may be. He himself has always shown respect for the right of anyone to work for social reform in his own way, just so long as the obligation is not smugly ignored. No other figure is at once so controversial and so well-liked. Even people who have never been able to understand his adherence to, let alone accept, his socialist views will add: "But he is a wonderful *person*." This is due to nothing so superficial as charm—though Fischer has plenty of that; there has been, about Abram Fischer and his wife and children, the particular magnetism of deeply honest lives. Paradoxically, the pull is strong in a country where so many compromises with conscience are made by so many decent citizens.

In his profession, as well, Fischer has borne something of a charmed life. From the fifties, when political trials got under way in South Africa, he would refuse conventionally important briefs in order to take time to defend rank-and-file Africans, Indians and whites on political charges. Such was his professional prestige that the financial Establishment continued to seek his services as before. From 1958 to 1961 he devoted himself to the defence of Nelson Mandela, the African National Congress leader, and twenty-nine others accused in the first mass political trial that, because it represented so many shades—both skin and ideological—of political thought, became known as "the Opposition on trial." In 1964 Fischer was leading defence counsel at the trial of the "High Command" of combined liberation movements, which had been based at Rivonia, north of Johannesburg. Later that year, his invisible armour was pierced for the first time; he was imprisoned, briefly, under the ninety-day-detention law. And then, in September of 1964 he was arrested, with thirteen others, on five charges including those of being a member and furthering the objects of the Communist Party.

Because of the esteem in which Fischer was held, his request for bail was supported by many of his legal colleagues and granted by the court, although he had been named chief accused. During the course of the trial, he was even given a temporary passport to enable him to go to London to represent an internationally known pharmaceutical company at the Privy Council. He could expect as much as a five-year sentence at his own trial: would he come back? He had given his word, and he did. Having won the case, he returned discussing the new plays he had seen in the West End, just as if he had come home to face nothing more than the letdown after a holiday.

He had been in South Africa a month or so when, on January 25, 1965, he disappeared overnight, leaving a letter to the court saying that he was aware that his eventual punishment would be increased by his action, but that he believed it was his duty both to remain in South Africa and to continue to oppose apartheid by carrying on with his political work as long as he was physically able. He referred to his career at the Bar, in relation to the injustice of apartheid upheld by the law: "I can no longer serve justice in the way I have attempted to do during the past 30 years. I can do it only in the way I have now chosen."

For ten months he eluded a police hunt that poked into every 20 backyard and farmhouse in the country, and brought into detention anyone suspected of being able to blurt out, under persuasion of solitary confinement, Fischer's whereabouts. On November 11 last year, he was arrested in Johannesburg, thin, bearded, his hair dyed. Except for the eyes, he was unrecognisable as the short but well-set, handsome man with curly white hair that he had been—and was to be again, by the time he appeared in court on January 26 of this year to face fifteen instead of the original five charges against him.

Why did Abram Fischer abscond? What did he achieve by it? So far as is known, he does not seem to have managed to initiate any significant new political activity while in hiding.

His fellow white South Africans, the majority of whom are indifferent to the quality of life on the other side of the colour bar, living their comfortable lives in the segregated suburbs where, once, he too had a house with a swimming pool, and among whom, last year, he lived as a fugitive, express strong opinions about what he had done with his life. His colleagues at the Bar, taking the position that absconding from his original trial was conduct unseemly to the dignity of the profession, hurriedly applied within days of his disappearance to have him disbarred. Some people assure themselves that he acted in blind obedience to "orders from Moscow"—the purpose of which they cannot suggest. Well-meaning people who cannot conceive that anyone would sacrifice profession, home, family, and ultimately personal liberty for a gesture affirming what he believed to be right, say that the tragic death of his wife, Molly, in a motor accident in 1964, must have disorientated him. Others, who have themselves suffered bans and lost passports as a result of courageous opposition to apartheid, feel that Fischer's final defiance of the law was a gratuitous act, ending in senseless tragedy: "Why has Bram thrown himself away?"

While Fischer was "at large" for those ten months, some people were saying, "Now he is our Mandela." (The reference was to the period when Nelson Mandela escaped a police net for more than a year, travelled abroad, and worked among his people from "underground.") In the jails last year (where there were more than three thousand political prisoners), when African politicals were allowed to see anybody, their first question was commonly not about their families but whether "Bram" was still "all right." And a few days before sentence was to be passed on him, an African couple begged his daughter to let them borrow one of his suits, so that a witchdoctor might use it in a spell to influence the judge to give a deferred sentence.

For the Fischer family, 1964–5 was a year to turn distraught any but the most tough and selfless minds. It has since become clear that, as defence counsel at the Rivonia Trial, Fischer had to muster the nerve and daring to handle evidence that might at any moment involve himself. Directly after the trial, he and his wife were driving to Cape Town to celebrate the twenty-first birthday of their daughter Ilse, a student at the University of Cape Town, and to enable Fischer to visit Mandela and the other convicted trial defendants imprisoned off the coast on Robben Island, when his car plunged into a deep pool by the side of the road and Molly Fischer was drowned.

The Fischers have always been an exceptionally devoted family, sharing as well as family love a working conviction that daily life must realise in warm, human action any theoretical condemnation of race discrimination. In Molly Fischer the very real tradition of Afrikaner hospitality triumphantly burst the barriers it has imposed on itself; her big house was open to people of all races, and, unmindful of what the neighbours would say, she and her husband brought up along with their own daughters and son an orphaned African child. 25

Molly Fischer taught Indian children, worked with women's non-racial movements and spent five months in prison, detained without trial, during the 1960 State of Emergency. At her huge funeral people of all races mourned together, as if apartheid did not exist. No one who saw him at that time can forget the terrible courage with which Fischer turned loss into concern for the living; neither could they confuse this with the workings of an unhinged mind. Almost at once, he set out again for Cape Town to visit the men on Robben Island.

If one wants to speculate why he disappeared in the middle of his trial and yet stayed in South Africa, fully aware that when, inevitably, he was caught he would incur greatly increased punishment, one must surely also ask oneself why, when he was allowed to go abroad while on bail, he ever came back. Some friends half hoped he wouldn't; a government supporter nervously remarked that there was nothing to stop Fischer turning up at The Hague, where, at the time, the World Court was hearing the question of South Africa's right to impose apartheid on the mandated territory of South West Africa [Namibia]. There would have been no extradition, but a hero's role for him there.

People of different backgrounds who know Fischer best seem to agree that what brought him back from Europe and what made him turn fugitive were one and the same thing, the touchstone of his personality: absolute faith in human integrity. It seems reasonable to conclude that he came back because he believed that this integrity was mutual and indivisible—he believed he would never be betrayed by the people with whom he was working in opposition to apartheid, and, in turn, he owed them the guarantee of his presence.

As for the 'gesture' of the ten months he spent in hiding, he has given, in court, his own answer to those fellow citizens—legal colleagues, firms, enemies, the white people of South Africa—who seek to judge him:

> It was to keep faith with all those dispossessed by apartheid that I broke my undertaking to the court, separated myself from my family, pretended I was someone else, and accepted the life of a fugitive. I owed it to the political prisoners, to the banished, to the silenced and to those under house arrest not to remain a spectator, but to act. I knew what they expected of me, and I did it. I felt responsible, not to those who are indifferent to the sufferings of others, but to those who are concerned. I knew that by valuing, above all, their judgment, I would be condemned by people who are content to see themselves as respectable and loyal citizens. I cannot regret any such condemnation that may follow me.

The judge sentenced him to prison "for life" and, while others wept, Fischer himself received the pronouncement with fortitude. No one can guess what goes on in a man's mind when he hears such words; but perhaps Abram Fischer, sitting it out in prison, now, may ask himself, taking courage, "Whose life? Theirs—the government's—or mine?"°   *30*

Questions for Understanding

1. What was the long-range objective of Bram Fischer's "criminal" conduct that led the government to bring charges against him?
2. What was Bram Fischer's social standing in South Africa's Afrikaner society?
3. What attracted Bram Fischer to the South African Communist Party?
4. Why did those Afrikaners who strongly opposed Fischer politically nevertheless feel much affection for him?
5. Why did Bram Fischer become a fugitive?

"Whose life? Theirs—the government's—or mine?": While in prison, Bram Fischer became ill with cancer. He was released from prison shortly before he died in 1975.

Suggestions for Writing

1. Describe a person you know who has forsaken for an ideal the privileges he or she would be entitled to by virtue of family background or education.
2. Describe a person you know who pretends to be a "Bram Fischer" but really is not.
3. Describe a married couple who are as well matched in their ideals as Bram and Molly Fischer were.
4. Discuss a historical person who in important ways resembles Bram Fischer.
5. Have you ever faced the dilemma of whether to be true to your ideals and accept stern punishment or to compromise your ideals and avoid punishment? Discuss the predicament you found yourself in.

A BOLTER AND THE INVINCIBLE SUMMER

1963

My writing life began long before I left school, and I began to leave   *1*
school (frequently) long before the recognized time came, so there is no real
demarcation, for me, between school and "professional" life. The quotes are
there because I think of professional life as something one enters by way of
an examination, not as an obsessional occupation like writing for which you
provide your own, often extraordinary or eccentric, qualifications as you go
along. And I'm not flattered by the idea of being presented with a
"profession," *honoris causa;* every honest writer or painter wants to achieve the
impossible and needs no minimum standard laid down by an establishment
such as a profession.

This doesn't mean that I think a writer doesn't need a good education
in general, and that I don't wish I had had a better one. But maybe my own
regrets arise out of the common impulse to find a justification, outside the
limits of one's own talent, for the limits of one's achievement.

I was a bolter, from kindergarten age, but unlike most small children
rapidly accustoming their soft, round selves to the sharp angles of desks and
discipline, I went on running away from school, year after year. I was a day
scholar at a convent in Springs, the Transvaal gold-mining town where we
lived, and when I was little I used to hide until I heard the hive of voices start
up "Our Father" at prayers, and then I would walk out of the ugly iron gates
and spend the morning on the strip of open veld that lay between the
township where the school was and the township where my home was. I
remember catching white butterflies there, all one summer morning, until,
in the quiet when I had no shadow, I heard the school bell, far away, clearly,
and I knew I could safely appear at home for lunch. When I was older I used
to take refuge for hours in the lavatory block, waiting in the atmosphere of
Jeyes' Fluid for my opportunity to escape. By then I no longer lived from
moment to moment, and could not enjoy the butterflies; the past, with the
act of running away contained in it, and the future, containing discovery and
punishment, made freedom impossible; the act of seizing it was merely a
desperate gesture.

What the gesture meant, I don't know. I managed my school work
easily, and among the girls of the class I had the sort of bossy vitality that makes
for popularity; yet I was overcome, from time to time, by what I now can at
least label as anxiety states. Speculation about their cause hasn't much place
here, which is lucky, for the people who were around me then are still alive.
Autobiography can't be written until one is old, can't hurt anyone's feelings,
can't be sued for libel, or, worse, contradicted.

There is just one curious aspect of my bolting that seems worth   *5*
mentioning because it reveals a device of the personality that, beginning at

that very time, perhaps, as a dream-defence, an escape, later became the practical sub-cónscious cunning that enabled me to survive and grow in secret while projecting a totally different, camouflage image of myself. I ran away from school; yet there was another school, the jolly, competitive, thrillingly loyal, close-knit world of schoolgirl books, to which I felt that I longed to belong. (At one time I begged to go to boarding school, believing, no doubt, that I should find it there.) Of course, even had it existed, that *School Friend* world would have been the last place on earth for me. I should have found there, far more insistently, the walls, the smell of serge and floor polish, the pressure of uniformity and the tyranny of bell-regulated time that set off revolt and revulsion in me. What I did not know—and what a child never knows—is that there is more to the world than what is offered to him; more choices than those presented to him; more kinds of people than those (the only ones he knows) to which he feels but dares not admit he does not belong. I thought I *had* to accept school and all the attitudes there that reflected the attitudes of home; therefore, in order to be a person I had to have *some* sort of picture of a school that would be acceptable to me; it didn't seem possible to live without it. Stevie Smith once wrote that all children should be told of the possibility of committing suicide, to console them in case they believed there was no way out of the unbearable; it would be less dramatic but far more consoling if a child could be told that there is an aspect of himself he *does not know is permissible.*

The conclusion my bolting school drew from the grown-ups around me was that I was not the studious type and simply should be persuaded to reconcile myself to the minimum of learning. In our small town many girls left school at fifteen or even before. Then, after a six-week course at the local commercial college, a girl was ready for a job as a clerk in a shop or in the offices of one of the gold mines which had brought the town into being. And the typewriter itself merely tapped a mark-time for the brief season of glory, self-assertion and importance that came with the engagement party, the pre-nuptial linen "shower," and culminated not so much in the wedding itself as in the birth, not a day sooner than nine months and three weeks later, of the baby. There wasn't much point in a girl keeping her head stuck in books anyway, even if she chose to fill the interim with one of the occupations that carried a slightly higher prestige, and were vaguely thought of as artistic—teaching tap-dancing, the piano, or "elocution."

I suppose I must have been marked out for one of these, because, although I had neither talent nor serious interest in drumming my toes, playing Czerny, or rounding my vowels, I enjoyed using them all as material in my talent for showing off. As I grew toward adolescence I stopped the home concerts and contented myself with mimicking, for the entertainment of one group of my parents' friends, other friends who were not present. It did not seem to strike those who were there that, in their absence, they would change places with the people they were laughing at; or perhaps it did, I do them an injustice, and they didn't mind.

All the time it was accepted that I was a candidate for home-dressmaking or elocution whom there was no point in keeping at school too long, I was reading and writing not in secret, but as one does, openly, something that is not taken into account. It didn't occur to anyone else that these activities were connected with learning, so why should it have occurred to me? And although I fed on the attention my efforts at impersonation brought me, I felt quite differently about any praise or comment that came when my stories were published in the children's section of a Sunday paper. While I was terribly proud to see my story in print—for only in print did it become "real," did I have proof of the miracle whereby the thing created has an existence of its own—I had a jealous instinct to keep this activity of mine from the handling that would pronounce it "clever" along with the mimicry and the home concerts. It was the beginning of the humble arrogance that writers and painters have, knowing that it is hardly likely that they will ever do anything really good, and not wanting to be judged by standards that will accept anything less. Is this too high-falutin' a motive to attribute to a twelve-year-old child? I don't think so. One can have a generalised instinct toward the unattainable long before one has actually met with it. When, not many years later, I read *Un Cœur simple* or *War and Peace*—O, I knew this was it, without any guidance from the list of the World's Hundred Best Books that I once tried to read through!

I started writing at nine, because I was surprised by a poem I produced as a school exercise. The subject prescribed was "Paul Kruger,"° and although an item of earliest juvenilia, in view of what has happened between people like myself and our country since then, I can't resist quoting, just for the long-untasted patriotic flavour:

Noble in heart,
Noble in mind,
Never deceitful,
Never unkind . . .

It was the dum-de-de-dum that delighted me rather than the senti-   10
ments or the subject. But soon I found that what I really enjoyed was making up a story, and that this was more easily done without the restrictions of dum-de-de-dum. After that I was always writing something, and from the age of twelve or thirteen, often publishing. My children's stories were anthropomorphic, with a dash of the Edwardian writers' Pan-cult paganism as it had been shipped out to South Africa in Kenneth Grahame's books, though already I used the background of mine dumps and veld animals that was familiar to me, and not the European one that provided my literary background, since there were no books about the world I knew. I wrote my

Paul Kruger: Perhaps the greatest hero of Afrikaners, Kruger (1825–1904) was the four-term president of Transvaal, the former Afrikaans-speaking republic.

elder sister's essays when she was a student at the Witwatersrand University, and kept up a fair average for her. I entered an essay in the literary section of the Eisteddfod run by the Welsh community in Johannesburg and bought with the prize chit *War and Peace, Gone with the Wind,* and an Arthur Ransome.

I was about fourteen then, and a happy unawareness of the strange combination of this choice is an indication of my reading. It was appetite rather than taste, that I had; yet while it took in indiscriminately things that were too much for me, the trash tended to be crowded out and fall away. Some of the books I read in my early teens puzzle me, though. Why Pepys's *Diary?* And what made me plod through *The Anatomy of Melancholy?* Where did I hear of the existence of these books? (That list of the World's One Hundred Best, maybe.) And once I'd got hold of something like Burton, what made me go on from page to page? I think it must have been because although I didn't understand all that I was reading, and what I did understand was remote from my experience in the way that easily assimilable romance was not, the half-grasped words dealt with the world of ideas, and so confirmed the recognition, somewhere, of that part of myself that I did not know was permissible.

All the circumstances and ingredients were there for a small-town prodigy, but, thank God, by missing the encouragement and practical help usually offered to "talented" children, I also escaped the dwarf status that is clapped upon the poor little devils before their time (if it ever comes). It did not occur to anyone that if I wanted to try to write I ought to be given a wide education in order to develop my powers and to give me some cultural background. But this neglect at least meant that I was left alone. Nobody came gawping into the private domain that was no dream-world, but, as I grew up, the scene of my greatest activity and my only disciplines. When school-days finally petered out (I had stopped running away, but various other factors had continued to make attendance sketchy) I did have some sort of show of activity that passed for my life in the small town. It was so trivial that I wonder how it can have passed, how family or friends can have accepted that any young person could expend vitality at such a low hum. It was never decided what I should "take up" and so I didn't have a job. Until, at twenty-two, I went to the University, I led an outward life of sybaritic meagreness that I am ashamed of. In it I did not one thing that I wanted wholeheartedly to do; in it I attempted or gratified nothing (outside sex) to try out my reach, the measure of aliveness in me. My existential self was breathing but inert, like one of those unfortunate people who has had a brain injury in a motor accident and lies unhearing and unseeing, though he will eat when food comes and open his eyes to a light. I played golf, learnt to drink gin with the RAF pupil pilots from the nearby air station, and took part in amateur theatricals to show recognisable signs of life to the people around me. I even went to first aid and nursing classes because this was suggested as an "interest" for me; it did not matter to me what I did, since I could not admit that there was nothing, in the occupations and diversions offered to me, that really did interest me, and I was not sure—the only evidence was in books—that anything else was possible.

I am ashamed of this torpor nevertheless, setting aside what I can now see as probable reasons for it, the careful preparation for it that my childhood constituted. I cannot understand why I did not free myself in the most obvious way, leave home and small town and get myself a job somewhere. No conditioning can excuse the absence of the simple act of courage that would resist it. My only overt rejection of my match-box life was the fact that, without the slightest embarrassment or conscience, I let my father keep me. Though the needs provided for were modest, he was not a rich man. One thing at least I would not do, apparently—I would not work for the things I did not want. And the camouflage image of myself as a dilettantish girl, content with playing grown-up games at the end of my mother's apron strings—at most a Bovary in the making—made this possible for me.

When I was fifteen I had written my first story about adults and had sent it off to a liberal weekly that was flourishing in South Africa at the time. They published it. It was about an old man who is out of touch with the smart, prosperous life he has secured for his sons, and who experiences a moment of human recognition where he least expects it—with one of their brisk young wives who is so unlike the wife he remembers. Not a bad theme, but expressed with the respectable bourgeois sentiment which one would expect. That was in 1939, two months after the war had broken out, but in the years that followed the stories that I was writing were not much influenced by the war. It occupied the news bulletins on the radio, taking place a long way off, in countries I had never seen; later, when I was seventeen or eighteen, there were various boyfriends who went away to Egypt and Italy and sent back coral jewellery and leather bags stamped with a sphinx.

Oddly enough, as I became engaged with the real business of learning how to write, I became less prompt about sending my efforts off to papers and magazines. I was reading Maupassant, Chekhov, Maugham and Lawrence, now, also discovering O. Henry, Katherine Anne Porter and Eudora Welty, and the stories in *Partisan Review, New Writing* and *Horizon.* Katherine Mansfield and Pauline Smith, although one was a New Zealander, confirmed for me that my own "colonial" background provided an experience that had scarcely been looked at, let alone thought about, except as a source of adventure stories. I had read "The Death of Ivan Ilyich" and "The Child of Queen Victoria," the whole idea of what a story could do, be, swept aside the satisfaction of producing something that found its small validity in print. From time to time I sent off an attempt to one of the short-lived local politico-literary magazines—meant chiefly as platforms for liberal politics, they were the only publications that published poetry and stories outside the true romance category—but these published stories were the easy ones. For the other I had no facility whatever, and they took months, even years, to cease changing shape before I found a way of getting hold of them in my mind, let alone nailing the words down around them. And then most of them were too long, or too outspoken (not always in the sexual sense) for these magazines. In a fumbling way that sometimes slid home in an unexpected strike, I was looking for what people meant but didn't say, not only about sex, but also about politics and their relationship with the black people among whom we lived as people live in a forest among trees. So it was that I didn't wake up to Africans and the shameful enormity of the colour bar through a youthful spell in the Communist Party, as did some of my contemporaries with whom I share the rejection of white supremacy, but through the apparently esoteric speleology of doubt, led by Kafka rather than Marx. And the "problems" of my country did not set me writing; on the contrary, it was learning to write that sent me falling, falling through the surface of "the South African way of life."

It was about this time, during a rare foray into the nursery bohemia of university students in Johannesburg, that I met a boy who believed I was a writer. Just that; I don't mean he saw me as Chosen for the Holy Temple of Art, or any presumptuous mumbo-jumbo of that kind. The cosmetic-counter sophistication that I hopefully wore to disguise my stasis in the world I knew and my uncertainty of the possibility of any other, he ignored as so much rubbish. This aspect of myself, that everyone else knew, he did not; what he recognised was my ignorance, my clumsy battle to chip my way out of shell after shell of ready-made concepts and make my own sense of life. He was often full of scorn, and jeered at the way I was going about it; but *he recognised the necessity*. It was through him, too, that I roused myself sufficiently to insist on going to the University; not surprisingly, there was opposition to this at home, since it had been accepted so long that I was not the studious type, as the phrase went. It seemed a waste, spending money on a university at twenty-two (surely I should be married soon?); it was suggested that (as distinct from the honourable quest for a husband) the real reason why I wanted to go was to look for men. It seems to me now that this would have been as good a reason as any. My one preoccupation outside the world of ideas was men, and I should have been prepared to claim my right to the one as valid as the other.

But my freedom did not come from my new life at university; I was too old, in many ways, had already gone too far, on my own scratched tracks, for what I might once have gained along the tarmac. One day a poet asked me to lunch. He was co-editor of yet another little magazine that was then halfway through the dozen issues that would measure its life. He had just published a story of mine and, like many editors when the contributor is known to be a young girl, was curious to meet its author. He was the Afrikaans poet and playwright Uys Krige, who wrote in English as well, had lived in France and Spain, spoke five languages, was familiar with their literature, and translated from three. He had been a swimming instructor on the Riviera, a football coach somewhere else, and a war correspondent with the International Brigade in Spain.

When the boy (that same boy) heard that I was taking the train into Johannesburg for this invitation—I still lived in Springs—he said: "I wouldn't go, if I were you, Nadine."

"For Pete's sake, why not?"

"Not unless you're prepared to change a lot of things. You may not feel   *20*
the same, afterwards. You may never be able to go back."

"What on *earth* are you talking about?" I made fun of him: "I'll take the
train back."

"No, once you see what a person like that is like, you won't be able to
stand your ordinary life. You'll be miserable. So don't go unless you're
prepared for this."

The poet was a small, sun-burned, blond man. While he joked, enjoyed
his food, had an animated discussion with the African waiter about the origin
of the name of a fruit, and said for me some translations of Lorca and Eluard,
first in Afrikaans and then, because I couldn't follow too well, in English, he
had the physical brightness of a fisherman. It was true; I had never met anyone
like this being before. I have met many poets and writers since, sick, tortured,
pompous, mousy; I know the morning-after face of Apollo. But that day I
had a glimpse of—not some spurious "artist's life," but, through the poet's
person, the glint of his purpose—what we are all getting at, Camus's
"invincible summer" that is there to be dug for in man beneath the grey of
suburban life, the numbness of repetitive labour, and the sucking mud of
politics.

Oh yes—not long after, a story of mine was published in an anthology,
and a second publisher approached me with the offer to publish a collection.
The following year I at last sent my stories where I had never been—across
the seas to England and America. They came back to me in due course, in
hard covers with my name printed on the coloured jacket. There were
reviews, and, even more astonishing, there was money. I was living alone in
Johannesburg by then, and was able to pay the rent and feed both myself and
the baby daughter I had acquired. These things are a convenient marker for
the beginning of a working life. But mine really began that day at lunch. I see
the poet occasionally. He's older now, of course; a bit seamed with
disappointments, something of a political victim, since he doesn't celebrate
his people's politics or the white man's colour bar in general. The truth isn't
always beauty, but the hunger for it is.

Questions for Understanding

1. As Gordimer uses it, what does the word *bolter* mean?
2. What was the attitude of Gordimer's family toward the reading and writing
   she did as an adolescent?
3. Gordimer says that, as a young writer of fiction, she could write some stories
   relatively easily, whereas others "took months, even years." What was the
   nature of the stories that she spent a lot of time on?
4. What does Gordimer mean when she says that her meeting with Uys Krige
   gave her a glimpse of the "invincible summer"? What, in other words, is an
   "invincible summer"?

5. What does Gordimer mean when she says, "The truth isn't always beauty, but the hunger for it is"?

Suggestions for Writing

1. Is *hooky player* a term that ever applied to you? If it did, what caused you to play hooky? What were some of the effects of your playing hooky?
2. Classify and discuss the kids in your school who were known to be hooky players.
3. Describe what you would do during a day of playing hooky.
4. Is there one book that you read as an adolescent that left you a significantly different person from the one you were before reading that book? Discuss what you were like before and what you were like after reading it.
5. Is there one person you encountered as an adolescent who had a profound effect on you? Describe the encounter and analyze the effect.

NUTS AND BOLTS 4: WHAT IS GOOD WRITING?

In "A Bolter and the Invincible Summer," Nadine Gordimer says, "there is no real demarcation, for me, between school and 'professional' life." In other words, she had been writing—voluntarily and seriously—almost from the time she was first able to pick up a pencil, and, without any conscious decision on her part, that childhood activity evolved into the writing she went on to do as an adult. Gordimer seems to have been destined to become a writer.

Unlike Nadine Gordimer, most people begin to write when they begin school. Writing is a classroom activity or a homework assignment. As the years pass, writing continues to be a chore. Indeed, for most people writing causes a certain level of anxiety because there are so many ways a given piece of writing—be it a freshman composition, an answer to an essay question, a report for an employer—is open to criticism. Surprisingly, Gordimer, too, came to be apprehensive about what she put on paper, even though writing had been second nature since her early years.

What caused Gordimer apprehension was very different from what worries most student writers. Gordimer didn't worry about spelling, punctuation errors, or constructing ungrammatical sentences. For beginning writers, such concerns are important, but a piece of writing that is free of those kinds of errors is not necessarily a good piece of writing. A really good piece of writing—of any kind, on any level—is one that does more than just avoid mistakes.

Gordimer started publishing short stories when she was fifteen. But as she got more involved in reading the great modern writers, she realized that the stories she had published were "easy," that they lacked a quality she found in the work of the great writers. She says she "had no facility whatever" for that quality and that it "took months, even years," to find it for some of the stories she had been working on. She says, "I was looking for what people meant but didn't say. . . ." That modest remark is loaded with meaning. Gordimer wanted to do more than simply describe what she observed; she wanted to reveal what was going on beneath the surface of people's lives.

She listened as people spoke, and it was the most natural thing in the world to assume that what was said was truthful. She did not doubt that what a person said he or she believed or felt was an accurate representation of what was really going on inside the person. But the more Gordimer read of the great writers, the more she became aware that there often were significant differences between outside and inside, between how things appeared and what they really were. The difference between appearance and reality, she realized, is an ever-recurring theme among great writers.

It was necessary to go beyond mere recording. She wanted to be able to reveal what wasn't readily apparent, and that is the lesson here for student writers, regardless of the kind of writing to be done. A good writer does more than merely record what the eyes see or the ears hear. A good writer goes beneath the surface. A good writer doesn't just describe what a person or a building looks like but attempts to reveal what is not obvious. A good writer doesn't just record what the hooky player did during the day away from school but tells more—possibly about the causes and effects of playing hooky. In dealing with information uncovered through research, a good writer not only presents the facts in an orderly way but also reveals what they mean. An accountant or lawyer who studies a client's ledgers and documents is not worth very much if all he or she does afterwards is sum up. Summing up may be necessary, but the distinguishing quality of a professional's work lies in what else he or she contributes—in the ability to see below the surface. A professional, like a good writer, deals with such questions as, Is there some kind of pattern in what is being done? What effects are likely to follow from such a pattern?

Gordimer tells us that, when she went to Johannesburg and met the university student who believed she was a real writer, he saw through the surface she presented to the world—"the cosmetic-counter sophistication." "What he recognized was my ignorance, my clumsy battle to chip my way out of shell after shell of ready-made concepts and make my own sense of life." Good writers of all kinds are very wary of ready-made concepts. Such concepts might fit a couple of situations, but good writers know that such concepts should not be applied to all similar situations. Among similar things, persons, or ideas, the differences may be much more interesting and important than the similarities. It is in seeing those differences and in interpreting them in our own unique way that we achieve our individuality—our own sense of life.

APARTHEID

1959

Men are not born brothers; they have to discover each other, and it is   *1*
this discovery that apartheid seeks to prevent. . . . What is apartheid?

It depends who's answering. If you ask a member of the South African
government, he will tell you that it is separate and parallel development of
white and black—that is the official, legal definition. If you ask an ordinary
white man who supports the policy, he will tell you that it is the means of
keeping South Africa white. If you ask a black man, he may give you any one
of a dozen answers, arising out of whatever aspect of apartheid he has been
brought up short against that day, for to him it is neither an ideological
concept nor a policy, but a context in which his whole life, learning, working,
loving, is rigidly enclosed.

He could give you a list of the laws that restrict him from aspiring
to most of the aims of any civilized person, or enjoying the pleasures
that every white person takes for granted. But it is unlikely that he will.
What may be on his mind at the moment is the problem of how to save
his child from the watered-down "Bantu Education" which is now standard
in schools for black children—inferior schooling based on a reduced
syllabus that insists the black child cannot attain the same standard of
education as the white child, and places emphasis on practical and menial
skills. Or perhaps you've merely caught him on the morning after he's spent
a night in the police cells because he was out after curfew hours without
a piece of paper bearing a white man's signature permitting him to be so.
Perhaps (if he's a man who cares for such things) he's feeling resentful
because there's a concert in town he would not be permitted to attend,
or (if he's that kind of man, and who isn't?) he's irked at having to pay
a black-market price for the bottle of brandy he is debarred from buying
legitimately. That's apartheid, to him. All these things, big and little, and
many more.

If you want to know how Africans—black men—live in South Africa,
you will get in return for your curiosity an exposition of apartheid in action,
for in all of a black man's life—all his life—rejection by the white man has the
last word. With this word of rejection apartheid began, long before it
hardened into laws and legislation, long before it became a theory of racial
selectiveness and the policy of a government. The Afrikaner Nationalists (an
Afrikaner is a white person of Dutch descent whose mother tongue is
Afrikaans; a Nationalist is a member or supporter of the National Party, at
present in power) did not invent it, they merely developed it, and the impulse
of Cain from which they worked lives in many white South Africans today,
English-speaking as well as Afrikaner.

Shall I forget that when I was a child I was taught that I must never use   *5*
a cup from which our black servant had drunk?

I live in the white city of Johannesburg, the largest city in South Africa. Around the white city, particularly to the west and north, is another city, black Johannesburg. This clear picture of black and white is blurred only a little at the edges by the presence of small Coloured—mixed blood—and Indian communities, also segregated, both from each other and from the rest. You will see Africans in every house in the white city, of course, for servants live in, and every house has its servants' quarters, in a building separate from the white house. Sophisticated Africans call this back-yard life "living dogs-meat"—closer to the kennel and the outhouses than to the humans in the house.

But no black man has his *home* in the white city; neither wealth nor honor nor distinction of any kind could entitle him to move into a house in the street where I or any other white person lives. So it easily happens that thousands of white people live their whole lives without ever exchanging a word with a black man who is on their own social and cultural level; and for them, the whole African people is composed of servants and the great army of "boys" who cart away or deliver things—the butcher's boy, the grocer's boy, the milk boy, the dust boy. On the basis of this experience, you will see that it is simple for white men and women to deduce that black men and women are an inferior race. Out of this experience all the platitudes of apartheid sound endlessly, like the bogus sea from the convolutions of a big shell: *they're like children . . . they don't think the way we do . . . they're not ready.*

Black men do all the physical labor in our country, because no white man wants to dig a road or load a truck. But in every kind of work a white man *wants* to do, there are sanctions and job reservations to shut the black man out. In the building trade, and in industry, the Africans are the unskilled and semiskilled workers, and they cannot, by law, become anything else. They cannot serve behind the counters in the shops, and cannot be employed alongside white clerks. Wherever they work, they cannot share the washrooms or the canteens of the white workers. But they may buy in the shops. Oh yes, once the counter is between the black customer and the white shopkeeper, the hollow murmur of the apartheid shell is silenced—they *are* ready, indeed, to provide a splendid market, they *do* think enough like white people to want most of the things that white people want, from LP recordings to no-iron shirts.

The real life of any community—restaurants, bars, hotels, clubs and coffee bars—has no place for the African man or woman. They serve in all these, but they cannot come in and sit down. Art galleries, cinemas, theaters, golf courses and sports clubs, even the libraries are closed to them. In the post offices and all other government offices, they are served at segregated counters. They have no vote.

What it means to live like this, from the day you are born until the day you die, I cannot tell you. No white person can. I think I know the lives of my African friends, but time and again I find that I have assumed—since it was so ordinary a part of the average white person's life—that they had knowledge of some commonplace experience that, in fact, they could never have had. How am I to remember that Danny, who is writing his Ph.D. thesis on industrial psychology, has never seen the inside of a museum? How am I to remember that John, who is a journalist on a lively newspaper, can never hope to see the film I am urging him not to miss, since the township cinemas are censored and do not show what one might call adult films? How am I to remember that Alice's charming children, playing with my child's toy elephant, will never be able to ride on the elephant in the Johannesburg Zoo?

The humblest laborer will find his life the meaner for being black. If he were a white man, at least there would be no ceiling to his children's ambitions. But it is in the educated man that want and need stand highest on the wrong side of the color bar. Whatever he achieves as a man of learning, *as a man* he still has as little say in the community as a child or a lunatic. Outside the gates of the university (soon he may not be able to enter them at all; the two "open" universities are threatened by legislation that will close them to all who are not white), white men will hail him as "boy." When the first African advocate was called to the Johannesburg bar, back in 1956, government officials raised objections to his robing and disrobing in the same chamber as the white advocates. His colleagues accepted him as a man of the law; but the laws of apartheid saw him only as a black man. Neither by genius nor cunning, by sainthood or thuggery, is there a way in which a black man can earn the right to be regarded as any other man.

Of course, the Africans have made some sort of life of their own. It's a slum life, a make-do life, because, although I speak of black cities outside white cities, these black cities—known as "the townships"—are no Harlems. They are bleak rectangular patterns of glum municipal housing, or great smoky proliferations of crazy, chipped brick and tin huts, with few street lights, few shops. The life there is robust, ribald and candid. All human exchange of the extrovert sort flourishes; standing in a wretched alley, you feel the exciting blast of a great vitality. Here and there, in small rooms where a candle makes big shadows, there is good talk. It is attractive, especially if you are white; but it is also sad, bleak and terrible. It may not be a bad thing to be a township Villon; but it is tragic if you can never be anything else. The penny whistle is a charming piece of musical ingenuity; but it should not always be necessary for a man to make his music out of nothing.

Some Africans are born, into their segregated townships, light enough to pass as Coloured. They play Coloured for the few privileges—better jobs, better housing, more freedom of movement—that this brings, for the nearer you can get to being white, the less restricted your life is. Some Coloureds are born, into their segregated townships, light enough to pass as white. A fair skin is the equivalent of a golden spoon in the child's mouth; in other countries colored people may be tempted to play white for social reasons, but in South Africa a pale face and straight hair can gain the basic things—a good school, acceptance instead of rejection all the way along the line.

It is the ambition of many Coloured parents to have a child light enough to cross the color bar and live the precarious lie of pretending to be white; their only fear is that the imposture will be discovered. But the other night

I was made aware of a different sort of fear and a new twist to the old game of play-white. An Indian acquaintance confessed to me that he was uneasy because his thirteen-year-old son has turned out to have the sort of face and complexion that could pass for white. "He's only got to slip into a white cinema or somewhere, just once, for the fun of it. The next thing my wife and I know, he'll be starting to play white. Once they've tried what it's like to be a white man, how are you to stop them? Then it's lies, and not wanting to know their own families, and misery all round. That's one of the reasons why I want to leave South Africa, so my kids won't want to grow up to be something they're not."

I've talked about the wrong side of the color bar, but the truth is that   15
both are wrong sides. Do not think that we, on the white side of privilege, are the people we might be in a society that has no sides at all. We do not suffer, but we are coarsened. Even to continue to live here is to acquiesce in some measure to apartheid—to a sealing off of responses, the cauterization of the human heart. Our children grow up accepting as natural the fact that they are well clothed and well fed, while black children are ragged and skinny. It cannot occur to the white child that the black one has any rights outside of charity; you must explain to your child, if you have the mind to, that men have decided this, that the white shall have and the black shall have not, and it is not an immutable law, like the rising of the sun in the morning. Even then it is not possible entirely to counter with facts an emotional climate of privilege. We have the better part of everything, and it is difficult for us not to feel, somewhere secretly, that we *are* better.

Hundreds of thousands of white South Africans are concerned only with holding on to white privilege. They believe that they would rather die holding on to it than give up the smallest part of it; and I believe they would. They cannot imagine a life that would be neither their life nor the black man's life, but another life altogether. How can they imagine freedom, who for years have been so vigilant to keep it only to themselves?

No one of us, black or white, can promise them that black domination will not be the alternative to white domination, and black revenge the long if not the last answer to all that the whites have done to the blacks. For—such is the impact of apartheid—there are many blacks, as well as many whites, who cannot imagine a life that would be neither a black man's life nor a white man's life.

Those white South Africans who want to let go—leave hold—are either afraid of having held on too long, or are disgusted and ashamed to go on living as we do. These last have become color-blind, perhaps by one of those freaks by which desperate nature hits upon a new species. They want another life altogether in South Africa. They want people of all colors to use the same doors, share the same learning, and give and take the same respect from each other. They don't care if the government that guarantees these things is white or black. A very few of these people go so far as to go to prison, in the name of one political cause or another, in attempts that they believe will help to bring about this new sort of life. The rest make, in one degree or another, an effort to live, within an apartheid community, the decent life that apartheid prohibits.

Of course, I know that no African attaches much importance to what apartheid does to the white man, and no one could blame him for this. What does it signify to him that your sense of justice is outraged, your conscience is troubled, and your friendships are restricted by the color bar? All this lies heavily, mostly unspoken, between black and white friends. My own friends among Africans are people I happen to like, my kind of people, whose friendship I am not prepared to forgo because of some racial theory I find meaningless and absurd. Like that of many others, my opposition to apartheid is compounded not only out of a sense of justice but also out of a personal, selfish and extreme distaste for having the choice of my friends dictated to me, and the range of human intercourse proscribed for me.

Questions for Understanding

1. What were the different racial groups recognized by the white government of South Africa?
2. Where did blacks in Johannesburg live?
3. According to Gordimer, what did whites deduce as a result of the limited job opportunities available to blacks?
4. According to Gordimer, what was the disadvantage to whites of limiting the job opportunities of blacks?
5. What loss does Gordimer believe she suffered as a result of apartheid?

Suggestions for Writing

1. Write an essay in which you discuss the degree to which there is racial integration in housing in your hometown.
2. Write an essay in which you discuss the degree to which there is racial integration in housing on your campus.
3. Write an essay in which you discuss the degree to which there is racial integration at social events at your college.
4. "We have the better part of everything, and it is difficult for us not to feel, somewhat secretly, that we *are* better. . . ." Does this statement also apply to you and your family? If so, write an essay in which you compare and contrast what you have and what *they* have, and discuss the effects of an awareness of such differences.
5. Have you ever been in a friendship with a person of another race? If so, write an essay in which you discuss the rewards of a biracial friendship and some of the obstacles that had to be overcome to keep the friendship going.

George Orwell

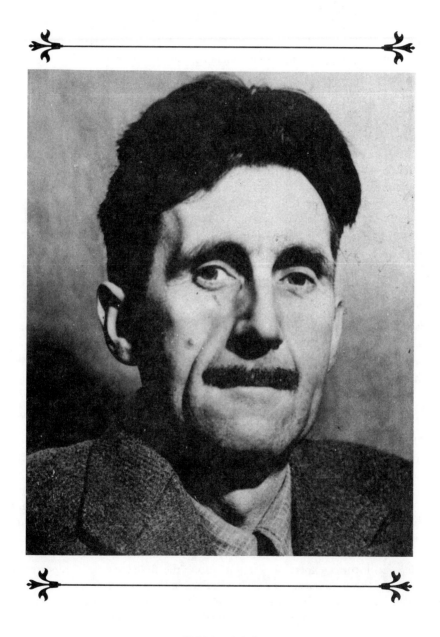

[1903–1950]

George Orwell was a man who easily could be made happy but who more easily could be made unhappy—not by things that happened to him, but by how people treated their fellow human beings. During his relatively brief life, cut short by a fatal case of tuberculosis, he saw the need so many people have to feel superior to other people; he saw callous indifference to poverty and suffering, he saw the determination of those with power to preserve that power by any means, and he heard very intelligent people who were nevertheless unable to distinguish fact from idea. He wished the world were a better place, and he hoped his writings would help make it so.

At age eight, Orwell was enrolled in a private boarding school—St. Cyprian's, in the south of England. He attended the school for about five years and hated it. As was often the case with English boarding schools, the place was a hotbed of snobbery. A student's treatment there depended on his or her family's social position. Orwell's father was a respected civil servant for the British government in India, and the family was far from being impoverished. But almost everyone at school was upper middle class, and Orwell was made to feel he was *lower* upper middle class. Years later, he wrote about his time at the school, "I had no money, I was weak, I was ugly, I was unpopular, I had a chronic cough, I smelt."

Eton, founded in 1440, is the most highly regarded English prep school. Orwell attended Eton on a scholarship, but for him it was only a more acute version of St. Cyprian's. Whereas most graduates of Eton go on to either Oxford or Cambridge, both elite universities, Orwell chose to see what the British Empire was all about. Following in his father's footsteps, he went to work as a civil servant in British Asia—but in adjacent Burma rather than India. In Burma, between the ages of nineteen and twenty-four, Orwell came to despise the system that made the English rulers of the Burmese. When he returned to England on leave in 1927, he decided he could "not go on any longer serving an imperialism I had come to regard as very largely a racket." Instead of returning to Burma, he began his career as a writer. The essays titled "A Hanging" and "Shooting an Elephant"—both set in Burma and both remarkable in their rendering of detail and attitude—were written not on the spot but only after Orwell was back in England.

As a gesture of compassion and as a way of finding material to write about, Orwell immersed himself in the life of the downtrodden, first in England and then in Paris, where he worked as a dishwasher and kitchen helper. While in Paris he contracted pneumonia and was taken to a hospital that mainly served poor people. His experience there was later described in the essay "How the Poor Die." His broader experiences living among the underclass were reported in *Down and Out in Paris and London* (1933). Back in England, Orwell wrote his first novel, *Burmese Days* (1934), about the unpleasantness of both the rulers and the ruled in Burma. It was with the publication of *Down and Out* that Orwell, whose real name was Eric Arthur Blair, adopted his pseudonym; Orwell is the name of the river that runs through Suffolk, where his parents lived.

In 1936 Orwell lived among unemployed coal miners in the northern English borough of Wigan, an experience he wrote about in *The Road to Wigan Pier* (1937). Orwell offered this explanation of the meaning of his title: "Wigan is in the middle of the mining areas. . . . The landscape is mostly slag-heaps, looking like the mountains of the moon. . . . At one time, on one of the little muddy canals that run round the town, there used to be a tumble-down wooden jetty; and by way of a joke someone nicknamed this Wigan Pier." The little jetty is long gone, but *Wigan Pier* remains as a symbol for pretension amidst squalor.

The civil war in Spain raged between 1936 and 1939. Like America's Ernest Hemingway, George Orwell thought he belonged in Spain, fighting to preserve a democratic government against Franco and fascism. Orwell's experiences in Spain had a profound effect on him and are reported in *Homage to Catalonia* (1938). From what he saw of the lives of the peasants in the Spanish countryside and of working people in the city of Barcelona, then ruled by the people themselves, he came to believe that democratic socialism was a desirable—and possible—political goal. Among the several left-wing groups fighting the fascists, the communists were dominant. But the communists were as interested in suppressing their allies as they were in defeating the fascists. To Orwell and many others, the words and actions of the communists were full of duplicity and bespoke a greater concern for the interests of the Soviet Union than for democracy in Spain.

A sentence near the end of *Homage to Catalonia* reveals a great deal about George Orwell as a man and as a writer: "In case I have not said this somewhere earlier in the book I will say it now: beware of my partisanship, my mistakes of fact and the distortion inevitably caused by my having seen only one corner of the events." Six months after he arrived in Spain, a sniper's bullet through the throat put an end to Orwell's soldiering but left him alive.

Orwell's most famous work is *Nineteen Eighty-Four* (1949). Convinced that human beings would flourish under a political and social system based on liberty, democracy, and socialism, Orwell was horrified by the slaughter of liberty and democracy in the one major country that professed socialism, the Soviet Union. Yet these tyrannical practices were frequently defended and rationalized by left-wing intellectuals in the West. Rather than acknowledge unpleasant realities for what they were, such intellectuals eagerly threw up a smokescreen of words and ideas. They refused to see the totalitarianism of the Soviet Union; instead they saw a smiling, pipe-smoking Uncle Joe Stalin, who, despite his responsibility for the deaths of millions, had the welfare of workers and peasants at heart. In *Nineteen Eighty-Four,* Orwell imagines the nightmarish consequences for England of such willing delusion. Big Brother is everywhere.

ANTISEMITISM IN BRITAIN

1945

There are about 400,000 known Jews in Britain, and in addition some   *1*
thousands or, at most, scores of thousands of Jewish refugees who have
entered the country from 1934 onwards. The Jewish population is almost
entirely concentrated in half a dozen big towns and is mostly employed in the
food, clothing and furniture trades. A few of the big monopolies, such as the
ICI°, one or two leading newspapers and at least one big chain of department
stores are Jewish-owned or partly Jewish-owned, but it would be very far
from the truth to say that British business life is dominated by Jews. The Jews
seem, on the contrary, to have failed to keep up with the modern tendency
towards big amalgamations and to have remained fixed in those trades which
are necessarily carried out on a small scale and by old-fashioned methods.

I start off with these background facts, which are already known to any
well-informed person, in order to emphasise that there is no real Jewish
"problem" in England. The Jews are not numerous or powerful enough, and
it is only in what are loosely called "intellectual circles" that they have any
noticeable influence. Yet it is generally admitted that antisemitism is on the
increase, that it has been greatly exacerbated by the war, and that humane and
enlightened people are not immune to it. It does not take violent forms
(English people are almost invariably gentle and law-abiding), but it is
ill-natured enough, and in favorable circumstances it could have political
results. Here are some samples of antisemitic remarks that have been made to
me during the past year or two:

> Middle-aged office employee: "I generally come to work by bus. It
> takes longer, but I don't care about using the Underground from
> Golders Green nowadays. There's too many of the Chosen Race
> travelling on that line."
>
> Tobacconist (woman): "No, I've got no matches for you. I should
> try the lady down the street. *She's* always got matches. One of the
> Chosen Race, you see."
>
> Young intellectual, Communist or near-Communist: "No, I do   *5*
> *not* like Jews. I've never made any secret of that. I can't stick
> them. Mind you, I'm not antisemitic, of course."
>
> Middle-class woman: "Well, no one could call me antisemitic, but I
> do think the way these Jews behave is too absolutely stinking. The
> way they push their way to the head of queues, and so on. They're
> so abominably selfish. I think they're responsible for a lot of what
> happens to them."

ICI: International Chemical Industries, a large manufacturer of chemicals.

Milk roundsman: "A Jew don't do no work, not the same as what an Englishman does. 'E's too clever. We work with this 'ere" (flexes his biceps). "They work with that there" (taps his forehead).

Chartered accountant, intelligent, left-wing in an undirected way: "These bloody Yids are all pro-German. They'd change sides tomorrow if the Nazis got here. I see a lot of them in my business. They admire Hitler at the bottom of their hearts. They'll always suck up to anyone who kicks them."

Intelligent woman, on being offered a book dealing with antisemitism and German atrocities: "Don't show it me, *please* don't show it to me. It'll only make me hate the Jews more than ever."

I could fill pages with similar remarks, but these will do to go on with. 10 Two facts emerge from them. One—which is very important and which I must return to in a moment—is that above a certain intellectual level people are ashamed of being antisemitic and are careful to draw a distinction between "antisemitism" and "disliking Jews." The other is that antisemitism is an irrational thing. The Jews are accused of specific offences (for instance, bad behaviour in food queues) which the person speaking feels strongly about, but it is obvious that these accusations merely rationalise some deep-rooted prejudice. To attempt to counter them with facts and statistics is useless, and may sometimes be worse than useless. As the last of the above-quoted remarks shows, people can remain antisemitic, or at least anti-Jewish, while being fully aware that their outlook is indefensible. If you dislike somebody, you dislike him and there is an end of it: your feelings are not made any better by a recital of his virtues.

It so happens that the war has encouraged the growth of antisemitism and even, in the eyes of many ordinary people, given some justification for it. To begin with, the Jews are one people of whom it can be said with complete certainty that they will benefit by an Allied victory. Consequently the theory that "this is a Jewish war" has a certain plausibility, all the more so because the Jewish war effort seldom gets its fair share of recognition. The British Empire is a huge heterogeneous organisation held together largely by mutual consent, and it is often necessary to flatter the less reliable elements at the expense of the more loyal ones. To publicise the exploits of Jewish soldiers, or even to admit the existence of a considerable Jewish army in the Middle East, rouses hostility in South Africa, the Arab countries and elsewhere: it is easier to ignore the whole subject and allow the man in the street to go on thinking that Jews are exceptionally clever at dodging military service. Then again, Jews are to be found in exactly those trades which are bound to incur unpopularity with the civilian public in war-time. Jews are mostly concerned with selling food, clothes, furniture and tobacco—exactly the commodities of which there is a chronic shortage, with consequent overcharging, black-marketing and favouritism. And again, the common charge that Jews behave in an exceptionally cowardly way during air raids was given a certain amount of colour by the big raids of 1940. As it happened, the

Jewish quarter of Whitechapel was one of the first areas to be heavily blitzed, with the natural result that swarms of Jewish refugees distributed themselves all over London. If one judged merely from these war-time phenomena, it would be easy to imagine that antisemitism is a quasi-rational thing, founded on mistaken premises. And naturally the antisemite thinks of himself as a reasonable being. Whenever I have touched on this subject in a newspaper article, I have always had a considerable "come-back," and invariably some of the letters are from well-balanced, middling people—doctors, for example—with no apparent economic grievance. These people always say (as Hitler says in *Mein Kampf*) that they started out with no anti-Jewish prejudice but were driven into their present position by mere observation of the facts. Yet one of the marks of antisemitism is an ability to believe stories that could not possibly be true. One could see a good example of this in the strange accident that occurred in London in 1942, when a crowd, frightened by a bomb-burst nearby, fled into the mouth of an Underground station, with the result that something over a hundred people were crushed to death. The very same day it was repeated all over London that "the Jews were responsible". Clearly, if people will believe this kind of thing, one will not get much further by arguing with them. The only useful approach is to discover *why* they can swallow absurdities on one particular subject while remaining sane on others.

But now let me come back to that point I mentioned earlier—that there is widespread awareness of the prevalence of antisemitic feeling, and un-willingness to admit sharing it. Among educated people, antisemitism is held to be an unforgivable sin and in a quite different category from other kinds of racial prejudice. People will go to remarkable lengths to dem-onstrate that they are *not* antisemitic. Thus, in 1943 an intercession service on behalf of the Polish Jews was held in a synagogue in St. John's Wood. The local authorities declared themselves anxious to participate in it, and the service was attended by the mayor of the borough in his robes and chain, by representatives of all the churches, and by detachments of RAF,° Home Guards, nurses, Boy Scouts and what not. On the surface it was a touching demonstration of solidarity with the suffering Jews. But it was essentially a *conscious* effort to behave decently by people whose subjective feelings must in many cases have been very different. That quarter of London is partly Jewish, antisemitism is rife there, and, as I well knew, some of the men sitting round me in the synagogue were tinged by it. Indeed, the commander of my own platoon of Home Guards, who had been especially keen beforehand that we should "make a good show" at the intercession service, was an ex-member of Mosley's Blackshirts. While this division of feeling exists, tolerance of mass violence against Jews, or, what is more important, antisemitic legislation, are not possible in England. It is not at present possible, indeed, that antisemitism should *become respectable*. But this is less of an advantage than it might appear.

RAF: The Royal Air Force.

One effect of the persecutions in Germany has been to prevent antisemitism from being seriously studied. In England a brief inadequate survey was made by Mass Observation a year or two ago, but if there has been any other investigation of the subject, then its findings have been kept strictly secret. At the same time there has been conscious suppression, by all thoughtful people, of anything likely to wound Jewish susceptibilities. After 1934 the "Jew joke" disappeared as though by magic from postcards, periodicals and the music-hall stage, and to put an unsympathetic Jewish character into a novel or short story came to be regarded as antisemitism. On the Palestine issue, too, it was *de rigueur* among enlightened people to accept the Jewish case as proved and avoid examining the claims of the Arabs—a decision which might be correct on its own merits, but which was adopted primarily because the Jews were in trouble and it was felt that one must not criticise them. Thanks to Hitler, therefore, you had a situation in which the press was in effect censored in favour of the Jews while in private antisemitism was on the up-grade, even, to some extent, among sensitive and intelligent people. This was particularly noticeable in 1940 at the time of the internment of the refugees. Naturally, every thinking person felt that it was his duty to protest against the wholesale locking-up of unfortunate foreigners who for the most part were only in England because they were opponents of Hitler. Privately, however, one heard very different sentiments expressed. A minority of the refugees behaved in an exceedingly tactless way, and the feeling against them necessarily had an antisemitic undercurrent, since they were largely Jews. A very eminent figure in the Labour Party—I won't name him, but he is one of the most respected people in England—said to me quite violently: "We never asked these people to come to this country. If they choose to come here, let them take the consequences." Yet this man would as a matter of course have associated himself with any kind of petition or manifesto against the internment of aliens. This feeling that antisemitism is something sinful and disgraceful something that a civilised person does not suffer from, is unfavourable to a scientific approach, and indeed many people will admit that they are frightened of probing too deeply into the subject. They are frightened, that is to say, of discovering not only that antisemitism is spreading, but that they themselves are infected by it.

To see this in perspective one must look back a few decades, to the days when Hitler was an out-of-work house-painter whom nobody had heard of. One would then find that though antisemitism is sufficiently in evidence now, it is probably *less* prevalent in England than it was thirty years ago. It is true that antisemitism as a fully thought-out racial or religious doctrine has never flourished in England. There has never been much feeling against intermarriage, or against Jews taking a prominent part in public life. Nevertheless, thirty years ago it was accepted more or less as a law of nature that a Jew was a figure of fun and—though superior in intelligence—slightly deficient in "character". In theory a Jew suffered from no legal disabilities, but in effect he was debarred from certain professions. He would probably not have been accepted as an officer in the navy, for instance, nor in what is called a "smart" regiment in the army. A Jewish boy at a public school° almost invariably had a bad time. He could, of course, live down his Jewishness if he was exceptionally charming or athletic, but it was an initial disability comparable to a stammer or a birthmark. Wealthy Jews tended to disguise themselves under aristocratic English or Scottish names, and to the average person it seemed quite natural that they should do this, just as it seems natural for a criminal to change his identity if possible. About twenty years ago, in Rangoon, I was getting into a taxi with a friend when a small ragged boy of fair complexion rushed up to us and began a complicated story about having arrived from Colombo on a ship and wanting money to get back. His manner and appearance were difficult to "place", and I said to him:

"You speak very good English. What nationality are you?"   15

He answered eagerly in his chi-chi accent: "I am a *Joo,* sir!"

And I remember turning to my companion and saying, only partly in joke, "He admits it openly." All the Jews I had known till then were people who were ashamed of being Jews, or at any rate preferred not to talk about their ancestry, and if forced to do so tended to use the word "Hebrew."

The working-class attitude was no better. The Jew who grew up in Whitechapel took it for granted that he would be assaulted, or at least hooted at, if he ventured into one of the Christian slums nearby, and the "Jew joke" of the music halls and the comic papers was almost consistently ill-natured.[1] There was also literary Jew-baiting, which in the bands of Belloc, Chesterton and their followers reached an almost continental level of scurrility. Non-Catholic writers were sometimes guilty of the same thing in a milder form. There has been a perceptible antisemitic strain in English literature from Chaucer onwards, and without even getting up from this table to consult a book I can think of passages which *if written now* would be stigmatised as antisemitism, in the works of Shakespeare, Smollett, Thackeray, Bernard Shaw, H. G. Wells, T. S. Eliot, Aldous Huxley and various others. Offhand, the only English writers I can think of who, before the days of Hitler, made a definite effort to stick up for Jews are Dickens and Charles Reade. And however little the average intellectual may have agreed with the opinions of Belloc and Chesterton, he did not acutely disapprove of them. Chesterton's endless tirades against Jews, which he thrust into stories and essays upon the flimsiest pretexts, never got him into trouble—indeed Chesterton was one of the most generally respected figures in English literary

---

public school: An English public school is like an American private school.

[1]It is interesting to compare the "Jew joke" with that other stand-by of the music halls, the "Scotch joke", which superficially it resembles. Occasionally a story is told (e.g. the Jew and the Scotsman who went into a pub together and both died of thirst) which puts both races on an equality, but in general the Jew is credited *merely* with cunning and avarice while the Scotsman is credited with physical hardihood as well. This is seen, for example, in the story of the Jew and the Scotsman who go together to a meeting which has been advertised as free. Unexpectedly there is a collection, and to avoid this the Jew faints and the Scotsman carries him out. Here the Scotsman performs the athletic feat of carrying the other. It would seem vaguely wrong if it were the other way about.

life. Anyone who wrote in that strain *now* would bring down a storm of abuse upon himself, or more probably would find it impossible to get his writings published.

If, as I suggest, prejudice against Jews has always been pretty widespread in England, there is no reason to think that Hitler has genuinely diminished it. He has merely caused a sharp division between the politically conscious person who realises that this is not a time to throw stones at the Jews, and the unconscious person whose native antisemitism is increased by the nervous strain of the war. One can assume, therefore, that many people who would perish rather than admit to antisemitic feelings are secretly prone to them. I have already indicated that I believe antisemitism to be essentially a neurosis, but of course it has its rationalisations, which are sincerely believed in and are partly true. The rationalisation put forward by the common man is that the Jew is an exploiter. The partial justification for this is that the Jew, in England, is generally a small businessman—that is to say a person whose depredations are more obvious and intelligible than those of, say, a bank or an insurance company. Higher up the intellectual scale, antisemitism is rationalised by saying that the Jew is a person who spreads disaffection and weakens national morale. Again there is some superficial justification for this. During the past twenty-five years the activities of what are called "intellectuals" have been largely mischievous. I do not think it an exaggeration to say that if the "intellectuals" had done their work a little more thoroughly, Britain would have surrendered in 1940. But the disaffected intelligentsia inevitably included a large number of Jews. With some plausibility it can be said that the Jews are the enemies of our native culture and our national morale. Carefully examined, the claim is seen to be nonsense, but there are always a few prominent individuals who can be cited in support of it. During the past few years there has been what amounts to a counter-attack against the rather shallow Leftism which was fashionable in the previous decade and which was exemplified by such organisations as the Left Book Club. This counter-attack (see for instance such books as Arnold Lunn's *The Good Gorilla* or Evelyn Waugh's *Put Out More Flags*) has an antisemitic strain, and it would probably be more marked if the subject were not so obviously dangerous. It so happens that for some decades past Britain has had no nationalist intelligentsia worth bothering about. But British nationalism, i.e. nationalism of an intellectual kind, may revive, and probably will revive if Britain comes out of the present war greatly weakened. The young intellectuals of 1950 may be as naively patriotic as those of 1914. In that case the kind of antisemitism which flourished among the anti-Dreyfusards in France, and which Chesterton and Belloc tried to import into this country, might get a foothold.

I have no hard-and-fast theory about the origins of antisemitism. The two current explanations, that it is due to economic causes, or on the other hand, that it is a legacy from the Middle Ages, seem to me unsatisfactory, though I admit that if one combines them they can be made to cover the facts. All I would say with confidence is that antisemitism is part of the larger

20

problem of nationalism, which has not yet been seriously examined, and that the Jew is evidently a scapegoat, though for what he is a scapegoat we do not yet know. In this essay I have relied almost entirely on my own limited experience, and perhaps every one of my conclusions would be negatived by other observers. The fact is that there are almost no data on this subject. But for what they are worth I will summarise my opinions. Boiled down, they amount to this:

There is more antisemitism in England than we care to admit, and the war has accentuated it, but it is not certain that it is on the increase if one thinks in terms of decades rather than years.

It does not at present lead to open persecution, but it has the effect of making people callous to the suffering of Jews in other countries.

It is at bottom quite irrational and will not yield to argument.

The persecutions in Germany have caused much concealment of antisemitic feeling and thus obscured the whole picture.

The subject needs serious investigation.   25

Only the last point is worth expanding. To study any subject scientifically one needs a detached attitude, which is obviously harder when one's own interests or emotions are involved. Plenty of people who are quite capable of being objective about sea urchins, say, or the square root of 2, become schizophrenic if they have to think about the sources of their own income. What vitiates nearly all that is written about antisemitism is the assumption in the writer's mind that *he himself* is immune to it. "Since I know that antisemitism is irrational," he argues, "it follows that I do not share it." He thus fails to start his investigation in the one place where he could get hold of some reliable evidence—that is, in his own mind.

It seems to me a safe assumption that the disease loosely called nationalism is now almost universal. Antisemitism is only one manifestation of nationalism, and not everyone will have the disease in that particular form. A Jew, for example, would not be antisemitic: but then many Zionist Jews seem to me to be merely antisemites turned upside-down, just as many Indians and Negroes display the normal colour prejudices in an inverted form. The point is that something, some psychological vitamin, is lacking in modern civilisation, and as a result we are all more or less subject to this lunacy of believing that whole races or nations are mysteriously good or mysteriously evil. I defy any modern intellectual to look closely and honestly into his own mind without coming upon nationalistic loyalties and hatreds of one kind or another. It is the fact that he can feel the emotional tug of such things, and yet see them dispassionately for what they are, that gives him his status as an intellectual. It will be seen, therefore, that the starting point for any investigation of antisemitism should not be "Why does this obviously irrational belief appeal to other people?" but "Why does antisemitism appeal to *me*? What is there about it that I feel to be true?" If one asks this question one at least discovers one's own rationalisations, and it may be possible to find out what lies beneath them. Antisemitism should be investigated—and I will not say by antisemites, but at any rate by people who know that they are not immune to that kind of emotion. When Hitler has disappeared a real enquiry into this subject will be possible, and it would probably be best to start not by debunking antisemitism, but by marshalling all the justifications for it that can be found, in one's own mind or anybody else's. In that way one might get some clues that would lead to its psychological roots. But that antisemitism will be definitively *cured,* without curing the larger disease of nationalism, I do not believe.

Questions for Understanding

1. Why does Orwell believe that "facts" will have no effect on people who are antisemitic?
2. According to Orwell, what in general is the position of educated English people regarding Jews?
3. What were the effects on English attitudes of Hitler's campaign against the Jews?
4. One meaning of the word *disability* for the English is disqualification. What were the disabilities suffered by Jews in England before World War II?
5. Orwell writes, "With some plausibility it can be said that the Jews are the enemies of our native culture and our national morale." How much plausibility does Orwell ascribe to the sentiment expressed in this sentence?

Suggestions for Writing

1. Using the process of induction, as Orwell does at the beginning of "Antisemitism in Britain," write an essay in which you demonstrate that there is a widespread feeling toward a particular minority.
2. Write an essay in which you demonstrate that what seems to be a common attitude toward a minority group is irrational.
3. Pick an unpleasant occurrence that you witnessed firsthand, and demonstrate that the conclusion most people arrived at about the cause is wrong.
4. Discuss the ways in which you deal with people who have irrational attitudes toward you.
5. Describe a highly regarded person in your community who seems completely unaware of the prejudice he or she reveals. Why is the person unaware of his or her prejudice?

SHOOTING AN ELEPHANT

1936

In Moulmein, in Lower Burma,° I was hated by large numbers of   1
people—the only time in my life that I have been important enough for this
to happen to me. I was sub-divisional police officer of the town, and in an
aimless, petty kind of way anti-European feeling was very bitter. No one had
the guts to raise a riot, but if a European woman went through the bazaars
alone somebody would probably spit betel juice over her dress. As a police
officer I was an obvious target and was baited whenever it seemed safe to do
so. When a nimble Burman tripped me up on the football field and the
referee (another Burman) looked the other way, the crowed yelled with
hideous laughter. This happened more than once. In the end the sneering
yellow faces of young men that met me everywhere, the insults hooted after
me when I was at a safe distance, got badly on my nerves. The young Buddhist
priests were the worst of all. There were several thousands of them in the town
and none of them seemed to have anything to do except stand on street
corners and jeer at Europeans.

All this was perplexing and upsetting. For at that time I had already
made up my mind that imperialism was an evil thing and the sooner I chucked
up my job and got out of it the better. Theoretically—and secretly, of
course—I was all for the Burmese and all against their oppressors, the British.
As for the job I was doing, I hated it more bitterly than I can perhaps make
clear. In a job like that you see the dirty work of Empire at close quarters. The
wretched prisoners huddling in the stinking cages of the lock-ups, the grey,
cowed faces of the long-term convicts, the scarred buttocks of the men who
had been flogged with bamboos—all these oppressed me with an intolerable
sense of guilt. But I could get nothing into perspective. I was young and
ill-educated and I had had to think out my problems in the utter silence that
is imposed on every Englishman in the East. I did not even know that the
British Empire is dying, still less did I know that it is a great deal better than
the younger empires that are going to supplant it. All I knew was that I was
stuck between my hatred of the empire I served and my rage against the
evil-spirited little beasts who tried to make my job impossible. With one part
of my mind I thought of the British Raj as an unbreakable tyranny, as
something clamped down, *in saecula saeculorum,*° upon the will of prostrate
peoples; with another part I thought that the greatest joy in the world would
be to drive a bayonet into a Buddhist priest's guts. Feelings like these are the
normal by-products of imperialism; ask any Anglo-Indian official, if you can
catch him off duty.

Lower Burma: What was then Burma, a British colony in Southern Asia, in now Myanmar, an
independent nation.
in saecula saeculorum: For ever and ever.

One day something happened which in a roundabout way was enlightening. It was a tiny incident in itself, but it gave me a better glimpse than I had had before of the real nature of imperialism—the real motives for which despotic governments act. Early one morning the sub-inspector at a police station the other end of the town rang me up on the phone and said that an elephant was ravaging the bazaar. Would I please come and do something about it? I did not know what I could do, but I wanted to see what was happening and I got on to a pony and started out. I took my rifle, an old .44 Winchester and much too small to kill an elephant, but I thought the noise might be useful *in terrorem*. Various Burmans stopped me on the way and told me about the elephant's doings. It was not, of course, a wild elephant, but a tame one which had gone "must." It had been chained up as tame elephants always are when their attack of "must" is due, but on the previous night it had broken its chain and escaped. Its mahout, the only person who could manage it when it was in that state, had set out in pursuit, but he had taken the wrong direction and was now twelve hours' journey away, and in the morning the elephant had suddenly reappeared in the town. The Burmese population had no weapons and were quite helpless against it. It had already destroyed somebody's bamboo hut, killed a cow and raided some fruit-stalls and devoured the stock; also it had met the municipal rubbish van, and, when the driver jumped out and took to his heels, had turned the van over and inflicted violence upon it.

The Burmese sub-inspector and some Indian constables were waiting for me in the quarter where the elephant had been seen. It was a very poor quarter, a labyrinth of squalid bamboo huts, thatched with palm-leaf, winding all over a steep hillside. I remember that it was a cloudy stuffy morning at the beginning of the rains. We began questioning the people as to where the elephant had gone, and, as usual, failed to get any definite information. That is invariably the case in the East; a story always sounds clear enough at a distance, but the nearer you get to the scene of events the vaguer it becomes. Some of the people said that the elephant had gone in one direction, some said that he had gone in another, some professed not even to have heard of any elephant. I had almost made up my mind that the whole story was a pack of lies, when we heard yells a little distance away. There was a loud, scandalised cry of "Go away, child! Go away this instant!" and an old woman with a switch in her hand came round the corner of a hut, violently shooing away a crowd of naked children. Some more women followed, clicking their tongues and exclaiming; evidently there was something there that the children ought not to have seen. I rounded the hut and saw a man's dead body sprawling in the mud. He was an Indian, a black Dravidian coolie, almost naked, and he could not have been dead many minutes. The people said that the elephant had come suddenly upon him round the corner of the hut, caught him with its trunk, put its foot on his back and ground him into the earth. This was the rainy season and the ground was soft, and his face had scored a trench a foot deep and a couple of yards long. He was lying on his belly with arms crucified and head sharply twisted to one side. His face was coated with mud, the eyes wide open, the teeth bared and grinning with an expression of unendurable agony. (Never tell me, by the way, that the dead look peaceful. Most of the corpses I have seen looked devilish.) The friction of the great beast's foot had stripped the skin from his back as neatly as one skins a rabbit. As soon as I saw the dead man I sent an orderly to a friend's house nearby to borrow an elephant rifle. I had already sent back the pony, not wanting it to go mad with fright and throw me if it smelled the elephant.

The orderly came back in a few minutes with a rifle and five cartridges,   5 and meanwhile some Burmans had arrived and told us that the elephant was in the paddy fields below, only a few hundred yards away. As I started forward practically the whole population of the quarter flocked out of their houses and followed me. They had seen the rifle and were all shouting excitedly that I was going to shoot the elephant. They had not shown much interest in the elephant when he was merely ravaging their homes, but it was different now that he was going to be shot. It was a bit of fun to them, as it would be to an English crowd; besides, they wanted the meat. It made me vaguely uneasy. I had no intention of shooting the elephant—I had merely sent for the rifle to defend myself if necessary—and it is always unnerving to have a crowd following you. I marched down the hill, looking and feeling a fool, with the rifle over my shoulder and an evergrowing army of people jostling at my heels. At the bottom, when you got away from the huts, there was a metalled road and beyond that a miry waste of paddy fields a thousand yards across, not yet ploughed but soggy from the first rains and dotted with coarse grass. The elephant was standing eighty yards from the road, his left side towards us. He took not the slightest notice of the crowd's approach. He was tearing up bunches of grass, beating them against his knees to clean them and stuffing them into his mouth.

I had halted on the road. As soon as I saw the elephant I knew with perfect certainty that I ought not to shoot him. It is a serious matter to shoot a working elephant—it is comparable to destroying a huge and costly piece of machinery—and obviously one ought not to do it if it can possibly be avoided. And at that distance, peacefully eating, the elephant looked no more dangerous than a cow. I thought then and I think now that his attack of "must" was already passing off; in which case he would merely wander harmlessly about until the mahout came back and caught him. Moreover, I did not in the least want to shoot him. I decided that I would watch him for a little while to make sure that he did not turn savage again, and then go home.

But at that moment I glanced round at the crowd that had followed me. It was an immense crowd, two thousand at the least and growing every minute. It blocked the road for a long distance on either side. I looked at the sea of yellow faces above the garish clothes—faces all happy and excited over this bit of fun, all certain that the elephant was going to be shot. They were watching me as they would watch a conjuror about to perform a trick. They did not like me, but with the magical rifle in my hands I was momentarily worth watching. And suddenly I realised that I should have to shoot the elephant after all. The people expected it of me and I had got to do it; I could feel their two thousand wills pressing me forward, irresistibly. And it was at this moment, as I stood there with the rifle in my hands, that I first grasped the hollowness, the futility of the white man's dominion in the East. Here was I, the white man with his gun, standing in front of the unarmed native crowd—seemingly the leading actor of the piece; but in reality I was only an absurd puppet pushed to and fro by the will of those yellow faces behind. I perceived in this moment that when the white man turns tyrant it is his own freedom that he destroys. He becomes a sort of hollow, posing dummy, the conventionalised figure of a sahib. For it is the condition of his rule that he shall spend his life in trying to impress the "natives" and so in every crisis he has got to do what the "natives" expect of him. He wears a mask, and his face grows to fit it. I had got to shoot the elephant. I had committed myself to doing it when I sent for the rifle. A sahib has got to act like a sahib; he has got to appear resolute, to know his own mind and do definite things. To come all that way, rifle in hand, with two thousand people marching at my heels, and then to trail feebly away, having done nothing—no, that was impossible. The crowd would laugh at me. And my whole life, every white man's life in the East, was one long struggle not to be laughed at.

But I did not want to shoot the elephant. I watched him beating his bunch of grass against his knees, with that preoccupied grandmotherly air that elephants have. It seemed to me that it would be murder to shoot him. At that age I was not squeamish about killing animals, but I had never shot an elephant and never want to. (Somehow it always seems worse to kill a *large* animal.) Besides, there was the beast's owner to be considered. Alive, the elephant was worth at least a hundred pounds; dead, he would only be worth the value of his tusks--five pounds, possibly. But I had got to act quickly. I turned to some experienced-looking Burmans who had been there when we arrived, and asked them how the elephant had been behaving. They all said the same thing: he took no notice of you if you left him alone, but he might charge if you went too close to him.

It was perfectly clear to me what I ought to do. I ought to walk up to within say, twenty-five yards of the elephant and test his behavior. If he charged I could shoot, if he took no notice of me it would be safe to leave him until the mahout came back. But also I knew that I was going to do no such thing. I was a poor shot with a rifle and the ground was soft mud into which one would sink at every step. If the elephant charged and I missed him, I should have about as much chance as a toad under a steam-roller. But even then I was not thinking particularly of my own skin, only the watchful yellow faces behind. For at that moment, with the crowd watching me, I was not afraid in the ordinary sense, as I would have been if I had been alone. A white man mustn't be frightened in front of "natives"; and so, in general, he isn't frightened. The sole thought in my mind was that if anything went wrong those two thousand Burmans would see me pursued, caught, trampled on and reduced to a grinning corpse like that Indian up the hill. And if that happened it was quite probable that some of them would laugh. That would never do. There was only one alternative. I shoved the cartridges into the magazine and lay down on the road to get a better aim.

The crowd grew very still, and a deep, low, happy sigh, as of people who   *10* see the theatre curtain go up at last, breathed from innumerable throats. They were going to have their bit of fun after all. The rifle was a beautiful German thing with cross-hair sights. I did not then know that in shooting an elephant one should shoot to cut an imaginary bar running from ear-hole to ear-hole. I ought therefore, as the elephant was sideways on, to have aimed straight at his ear-hole; actually I aimed several inches in front of this, thinking the brain would be further forward.

When I pulled the trigger I did not hear the bang or feel the kick—one never does when a shot goes home—but I heard the devilish roar of glee that went up from the crowd. In that instant, in too short a time, one would have thought, even for the bullet to get there, a mysterious, terrible change had come over the elephant. He neither stirred nor fell, but every line of his body had altered. He looked suddenly stricken, shrunken, immensely old, as though the frightful impact of the bullet had paralysed him without knocking him down. At last, after what seemed a long time—it might have been five seconds, I dare say—he sagged flabbily to his knees. His mouth slobbered. An enormous senility seemed to have settled upon him. One could have imagined him thousands of years old. I fired again into the same spot. At the second shot he did not collapse but climbed with desperate slowness to his feet and stood weakly upright, with legs sagging and head drooping. I fired a third time. That was the shot that did for him. You could see the agony of it jolt his whole body and knock the last remnant of strength from his legs. But in falling he seemed for a moment to rise, for as his hind legs collapsed beneath him he seemed to tower upwards like a huge rock toppling, his trunk reaching skyward like a tree. He trumpeted, for the first and only time. And then down he came, his belly towards me, with a crash that seemed to shake the ground even where I lay.

I got up. The Burmans were already racing past me across the mud. It was obvious that the elephant wound never rise again, but he was not dead. He was breathing very rhythmically with long rattling gasps, his great mound of a side painfully rising and falling. His mouth was wide open—I could see far down into caverns of pale pink throat. I waited a long time for him to die, but his breathing did not weaken. Finally I fired my two remaining shots into the spot where I thought his heart must be. The thick blood welled out of him like red velvet, but still he did not die. His body did not even jerk when the shots hit him, the tortured breathing continued without a pause. He was dying, very slowly and in great agony, but in some world remote from me where not even a bullet could damage him further. I felt that I had got to put an end to that dreadful noise. It seemed dreadful to see the great beast lying there, powerless to move and yet powerless to die, and not even to be able to finish him. I sent back for my small rifle and poured shot after shot into his heart and down his throat. They seemed to make no impression. The tortured gasps continued as steadily as the ticking of a clock.

In the end I could not stand it any longer and went away. I heard later that it took him half an hour to die. Burmans were arriving with dahs and baskets even before I left, and I was told they had stripped his body almost to the bones by the afternoon.

Afterwards, of course, there were endless discussions about the shooting of the elephant. The owner was furious, but he was only an Indian and could do nothing. Besides, legally I had done the right thing, for a mad elephant has to be killed, like a mad dog, if its owner fails to control it. Among the Europeans opinion was divided. The older men said I was right, the younger men said it was a damn shame to shoot an elephant for killing a coolie, because an elephant was worth more than any damn Coringhee coolie. And afterwards I was very glad that the coolie had been killed; it put me legally in the right and it gave me a sufficient pretext for shooting the elephant. I often wondered whether any of the others grasped that I had done it solely to avoid looking a fool.

Questions for Understanding

1. What are the main elements of imperialism?
2. Why did Orwell think that "the greatest joy in the world would be to drive a bayonet into a Buddhist priest's guts"?
3. Why did Orwell decide to send for the elephant rifle?
4. "I knew with perfect certainty that I ought not to shoot him," Orwell thinks when he first sees the elephant in the paddy fields. Why was this conviction so strong?
5. Why does Orwell shoot the elephant?

Suggestions for Writing

1. Orwell says that he bitterly hated his job as a policeman, but that, of course, he could not show it. Have you been in a similar situation? If so, write an essay in which you describe the circumstances, your feelings and thoughts, and your solution.
2. Are you aware of a situation in which you fired a gun but with hindsight know that you should not have? If so, write an essay in which you describe the situation, explain why you fired the gun, and give the reasons why you should not have.
3. Are you aware of having done something that had serious consequences because you were unable to act contrary to the expectations of others? If so, write an essay in which you describe the situation, explain what was expected of you, and explain why your action was wrong.
4. Are you aware of a time in your life when your resisted powerful peer pressure to do something against your better judgment? If so, write an essay in which you describe the situation, explain what was expected of you, and explain why you were able to resist.

5. Orwell says of the white man in Burma, "He wears a mask, and his face grows to fit it." Are you aware of a time in your life when you felt as if you were wearing a mask? If so, to what extent did your face grow to fit it? Write an essay in which you describe the situation, give your reasons for wearing the mask, and explain the extent to which wearing the mask changed you.

NUTS AND BOLTS 5: PARALLELISM

Parallelism in writing is the repetition of a grammatical form. Within a sentence, parallelism is the repeating, in the same grammatical context, of nouns or verbs, adjectives or adverbs. It may also be the repeating, in the same grammatical context, of combinations of words such as phrases, predicates, or clauses. Sometimes the term is used to refer to what happens within a paragraph; that is, within a paragraph, whole sentences can be parallel—can have the same basic structure. Whether within a sentence or a paragraph, repetition of the form is the essence of parallelism.

Unfortunately, most student writers come to college with a prejudice against repetition. They think that it is not good to repeat and that repeating will cause monotony. Usually, this prejudice is most consciously applied to the repetition of individual words. Then the prejudice against repeating words leads to the corollary idea that repeating a grammatical form is also undesirable. Reinforcing that idea is the principle that says variation of sentence structure is a mark of good writing. Varied sentence structure *is* a mark of good writing—but so is the skillful use of repetition. Two railroad tracks paralleling each other for miles, curving, climbing, and descending together, make a good analogy to verbal parallelism. But really skillful verbal parallelism usually involves the use of more than two parallel elements—of three, four, or even more.

In "Shooting an Elephant," George Orwell tells the story of how he felt pressured by the people of Moulmein into killing a valuable elephant to avoid looking like a fool. His narrative begins with a phone call early in the morning and ends in the afternoon, by which time the elephant's body has been stripped of its meat. The excellence of the essay lies partly in its enlightening treatment of the theme of the relationship of the governors to the governed under imperialism and partly in the effectiveness of the narrative. Orwell's use of parallelism contributes greatly to the effectiveness of the narrative.

Let us look closely at four instances of Orwell's use of parallelism. In paragraph 11, Orwell describes the effect of his bullets on the elephant. He wants to convey to the reader exactly what he saw. Conveying exactly what was seen is something anyone who writes will frequently want to do. Using parallelism helps. After the first shot, Orwell tells us, the elephant looked "stricken, shrunken, immensely old, as though the frightful impact of the bullet had paralyzed him without knocking him down." Orwell gives us four descriptions of how the elephant looked to him. When a person, place, or thing is described, the word that does the describing is called an adjective: *stricken, shrunken,* and *old* are adjectives. Sometimes, though, getting an aspect of description right requires not just one word but several; those several words are said to act in an *adjectival* way—like an adjective. Thus, "as though the frightful impact of the bullet had paralyzed him without knocking him down" is a clause that does the same thing the one-word adjectives do: it describes an aspect of how the elephant looked.

Paragraph 9 contains this sentence (italics added): "The sole thought in my mind was that if anything went wrong those two thousand Burmans would see me *pursued, caught, trampled on, and reduced to a grinning corpse* like that Indian up the hill." Here Orwell describes how he imagined he would look if the elephant turned on him. He first uses two one-word adjectives, then a two-word adjectival phrase, then a multiple-word adjectival phrase. That's what it took to convey how Orwell thought he would be seen. An interesting twist here is that Orwell's key descriptive words are forms of verbs. Using forms of verbs to describe is perfectly legitimate.

In paragraph 4, Orwell tells of his frustration when he tried to find out from the people where the elephant had gone. He doesn't think he conveys the depth of his frustration by simply saying that he "as usual, failed to get any definitive information" or even by going on to say, "That is invariably the case in the East; a story always sounds clear enough at a distance but the nearer you get to the scene of events the vaguer it becomes." He feels compelled to give some examples, but he doesn't want to devote a whole sentence to each example. So he uses just one sentence with three parallel independent clauses: "Some of the people said that the elephant had gone in one direction, some said that he had gone in another, some professed not even to have heard of any elephant."

Later in paragraph 4, Orwell tells about coming upon the body of the coolie killed by the elephant. He reports what the people said the elephant did. The elephant (numerals added) (1) "had come suddenly upon him round the corner of the hut, (2) caught him with its trunk, (3) put its foot on his back and (4) ground him into the earth." Here the parallelism consists of a series of four predicates.

To write at your best, be alert for opportunities to use parallelism, to come in with a series. To get your third or fourth or fifth element in the series, you must force yourself to have a better look, to focus more tightly, to examine more carefully. When you look closer, you will find more detail. Giving your reader more detail will enable the reader to see almost as much as you saw or come closer to feeling what you felt.

A HANGING

1931

It was in Burma, a sodden morning of the rains. A sickly light, like   *1*
yellow tinfoil, was slanting over the high walls into the jail yard. We were
waiting outside the condemned cells, a row of sheds fronted with double bars,
like small animal cages. Each cell measured about ten feet by ten and was quite
bare within except for a plank bed and a pot of drinking water. In some of
them brown silent men were squatting at the inner bars, with their blankets
draped round them. These were the condemned men, due to be hanged
within the next week or two.

One prisoner had been brought out of his cell. He was a Hindu, a puny
wisp of a man, with a shaven head and vague liquid eyes. He had a thick,
sprouting moustache, absurdly too big for his body, rather like the moustache
of a comic man on the films. Six tall Indian warders were guarding him and
getting him ready for the gallows. Two of them stood by with rifles and fixed
bayonets, while the others handcuffed him, passed a chain through his
handcuffs and fixed it to their belts, and lashed his arms tight to his sides. They
crowded very close about him, with their hands always on him in a careful,
caressing grip, as though all the while feeling him to make sure he was there.
It was like men handling a fish which is still alive and may jump back into the
water. But he stood quite unresisting, yielding his arms limply to the ropes,
as though he hardly noticed what was happening.

Eight o'clock struck and a bugle call, desolately thin in the wet air,
floated from the distant barracks. The superintendent of the jail, who was
standing apart from the rest of us, moodily prodding the gravel with his stick,
raised his head at the sound. He was an army doctor, with a grey toothbrush
moustache and a gruff voice. "For God's sake hurry up, Francis," he said
irritably. "The man ought to have been dead by this time. Aren't you ready
yet?"

Francis, the head jailer, a fat Dravidian in a white drill suit and gold
spectacles, waved his black hand, "Yes sir, yes sir," he bubbled. "All iss
satisfactorily prepared. The hangman iss waiting. We shall proceed."

"Well, quick march, then. The prisoners can't get their breakfast till this   *5*
job's over."

We set out for the gallows. Two warders marched on either side of the
prisoner, with their rifles at the slope; two others marched close against him,
gripping him by arm and shoulder, as though at once pushing and supporting
him. The rest of us, magistrates and the like, followed behind. Suddenly,
when we had gone ten yards, the procession stopped short without any order
or warning. A dreadful thing had happened—a dog, come goodness knows
whence, had appeared in the yard. It came bounding among us with a loud
volley of barks, and leapt round us wagging its whole body, wild with glee at
finding so many human beings together. It was a large woolly dog, half
Airedale, half pariah. For a moment it pranced round us, and then, before

anyone could stop it, it had made a dash for the prisoner, and jumping up tried to lick his face. Everyone stood aghast, too taken aback even to grab at the dog.

"Who let that bloody brute in here?" said the superintendent angrily. "Catch it, someone!"

A warder, detached from the escort, charged clumsily after the dog, but it danced and gambolled just out of his reach, taking everything as part of the game. A young Eurasian jailer picked up a handful of gravel and tried to stone the dog away, but it dodged the stones and came after us again. Its yaps echoed from the jail walls. The prisoner, in the grasp of the two warders, looked on incuriously, as though this was another formality of the hanging. It was several minutes before someone managed to catch the dog. Then we put my handkerchief through its collar and moved off once more, with the dog still straining and whimpering.

It was about forty yards to the gallows. I watched the bare brown back of the prisoner marching in front of me. He walked clumsily with his bound arms, but quite steadily, with the bobbing gait of the Indian who never straightens his knees. At each step his muscles slid neatly into place, the lock of hair on his scalp danced up and down, his feet printed themselves on the wet gravel. And once, in spite of the men who gripped him by each shoulder, he stepped slightly aside to avoid a puddle on the path.

It is curious, but till that moment I had never realised what it means to destroy a healthy, conscious man. When I saw the prisoner step aside to avoid the puddle, I saw the mystery, the unspeakable wrongness, of cutting a life short when it is in full tide. This man was not dying, he was alive just as we were alive. All the organs of his body were working—bowels digesting food, skin renewing itself, nails growing, tissue forming—all toiling away in solemn foolery. His nails would still be growing when he stood on the drop, when he was falling through the air with a tenth of a second to live. His eyes saw the yellow gravel and the grey walls, and his brain still remembered, foresaw, reasoned—reasoned even about puddles. He and we were a party of men walking together, seeing, hearing, feeling, understanding the same world; and in two minutes, with a sudden snap, one of us would be gone—one mind less, one world less.

The gallows stood in a small yard, separate from the main grounds of the prison, and overgrown with tall prickly weeds. It was a brick erection like three sides of a shed, with planking on top, and above that two beams and a crossbar with the rope dangling. The hangman, a grey-haired convict in the white uniform of the prison, was waiting beside his machine. He greeted us with a servile crouch as we entered. At a word from Francis the two warders, gripping the prisoner more closely than ever, half led, half pushed him to the gallows and helped him clumsily up the ladder. Then the hangman climbed up and fixed the rope round the prisoner's neck.

We stood waiting, five yards away. The warders had formed in a rough circle round the gallows. And then, when the noose was fixed, the prisoner began crying out on his god. It was a high, reiterated cry of "Ram! Ram!

Ram! Ram!", not urgent and fearful like a prayer or a cry for help, but steady, rhythmical, almost like the tolling of a bell. The dog answered the sound with a whine. The hangman, still standing on the gallows, produced a small cotton bag like a flour bag and drew it down over the prisoner's face. But the sound, muffled by the cloth, still persisted, over and over again: "Ram! Ram! Ram! Ram! Ram!"

The hangman climbed down and stood ready, holding the lever. Minutes seemed to pass. The steady, muffled crying from the prisoner went on and on, "Ram! Ram! Ram!" never faltering for an instant. The superintendent, his head on his chest, was slowly poking the ground with his stick; perhaps he was counting the cries, allowing the prisoner a fixed number—fifty, perhaps, or a hundred. Everyone had changed colour. The Indians had gone grey like bad coffee, and one or two of the bayonets were wavering. We looked at the lashed, hooded man on the drop, and listened to his cries—each cry another second of life; the same thought was in all our minds: oh, kill him quickly, get it over, stop that abominable noise!

Suddenly the superintendent made up his mind. Throwing up his head he made a swift motion with this stick. "Chalo!" he shouted almost fiercely.

There was a clanking noise, and then dead silence. The prisoner had vanished, and the rope was twisting on itself. I let go of the dog, and it galloped immediately to the back of the gallows; but when it got there it stopped short, barked, and then retreated into a corner of the yard, where it stood among the weeds, looking timorously out at us. We went round the gallows to inspect the prisoner's body. He was dangling with his toes pointed straight downwards, very slowly revolving, as dead as a stone. 15

The superintendent reached out with his stick and poked the bare body; it oscillated, slightly. "*He's* all right," said the superintendent. He backed out from under the gallows, and blew out a deep breath. The moody look had gone out of his face quite suddenly. He glanced at his wrist-watch. "Eight minutes past eight. Well, that's all for this morning, thank God."

The warders unfixed bayonets and marched away. The dog, sobered and conscious of having misbehaved itself, slipped after them. We walked out of the gallows yard, past the condemned cells with their waiting prisoners, into the big central yard of the prison. The convicts, under the command of warders armed with laths, were already receiving their breakfast. They squatted in long rows, each man holding a tin pannikin, while two warders with buckets marched round ladling out rice; it seemed quite a homely, jolly scene, after the hanging. An enormous relief had come upon us now that the job was done. One felt an impulse to sing, to break into a run, to snigger. All at once everyone began chattering gaily.

The Eurasian boy walking beside me nodded towards the way we had come, with a knowing smile: "Do you know, sir, our friend (he meant the dead man), when he heard his appeal had been dismissed, he pissed on the floor of his cell. From fright.—Kindly take one of my cigarettes, sir. Do you not admire my new silver case, sir? From the boxwallah, two rupees eight annas. Classy European style."

Several people laughed—at what, nobody seemed certain.

Francis was walking by the superintendent, talking garrulously: "Well, sir, all hass passed off with the utmost satisfactoriness. It wass all finished— flick! like that. It iss not always so—oah, no! I have known cases where the doctor wass obliged to go beneath the gallows and pull the prisoner's legs to ensure decease. Most disagreeable!"   *20*

"Wriggling about, eh? That's bad," said the superintendent.

"Ach, sir, it iss worse when they become refractory! One man, I recall, clung to the bars of hiss cage when we went to take him out. You will scarcely credit, sir, that it took six warders to dislodge him, three pulling at each leg. We reasoned with him. 'My dear fellow,' we said, 'think of all the pain and trouble you are causing to us!' But no, he would not listen! Ach, he wass very troublesome!"

I found that I was laughing quite loudly. Everyone was laughing. Even the superintendent grinned in a tolerant way. "You'd better all come out and have a drink," he said quite genially. "I've got a bottle of whisky in the car. We could do with it."

We went through the big double gates of the prison, into the road. "Pulling at his legs!" exclaimed a Burmese magistrate suddenly, and burst into a loud chuckling. We all began laughing again. At that moment Francis's anecdote seemed extraordinarily funny. We all had a drink together, native and European alike, quite amicably. The dead man was a hundred yards away.

Questions for Understanding

1. What does Orwell accomplish by describing the condemned man's moustache?
2. From the way they handle him, what seem to be the expectations the six Indian warders have about how the condemned man will behave?
3. What is accomplished by bringing the dog into the narrative?
4. After stating that "a healthy, conscious man" was about to be destroyed, Orwell goes on to specify certain organs that continued to function, "all toiling away in solemn foolery." What does Orwell mean by "solemn foolery"?
5. Would Orwell think it a good idea for judges who sentence criminals to death to attend the executions?

Suggestions for Writing

1. Making use of some aspects of "A Hanging," write an essay in which you argue for or against capital punishment.
2. Justice is served, it is said, when the punishment fits the crime. Discuss an instance in which, in your opinion, the punishment for a crime was excessive, or discuss an instance in which the punishment fell short of what the crime warranted.

3. When an American youth in Singapore was punished by caning, many Americans thought caning an appropriate punishment for acts of vandalism. Write an essay in which you argue that caning is, or is not, "cruel and unusual punishment."

4. The philosopher Nietzsche wrote, "Punishment tames man, but does not make him 'better.' " Is there a way to deal with criminals that will make them better human beings? Discuss.

5. The Englishman G. Lowes Dickinson wrote the following: "A fundamental, and as many believe, the most essential part of Christianity, is its doctrine of reward and punishment in the world beyond; and a religion which has nothing at all to say about this great enigma we should hardly feel to be a religion at all." Discuss the extent to which, according to what you have observed, the idea of reward and punishment in the hereafter affects human behavior.

E. B. White

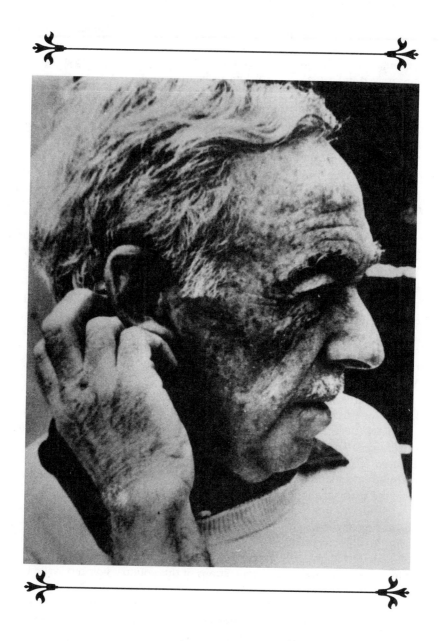

[1899–1985]

One of the best ways to launch a career as a writer is to work on a college newspaper. E. B. White did that at Cornell University in Ithaca, New York, where he became editor-in-chief of the *Daily Sun*. Upon graduation, White moved to Manhattan and found work as a reporter for the United Press. After a couple of years and a series of jobs in Manhattan, however, White and a friend decided to find out about the rest of the country. They headed west in a Model T, and after six months of traveling and working at odds jobs, they arrived in Seattle, where White again worked as a reporter—this time for the *Seattle Times*.

After returning to New York, White bought a copy of the very first issue of *The New Yorker* in February, 1925. Within weeks, Harold Ross, the editor, accepted a brief essay and offered White additional writing opportunities. *The New Yorker* began as a humor magazine; White's wit and wry view of the world gained a substantial following for his brief essays in the "Talk of the Town" section. He also wrote light verse, cartoon captions, and taglines for the reproduced gaffes of other publications. Along with James Thurber, he became one of the magazine's mainstays.

In 1933, White and his wife, Katherine Angell (who was literary editor of *The New Yorker*) bought a waterfront farm in Maine. In 1938, White left *The New Yorker* for *Harper's Magazine,* for which he was to write a monthly column in his own voice rather than assuming the editorial "we" of *The New Yorker*. White wrote for *Harper's* for five years and then returned to *The New Yorker*. Most of the essays written for *Harper's* are about his experiences in Maine; these were gathered in *One Man's Meat* (1942). "Camp Meeting" is one such essay. "Once More to the Lake" is also set in Maine—in North Belgravia, on Great Pond—but that essay, along with the two others that follow here, was published in *The New Yorker* during White's second stint there.

For Americans who are unfamiliar with his essays, White is probably best known for his children's books and for being the White of Strunk and White's *The Elements of Style*. *Stuart Little* (1945), *Charlotte's Web* (1952), and *The Trumpet of the Swan* (1970) have been read by or to hundreds of thousands of children. *The Elements of Style* is White's 1959 revision of a writing handbook originally prepared by a Cornell professor of White's, William Strunk; since 1959, it has been the trusty handbook of hundreds of thousands of college students.

When White died in 1985, William Shawn, *The New Yorker's* very demanding editor-in-chief, said this: "E. B. White was a great essayist, a supreme stylist. His literary style was as pure as any in our language. It was singular, colloquial, clear, unforced, thoroughly American and utterly beautiful. Because of his quiet influence, several generations of this country's writers write better than they might have done. . . . "

Although E. B. White, unlike many writers, did not face much outward adversity during his lifetime, he was far from being carefree or pleased with himself. He once wrote, "I have always been aware that I am by nature self-absorbed and egotistical; to write of myself to the extent I have done indicates a too-great attention to my own life, not enough to the lives of others. I have worn many shirts, and not all of them have been a good fit. But when I am discouraged or downcast I need only fling open the door of my closet, and there, hidden behind everything else, hangs the mantle of Michel de Montaigne. . . ." In other words, whenever a mood of depression began to overtake him, he would pick up the essays of Montaigne, and in them, he would find reassurance. Three of the essays of Montaigne, the sixteenth-century father of the essay (who also wrote primarily about himself) appear at the end of this book.

THE MOTORCAR

1958

The automobile industry, according to the newspaper that usurps my bed, is facing a period of crucial decisions. On the whole, this is good news. There is always the chance that during a time of crisis some car manufacturer will shake free from the vision of stratocruisers and rockets and at last see the automobile for what it is—a handy little four-wheeled contraption that moves along the surface of the earth carrying an American family on errands of an inconsequential nature, a vehicle requiring no wings for rising into the air, no fins for diving into the sea. The determination to resist the queer, corrupting conception of the automobile as a winged thing or a finny thing should be the first crucial decision the industry makes.

For twenty-five years car makers have foolishly pursued two false and seductive ideas: first, that the stature of man is decreasing; second, that the way to create beauty is to turn the matter over to a style department after consulting a few motivational-research monkeys and a covey of social psychologists. Everyone should know that the stature of man is *not* decreasing (if anything, men and women are somewhat taller than they used to be), and anyone who has eyes in his head should know that beauty is the child of truth, not to be had by last-minute scheming and conniving. I do not recall ever seeing a properly designed boat that was not also a beautiful boat. Purity of line, loveliness, symmetry—these arrive mysteriously whenever someone who knows and cares creates something that is perfectly fitted to do its work, whether the object is a grain scoop, a suspension bridge, or a guillotine. Nobody styled the orb web of a spider, nobody styled the sixteen-foot canoe. Both are beautiful, and for a common reason: each was designed to perform a special task under special conditions. I think it would be impossible to build a thoroughly honest and capable motorcar, correctly designed to meet the conditions a car must meet, and have it turn out to be anything but good-looking. But the method used in Detroit is to turn some engineers loose in one room and some stylists in another room, while the motivational pixies scamper back and forth whispering secrets in everybody's ear, and after months of such fooling and plotting and compromising and adjusting, then out comes the new automobile, and no wonder it carries the telltale marks of monstrosity on its poor tortured body. In many cases it looks as though the final licks had been given it by a group of emotionally disturbed children.

Not only have car makers lacked faith in the essential truth of a motor vehicle but they have painted their lily so lavishly and so drunkenly that they have ruined its appearance and added greatly to its cost. A garbage scow carries a filthy cargo but it has clean lines—cleaner by far than the lines of the 1958 automobile.

The mess the car makers find themselves in today bears a strong likeness to the pickle the motion-picture industry got into ten or a dozen years ago. That, too, was the direct result of indulging in dream life and underestimating the intelligence and stature of the people. The movie makers, if you remember, got so absorbed in the work of examining the entrails of pollsters and taking everybody's pulse in America to see what the average heartbeat was, they had no time to examine their own innards for a subject worth filming. It took them a number of years to pull out of their queer preoccupation with the human circulatory system and get back into the simple creative life. Now it's the car makers whose fingers are wrapped around my wrist in what feels like the grip of death. If they really want to know the state of my health and the shape of my desires, I shall be happy to accommodate them, but I warn them it's not the way to go about designing and building an automobile.

I sit here in this pavilion, running a low fever and looking out at the world from a high window. My view includes a small slice of the West Side Highway, southbound. The cars pass in an endless parade, and there is a terrible sameness to them—a litter of lively pigs from the brood sow in Detroit. Some are slightly upswept, some are slightly downcast (like the industry itself). But almost all of them seem to have been poured from the same mold: the Cadillac is blood brother to the Ford, the Lincoln and the Plymouth could lie down together in a field of daisies and you'd hardly know they weren't twins.

My newspaper says that the atmosphere in the hub of the auto industry is one of gloom. The bedtime story I am about to tell, revealing my pulse rate, my prejudices, and the state of my dreams, is not calculated to lift the industry's spirits, but it is a true story, and it concerns a man and his search for a car, and on that account it does bear on the vexing problems of these troubled times. I'll begin at the beginning, it's so soothing to do it that way.

In the summer of 1949, being then of sound mind and in good pocket, I purchased a four-door De Soto sedan in a pleasing shade of green—a green as rich as the new growth of a spruce tree in the spring. I mention the name De Soto hesitantly, for I have no wish to send a convulsion of pain through the bodies of Harlow Curtice° and Henry Ford II, and indeed the name of the car could as well be Oldsmobile or Mercury and make no difference; it's the year 1949 that is the pertinent fact here. At any rate, my new car seemed at the time a very agreeable and serviceable automobile, and so it turned out to be. For this beauty I paid the handsome sum, in cash, of two thousand four hundred and ninety-five dollars, a veritable pile. I took possession of the car in Bangor, Maine, a few blocks from the railroad station. Through the years that have intervened, having through God's grace remained of sound mind,

Harlow Curtis: President of General Motors.

I have managed not to lose possession of the car, although there have been a couple of narrow squeaks in recent months.

I now skip lightly over eight years and we come to the summer of 1957. Last August, when somebody else was at the wheel, my car met with a slight accident involving another vehicle. The whole affair was on a very low pitch of disaster: the other car was motionless at the time, and my own car was moving at the rate of about seven miles per hour. But despite the trivial nature of the encounter, my right front fender received a long, straight slash the whole length of it, raked fore and aft by the strong, sharp blade of the opponent's rear bumper. I was so impressed by the neatness of the stroke that I drove to a local garage and instructed the mechanic to finish the job off with his shears and then weld a temporary bracket to the frame, to support what was left of the fender; namely, its upper part. When this was accomplished, the first discovery I made was that the right, or damaged, side of my car presented a better appearance, on the whole, than the left, or undamaged, side. The right front wheel had been exposed to view by the loss of the lower half of the fender, and I noted with satisfaction that a wheel revealed is more exciting to the eye than a wheel concealed.

For a few days, neither my wife nor I paid any particular attention to the fact that our family automobile was now asymmetrical and beat up. Our minds were on other matters, and when we wanted to go somewhere we would simply get in the car and go, enjoying the same inward elegance to which we had long been accustomed. But then one day the subject came up, as it was bound to sooner or later, and the phrase "new car" escaped from our lips and went darting about the rooms like Tinker Bell. "New car"! What an intoxicating sound the words make—like the jingle of frogs! What hot thoughts course through the mind! Before embarking on the golden adventure of shopping for an automobile, however, we strolled out together one morning to take a long, hard look at what we had in hand (a 1949 De Soto) and size up the true situation in a mood of cold sobriety.

The busted fender was, of course, a brilliant reality. And there was also the little matter of the torn upholstery on the front seat, which looked like the work of squirrels but was actually *my* work. I habitually carry a jackknife in my right-hand trousers pocket, and the bony structure of this useful tool, working through to the cloth of the seat, had taken it toll over the years. Also, on one occasion I had deliberately cut a swatch from the seat, to give to an upholsterer as a sample. This was during a phase when we were entertaining the idea of reupholstering the car. Nothing came of the reupholstery project at the time; it died of its own weight, leaving the front seat with its swatch-hole as a reminder of our good intentions and untapped resourcefulness.

After studying our car for a few minutes, we decided that the word for it was "shabby." Both of us knew, though, that we were looking at an automobile the likes of which (if we were to lose it) we might not see again, a car that had not given us a moment's anxiety or pain in the whole time we

10

had owned it and that still served us in an almost perfect manner. Its paint, after eight years, compared favorably with the paint on the new crop of cars; its metal seemed somehow stronger and heavier; all the doors worked with precision; and the only rattle it had was one it had had from the very beginning—a built-in rattle caused by a small glass plate on the instrument panel framing the legend "DE LUXE." I had always rather enjoyed this rattle as a piece of audible irony; it made me chuckle to observe that the only cheap streak in the entire car was caused by the stylist's written proclamation of swank. Every now and again I'd tire of the noise and plug the glass plate with a paper match or a tiny wad of Kleenex, but sooner or later DE LUXE would sound off again. DE LUXE was all that ever broke the silence of De Soto.

The upshot of our conference was this: Because of "shabbiness" we would look for a new car, but we would take our time about it. We were not faced with a crisis in transportation (the car ran fine), and we agreed that we would trade in our old automobile on a new one only if we could find a new one that seemed to be at least as good as what we had. We would not buy a new car merely because it bore the label "1957" or the label "1958." We would not let shabbiness embarrass us into doing anything foolish. That was the way we talked in our pride.

My wife is the sort of woman who does not notice automobiles except during the infrequent periods when we are in the process of selecting one. She has never counted on an automobile to invest her with prestige. (She was a distinguished woman at birth and needed no help from Detroit.) Motorcars simply do not attract her attention or excite her fancy, and I knew well enough that it was eight years since she'd last examined an automobile with eyes that see, and that she was in for a number of surprises, most of them unpleasant. The three things that especially interest her in a car are whether she can see out when at the wheel, whether she can ride in the front seat for any length of time without getting a pain in her back, and whether she can enter the car in a forthright manner, without turning around and going in backwards. She has never been willing to slink into an automobile fanny first, as millions of spineless and adjustable American women have learned to do, and I greatly respect this quality in her.

To prepare for what lay ahead I went to my workbench, got a spirit level and a two-foot rule, and carefully measured the height of the driver's seat from the floor. It measured fourteen and three-quarters inches.

From the end of August till the middle of January, whenever we could find a spare hour or two, we drove about the countryside, visiting nearby towns and cities in search of a car. We would pull in to a dealer's place with our naked right front wheel gleaming in the beautiful light and illuminating the car the way a cauliflower ear illuminates the face of an old fighter, and I would watch the dealer's eye rove furtively over the injured fender and see him make a mental note to knock an extra hundred dollars off the trade-in allowance. A new car would be trotted out for our inspection, and each of us in turn would sit in the driver's seat to get the feel of the thing. In most instances my wife lasted only a fraction of a minute at the wheel and came sliding and slithering out amid little stifled cries of alarm and disgust. Front seats had sunk in eight years, some of them a few inches, many of them without a trace. In several of the cars we looked at, the front seat was little more than a tilted hassock—a hassock that answered to the touch of a button, gliding forward and back, up and down, and leaving you either with your legs stretched straight out in front of you as though you were sitting on the floor, or with your knees pinned in a vicious grip under the steering wheel as though you were in the stocks.

At first we were shown 1957 automobiles, but soon after Labor Day we began encountering cars that were called 1958, among them the Edsel of great renown. It was an autumn rich in new experience for us. Everywhere we were courteously treated and everywhere we were bitterly disappointed. We ran through General Motors, we ran through Chrysler, we ran through Ford, we rambled through Rambler, and we poked around among foreign cars. A friend of ours who runs the general store where we trade let me drive his Lincoln, and another friend, just home from Germany, let me drive the Mercedes that he had brought back with him. (This last car, incidentally, felt more like our old 1949 sedan than anything else we had tried, but its manual gearshift seemed to me so delicately selective as to require the sandpapered fingers of a lock picker, and I felt fairly certain that even if I got together enough money to buy such a car, my wife would strip the gears out of it inside of a day, unless I managed to beat her to it myself.)

I usually carried my two-foot rule with me on our excursions and would make quick measurements of the front seat when nobody was looking, hoping to run across a car that could touch the fourteen-and-three-quarters-inch mark. The little Hillman, curiously enough, came close, and we were so impressed by this single fact we almost bought the car on the spot. But the same thing happened at the Hillman place that happened at all the other agencies: we took a short ride, with me at the wheel; then we thanked the man and said we wanted time to think it over; then we climbed back into the De Soto and started for home in an easy glide. Almost immediately the subtle superiority of our 1949 car to the one we had just been testing infected us, manifesting itself in a dozen indescribable ways and stirring our blood, and we felt relieved and happy and exhilarated by the rediscovery of old familiar virtues and properties, and this made us lightheaded and gay, and I stepped down on the accelerator and gradually the old automobile responded to the surge of gasoline until we were rushing along at the speed of the wind (forty-five miles an hour), singing and clowning and admiring the wonderful sheen of the green hood that stretched out in front of us, a green as rich as the new growth of a spruce tree in the spring. Even the holes in the upholstery were in perfect concealment; I sat on the knife-hole, my bride on the swatch-hole. Not a sign of shabbiness was apparent, the missing section of the fender being well out of view over the curve of the machine.

Sometime in January we tired of the rigmarole of buying a new car and decided to wait patiently for a turn in the automotive tide. I treated our sedan

to a new front fender, had a few minor dents smoothed out, installed a pair
of new front springs, and commissioned our upholsterer to re-cover the seats.
(He told us that he was about to leave for Cape Canaveral to visit a son who
is engaged in Space but that he would tend to our car when he returned to
Maine and to terrestrial affairs.) I also arranged for another coat of Turtle Wax
to be applied to the surface of Old Shabby. And that is where the matter stands
now, and that is the end of my story.

Thirty or forty years ago, when a man wanted a car, he had a fabulous
assortment to choose from—everything from a jackrabbit to a bearcat. Big
cars, small cars, medium-size cars, cheap cars, expensive cars, moderate-
priced cars, high cars, low cars, open cars, closed cars, gas cars, steam cars,
electric cars: it was paradise. The trend in manufacturing has been to
standardize the automobile, as though the consumer were himself standard
and fixed. Big cars have grown smaller, small cars have grown bigger, all cars
have grown lower, all cars have gone up in price. Sales of most American cars
are lagging; only the foreign cars are enjoying an active market.

My newspaper says that Detroit is reappraising the scene. Car makers are   *20*
asking, "Do people want expensive chrome-covered, prestige-laden big cars,
or do they want smaller and more economical basic transportation?" I think
the answer to that is, there is no such thing as "people" in the sense that the
word is used here. Every person is different. Some want expensive
chrome-covered, prestige-laden cars; some want plain undecorated inexpensive cars that carry no more prestige than an old umbrella. Some want a
car that is spacious, to carry big loads long distances. Others want a small,
economical car for light going on short hauls.

For millions of men a motorcar is primarily a means of getting to and
from work. For millions of wives it is primarily a means of getting to and from
the nearby shops, churches, and schools. Yet from reading auto ads you would
think that the primary function of the motorcar in America was to carry its
owner first into a higher social stratum, then into an exquisite delirium of
high adventure.

In the New England village I live in, the automobile is used chiefly
for getting to and from a job and a store. The one car for which there
is always a brisk demand in my town is the Model A Ford, now about
thirty years old. Whenever a Model A comes on the market, it is snapped
up in no time, and usually there is a waiting list. People actually advertise
in the papers, wanting to buy a Model A. The reason the A is going strong
today is simple: the car is a triumph of honest, unfussy design and superior
materials. It doesn't look like a turbojet or like an elephant's ear, it drinks
gasoline in moderation, it puts on no airs, and when something gets out
of adjustment the owner can usually tinker it back to health himself. The
car is not long, it is not low, but it works and it is extremely durable. It
wouldn't fill the bill today for high-speed travel over superhighways, but
I am quite sure of one thing—if Ford could suddenly produce a new batch
of Model A's and put them up for sale some morning, at about double
what they cost originally, they'd be gone by nightfall. I'd be strongly

tempted to buy one myself. It isn't *exactly* what I'm looking for, but it's close. And the price would be so favorable I wouldn't have to turn in my old car but could keep it and become a two-car American, using the Ford for dashing to the store for a box of soap flakes and the De Soto for long-distance de-luxe occasions, such as running out to San Francisco to see the Giants play ball.

Whenever the automobile industry is in trouble, it's a serious matter for the country. The motorcar is really our No. 1 consumer item; when it languishes, everything languishes. I have contributed my tiny bit to the sickness in Detroit, because I haven't bought a car in nine years—an un-American way to act. But the fault is not mine. I think manufacturers should take a deep breath and start over, on new principles. They should regard the American motorist as an individual, not a type. They should respect his honesty and his intellect and his physical stature. They should abandon the cult of "lowness," as though lowness were synonymous with beauty and performance. (Every car should have a low center of gravity, but it isn't hard to come by. Virtually everything that's heavy about an automobile is in a naturally low position—engine, wheels, axles, frame, drive shaft, transmission, differential.)

The architect and his brother the engineer are perhaps the most valuable citizens we have. When they fail us, it affects our health and our purse. I believe that in motordom architects and engineers are not permitted to work undisturbed; their elbow is constantly being jiggled by tipsters, pollsters, motivationalists, and dream-mongers. To design a car is a responsible job, like designing a railroad bridge or a skyscraper. The motorcar is a killer and will always be a killer, but the death rate will always respond to responsible work at the drawing board. Where there are honesty and sincerity and technical skill and belief in the good traits of human beings, there is never any problem about beauty of form and line. The reason women's clothes are hideous this season is that the bag or sack is a betrayal of anatomy, and fails to translate the figure of a woman, merely caricaturing it. But it's one thing to pander to human foibles when creating a dress and quite another when creating a car. A car is a matter of life and death.

I didn't carry a two-foot rule around the countryside in order to annoy dealers. I did it because I was afraid we might have a terrible accident if my wife was obliged to sit almost at floor level while driving a high-powered car. This was a more compelling consideration than the slight increment of prestige I might gain by owning a vehicle my neighbors would think was smart because it was low. I'd rather stay down on a low level of society with a living wife than be up with the best of them as a widower. During our days of searching, I noticed that although dealers don't like two-foot rules, many of the ones I encountered were sympathetic to my cry. None of them gave me much of an argument, and several of them said they agreed.

I'll promise Detroit one thing: build me a car that's as comfortable, as safe, as durable, and as handsome as the one I have today, and I'll swap cars.

25

P.S. (May 1962).   The tide did turn, and I kept my promise to Detroit. The air in that city has changed; gloom has been dispersed, sales are brisk, and this spring is jubilee. Sylvia Porter° says it will last eleven months.

Cars are no longer uniform in size and shape. Today a man can find almost anything he wants—big, little, medium, fancy, plain, foreign, sporting, sedate. And if a conventional body fails to satisfy his needs, he can buy a minibus and sit well forward over the front wheels, while the children sit behind and leave the driving to him. The automotive scene is far healthier than it was in that grim springtime of 1958. There is real vigor in it.

Instead of trading in my old De Soto for a new car, I bought a new car outright and sold my De Soto to a friend who lives about a mile up the road and who had had his eye on my buggy for quite a while. I knew about his interest in the car, but he himself had never mentioned it to me. One afternoon, having made my mind up, I turned in at his place and stopped the car just short of the barn door and got out, and he came out of his kitchen and we stood together for a long while, leaning against the car and chinning. I am sure he knew perfectly well what the purpose of my visit was, and under the circumstances I felt as conspicuous coming into his yard with the De Soto as I would have felt if I had come in leading a Holstein bull. But although each of us knew what was in the other's mind, we both carefully avoided the subject, in the manner of traders the world over, as though the subject were indecent, or distasteful. Instead of discussing cars, we discussed bees. My friend is the foremost beeman in town: he loves to hunt wild honey in the fall of the year by tracking bees, and if you suddenly find yourself with a swarm of bees on your porch and are in trouble, he's the man you call on for help.

After we had covered the subject of bees thoroughly, and several other *30* subjects, I remarked casually that I had heard he might be interested in buying a car. "I might," he replied. "What price have you got on it?" All this without looking at the automobile. I named a figure. "I'll go in and write you a check," he said, as though he were saying, "Looks as though it might turn warmer tomorrow." The whole transaction was over in less time than it takes a bee to rifle a flower.

It is nice to have my old car so close by. The new owner and I pass each other several times a week on the road and always exchange a small salute. When I go past his place, I often catch a glimpse of the car's voluptuous green posterior through the open barn door.

For myself, after much hunting, I found a car with a front seat that is well up off the floor, thirteen inches exactly—a 1960 Lark, to mention no names. I have driven this car two years and am a satisfied customer. By American standards it is already an old automobile, ready for the used-car lot; but from the looks of things, it is going to be around for a while yet. Maybe not eleven years (I can't break Detroit's heart twice in one lifetime), but at any rate for a while.

Sylvia Porter: A well-known economics columnist.

Questions for Understanding

1. What was White's attitude toward automobile designers in 1958?
2. What is White's theory of aesthetics? In other words, what constitutes beauty, in his eyes?
3. Was the Whites' De Soto really "shabby"?
4. How did the Whites usually react after visiting an automobile dealership?
5. What does White believe is the fundamental flaw in the thinking of American automobile designers?

Suggestions for Writing

1. Discuss your own experience shopping for a car.
2. Compare and contrast two cars that look alike but are significantly different.
3. Discuss a product, other than a car, that you think is badly designed.
4. Discuss your own theory of aesthetics. In your eyes, what makes an item made by human hands beautiful?
5. Write a brief history of American automotive design since the 1950s.

DEATH OF A PIG

1947

I spent several days and nights in mid-September with an ailing pig and   *1*
I feel driven to account for this stretch of time, more particularly since the pig
died at last, and I lived, and things might easily have gone the other way round
and none left to do the accounting. Even now, so close to the event, I cannot
recall the hours sharply and am not ready to say whether death came on the
third night or the fourth night. This uncertainty afflicts me with a sense of
personal deterioration; if I were in decent health I would know how many
nights I had sat up with a pig.

The scheme of buying a spring pig in blossomtime, feeding it through
summer and fall, and butchering it when the solid cold weather arrives, is a
familiar scheme to me and follows an antique pattern. It is a tragedy enacted
on most farms with perfect fidelity to the original script. The murder, being
premeditated, is in the first degree but is quick and skillful, and the smoked
bacon and ham provide a ceremonial ending whose fitness is seldom
questioned.

Once in a while something slips—one of the actors goes up in his
lines and the whole performance stumbles and halts. My pig simply failed
to show up for a meal. The alarm spread rapidly. The classic outline of
the tragedy was lost. I found myself cast suddenly in the role of pig's friend
and physician—a farcical character with an enema bag for a prop. I had
a presentiment, the very first afternoon, that the play would never regain
its balance and that my sympathies were now wholly with the pig. This
was slapstick—the sort of dramatic treatment that instantly appealed to my
old dachshund, Fred, who jointed the vigil, held the bag, and, when all
was over, presided at the interment. When we slid the body into the grave,
we both were shaken to the core. The loss we felt was not the loss of ham
but the loss of pig. He had evidently become precious to me, not that he
represented a distant nourishment in a hungry time, but that he had suffered
in a suffering world. But I'm running ahead of my story and shall have
to go back.

My pigpen is at the bottom of an old orchard below the house. The pigs
I have raised have lived in a faded building that once was an ice-house. There
is a pleasant yard to move about in, shaded by an apple tree that overhangs the
low rail fence. A pig couldn't ask for anything better—or none has, at any rate.
The sawdust in the icehouse makes a comfortable bottom in which to root,
and a warm bed. This sawdust, however, came under suspicion when the pig
took sick. One of my neighbors said he thought the pig would have done
better on new ground—the same principle that applies in planting potatoes.
He said there might be something unhealthy about the sawdust, that he never
thought well of sawdust.

It was about four o'clock in the afternoon when I first noticed that there   *5*
was something wrong with the pig. He failed to appear at the trough for his

supper, and when a pig (or a child) refuses supper a chill wave of fear runs through any household, or ice-household. After examining my pig, who was stretched out in the sawdust inside the building, I went to the phone and cranked it four times. Mr. Dameron answered. "What's good for a sick pig?" I asked. (There is never any identification needed on a country phone; the person on the other end knows who is talking by the sound of the voice and by the character of the question.)

"I don't know, I never had a sick pig," said Mr. Dameron, "but I can find out quick enough. You hang up and I'll call Henry."

Mr. Dameron was back on the line again in five minutes. "Henry says roll him over on his back and give him two ounces of castor oil or sweet oil, and if that doesn't do the trick give him an injection of soapy water. He says he's almost sure the pig's plugged up, and even if he's wrong, it can't do any harm."

I thanked Mr. Dameron. I didn't go right down to the pig, though. I sank into a chair and sat still for a few minutes to think about my troubles, and then I got up and went to the barn, catching up on some odds and ends that needed tending to. Unconsciously I held off, for an hour, the deed by which I would officially recognize the collapse of the performance of raising a pig; I wanted no interruption in the regularity of feeding, the steadiness of growth, the even succession of days. I wanted no interruption, wanted no oil, no deviation. I just wanted to keep on raising a pig, full meal after full meal, spring into summer into fall. I didn't even know whether there were two ounces of castor oil on the place.

Shortly after five o'clock I remembered that we had been invited out to dinner that night and realized that if I were to dose a pig there was no time to lose. The dinner date seemed a familiar conflict: I move in a desultory society and often a week or two will roll by without my going to anybody's house to dinner or anyone's coming to mine, but when an occasion does arise, and I am summoned, something usually turns up (an hour or two in advance) to make all human intercourse seem vastly inappropriate. I have come to believe that there is in hostesses a special power of divination, and that they deliberately arrange dinners to coincide with pig failure or some other sort of failure. At any rate, it was after five o'clock and I knew I could put off no longer the evil hour.

When my son and I arrived at the pigyard, armed with a small bottle of castor oil and a length of clothesline, the pig had emerged from his house and was standing in the middle of his yard, listlessly. He gave us a slim greeting. I could see that he felt uncomfortable and uncertain. I had brought the clothesline thinking I'd have to tie him (the pig weighed more than a hundred pounds) but we never used it. My son reached down, grabbed both front legs, upset him quickly, and when he opened his mouth to scream I turned the oil into his throat—a pink, corrugated area I had never seen before. I had just time to read the label while the neck of the bottle was in his mouth. It said Puretest. The screams, slightly muffled by oil, were pitched in the hysterically high range of pig-sound, as though torture were being carried out, but they

10

didn't last long: it was all over rather suddenly, and, his legs released, the pig righted himself.

In the upset position the corners of his mouth had been turned down, giving him a frowning expression. Back on his feet again, he regained the set smile that a pig wears even in sickness. He stood his ground, sucking slightly at the residue of oil; a few drops leaked out of his lips while his wicked eyes, shaded by their coy little lashes turned on me in disgust and hatred. I scratched him gently with oily fingers and he remained quiet, as though trying to recall the satisfaction of being scratched when in health, and seeming to rehearse in his mind the indignity to which he had just been subjected. I noticed, as I stood there, four or five small dark spots on his back near the tail end, reddish brown in color, each about the size of a housefly, I could not make out what they were. They did not look troublesome but at the same time they did not look like mere surface bruises or chafe marks. Rather they seemed blemishes of internal origin. His stiff white bristles almost completely hid them and I had to part the bristles with my fingers to get a good look.

Several hours later, a few minutes before midnight, having dined well and at someone else's expense, I returned to the pighouse with a flashlight. The patient was asleep. Kneeling, I felt his ears (as you might put your hand on the forehead of a child) and they seemed cool, and then with the light made a careful examination of the yard and the house for sign that the oil had worked. I found none and went to bed.

We had been having an unseasonable spell of whether—hot, close days, with the fog shutting in every night, scaling for a few hours in midday, then creeping back again at dark, drifting in first over the trees on the point, then suddenly blowing across the fields, blotting out the world and taking possession of houses, men, and animals. Everyone kept hoping for a break, but the break failed to come. Next day was another hot one. I visited the pig before breakfast and tried to tempt him with a little milk in his trough. He just stared at it, while I made a sucking sound through my teeth to remind him of past pleasures of the feast. With very small, timid pigs, weanlings, this ruse is often quite successful and will encourage them to eat; but with a large, sick pig the ruse is senseless and the sound I made must have made him feel, if anything, more miserable. He not only did not crave food, he felt a positive revulsion to it. I found a place under the apple tree where he had vomited in the night.

At this point, although a depression had settled over me, I didn't suppose that I was going to lose my pig. From the lustiness of a healthy pig a man derives a feeling of personal lustiness; the stuff that goes into the trough and is received with such enthusiasm is an earnest of some later feast of his own, and when this suddenly comes to an end and the food lies stale and untouched, souring in the sun, the pig's imbalance becomes the man's, vicariously, and life seems insecure, displaced, transitory.

As my own spirits declined, along with the pig's, the spirits of my vile old dachshund rose. The frequency of our trips down the footpath through the orchard to the pigyard delighted him, although he suffers greatly from arthritis, moves with difficulty, and would be bedridden if he could find anyone willing to serve him meals on a tray.

He never missed a chance to visit the pig with one, and he made many professional calls on his own. You could see him down there at all hours, his white face parting the grass along the fence as he wobbled and stumbled about, his stethoscope dangling—a happy quack, writing his villainous prescriptions and grinning his corrosive grin. When the enema bag appeared, and the bucket of warm suds, his happiness was complete, and he managed to squeeze his enormous body between the two lowest rails of the yard and then assumed full charge of the irrigation. Once, when I lowered the bag to check the flow, he reached in and hurriedly drank a few mouthfuls of the suds to test their potency. I have noticed that Fred will feverishly consume any substance that is associated with trouble—the bitter flavor is to his liking. When the bag was above reach, he concentrated on the pig and was everywhere at once, a tower of strength and inconvenience. The pig, curiously enough, stood rather quietly through this colonic carnival, and the enema, though ineffective, was not as difficult as I had anticipated.

I discovered, though, that once having given a pig an enema there is no turning back, no chance of resuming one of life's more stereotyped roles. The pig's lot and mine were inextricably bound now, as though the rubber tube were the silver cord. From then until the time of his death I held the pig steadily in the bowl of my mind; the task of trying to deliver him from his misery became a strong obsession. His suffering soon became the embodiment of all earthly wretchedness. Along toward the end of the afternoon, defeated in physicking, I phoned the veterinary twenty miles away and placed the case formally in his hands. He was full of questions, and when I casually mentioned the dark spots on the pig's back, his voice changed its tone.

"I don't want to scare you," he said, "but when there are spots, erysipelas has to be considered."

Together we considered erysipelas, with frequent interruptions from the telephone operator, who wasn't sure the connection had been established.

"If a pig has erysipelas can he give it to a person?" I asked.   20

"Yes, he can," replied the vet.

"Have they answered?" asked the operator.

"Yes, they have," I said. Then I addressed the vet again. "You better come over here and examine this pig right away."

"I can't come myself," said the vet, "but McFarland can come this evening if that's all right. Mac knows more about pigs than I do anyway. You needn't worry too much about the spots. To indicate erysipelas they would have to be deep hemorrhagic infarcts."

"Deep hemorrhagic what?" I asked.   25

"Infarcts," said the vet.

"Have they answered?" asked the operator.

"Well," I said, "I don't know what you'd call these spots, except they're about the size of a housefly. If the pig has erysipelas I guess I have it, too, by this time, because we've been very close lately."

"McFarland will be over," said the vet.

I hung up. My throat felt dry and I went to the cupboard and got a bottle *30* of whiskey. Deep hemorrhagic infarcts—the phrase began fastening its hooks in my head. I had assumed that there could be nothing much wrong with a pig during the months it was being groomed for murder; my confidence in the essential health and endurance of pigs had been strong and deep, particularly in the health of pigs that belonged to me and that were part of my proud scheme. The awakening had been violent and I minded it all the more because I knew that what could be true of my pig could be true also of the rest of my tidy world. I tried to put this distasteful idea from me, but it kept recurring. I took a short drink of the whiskey and then, although I wanted to go down to the yard and look for fresh signs, I was scared to. I was certain I had erysipelas.

It was long after dark and the supper dishes had been put away when a car drove in and McFarland got out. He had a girl with him. I could just make her out in the darkness—she seemed young and pretty. "This is Miss Owen," he said. "We've been having a picnic supper on the shore, that's why I'm late."

McFarland stood in the driveway and stripped off his jacket, then his shirt. His stocky arms and capable hands showed up in my flashlight's gleam as I helped him find his coverall and get zipped up. The rear seat of his car contained an astonishing amount of paraphernalia, which he soon overhauled, selecting a chain, a syringe, a bottle of oil, a rubber tube, and some other things I couldn't identify. Miss Owen said she'd go along with us and see the pig. I led the way down the warm slope of the orchard, my light picking out the path for them, and we all three climbed the fence, entered the pighouse, and squatted by the pig while McFarland took a rectal reading. My flashlight picked up the glitter of an engagement ring on the girl's hand.

"No elevation," said McFarland, twisting the thermometer in the light. "You needn't worry about erysipelas." He ran his hand slowly over the pig's stomach and at one point the pig cried out in pain.

"Poor piggledy-wiggledy!" said Miss Owen.

The treatment I had been giving the pig for two days was then repeated, *35* somewhat more expertly, by the doctor, Miss Owen and I handing him things as he needed them—holding the chain that he had looped around the pig's upper jaw, holding the syringe, holding the bottle stopper, the end of the tube, all of us working in darkness and in comfort, working with the instinctive teamwork induced by emergency conditions, the pig unprotesting, the house shadowy, protecting, intimate. I went to bed tired but with a feeling of relief that I had turned over part of the responsibility of the case to a licensed doctor. I was beginning to think, though, that the pig was not going to live.

He died twenty-four hours later, or it might have been forty-eight—there is a blur in time here, and I may have lost or picked up a day in the telling and the pig one in the dying. At intervals during the last day I took cool fresh water down to him and at such times as he found the strength to get to his feet he would stand with head in the pail and snuffle his snout around. He drank a few sips but no more; yet it seemed to comfort him to dip his nose in water and bobble it about, sucking in and blowing out through his teeth. Much of the time, now, he lay indoors half buried in sawdust. Once, near the last, while I was attending him I saw him try to make a bed for himself but he lacked the strength, and when he set his snout into the dust he was unable to plow even the little furrow he needed to lie down in.

He came out of the house to die. When I went down, before going to bed, he lay stretched in the yard a few feet from the door. I knelt, saw that he was dead, and left him there: his face had a mild look, expressive neither of deep peace nor of deep suffering, although I think he had suffered a good deal. I went back up to the house and to bed, and cried internally—deep hemorrhagic intears. I didn't wake till nearly eight the next morning, and when I looked out the open window the grave was already being dug, down beyond the dump under a wild apple. I could hear the spade strike against the small rocks that blocked the way. Never send to know for whom the grave is dug, I said to myself, it's dug for thee. Fred, I well knew, was supervising the work of digging, so I ate breakfast slowly.

It was a Saturday morning. The thicket in which I found the gravediggers at work was dark and warm, the sky overcast. Here, among alders and young hackmatacks, at the foot of the apple tree, Lennie had dug a beautiful hole, five feet long, three feet wide, three feet deep. He was standing in it, removing the last spadefuls of earth while Fred patrolled the brink in simple but impressive circles, disturbing the loose earth of the mound so that it trickled back in. There had been no rain in weeks and the soil, even three feet down, was dry and powdery. As I stood and stared, an enormous earthworm which had been partially exposed by the spade at the bottom dug itself deeper and made a slow withdrawal, seeking even remoter moistures at even lonelier depths. And just as Lennie stepped out and rested his spade against the tree and lit a cigarette, a small green apple separated itself from a branch overhead and fell into the hole. Everything about this last scene seemed overwritten—the dismal sky, the shabby woods, the imminence of rain, the worm (legendary bedfellow of the dead), the apple (conventional garnish of a pig).

But even so, there was a directness and dispatch about animal burial, I thought, that made it a more decent affair than human burial: there was no stopover in the undertaker's foul parlor, no wreath nor spray; and when we hitched a line to the pig's hind legs and dragged him swiftly from his yard, throwing our weight into the harness and leaving a wake of crushed grass and smoothed rubble over the dump, ours was a businesslike procession, with Fred, the dishonorable pallbearer, staggering along in the rear, his perverse bereavement showing in every seam in his face; and the post-mortem performed handily and swiftly right at the edge of the grave, so that the inwards that had caused the pig's death preceded him into the ground and he lay at last resting squarely on the cause of his own undoing.

I threw in the first shovelful, and then we worked rapidly and without   *40* talk, until the job was complete. I picked up the rope, made it fast to Fred's collar (he is a notorious ghoul), and we all three filed back up the path to the house, Fred bringing up the rear and holding back every inch of the way, feigning unusual stiffness. I noticed that although he weighed far less than the pig, he was harder to drag, being possessed of the vital spark.

The news of the death of my pig traveled fast and far, and I received many expressions of sympathy from friends and neighbors, for no one took the event lightly and the premature expiration of a pig is, I soon discovered, a departure which the community marks solemnly on its calendar, a sorrow in which it feels fully involved. I have written this account in penitence and in grief, as a man who failed to raise his pig, and to explain my deviation from the classic course of so many raised pigs. The grave in the woods is unmarked, but Fred can direct the mourner to it unerringly and with immense good will, and I know he and I shall often revisit it, singly and together, in seasons of reflection and despair, on flagless memorial days of our own choosing.

Questions for Understanding

1. What is the "classic outline of the tragedy" involving a pig?
2. Why did White procrastinate before he went down to "dose" the pig?
3. In what ways does White anthropomorphize the pig after giving him the castor oil?
4. What is White's point when, on the morning after the pig's death, he says to himself, "Never send to know for whom the grave is dug . . . it's dug for thee"?
5. At the pig's grave, why does White think, "Everything about this last scene seemed overwritten"?

Suggestions for Writing

1. Describe the effects on you of a relationship you had with an animal.
2. Is anthropomorphizing a way of deceiving oneself?
3. White raised his pig to be "murdered" and then eaten. Apparently he would not have been at all upset by eating his pig. Discuss the extent to which you would be bothered by eating an animal you had raised.
4. Are all forms of animal life to be valued equally? If not, what is the basis for valuing some animals more than others?
5. Are human beings, like pigs, just a link in the food chain? Discuss.

ONCE MORE TO THE LAKE

1941

One summer, along about 1904, my father rented a camp on a lake in   1
Maine and took us all there for the month of August. We all got ringworm
from some kittens and had to rub Pond's Extract on our arms and legs at night
and morning, and my father rolled over in a canoe with all his clothes on; but
outside of that the vacation was a success and from then on none of us ever
thought there was any place in the world like that lake in Maine. We returned
summer after summer—always on August 1 for one month. I have since
become a salt-water man, but sometimes in summer there are days when the
restlessness of the tides and the fearful cold of the sea water and the incessant
wind that blows across the afternoon and into the evening make me wish for
the placidity of a lake in the woods. A few weeks ago this feeling got so strong
I bought myself a couple of bass hooks and a spinner and returned to the lake
where we used to go, for a week's fishing and to revisit old haunts.

I took along my son, who had never had any fresh water up his nose and
who had seen lily pads only from train windows. On the journey over to the
lake I began to wonder what it would be like. I wondered how time would
have marred this unique, this holy spot—the coves and streams, the hills that
the sun set behind, the camps and the paths behind the camps. I was sure that
the tarred road would have found it out, and I wondered in what other ways
it would be desolated. It is strange how much you can remember about places
like that once you allow your mind to return into the grooves that lead back.
You remember one thing, and that suddenly reminds you of another thing.
I guess I remembered clearest of all the early mornings, when the lake was
cool and motionless, remembered how the bedroom smelled of the lumber
it was made of and of the wet woods whose scent entered through the screen.
The partitions in the camp were thin and did not extend clear to the top of
the rooms, and as I was always the first up I would dress softly so as not to wake
the others, and sneak out into the sweet outdoors and start out in the canoe,
keeping close along the shore in the long shadows of the pines. I remembered
being very careful never to rub my paddle against the gunwale for fear of
disturbing the stillness of the cathedral.

The lake had never been what you would call a wild lake. There were
cottages sprinkled around the shores, and it was in farming country although
the shores of the lake were quite heavily wooded. Some of the cottages were
owned by nearby farmers, and you would live at the shore and eat your meals
at the farmhouse. That's what our family did. But although it wasn't wild, it
was a fairly large and undisturbed lake and there were places in it that, to a
child at least, seemed infinitely remote and primeval.

I was right about the tar: it led to within half a mile of the shore. But
when I got back there, with my boy, and we settled into a camp near a
farmhouse and into the kind of summertime I had known, I could tell that
it was going to be pretty much the same as it had been before—I knew it, lying

in bed the first morning, smelling the bedroom and hearing the boy sneak quietly out and go off along the shore in a boat. I began to sustain the illusion that he was I, and therefore, by simple transposition, that I was my father. This sensation persisted, kept cropping up all the time we were there. It was not an entirely new feeling, but in this setting it grew much stronger. I seemed to be living a dual existence. I would be in the middle of some simple act, I would be picking up a bait box or laying down a table fork, or I would be saying something, and suddenly it would be not I but my father who was saying the words or making the gesture. It gave me a creepy sensation.

We went fishing the first morning. I felt the same damp moss covering   5 the worms in the bait can, and saw the dragonfly alight on the tip of my rod as it hovered a few inches from the surface of the water. It was the arrival of this fly that convinced me beyond any doubt that everything was as it always had been, that the years were a mirage and that there had been no years. The small waves were the same, chucking the rowboat under the chin as we fished at anchor, and the boat was the same boat, the same color green and the ribs broken in the same places, and under the floorboards the same fresh-water leavings and debris—the dead helgramite, the wisps of moss, the rusty discarded fishhook, the dried blood from yesterday's catch. We stared silently at the tips of our rods, at the dragonflies that came and went. I lowered the tip of mine into the water, tentatively, pensively dislodging the fly, which darted two feet away, poised, darted two feet back, and came to rest again a little farther up the rod. There had been no years between the ducking of this dragonfly and the other one—the one that was part of memory. I looked at the boy, who was silently watching his fly, and it was my hands that held his rod, my eyes watching. I felt dizzy and didn't know which rod I was at the end of.

We caught two bass, hauling them in briskly as though they were mackerel, pulling them over the side of the boat in a businesslike manner without any landing net, and stunning them with a blow on the back of the head. When we got back for a swim before lunch, the lake was exactly where we had left it, the same number of inches from the dock, and there was only the merest suggestion of a breeze. This seemed an utterly enchanted sea, this lake you could leave to its own devices for a few hours and come back to, and find that it had not stirred, this constant and trustworthy body of water. In the shallows, the dark, watersoaked sticks and twigs, smooth and old, were undulating in clusters on the bottom against the clean ribbed sand, and the track of the mussel was plain. A school of minnows swam by, each minnow with its small individual shadow, doubling the attendance, so clear and sharp in the sunlight. Some of the other campers were in swimming, along the shore, one of them with a cake of soap, and the water felt thin and clear and unsubstantial. Over the years there had been this person with the cake of soap, this cultist, and here he was. There had been no years.

Up to the farmhouse to dinner through the teeming, dusty field, the road under our sneakers was only a two-track road. The middle track was missing, the one with the marks of the hooves and the splotches of dried, flaky manure. There had been three tracks to choose from in choosing which track to walk in; now the choice was narrowed down to two. For a moment I missed terribly the middle alternative. But the way led past the tennis court, and something about the way it lay there in the sun reassured me; the tape had loosened along the backline, the alleys were green with plantains and other weeds, and the net (installed in June and removed in September) sagged in the dry noon, and the whole place steamed with midday heat and hunger and emptiness. There was a choice of pie for dessert, and one was blueberry and one was apple, and the waitresses were the same country girls, there having been no passage of time, only the illusion of it as in a dropped curtain—the waitresses were still fifteen; their hair had been washed, that was the only difference—they had been to the movies and seen the pretty girls with clean hair.

Summertime, oh, summertime, pattern of life indelible, the fade-proof lake, the woods unshatterable, the pasture with the sweetfern and the juniper forever and ever, summer without end; this was the background, and the life along the shore was the design, the cottagers with their innocent and tranquil design, their tiny docks with the flagpole and the American flag floating against the white clouds in the blue sky, the little paths over the roots of the trees leading from camp to camp and the paths leading back to the outhouses and the can of lime for sprinkling, and at the souvenir counters at the store the miniature birchbark canoes and the postcards that showed things looking a little better than they looked. This was the American family at play, escaping the city heat, wondering whether the newcomers in the camp at the head of the cove were "common" or "nice," wondering whether it was true that the people who drove up for Sunday dinner at the farmhouse were turned away because there wasn't enough chicken.

It seemed to me, as I kept remembering all this, that those times and those summers had been infinitely precious and worth saving. There had been jollity and peace and goodness. The arriving (at the beginning of August) had been so big a business in itself, at the railway station the farm wagon drawn up, the first smell of the pine-laden air, the first glimpse of the smiling farmer, and the great importance of the trunks and your father's enormous authority in such matters, and the feel of the wagon under you for the long ten-mile haul, and at the top of the last long hill catching the first view of the lake after eleven months of not seeing this cherished body of water. The shouts and cries of the other campers when they saw you, and the trunks to be unpacked, to give up their rich burden. (Arriving was less exciting nowadays, when you sneaked up in your car and parked it under a tree near the camp and took out the bags and in five minutes it was all over, no fuss, no loud wonderful fuss about trunks.)

Peace and goodness and jollity. The only thing that was wrong now, really, was the sound of the place, an unfamiliar nervous sound of the outboard motors. This was the note that jarred, the one thing that would sometimes break the illusion and set the years moving. In those other summertimes all motors were inboard; and when they were at a little distance, 10 the noise they made was a sedative, an ingredient of summer sleep. They were one-cylinder and two-cylinder engines, and some were make-and-break and some were jump-spark, but they all made a sleepy sound across the lake. The one-lungers throbbed and fluttered, and the twin-cylinder ones purred and purred, and that was a quiet sound, too. But now the campers all had outboards. In the daytime, in the hot mornings, these motors made a petulant, irritable sound; at night, in the still evening when the afterglow lit the water, they whined about one's ears like mosquitoes. My boy loved our rented outboard, and his great desire was to achieve single-handed mastery over it, and authority, and he soon learned the trick of choking it a little (but not too much), and the adjustment of the needle valve. Watching him I would remember the things you could do with the old one-cylinder engine with the heavy flywheel, how you could have it eating out of your hand if you got really close to it spiritually. Motorboats in those days didn't have clutches, and you would make a landing by shutting off the motor at the proper time and coasting in with a dead rudder. But there was a way of reversing them, if you learned the trick, by cutting the switch and putting it on again exactly on the final dying revolution of the flywheel, so that it would kick back against compression and begin reversing. Approaching a dock in a strong following breeze, it was difficult to slow up sufficiently by the ordinary coasting method, and if a boy felt he had complete mastery over his motor, he was tempted to keep it running beyond its time and then reverse it a few feet from the dock. It took a cool nerve, because if you threw the switch a twentieth of a second too soon you would catch the flywheel when it still had speed enough to go up past center, and the boat would leap ahead, charging bull-fashion at the dock.

We had a good week at the camp. The bass were biting well and the sun shone endlessly, day after day. We would be tired at night and lie down in the accumulated heat of the little bedrooms after the long hot day and the breeze would stir almost imperceptibly outside and the smell of the swamp drift in through the rusty screens. Sleep would come easily and in the morning the red squirrel would be on the roof, tapping out his gay routine. I kept remembering everything, lying in bed in the mornings—the small steamboat that had a long rounded stern like the lip of a Ubangi, and how quietly she ran on the moonlight sails, when the older boys played their mandolins and the girls sang and we ate doughnuts dipped in sugar, and how sweet the music was on the water in the shining night, and what it had felt like to think about girls then. After breakfast we would go up to the store and the things were in the same place—the minnows in a bottle, the plugs and spinners disarranged and pawed over by the youngsters from the boys' camp, the Fig Newtons and the Beeman's gum. Outside, the road was tarred and cars stood in front of the store. Inside, all was just as it had always been, except there was more Coca-Cola and not so much Moxie and root beer and birch beer and sarsaparilla. We would walk out with the bottle of pop apiece and sometimes the pop would backfire up our noses and hurt. We explored the streams, quietly, where the turtles slid off the sunny logs and dug their way into the soft bottom; and we lay on the town wharf and fed worms to the tame bass. Everywhere we went I had trouble making out which was I, the one walking at my side, the one walking in my pants.

One afternoon while we were there at that lake a thunderstorm came up. It was like the revival of an old melodrama that I had seen long ago with childish awe. The second-act climax of the drama of the electrical disturbance over a lake in America had not changed in any important respect. This was the big scene, still the big scene. The whole thing was so familiar, the first feeling of oppression and heat and a general air around camp of not wanting to go very far away. In mid-afternoon (it was all the same) a curious darkening of the sky, and a lull in everything that had made life tick; and then the way the boats suddenly swung the other way at their moorings with the coming of a breeze out of the new quarter, and the premonitory rumble. Then the kettle drum, then the snare, then the bass drum and cymbals, then crackling light against the dark, and the gods grinning and licking their chops in the hills. Afterward the calm, the rain steadily rustling in the calm lake, the return of light and hope and spirits, and the campers running out in joy and relief to go swimming in the rain, their bright cries perpetuating the deathless joke about how they were getting simply drenched, and the children screaming with delight at the new sensation of bathing in the rain, and the joke about getting drenched linking the generations in a strong indestructible chain. And the comedian who waded in carrying an umbrella.

When the others went swimming, my son said he was going in, too. He pulled his dripping trunks from the line where they had hung all through the shower and wrung them out. Languidly, and with no thought of going in, I watched him, his hard little body, skinny and bare, saw him wince slightly as he pulled up around his vitals the small, soggy, icy garment. As he buckled the swollen belt, suddenly my groin felt the chill of death.

Questions for Understanding

1. Near the beginning of his description of the return to the lake, White says he wondered "how time would have marred this unique, this holy spot." What is unique and holy about this spot?

2. In his description of the first morning out fishing with his son, White says they "stared silently" at the tips of their rods and that, in dislodging the dragonfly, he lowered the tip of his rod "tentatively" and "pensively." Are those two adverbs necessary? Would the sentence and paragraph lose anything if they were omitted?

3. Later that first morning, White and his son return to the lake for a swim, and White says the following about the lake: "The lake was exactly where we had left it, the same number of inches from the dock, and there was only the merest suggestion of a breeze. This seemed an utterly enchanted sea, this lake you could leave to its own devices for a few hours and come back to, and find that it had not stirred, this constant and trustworthy body of water." How does this description of the lake mesh with White's overall purpose in this essay?

4. The last sentence of paragraph 8 goes on for fifty-three words. Is this a successful sentence?
5. The first sentence of paragraph 11 has only eight words. Is this a successful sentence?

Suggestions for Writing

1. Describe a place you know that has remained the same while its surroundings have changed.
2. Describe a place you know that has changed, making clear the difference between what it is like now and what it was like before.
3. Members of the same family usually are alike in some ways but different in others. Describe two such family members, and point out interesting similarities and differences.
4. Members of a family often have very different notions about what constitutes an ideal vacation. Describe what your ideal vacation is like, and point out how your ideal differs from that of another member of your family.
5. White seems to take pride in providing his son with an experience similar to the one his own father provided to him. Is it a good idea for parents to try to guide the lives of their children onto paths they themselves have followed? To what extent does one of your parents want you to experience what he or she experienced? To what extent does one of your parents have a plan for your future? To what extent does your plan for yourself differ from that plan?

NUTS AND BOLTS 6: REPETITION OF WORDS AND VARYING SENTENCE LENGTHS

"Correct" English changes over time. For most people with an ear or an eye for the English language, what well-educated people say or do in speaking or writing is assumed to be correct. But that is not always true. The ultimate standard of correct English in America is what our best editors allow into print. They are the editors of the country's most prestigious magazines and newspapers; they are the editors of books published by our most respected publishing houses. Many well-educated people now say "between you and I," and lots of people who want to speak and write correctly assume they are doing so when they say "between you and I." But as long as America's top editors do not allow "between you and I" onto their pages, "between you and I" is not correct English. On the other hand, if the editors do approve of a way of saying something, then that phrase, word, punctuation, or form of sentence will have a "good English" stamp of approval. These editors don't hold meetings or take votes, but they read carefully what their colleagues print. Sometimes they resist something new, and it remains incorrect. Sometimes they go along, and what had been forbidden comes to be considered correct. Slowly, slowly, professors of English follow the editors.

The editors of the *Washington Post*, the *Los Angeles Times*, and especially *The New York Times* are very influential. So are the editors of three magazines: *Time*, *Newsweek*, and *The New Yorker*. The editors of *The New Yorker*, which started out in 1925 as a humor magazine, are the most influential because their magazine has gained the reputation of being the best-edited magazine in America. What does "best-edited" mean? It means, first of all, respect for the magazine's readers. It means caring passionately about the types of words, sentences, and paragraphs that are allowed into the magazine. It means being vigilant to exclude shoddy, tasteless, confusing, uninformed work. It also means keeping an open mind and allowing change when the change makes sense, when the change facilitates communication between writers and readers. It means encouraging freshness and genuine originality. Writers who hope to be published in *The New Yorker* know what its editors expect.

E. B. White wrote for *The New Yorker* for over fifty years, and his name is more closely associated with the magazine than is the name of any other writer. White's reputation as an essayist is to a great extent based on the freshness and elegance of his style. Therefore, that style—White's use of words and his ways of constructing sentences and paragraphs—can be a very useful model. Of course, writing style (like style in the arts or even in personal appearance) is highly individualized and won't necessarily work for anyone who happens to like it. Even so, a great deal can be learned from analysis of an excellent writer's style, just as a lot can be learned from close observation of someone whose style of dress we admire.

White characteristically does several things with his sentences that student writers can also do to great advantage. Look at paragraphs 4, 5, and 6 of "Once More to the Lake." Clearly, White is not afraid of repetition. Excess is bad, but repetition that is not excessive usually is effective. In the long next-to-last sentence of paragraph 4, White has four main clauses; three of them begin with "I would be," and the fourth begins with "It would be." There's nothing wrong with that. Through the repetition, White conveys how commonplace it became for him to feel as though he were living more than one life. If, in an essay you are writing, you reach a point where you think repetition would be effective, don't be inhibited. Go ahead and use the phrase or grammatical form three, four, or even more times.

Another characteristic of White's style is that the lengths of his sentences vary dramatically. Some sentences are quite brief, some are long. The "I would" sentence contains forty-nine words, but the sentence that precedes it contains eight words, and the sentence that follows it contains only six. Variations in sentence length help to build pleasing rhythms in paragraphs. They also play a role in creating emphasis. As a general rule, the briefer the sentence, the greater the emphasis on its point. In a longer sentence, emphasis is generally diffused. But because longer sentences usually say more, and because working out the grammar and internal punctuation takes skill and knowledge, the experienced reader usually finishes reading a successful longer sentence with a feeling of admiration—and sometimes awe—for what the writer has accomplished.

Although the history of art is filled with wonderful paintings of a single face, a painting that includes several interesting faces clearly requires more skill.

White does something else with sentence length that can be very helpful to the less experienced writer. He frequently uses brief sentences at the beginning and at the end of a paragraph. Both are positions of special emphasis. The final sentence in paragraph 4 contains six words. The first sentence contains sixteen—but could have stopped after six. The first sentence in paragraph 5 contains six words. Usually, the first sentence in a paragraph is the topic sentence. As a general rule for the less experienced writer, the briefer the topic sentence, the better the paragraph will be. If you can reduce your point to a brief sentence—let's say a sentence with only one clause—then you will know exactly what you need to do in the paragraph. Similarly, at the end of the paragraph, a brief sentence can clinch your point with clarity and force.

Repetition can be effective, and so can variation. A skillful writer uses both. Repetition of words, phrases, and grammatical forms gives emphasis. Varying the lengths of sentences so that the briefer ones state the more important points makes those points stand out, giving emphasis and sharpening focus.

CAMP MEETING

1939

Over in the next county the Methodists have a camp ground, in a clump   1
of woods near East Machias.° They were in session there for about a week,
and I went over on Saturday for the *pièce de résistance*—Dr. Francis E.
Townsend° (himself) of California. I had long wanted to see the author of
America's favorite plan, and there he was, plain as day, right under the GOD
IS LOVE sign.

It was a peaceful spot, though it gave one a sultry, hemmed-in feeling,
as hardwood jingles often do. There was a ticket booth, where I paid my
quarter; and beyond was a lane opening out into the *al fresco* temple where
about six hundred people were gathered to hear the good news. They were
Methodist farmers and small-town merchants and their Methodist wives
and children and dogs, Townsendites from Townsend Club Number One
of East Machias, pilgrims from all over the State, honest, hopeful folks,
their faces grooved with the extra lines that come from leading godly,
toilsome lives. The men sat stiffly in the dark-blue suits that had carried
them through weddings, funerals, and Fair days. In a big circle surrounding
the temple were the cottages (seventy or eighty of them), little two-storey
frame shacks, set ten or a dozen feet apart, each with its front porch, its
stuffy upstairs bedroom, and its smell from the kitchen. Beyond, in a nobler
circle, were the backhouses, at the end of the tiny trails. The whole place,
even with hymns rising through the leafy boughs, had the faintly disreputable air which pervades any woodland rendezvous where the buildings
stand unoccupied for most of the year, attracting woodpeckers, sneak
thieves, and lovers in season.

On the dais, behind some field flowers, sat the Doctor, patiently
awaiting his time—a skinny, bespectacled little savior, with a big jaw, like
the Tin Woodman. He had arrived by plane the night before at the Bangor
airport a hundred miles away, and had driven over that morning for the
meeting. As I sat down a voice was lifted in prayer, heads were bowed.
The voice came from a loudspeaker suspended from the branch of an elm,
and the speaker was talking pointedly of milk and honey. When he quit,
Dr. Townsend's henchman, a baldish fellow with a businesslike manner,
took the stand and introduced the man who needed no introduction, Dr.
Francis E. Townsend, of California, the world's greatest humanitarian. We
all rose and clapped. Children danced on the outskirts, dogs barked, and
faces appeared in the windows of some of the nearest cottages. The Doctor
held out his hands for silence. He stood quietly, looking round over the

---

Machias: On the coast of northern Maine.

Dr. Francis E. Townsend: Dr. Townsend (1867–1960), in 1933, announced the Townsend
Plan, described in the essay, which was designed as a way to end the Great Depression.

assemblage. And then, to the old folks with their troubled, expectant faces, he said, simply:

"I like you people very much"

It was like a handclasp, a friendly arm placed round the shoulder.   *5*
Instantly his listeners warmed, and smiled, and wriggled with sudden newfound comfort.

"I have come nearly four thousand miles to see you," continued the Doctor. "You look like good Methodists, and I like that. I was raised in a Methodist family, so I know what it means."

He spoke calmly, without any platform tricks, and he sounded as though this was the first time he had ever expounded Townsendism. In words of one syllable he unfolded the plan which he had conceived, the plan which he knew would work, the plan which he promised to see enacted into law, so that all people might enjoy equally the good things of this life.

"The retirement of the elders is a matter of concern to the entire population." Grizzly heads nodded assent. Old eyes shone with new light.

"In a nation possessed of our natural resources, with great masses of gold and money at our command, it is unthinkable that conditions such as exist to-day should be tolerated. There is something radically wrong with any political philosophy which permits this to exist. Now, then, how did it come about?"

Dr. Townsend explained how it had come about. Flies buzzed in the   *10*
clearing. The sun pierced the branches overhead, struck down on the folding music stands of the musicians, gleamed on the bare thighs of young girls in shorts, strolling with their fellows outside the pale of economics. The world, on this hot Saturday afternoon, seemed very old and sad, very much in need of something. Maybe this Plan was it. I never heard a milder-mannered economist, nor one more fully convinced of the right and wisdom of his proposal. I looked at the audience, at the faces. They were the faces of men and women reared on trouble, and now they wanted a few years of comfort on earth, and then to be received into the lap of the Lord. I think Dr. Townsend wanted this for them: I'm sure *I* did.

"Business is stymied," murmured the Doctor. "Almost half the population is in dire want. Sixty millions of people cannot buy the products of industry." The Doctor's statistics were staggering and loose-jointed, but his tone was quietly authoritative. There could be small room for doubt.

He spoke disparagingly of the New Deal, and knocked all the alphabetical schemes for employing idle men. "Do you want to be taxed for these useless and futile activities?"

His audience shook their heads.

And all the while he spoke, the plan itself was unfolding—simply, logically. A child could have understood it. Levy a two per cent tax on the gross business of the country and divide the revenue among persons over sixty years of age, with the one stipulation that they spend the money ($200 a month) within a certain number of days.

"And mind you," said the Doctor, with a good-natured grin, "we don't   15
care a rap what you spend it for!"

The old folks clapped their hands and winked at one another. They
were already buying pretty things, these Methodists, were already paying off
old cankerous debts.

"We want you to have new homes, new furniture, new shoes and
clothes. We want you to travel and go places. You old folks have earned the
right to loaf, and you're going to do it luxuriously in the near future. The
effect on business, when all this money is put into circulation, will be
tremendous. Just let us have two billion dollars to distribute this month, and
see what happens!"

The sound of the huge sum titivated the group; two billion dollars
flashed across the clearing like a comet, trailing a wispy tail of excitement,
longing, hope.

"It may even be three," said the Doctor, thoughtfully, as though the
possibility had just occurred to him. "America has the facilities, all we need
is the sense to use them."

He said he was reminded of a story in the old McGuffey's Reader. The   20
one about the ship flying a distress signal, and another ship came to its
assistance. "Get us water!" shouted the captain. "We are perishing of thirst."

"Dip up and drink, you fools!" answered the captain of the other ship.
"You're in the mouth of the Amazon River."

"Friends," said the good Doctor, "we are in the mouth of the Amazon
River of Abundance. But we haven't the sense to dip up and drink."

It was a nice story, and went well.

Suddenly the Doctor switched from the words of promise to words
of threat. Lightly, with bony fingers, he strummed the strings of terror.
If we're going to save this democracy of ours (he said), we shall have to
begin soon. You've read about strikes in the great industrial centers; in a
very brief time you will read of riots. And when rioting starts, it will be
an easy matter for someone to seize the armed forces of the country and
put them to his own use. This has happened in Europe. It can happen
here.

The glade darkened ominously. Trees trembled in all their limbs. The   25
ground, hard-packed under the Methodist heel, swam in the vile twilight of
Fascist doom. Still the little Doctor's voice droned on—calm, full of humility,
devoid of theatrics. Just the simple facts, simply told.

And then the vexatious question of money to carry on with. The
audience shifted, got a new grip on their seats with their behinds. The ancient
ceremony of plate-passing was a familiar and holy rite that had to be gone
through with. The Doctor carefully disclaimed any personal ambitions,
financial or political. "I don't want a fortune," he said, confidentially. "I mean
that. I don't seek wealth. For one thing, it might ruin my fine son. But it does
take money to educate people to a new idea. Give us a penny a day and we'll
educate the next Congress."

A joke or two, to restore amiability; another poke at Uncle Sam; another mention of the need for funds to carry on with; and the speech was over.

It had been an impressive performance. Most speeches lack the sincerity the Doctor had given his; not many speeches are so simply made and pleasantly composed. It had been more like a conversation with an old friend. I had listened, sitting there near the musicians, with all the sympathy that within me lay, and (I trust) with an open mind. Even a middle-aged hack has his moments of wanting to see the world get along. After all, this was no time for cynicism; most of what Dr. Townsend had said, God knows, was true enough. If anybody could devise a system for distributing wealth more evenly, more power to him. One man's guess was as good as another's. Well, pretty nearly as good. I pocketed the few scribbled notes I had made and gave myself over to a mood of summer afternoon despondency and world decay.

The chairman rose and announced that the meeting would be thrown open to questions, but that the time was short, so please speak right up. It was at this point that Dr. Francis E. Townsend (of California) began quietly to come apart, like an inexpensive toy. The questions came slowly, and they were neither very numerous nor very penetrating. Nor was there any heckling spirit in the audience: people were with him, not against him. But in the face of inquiry, the Doctor's whole manner changed. He had apparently been through this sort of thing before and was as wary as a squirrel. It spoiled his afternoon to be asked anything. Details of Townsendism were irksome in the extreme—he wanted to keep the Plan simple and beautiful, like young love before sex has reared its head. And now he was going to have to answer a lot of nasty old questions.

"How much would it cost to administer?" inquired a thrifty grand-   *30*
mother, rising to her feet.

The Doctor frowned, "Why, er," he said. (This was the first "er" of the afternoon.) "Why, not a great deal. There's nothing about it, that is, there's no reason why it needs to cost much." He then explained that it was just a matter of the Secretary of the Treasury making out forty-eight checks each month, one to each State. Surely that wouldn't take much of the Secretary's time. Then these big checks would be broken up by the individual State administrators, who would pay out the money to the people over sixty years of age who qualified. "We're not going to have any administrative problems to speak of, at all," said the Doctor, swallowing his spit. The little grandmother nodded and sat down.

"Can a person get the pension if they hold property?" inquired an old fellow who had suddenly remembered his home, and his field of potatoes.

"Yes, certainly," replied the Doctor, shifting from one foot to the other. "But we *do* have a stipulation; I mean, in our plan we are going to say that the money shall not go to anybody who has a gainful pursuit." An uneasy look crossed the farmer's face: very likely he was wondering whether his field of potatoes was gainful. Maybe his potato bugs would stand him in good stead at last. Things already didn't look so simple.

"How much bookkeeping would it mean for a business man?" asked a weary capitalist.

"Bookkeeping?" repeated the Doctor vaguely. "Oh, I don't think   *35* there will be any trouble about bookkeeping. It is so simple. Every business man just states what his gross is for the thirty-day period, and two per cent of it goes to pay the old people. In the Hawaiian Islands they already have a plan much like mine in operation. It works beautifully, and I was amazed, when I was there, at how few people it took to administer it. No, there'll be no difficulty about bookkeeping."

"How will the Townsend Plan affect foreign trade?" asked an elderly thinker on Large Affairs.

Doctor Townsend gave him a queer look—not exactly hateful, but the kind of look a parent sometimes gives a child on an off day.

"Foreign trade?" he replied, somewhat weakly. "Foreign trade? Why should we concern ourselves with foreign trade?" He stopped. But then he thought maybe he had given short measure on that one, so he told a story of a corn-flakes factory, and all the corn came from some foreign country. What kind of way was that—buying corn from foreigners?

Next question: "Would a person receiving the pension be allowed to use it to pay off a mortgage?"

Answer: "Yes. Pay your debts. Let's set our government a good   *40* example!" (Applause.)

And now a gentleman down front—an apple-cheeked old customer with a twinkle: "Doctor, would buying a drink count as spending your money?"

"A drink?" echoed the Doctor. Then he put on a hearty manner. "Why, if anybody came to me and wanted to drink himself into an early grave with money from the fund, I'd say, 'Go to it, old boy!'" There was a crackle of laughter, but the Doctor knew he was on slippery footing. "Don't misunderstand me," he put in. "Let's not put too many restrictions on morality. The way to bring about temperance in this world is to bring up our young sons and daughters decently, and teach them the evils of abuse. (Applause.) And now, friends, I must go. It has been a most happy afternoon."

The meeting broke up. Townsendites rose and started down the aisles to shake hands reverently with their chief. The chairman announced a take of eighty dollars and three cents. Life began to settle into its stride again. Pilgrims filed out of the pews and subsided in rocking chairs on the porches of the little houses. Red and white paper streamers, festooning the trees, trembled in the fitful air; and soft drinks began to flow at the booth beyond the Inner Circle. The Doctor, waylaid by a group of amateur photographers, posed in front of an American flag, and then departed in a Dodge sedan for the airport—a cloud-draped Messiah, his dream packed away in a brief case for the next performance. On the porch of a cottage called "Nest o'Rest" three old ladies rocked and rocked and rocked. And from a score of rusty stovepipes in the woods rose the first thick coils of smoke from the kitchen fires, where America's housewives, never quite giving up, were laboriously preparing one more meal in the long, long procession. The vision of milk and honey, it comes and goes. But the odor of cooking goes on forever.

Questions for Understanding

1. Where is the first clue to White's attitude toward Dr. Townsend and this meeting?
2. When Dr. Townsend began to speak, White says, "He spoke calmly, without any platform tricks. . . ." Is White referring to Dr. Townsend favorably in this part of his description?
3. Further on in his description of Dr. Townsend, White says, "And all the while he spoke, the plan itself was unfolding—simply, logically. A child could have understood it." Is this meant to be a favorable description?
4. What is White's attitude toward the six hundred people who have come to listen to Dr. Townsend?
5. Here are the final two sentences of the essay: "The vision of milk and honey, it comes and goes. But the odor of cooking goes on forever." What would you say White's tone and attitude are here?

Suggestions for Writing

1. Describe a public speaker you have recently heard. Did characteristics of the speaker's manner, body language, or choice of words make you skeptical of the truthfulness of what the speaker was saying?
2. Compare and contrast the diction and manner Dr. Townsend used to persuade his Methodist audience with the diction and manner of a hypothetical clergyman delivering a sermon to the same audience.
3. Compare and contrast Dr. Townsend's diction and manner with those of a current politician who is a strong advocate of a particular plan.
4. Write an essay in which you prove that Dr. Townsend either is or is not a demagogue.
5. Discuss the main similarities and differences between the Townsend Plan and Social Security. Which do you think is the better plan?

Katherine Anne Porter

[1890–1980]

ike Nadine Gordimer, Katherine Anne Porter is better known for her works of fiction than for her nonfiction. But with both these writers, as with others, the characteristics that make the fiction first rate also contribute to the quality of the nonfiction. One notable characteristic of Porter's fiction is its *translucence:* a highly polished surface objectivity that ultimately leads the reader to a sense of the protagonist's inner turmoil and failure of awareness. Such revelations are also frequent themes in Porter's essays.

Porter has said that the only character in her fiction who is autobiographical is the young woman Miranda, the main character in several stories and in the short novels *Pale Horse, Pale Rider* and *Old Mortality.* In spite of all the attractive qualities Miranda is given in *Old Mortality,* and in spite of her resolve to know the truth "about what happens to me," the closing words tell us that she makes this promise to herself "in her hopefulness, in her ignorance."

Here, in the essays "St. Augustine and the Bullfight" and "The Necessary Enemy," Porter also delves into the matter of awareness, of how difficult it is to know the truth about oneself and what one really feels. In "La Conquistadora," on the other hand, we meet a woman who has become so obsessed with the desire to possess that she is hardly aware of anything that is not related to what she owns or claims. In "Jacqueline Kennedy," surprisingly, Porter writes about a woman who has no shortage of awareness. As seen by Porter, Jackie exhibits not only consummate self-knowledge but also remarkable intuition about the perceptions of others.

Two of the four essays have a Mexican setting, as do several of Porter's short stories, including one of her very best, "Flowering Judas." Porter regarded Mexico as her "familiar country." As a Texan, she was born a neighbor, and as a girl she listened to her father tell "enchanting stories" of the "part of his youth" he had spent in Mexico. As a visitor during the Obregón Revolution, she witnessed changes that she hoped would bring social justice to the vast underclass. "It was as if an old field had been watered," she wrote, "and all the long-buried seeds flourished." She saw "the renascence of Mexican art—a veritable rebirth, very conscious, very powerful, of a deeply racial and personal art. . . . The Mexicans have enriched their national life through the medium of their native arts. It is in everything they do and are." About the Mexican temperament, she said that she especially liked the "aesthetic magnificence, and, above all, the passion for individual expression without hypocrisy, which is the true genius of the race." In 1922, in the employ of the Mexican government, Porter helped put together an exhibition of Mexican folk art in Los Angeles, and in conjunction with the exhibition, she wrote *Outline of Mexican Popular Arts and Crafts.* Porter's love of Mexico led to the circulation in Mexico of a song about her, "La Norteña."

Porter was born in Indian Creek, Texas, the fourth of five children. In earlier generations, her family had lived in Virginia, Kentucky, and Louisiana. Among her distant relatives were the pioneer Daniel Boone and the writer

Sidney Porter (O. Henry). Her mother died when Porter was two years old, and the responsibility for her upbringing fell largely to her paternal grandmother. When Porter was eleven, her grandmother died. Porter's father, who had become deeply melancholic after the death of his wife, sent her off to convent schools. At sixteen she ran away to get married, but the marriage ended in divorce at nineteen. In later years she married twice more, but each of those marriages also was brief.

In 1930, Porter published her first book, *Flowering Judas and Other Stories.* An enlarged version was published in 1935. She published *Pale Horse, Pale Rider: Three Short Novels* in 1939 and, in 1944, *The Leaning Tower and Other Stories.* The novel *Ship of Fools* came out in 1962, *The Collected Essays* in 1970.

JACQUELINE KENNEDY

1964

I saw Mrs. Kennedy only twice—first, at the Inaugural Ball in the   1
Armory in Washington; second, at the dinner in honor of the Nobel Prize
winners, in the White House. In each of these glimpses she looked like all her
photographs, those endless hundreds of images of her cast on screens and
printed pages everywhere through the short, brilliant years of her public
career beside her husband; only, in breathing life she was younger, more
tender and beautiful. She had the most generous and innocent smile in the
world, and her wide-set eyes really lighted up when she spoke to her guests.
Old-fashioned character readers of faces believed that this breadth between
the eyes was the infallible sign of a confiding, believing nature, one not given
to suspicions or distrust of the motives of others. It might very well be true.
On account of this feature, a girl reporter described her as resembling a
lioness. I do not think she resembles a lioness in the least, but I am ready to
say she is lionhearted. A merrier, sweeter face than hers never dawned upon
the official Washington scene—so poxed with hardbitten visages, male and
female, that bring joy to nobody—but even the swiftest of first glances could
not mistake it for a weak face. It was and is full of strong character and tragic
seriousness lying not quite dormant just under the surface, waiting for the
Furies to announce themselves.

Certain members of her family and long-term friends surmised these
latencies, but could not name them—someone of them called her a
"worrier." This is obviously not the word to name her special kind of
hand-to-hand immediate concentration on the varied demands and emer-
gencies of her days all through her life as we have known it—which may
be called the ordeal by camera—but it is easy to see how a bystander, no
matter how near the relationship, might misread her, never having seen
in action the austerity, the reserve force and the spiritual discipline which
no one expects in so young a creature. There had not been any occasion
sufficient to call them out. She had been such a fashionable sort of young
girl, brought up in the most conventional way: the good schools, the travel,
the accomplishments and sports, the prepared social life. The whole surface
was smooth as satin; she even wore clothes almost too well, a little too
near the professional model. But she outgrew this quickly and was
becoming truly elegant at an unusually early age. She had the mistaken
daydream that many very nice girls do have, that to be a newspaper reporter
and go about pointing cameras at perfect strangers was a romantic adventure. She got over this speedily too, and became herself the target of
every passing camera and every eager beaver of a reporter who could get
near her. And what a record they gave us of a life lived hourly in love
with joy, yet with every duty done and every demand fulfilled: nothing
overlooked or neglected.

Remember that veiled head going in and out of how many churches, to and from how many hospitals and institutions and official functions without number: that endless procession of newly sprung potentates to entertain royally! And always her splendid outdoor life—water-skiing with Caroline, both their faces serenely happy, fearless; driving a pony cartfull of Kennedy children, the infant John John on her lap; going headfirst off that hunter at the rail fence, and in perfect form too, her face perhaps not exactly merry, but calm, undismayed. An expert, trained fall that was; one would have to ride a horse to know how good it was, and what a superb rider Mrs. Kennedy is.

There is another snapshot of her going at a fine stride on her beautiful horse; and always that lovely look of quiet rapture in her high-spirited, high-stepping play. She never seemed happier than when swimming or skating or water-skiing, or sailing, or riding, or playing with her children. Who will forget the pictures of her in sopping wet slacks, bare feet, tangled hair, blissful smile, on the beach; with her husband nearby, rolling in the sand, holding Caroline, still in her baby-fat stage, at arm's length above him?

All of us heard, I'm sure, some lively stories of the pitched battles of early marriage, and there were dire predictions that little good would come of it. Nonsense! What would you expect of two high-strung, keen-witted, intensely conscious and gifted people deeply in love and both of them with notions of their own about almost everything? It was not in the stars for that pair to sink gently into each other's arms in a soft corner, murmuring a note of music in perfect key. It seems to have been a good, fair, running argument in the open—heaven knows there was no place for them to hide; eyes, ears and cameras were everywhere by then—and we know that things were coming out well. We could see it in their expressions as time ran on, and the cameras intercepted their glances at each other, saw them off guard at moments of greeting, of parting, their clasped hands as they came out of the hospital after Patrick was born—anybody could see that the marriage was growing into something grand and final, fateful and tragic, with birth and death and love in it at every step. Their lives were uniting, meshing firmly in the incessant uproar and confusions of the most incredibly complicated situation imaginable. But they were young, they were where they wanted to be, they loved what they were doing and felt up to it; and they dealt every day, together in their quite different ways, supporting and balancing each other, with a world in such disorder and in the presence of such danger, international and domestic, as we have not seen since Hitler's time. And the entertainments, the music, the dancing, the feasting—there hasn't been such a born giver of feasts in the White House, a First Lady who recognized that a good part of her duties were social, since Dolley Madison. Mrs. Kennedy had the womanly knack of making even dull parties appear to be pleasures. But the manner of the President and his wife to each other was always simple, courteous and pleasant, without gestures, without trying. It was a pleasant thing to see, and I began to be grateful for those swarming pestiferous cameras that could show me such reassuring steadfastness with such grace and goodness.

The only moment of uneasiness I ever saw in Mrs. Kennedy's pictured face was at the first showing of the *Mona Lisa* in Washington, when somebody concerned in the arrangements did something awkward, I forget what; she looked distressed. We know now she was expecting her fifth child, five within a period of little more than seven years: she had already lost two, and was to lose Patrick. Every child had cost her a major operation or a serious illness. This is real suffering, and yet she ceded nothing to the natural pains of women, but bore her afflictions as part of her human lot, rose and went about her life again.

I remember so vividly how she looked at the Inaugural Ball. In that vast place more fit for horse shows than balls, the stalls where we sat were railed in with raw pine, champagne was chilled in large zinc buckets such as they water horses in at country race tracks; there were miles and miles of droopy draperies and a lot of flags, and a quite impressive display of jewels and furs and seriously expensive-looking clothes. Also we listened to a peculiarly pointless program of popular songs: first, the Sidewalks of New York kind of stuff, then Negro jazz, not the best of its kind either; besides two or three bloodcurdling little ditties dedicated to Mrs. Kennedy; and I believe, I am not certain, that they were sung and played by the composers, young women who should have been warned off. It was acutely embarrassing; and altogether it was the oddest mixture of international grandeur and the tackiest little county fair you ever saw. I love county fairs, and I love grand occasions; but I don't like them mixed. So I remarked on the spot—still having the Coronation of Queen Elizabeth II in mind's eye—that we would never, it was clear, as a nation, learn how properly to conduct our ceremonial events.

The taking of the oath, outdoors in January, if you please, had been a series of gaffes. But that was over, and the young First Lady came to the big Ball at the Armory, one of five or six, I believe, going on all over town, and sat there in her white gown, motionless as a rose on its stem, watching her husband adoringly. She went away early, for John John had been born seven weeks before.

Later, by a year or more maybe, at the dinner given in the White House for the various Nobel Prize winners, and runners-up, we were having cocktails in the East Room, and I saw and greeted all sorts of delightful old acquaintances I hadn't seen for twenty years and may never see again—I seem nearly always to be somewhere else!—when the strains of "Hail to the Chief" gave us the cue to set down our glasses and turn toward the great door. There was no roll of drums, no silver trumpet fanfare, no; just a wistful, rather wiggly little tune, very appealing and sweet, and there stood the President and Mrs. Kennedy before us, amiable and so good-looking and so confident, with all the life and all the world before them, and why should it ever end? Very happily and easily we formed a long line and went past them shaking their hands lightly—think of all the hands they had to shake every day!—and then we went on to dinner and a merry party afterward, and it was all so gentle, and reassuring, in that lovely house, so well done and so easy.

Atmosphere, tone, are very elusive things in a house, and they depend   *10* entirely on the persons who live there. . . . The White House that evening was a most happy place to be, and I shall never see it again, for I wish to remember it as it was then. What style they had, those young people! And what looks. . . .

Then I went to Europe and came back a year later, on All Souls' Eve, to Washington. And now I am writing this, on the 22nd of December, 1963, on the day of the Month's Mind Mass, and the memorial lighting of candles at the Lincoln Memorial. The perpetual light that Mrs. Kennedy set at the President's grave can be seen from almost any point in this city. This light is only one of the many things Mrs. Kennedy asked for and received during that night of November 22.

I have a dear friend whose beloved wife died not long ago, and he wrote me an account of her going away, and he said: "I never heard of, or imagined, such an admirable performance!" I knew exactly what he meant, and within a few days I witnessed Mrs. Kennedy's performance, at the great crisis of her life, and it was flawless, and entirely admirable; I have no words good enough to praise it. The firmness with which she refused to leave the body of her husband, keeping her long vigil beside him, but not idly, not in tears, planning and arranging for his burial to the last detail. What relentless will she showed, fending off the officious sympathy of all those necessary persons who swarm about tragic occasions, each anxious to be of service, true, but all too ready to manage and meddle. She refused to be cheated of her right to this most terrible moment of her life, this long torment of farewell and relinquishment, of her wish to be conscious of every moment of her suffering: and this endurance did not fail her to the very end, and beyond, and will not fail her.

What I think of now is the gradual change in that lovely face through the fiercely shattering years when she and her husband raced like twin rockets to their blinding personal disaster which involved a whole world. Among the last pictures I remember is Mrs. Kennedy as she stood with her two children in the cold light of a late-fall day—and you don't have such perfectly well-behaved children at their age unless you have known how to love them and discipline them!—watching the President's coffin being carried from the White House on its way to the Rotunda. She stood there staring a little sidelong, as if she could not dare to look directly. The first shock was over, that head-on collision with death in one of its most wasteful and senseless forms had taken place without warning, as it always does, but the dazed blind look was gone from her eyes, replaced by a look of the full knowledge of the nature of Evil, its power and its bestial imbecility. She stared with dawning anger in her eyes, in the set of her mouth, yet with the deepest expression of grief I have ever seen, a total anguish of desolation, but proud, severe, implacable.

No one who witnessed that three-day funeral service, in presence or by screen, can ever say again that we, as a nation cannot properly conduct the ceremonies of our state. We have been well taught.

Questions for Understanding

1. Among Jacqueline Kennedy's favorable qualities, according to Porter, were her "austerity," "reserve force," and "spiritual discipline." What does Porter want these terms, individually, to convey about Mrs. Kennedy?
2. Why is Porter confident that the "pitched battles" early in the marriage of Jacqueline and John Kennedy were not a bad omen?
3. In concluding her description of the scene at the White House dinner for Nobel Prize winners, Porter offers this observation: "Atmosphere, tone, are very elusive things in a house, and they depend entirely on the persons who live there." What are some of the things that determine the atmosphere and tone of a house?
4. Porter quotes this sentence from a letter from a friend whose wife had died not long ago: "I never heard of, or imagined, such an admirable performance!" What are some of the images Porter assumes that sentence will allow her to share with her readers?
5. What does Porter suggest was Jacqueline Kennedy's greatest contribution to her country?

Suggestions for Writing

1. Porter devotes the first paragraph of the essay to describing Mrs. Kennedy's face, confident that it reveals a great deal about the kind of person she is. Have you ever studied a face and later discovered that the conclusions you came to about character and personality were wrong? Describe what you saw, tell what you concluded, and discuss the reality.
2. Have you observed someone at the great crisis of his or her life and, as a result, formed a strong judgment about the quality of the person? Describe the crisis, tell what revealing behavior you observed, and discuss the extent to which your judgment turned out to be correct.
3. In concluding her description of the White House on the night of the dinner for the Nobel Prize winners, Porter says, "The White House that evening was a most happy place to be, and I shall never see it again, for I wish to remember it as it was then." Can you remember an occasion in your life when you had a similar feeling? Describe what it was that gave the occasion its atmosphere and tone. Describe the moments that are indelibly impressed on your memory.
4. Porter was very impressed with the behavior of the young Kennedy children at their father's funeral. She says, "you don't have such perfectly well-behaved children at their age unless you have known how to love them and discipline them!" Write an essay in which you discuss how to love and discipline a young

child so that, at an important ceremonial or social occasion, it might be said that he or she was perfectly well-behaved.

5. Do you recall seeing or reading about another momentous ceremonial occasion in American history? Do some research to familiarize yourself again with what took place on that occasion. Then discuss whether the way that ceremony was conducted proved that the United States could, or could not, "properly conduct the ceremonies of our state."

ST. AUGUSTINE AND THE BULLFIGHT

1955

Adventure. The word has become a little stale to me, because it has been   *1*
applied too often to the dull physical exploits of professional "adventurers"
who write books about it, if they know how to write; if not, they hire ghosts
who quite often can't write either.

I don't read them, but rumors of them echo, and re-echo. The book
business at least is full of heroes who spend their time, money and energy
worrying other animals, manifestly their betters such as lions and tigers, to
death in trackless jungles and deserts only to be crossed by the stoutest
motorcar; or another feeds hooks to an inedible fish like the tarpon; another
crosses the ocean on a raft, living on plankton and seaweed, why ever, I
wonder? And always always, somebody is out climbing mountains, and
writing books about it, which are read by quite millions of persons who feel,
apparently, that the next best thing to going there yourself is to hear from
somebody who went. And I have heard more than one young woman remark
that, though she did not want to get married, still, she would like to have a
baby, for the adventure: not lately though. That was a pose of the 1920s and
very early '30s. Several of them did it, too, but I do not know of any who
wrote a book about it—good for them.

W. B. Yeats remarked—I cannot find the passage now, so must say it in
other words—that the unhappy man (unfortunate?) was one whose adventures outran his capacity for experience, capacity for experience being, I
should say, roughly equal to the faculty for understanding what has happened
to one. The difference then between mere adventure and a real experience
might be this? That adventure is something you seek for pleasure, or even for
profit, like a gold rush or invading a country; for the illusion of being more
alive than ordinarily, the thing you will to occur; but experience is what really
happens to you in the long run; the truth that finally overtakes you.

Adventure is sometimes fun, but not too often. Not if you can
remember what really happened; all of it. It passes, seems to lead nowhere
much, is something to tell friends to amuse them, maybe. "Once upon a
time," I can hear myself saying, for I once said it, "I scaled a cliff in Boulder,
Colorado, with my bare hands, and in Indian moccasins, bare-legged. And at
nearly the top, after six hours of feeling for toe- and fingerholds, and the
gayest feeling in the world that when I got to the top I should see something
wonderful, something that sounded awfully like a bear growled out of a cave,
and I scuttled down out of there in a hurry." This is a fact. I had never climbed
a mountain in my life, never had the least wish to climb one. But there I was,
for perfectly good reasons, in a hut on a mountainside in heavenly sunny
though sometimes stormy weather, so I went out one morning and scaled a
very minor cliff: alone, unsuitably clad, in the season when rattlesnakes are

casting their skins; and if it was not a bear in that cave, it was some kind of unfriendly animal who growls at people; and this ridiculous escapade, which was nearly six hours of the hardest work I ever did in my life, toeholds and fingerholds on a cliff, put me to bed for just nine days with a complaint the local people called "muscle poisoning." I don't know exactly what they meant, but I do remember clearly that I could not turn over in bed without help and in great agony. And did it teach me anything? I think not, for three years later I was climbing a volcano in Mexico, that celebrated unpronounceably named volcano, Popocatepetl which everybody who comes near it climbs sooner or later; but was that any reason for me to climb it? No. And I was knocked out for weeks, and that finally did teach me: I am not supposed to go climbing things. Why did I not know in the first place? For me, this sort of thing must come under the head of Adventure.

I think it is pastime of rather an inferior sort; yet I have heard men tell yarns like this only a very little better: their mountains were higher, or their sea was wider, or their bear was bigger and noisier, or their cliff was steeper and taller, yet there was no point whatever to any of it except that it had happened. This is not enough. May it not be, perhaps, that experience, that is, the thing that happens to a person living from day to day, is anything at all that sinks in? is, without making any claims, a part of your growing and changing life? what it is that happens in your mind, your heart?

Adventure hardly ever seems to be that at the time it is happening: not under that name, at least. Adventure may be an afterthought, something that happens in the memory with imaginative trimmings if not downright lying, so that one should suppress it entirely, or go the whole way and make honest fiction of it. My own habit of writing fiction has provided a wholesome exercise to my natural, incurable tendency to try to wangle the sprawling mess of our existence in this bloody world into some kind of shape: almost any shape will do, just so it is recognizably made with human hands, one small proof the more of the validity and reality of the human imagination. But even within the most limited frame what utter confusion shall prevail if you cannot take hold firmly, and draw the exact line between what really happened, and what you have since imagined about it. Perhaps my soul will be saved after all in spite of myself because now and then I take some unmanageable, indigestible fact and turn it into fiction; cause things to happen with some kind of logic—my own logic, of course—and everything ends as I think it should end and no back talk, or very little, from anybody about it. Otherwise, and except for this safety device, I should be the greatest liar unhung. (When was the last time anybody was hanged for lying?) What is Truth? I often ask myself. Who knows?

A publisher asked me a great while ago to write a kind of autobiography, and I was delighted to begin; it sounded very easy when he said, "Just start, and tell everything you remember until now!" I wrote about a hundred pages before I realized, or admitted, the hideous booby trap into which I had fallen. First place, I remember quite a lot of stupid and boring things: there were other times when my life seemed merely an endurance test, or a quite mysterious but not very interesting and often monotonous effort at survival on the most primitive terms. There are dozens of things that might be entertaining but I have no intention of telling them, because they are nobody's business; and endless little gossipy incidents that might entertain indulgent friends for a minute, but in print they look as silly as they really are. Then, there are the tremendous, unmistakable, life-and-death crises, the scalding, the bone-breaking events, the lightnings that shatter the landscape of the soul—who would write that by request? No, that is for a secretly written manuscript to be left with your papers, and if your executor is a good friend, who has probably been brought up on St. Augustine's *Confessions,* he will read it with love and attention and gently burn it to ashes for your sake.

Yet I intend to write something about my life, here and now, and so far as I am able without one touch of fiction, and I hope to keep it as shapeless and unforeseen as the events of life itself from day to day. Yet, look! I have already betrayed my occupation, and dropped a clue in what would be the right place if this were fiction, by mentioning St. Augustine when I hadn't meant to until it came in its right place in life, not in art. Literary art, at least, is the business of setting human events to rights and giving them meanings that, in fact, they do not possess, or not obviously, or not the meanings the artist feels they should have—we do understand so little of what is really happening to us in any given moment. Only by remembering, comparing, waiting to know the consequences can we sometimes, in a flash of light, see what a certain event really meant, what it was trying to tell us. So this will be notes on a fateful thing that happened to me when I was young and did not know much about the world or about myself. I had been reading St. Augustine's *Confessions* since I was able to read at all, and I thought I had read every word, perhaps because I did know certain favorite passages by heart. But then, it was something like having read the Adventures of Gargantua by Rabelais when I was twelve and enjoying it; when I read it again at thirty-odd. I was astounded at how much I had overlooked in the earlier reading, and wondered what I thought I had seen there.

So it was with St. Augustine and my first bullfight. Looking back nearly thirty-five years on my earliest days in Mexico, it strikes me that, for a fairly serious young woman who was in the country for the express purpose of attending a Revolution, and studying Mayan people art, I fell in with a most lordly gang of fashionable international hoodlums. Of course I had Revolutionist friends and artist friends, and they were gay and easy and poor as I was. This other mob was different: they were French, Spanish, Italian, Polish, and they all had titles and good names: a duke, a count, a marquess, a baron, and they all were in some flashy money-getting enterprise like importing cognac wholesale, or selling sports cars to newly rich politicians; and they all drank like fish and played fast games like polo or tennis or jai alai; they haunted the wings of theaters, drove slick cars like maniacs, but expert maniacs, never missed a bullfight or a boxing match; all were reasonably young and they had ladies to match, mostly imported and all speaking French. These persons stalked pleasure as if it were big game—they took their fun exactly where they found it, and the way they liked it, and they worked themselves to exhaustion at it. A fast, tough, expensive, elegant, high lowlife they led, for the ladies and gentlemen each in turn had other friends you would have had to see to believe; and from time to time, without being in any way involved or engaged, I ran with this crowd of shady characters and liked their company and ways very much. I don't like gloomy sinners, but the merry ones charm me. And one of them introduced me to Shelley. And Shelley, whom I knew in the most superficial way, who remained essentially a stranger to me to the very end, led me, without in the least ever knowing what he had done, into one of the most important and lasting experiences of my life.

He was British, a member of the poet's family; said to be authentic   *10* great-great-nephew; he was rich and willful, and had come to Mexico young and wild, and mad about horses, of course. Coldly mad—he bred them and raced them and sold them with the stony detachment and merciless appraisal of the true horse lover—they call it love, and it could be that: but he did not like them. "What is there to like about a horse but his good points? If he has a vice, shoot him or send him to the bullring; that is the only way to work a vice out of the breed!"

Once, during a riding trip while visiting a ranch, my host gave me a stallion to ride, who instantly took the bit in his teeth and bolted down a steep mountain trail. I managed to stick on, held an easy rein, and he finally ran himself to a standstill in an open field. My disgrace with Shelley was nearly complete. Why? Because the stallion was not a good horse. I should have refused to mount him. I said it was a question how to refuse the horse your host offered you—Shelley thought it no question at all. "A lady," he reminded me, "can always excuse herself gracefully from anything she doesn't wish to do." I said, "I wish that were really true," for the argument about the bullfight was already well started. But the peak of his disapproval of me, my motives, my temperament, my ideas, my ways, was reached when, to provide a diversion and end a dull discussion, I told him the truth: that I had liked being run away with, it had been fun and the kind of thing that had to happen unexpectedly, you couldn't arrange for it. I tried to convey to him my exhilaration, my pure joy when this half-broken, crazy beast took off down that trail with just a hoofhold between a cliff on one side and a thousand-foot drop on the other. He said merely that such utter frivolity surprised him in someone whom he had mistaken for a well-balanced, intelligent girl; and I remember thinking how revoltingly fatherly he sounded, exactly like my own father in his stuffier moments.

He was a stocky, red-faced, muscular man with broad shoulders, hard-jowled, with bright blue eyes glinting from puffy lids; his hair was a grizzled tan, and I guessed him about fifty years old, which seemed a great age to me then. But he mentioned that his Mexican wife had "died young" about three years before, and that his eldest son was only eleven years old. His whole appearance was so remarkably like the typical horsy, landed-gentry sort of Englishman one meets in books by Frenchmen or Americans, if this were fiction I should feel obliged to change his looks altogether, thus falling into one stereotype to avoid falling into another. However, so Shelley did look, and his clothes were magnificent and right beyond words, and never new-looking and never noticeable at all except one could not help observing sooner or later that he was beyond argument the best-dressed man in America, North or South; it was that kind of typical British inconspicuous good taste: he had it, superlatively. He was evidently leading a fairly rakish life, or trying to, but he was of a cast-iron conventionality even in that. We did not fall in love—far from it. We struck up a hands-off, quaint, farfetched, tetchy kind of friendship which consisted largely of good advice about worldly things from him, mingled with critical marginal notes on my character—a character of which I could not recognize a single trait; and if I said, helplessly, "But I am not in the least like that," he would answer, "Well, you should be!" or "Yes, you are, but you don't know it."

This man took me to my first bullfight. I'll tell you later how St. Augustine comes into it. It was the first bullfight of that season: Covadonga Day; April; clear, hot blue sky; and a long procession of women in flower-covered carriages; wearing their finest lace veils and highest combs and gauziest fans; but I shan't describe a bullfight. By now surely there is no excuse for anyone who can read or even hear or see not to know pretty well what goes on in a bullring. I shall say only that Sánchez Mejías and Rudolfo Gaona each killed a bull that day; but before the Grand March of the toreros, Hattie Weston rode her thoroughbred High School gelding into the ring to thunders of shouts and brassy music.

She was Shelley's idol. "Look at that girl, for God's sake," and his voice thickened with feeling, "the finest rider in the world," he said in his dogmatic way, and it is true I have not seen better since.

She was a fine buxom figure of a woman, a highly colored blonde with   15
a sweet, childish face; probably forty years old, and perfectly rounded in all directions; a big round bust, and that is the word, there was nothing plural about it, just a fine, warm-looking bolster straight across her front from armpit to armpit; fine firm round hips—again, why the plural? It was an ample seat born to a sidesaddle, as solid and undivided as the bust, only more of it. She was tightly laced and her waist was small. She wore a hard-brimmed dark gray Spanish sailor hat, sitting straight and shallow over her large golden knot of hair; a light gray bolero and a darker gray riding skirt—not a Spanish woman's riding dress, nor yet a man's, but something tight and fit and formal and appropriate. And there she went, the most elegant woman in the saddle I have ever seen, graceful and composed in her perfect style, with her wonderful, lightly dancing, learned horse, black and glossy as shoe polish, perfectly under control—no, not under control at all, you might have thought, but just dancing and showing off his paces by himself for his own pleasure.

"She makes the bullfight seem like an anticlimax," said Shelley, tenderly.

I had not wanted to come to this bullfight. I had never intended to see a bullfight at all. I do not like the slaughtering of animals as sport. I am carnivorous, I love all the red juicy meats and all the fishes. Seeing animals killed for food on the farm in summers shocked and grieved me sincerely, but it did not cure my taste for flesh. My family for as far back as I know anything about them, only about 450 years, were the huntin', shootin', fishin' sort: their houses were arsenals and their dominion over the animal kingdom was complete and unchallenged. When I was older, my father remarked on my tiresome timidity, or was I just pretending to finer feelings than those of the society around me? He hardly knew which was the more tiresome but that was perhaps only a personal matter. Morally, if I wished to eat meat I should be able to kill the animal—otherwise it appeared that I was willing to nourish myself on other people's sins? For he supposed I considered it a sin. Otherwise why bother about it? Or was it just something unpleasant I wished to avoid? Maintaining my own purity—and a very doubtful kind of purity he found it, too—at the expense of the guilt of others? Altogether, my father managed to make a very sticky question of it, and for some years at intervals I made it a matter of conscience to kill an animal or bird, something I intended to eat. I gave myself and the beasts some horrible times, through fright and awkwardness, and to my shame, nothing cured me of my taste for flesh. All forms of cruelty offend me bitterly, and this repugnance is inborn, absolutely impervious to any arguments, or even insults, at which the red-blooded lovers of blood sports are very expert; they don't admire me at all, any more than I admire them. . . . Ah, me, the contradictions, the paradoxes! I was once perfectly capable of keeping a calf for a pet until he outgrew the yard in the country and had to be sent to the pastures. His subsequent fate I leave you to guess. Yes, it is all revoltingly sentimental and, worse than that, confused. My defense is that no matter whatever else this world seemed to promise me, never once did it promise to be simple.

So, for a great tangle of emotional reasons I had no intention of going to a bullfight. But Shelley was so persistently unpleasant about my cowardice, as he called it flatly, I just wasn't able to take the thrashing any longer. Partly, too, it was his natural snobbery; smart people of the world did not have such feelings; it was to him a peculiarly provincial if not downright Quakerish attitude. "I have some Quaker ancestors," I told him. "How absurd of you!" he said, and really meant it.

The bullfight question kept popping up and had a way of spoiling other occasions that should have been delightful. Shelley was one of those men, of whose company I feel sometimes that I have had more than my fair share, who simply do not know how to drop a subject, or abandon a position once they have declared it. Constitutionally incapable of admitting defeat, or even its possibility, even when he had not the faintest shadow of right to expect a victory—for why should he make a contest of my refusal to go to a bullfight?—he would start an argument during the theater intermissions, at the fronton, at a street fair, on a stroll in the Alameda, at a good restaurant over coffee and brandy; there was no occasion so pleasant that he could not shatter it with his favorite gambit: "If you would only see one, you'd get over this nonsense."

So there I was, at the bullfight, with cold hands, trembling innerly, with   *20*
painful tinglings in the wrists and collarbone: yet my excitement was not
altogether painful; and in my happiness at Hattie Weston's performance I was
calmed and off guard when the heavy barred gate to the corral burst open and
the first bull charged through. The bulls were from the Duke of Veragua's°
ranch, as enormous and brave and handsome as any I ever saw afterward. (This
is not a short story, so I don't have to maintain any suspense.) This first bull
was a beautiful monster of brute courage: his hide was a fine pattern of black
and white, much enhanced by the goad with fluttering green ribbons stabbed
into his shoulder as he entered the ring; this in turn furnished an interesting
design in thin rivulets of blood, the enlivening touch of scarlet in his sober
color scheme, with highly aesthetic effect.

He rushed at the waiting horse, blindfolded in one eye and standing at
the proper angle for the convenience of his horns, the picador making only
the smallest pretense of staving him off, and disemboweled the horse with one
sweep of his head. The horse trod in his own guts. It happens at least once
every bullfight. I could not pretend not to have expected it; but I had not been
able to imagine it. I sat back and covered my eyes. Shelley, very deliberately
and as inconspicuously as he could, took both my wrists and held my hands
down on my knees. I shut my eyes and turned my face away, away from the
arena, away from him, but not before I had seen in his eyes a look of real, acute
concern and almost loving anxiety for me—he really believed that my
feelings were the sign of a grave flaw of character, or at least an unbecoming,
unworthy weakness that he was determined to overcome in me. He couldn't
shoot me, alas, or turn me over to the bullring; he had to deal with me in
human terms, and he did it according to his lights. His voice was hoarse and
fierce: "Don't you dare come here and then do this! You must face it!"

Part of his fury was shame, no doubt, at being seen with a girl who
would behave in such a pawky way. But at this point he was, of course, right.
Only he had been wrong before to nag me into this, and I was altogether
wrong to have let him persuade me. Or so I felt then. "You have got to face
this!" By then he was right; and I did look and I did face it, though not for
years and years.

During those years I saw perhaps a hundred bullfights, all in Mexico
City, with the finest bulls from Spain and the greatest bullfighters—but not
with Shelley—never again with Shelley, for we were not comfortable
together after that day. Our odd, mismatched sort of friendship declined and
neither made any effort to revive it. There was bloodguilt between us, we
shared an evil secret, a hateful revelation. He hated what he had revealed in
me to himself, and I hated what he had revealed to me about myself, and each
of us for entirely opposite reasons; but there was nothing more to say or do,
and we stopped seeing each other.

Duke of Veragua: Lineal descendant of Christopher Columbus.

I took to the bullfights with my Mexican and Indian friends. I sat with them in the cafés where the bullfighters appeared; more than once went at two o'clock in the morning with a crowd to see the bulls brought into the city; I visited the corral back of the ring where they could be seen before the corrida. Always, of course, I was in the company of impassioned adorers of the sport, with their special vocabulary and mannerisms and contempt for all others who did not belong to their charmed and chosen cult. Quite literally there were those among them I never heard speak of anything else; and I heard then all that can be said—the topic is limited, after all, like any other—in love and praise of bullfighting. But it can be tiresome, too. And I did not really live in that world, so narrow and so trivial, so cruel and so unconscious; I was a mere visitor. There was something deeply, irreparably wrong with my being there at all, something against the grain of my life; except for this (and here was the falseness I had finally to uncover): I loved the spectacle of the bullfights. I was drunk on it. I was in a strange, wild dream from which I did not want to be awakened. I was now drawn irresistibly to the bullring as before I had been drawn to the race tracks and the polo fields at home. But this had death in it, and it was the death in it that I loved. . . . And I was bitterly ashamed of this evil in me, and believed it to be in me only—no one had fallen so far into cruelty as this! These bullfight buffs I truly believed did not know what they were doing—but I did, and I knew better because I had once known better; so that spiritual pride got in and did its deadly work, too. How could I face the cold fact that at heart I was just a killer, like any other, that some deep corner of my soul consented not just willingly but with rapture? I still clung obstinately to my flattering view of myself as a unique case, as a humane, blood-avoiding civilized being, somehow a fallen angel, perhaps? Just the same, what was I doing there? And why was I beginning secretly to abhor Shelley as if he had done me a great injury, when in fact he had done me the terrible and dangerous favor of helping me to find myself out?

In the meantime I was reading St. Augustine; and if Shelley had helped me find myself out, St. Augustine helped me find myself again. I read for the first time then his story of a friend of his, a young man from the provinces who came to Rome and was taken up by the gang of clever, wellborn young hoodlums Augustine then ran with; and this young man, also wellborn but severely brought up, refused to go with the crowd to the gladiatorial combat; he was opposed to them on the simple grounds that they were cruel and criminal. His friends naturally ridiculed such dowdy sentiments; they nagged him slyly, bedeviled him openly, and, of course, finally some part of him consented—but only to a degree. He would go with them, he said, but he would not watch the games. And he did not, until the time for the first slaughter, when the howling of the crowd brought him to his feet, staring: and afterward he was more bloodthirsty than any.

Why, of course: oh, it might be a commonplace of human nature, it might be it could happen to anyone! I longed to be free of my uniqueness, to be a fellow-sinner at least with someone: I could not bear my guilt

25

alone—and here was this student, this boy at Rome in the fourth century, somebody I felt I knew well on sight, who had been weak enough to be led into adventure but strong enough to turn it into experience. For no matter how we both attempted to deceive ourselves, our acts had all the earmarks of adventure: violence of motive, events taking place at top speed, at sustained intensity, under powerful stimulus and a willful seeking for pure sensation; willful, I say, because I was not kidnapped and forced, after all, nor was that young friend of St. Augustine's. We both proceeded under the power of our own weakness. When the time came to kill the splendid black and white bull, I who had pitied him when he first came into the ring stood straining on tiptoe to see everything, yet almost blinded with excitement, and crying out when the crowd roared, and kissing Shelley on the cheekbone when he shook my elbow and shouted in the voice of one justified: "Didn't I tell you? Didn't I?"

Questions for Understanding

1. Why does Porter call adventure a "pastime of rather an inferior sort"?
2. What kind of person does Porter think Shelley perceived her to be?
3. What are the faults Porter finds with Shelley?
4. What does Porter think Shelley revealed to her about herself?
5. Why was Porter able to transform her attendance at bullfights from adventure into experience?

Suggestions for Writing

1. Recall two adventures, one of which became an experience. Describe what made each an adventure, and explain why one became an experience.
2. Shelley had a much greater influence over Porter than she ever intended him to have. Describe a person who had a much greater effect on you than you would have thought possible, and explain how that effect came about.
3. Porter says, "I loved the spectacle of the bullfight, I was drunk on it, I was in a strange, wild dream from which I did not want to be awakened." Has anything like that ever happened to you? Describe the spectacle and the degree of your "intoxication." Explain what the consequences were to you.
4. When she began attending the bullfights regularly, Porter says, she knew she was doing something against the grain of her life. Have you found yourself engaged in an activity that you knew went against the grain of your life? Describe the activity and explain why it went against the grain. Explain how you were able to disengage yourself from that activity—or why you have not been able to.
5. Porter says that reading St. Augustine helped her to find herself again. Has something you read ever had a similar effect on you—made you realize something about your life that otherwise might have remained obscure to you? Describe the situation you were in, and explain how what you read caused you to see the light.

THE NECESSARY ENEMY

1948

She is a frank, charming, fresh-hearted young woman who married   *1*
for love. She and her husband are one of those gay, good-looking young
pairs who ornament this modern scene rather more in profusion perhaps
than ever before in our history. They are handsome, with a talent for finding
their way in their world, they work at things that interest them, their tastes
agree and their hopes. They intend in all good faith to spend their lives
together, to have children and do well by them and each other—to be
happy, in fact, which for them is the whole point of their marriage. And
all in stride, keeping their wits about them. Nothing romantic, mind you;
their feet are on the ground.

Unless they were this sort of person, there would be not much point to
what I wish to say; for they would seem to be an example of the high-spirited,
right-minded young whom the critics are always invoking to come forth and
do their duty and practice all those sterling old-fashioned virtues which in
every generation seem to be falling into disrepair. As for virtues, these young
people are more or less on their own, like most of their kind; they get very
little moral or other aid from their society; but after three years of marriage
this very contemporary young woman finds herself facing the oldest and
ugliest dilemma of marriage.

She is dismayed, horrified, full of guilt and forebodings because she is
finding out little by little that she is capable of hating her husband, whom she
loves faithfully. She can hate him at times as fiercely and mysteriously, indeed
in terribly much the same way, as often she hated her parents, her brothers and
sisters, whom she loves, when she was a child. Even then it had seemed to her
a kind of black treacherousness in her, her private wickedness that, just the
same, gave her her only private life. That was one thing her parents never
knew about her, never seemed to suspect. For it was never given a name. They
did and said hateful things to her and to each other as if by right, as if in them
it was a kind of virtue. But when they said to her, "Control your feelings,"
it was never when she was amiable and obedient, only in the black times of
her hate. So it was her secret, a shameful one. When they punished her,
sometimes for the strangest reasons, it was, they said, only because they loved
her—it was for her good. She did not believe this, but she thought herself
guilty of something worse than ever they had punished her for. None of this
really frightened her: the real fright came when she discovered that at times
her father and mother hated each other; this was like standing on the doorsill
of a familiar room and seeing in a lightning flash that the floor was gone, you
were on the edge of a bottomless pit. Sometimes she felt that both of them
hated her, but that passed, it was simply not a thing to be thought of, much
less believed. She thought she had outgrown all this, but here it was again, an
element in her own nature she could not control, or feared she could not. She
would have to hide from her husband, if she could, the same spot in her

feelings she had hidden from her parents, and for the same no doubt disreputable, selfish reason: she wants to keep his love.

Above all, she wants him to be absolutely confident that she loves him, for that is the real truth, no matter how unreasonable it sounds, and no matter how her own feelings betray them both at times. She depends recklessly on his love; yet while she is hating him, he might very well be hating her as much or even more, and it would serve her right. But she does not want to be served right, she wants to be loved and forgiven—that is, to be sure he would forgive her anything, if he had any notion of what she had done. But best of all she would like not to have anything in her love that should ask for forgiveness. She doesn't mean about their quarrels—they are not so bad. Her feelings are out of proportion, perhaps. She knows it is perfectly natural for people to disagree, have fits of temper, fight it out; they learn quite a lot about each other that way, and not all of it disappointing either. When it passes, her hatred seems quite unreal. It always did.

Love. We are early taught to say it. I love you. We are trained to the thought of it as if there were nothing else, or nothing else worth having without it, or nothing worth having which it could not bring with it. Love is taught, always by precept, sometimes by example. Then hate, which no one meant to teach us, comes of itself. It is true that if we say I love you, it may be received with doubt, for there are times when it is hard to believe. Say I hate you, and the one spoken to believes it instantly, once for all.

Say I love you a thousand times to that person afterward and mean it every time, and still it does not change the fact that once we said I hate you, and meant that too. It leaves a mark on that surface love had worn so smooth with its eternal caresses. Love must be learned, and learned again and again; there is no end to it. Hate needs no instruction, but waits only to be provoked . . . hate, the unspoken word, the unacknowledged presence in the house, that faint smell of brimstone among the roses, that invisible tongue-tripper, that unkempt finger in every pie, that sudden oh-so-curiously *chilling* look—could it be boredom?—on your dear one's features, making them quite ugly. Be careful: love, perfect love, is in danger.

If it is not perfect, it is not love, and if it is not love, it is bound to be hate sooner or later. This is perhaps a not too exaggerated statement of the extreme position of Romantic Love, more especially in America, where we are all brought up on it, whether we know it or not. Romantic Love is changeless, faithful, passionate, and its sole end is to render the two lovers happy. It has no obstacles save those provided by the hazards of fate (that is to say, society), and such sufferings as the lovers may cause each other are only another word for delight: exciting jealousies, thrilling uncertainties, the ritual dance of courtship within the charmed closed circle of their secret alliance; all *real* troubles come from without, they face them unitedly in perfect confidence. Marriage is not the end but only the beginning of true happiness, cloudless, changeless to the end. That the candidates for this blissful condition have never seen an example of it, nor

5

ever knew anyone who had, makes no difference. That is the ideal and they will achieve it.

How did Romantic Love manage to get into marriage at last, where it was most certainly never intended to be? At its highest it was tragic: the love of Héloise and Abélard.° At its most graceful, it was the homage of the trouvère for his lady. In its most popular form, the adulterous strayings of solidly married couples who meant to stray for their own good reasons, but at the same time do nothing to upset the property settlements or the line of legitimacy; at its most trivial, the pretty trifling of shepherd and shepherdess.

This was generally condemned by church and state and a word of fear to honest wives whose mortal enemy it was. Love within the sober, sacred realities of marriage was a matter of personal luck, but in any case, private feelings were strictly a private affair having, at least in theory, no bearing whatever on the fixed practice of the rules of an institution never intended as a recreation ground for either sex. If the couple discharged their religious and social obligations, furnished forth a copious progeny, kept their troubles to themselves, maintained public civility and died under the same roof, even if not always on speaking terms, it was rightly regarded as a successful marriage. Apparently this testing ground was too severe for all but the stoutest spirits; it too was based on an ideal, as impossible in its way as the ideal Romantic Love. One good thing to be said for it is that society took responsibility for the conditions of marriage, and the sufferers within its bonds could always blame the system, not themselves. But Romantic Love crept into the marriage bed, very stealthily, by centuries, bringing its absurd notions about love as eternal springtime and marriage as a personal adventure meant to provide personal happiness. To a Western romantic such as I, though my views have been much modified by painful experience, it still seems to me a charming work of the human imagination, and it is a pity its central notion has been taken too literally and has hardened into a convention as cramping and enslaving as the older one. The refusal to acknowledge the evils in ourselves which therefore are implicit in any human situation is as extreme and unworkable a proposition as the doctrine of total depravity; but somewhere between them, or maybe beyond them, there does exist a possibility for reconciliation between our desires for impossible satisfactions and the simple unalterable fact that we also desire to be unhappy and that we create our own sufferings; and out of these sufferings we salvage our fragments of happiness.

Our young woman who has been taught that an important part of her human nature is not real because it makes trouble and interferes with her peace of mind and shakes her self-love, has been very badly taught; but she has arrived at a most important stage of her re-education. She is afraid her   *10*

Héloise and Abélard: In the Twelfth Century, the philosopher and teacher Abélard (1079–1142) fell in love with Héloise, whom he tutored, who gave birth to his child, and whose uncle had Abélard emasculated.

marriage is going to fail because she has not love enough to face its difficulties; and this because at times she feels a painful hostility toward her husband, and cannot admit its reality because such an admission would damage in her own eyes her view of what love should be, an absurd view, based on her vanity of power. Her hatred is real as her love is real, but her hatred has the advantage at present because it works on a blind instinctual level, it is lawless; and her love is subjected to a code of ideal conditions, impossible by their very nature of fulfillment, which prevents its free growth and deprives it of its right to recognize its human limitations and come to grips with them. Hatred is natural in a sense that love, as she conceives it, a young person brought up in the tradition of Romantic Love, is not natural at all. Yet it did not come by hazard, it is the very imperfect expression of the need of the human imagination to create beauty and harmony out of chaos, no matter how mistaken its notion of these things may be, nor how clumsy its methods. It has conjured love out of the air, and seeks to preserve it by incantations; when she spoke a vow to love and honor her husband until death, she did a very reckless thing, for it is not possible by an act of the will to fulfill such an engagement. But it was the necessary act of faith performed in defense of a mode of feeling, the statement of honorable intention to practice as well as she is able the noble, acquired faculty of love, that very mysterious overtone to sex which is the best thing in it. Her hatred is part of it, the necessary enemy and ally.

Questions for Understanding

1. What exactly is the "spot in her feelings" that Porter's hypothetical young wife will have to hide from her husband?
2. According to Porter, how well prepared are we to deal with the awareness that we feel hatred toward someone close?
3. What is Porter's attitude toward Romantic Love?
4. According to Porter, what were the roles the partners were expected to play in a traditional marriage?
5. What does Porter believe it is necessary to acknowledge about ourselves?

Suggestions for Writing

1. In discussing love and hate within marriage, Porter is discussing ambivalence, having strongly opposing feelings. Part of growing up is realizing that ambivalence, however unexpected, is unavoidable. Describe a situation in which you were surprised to discover your ambivalence. Tell what it was that made you aware that your feelings were not all in harmony.
2. Porter says that we seek to preserve ideal love through "incantations." Have you ever tried to make yourself believe you felt something through incantations? Describe the situation and tell what it was you were trying to persuade yourself that you felt. Discuss what your real feelings were.

3. At the end of the essay, Porter refers to love this way: "the noble, acquired faculty of love." In doing so, Porter suggests that love takes time to develop, that love grows. Can you recall coming to have a strongly positive feeling—like love—that grew from a most unlikely seed? That is, have you experienced the growth of a feeling that wasn't recognizable at the beginning? Describe the situation and discuss the evolution of the feeling.

4. Porter uses the word *reckless* in connection with marital vows. Have you ever taken a vow recklessly? Describe the situation and the vow you took. Tell how you came to realize that you had been reckless in taking such a vow.

5. Discuss a play, a movie, or a novel in which a wife or husband enters marriage believing in the ideal of Romantic Love and is unable to cope with a disillusioning experience.

NUTS AND BOLTS 7: METAPHORS

When Katherine Anne Porter speaks of hatred in marriage as a necessary "enemy," she is using a *metaphor*, a figure of speech that makes a comparison, as do the *simile* and the *analogy*. In its literal sense, *enemy* refers to an opponent, an opponent whose attitude is hostile and whose goal is to destroy. In its most common use, *enemy* means an opponent in warfare. But Porter is not writing about warfare; she is writing about a feeling a young woman is likely to have after three years of marriage, and that feeling is the enemy. Porter, in other words, is making a comparison between an opponent in war and a destructive feeling. This comparison enables Porter to convey just how destructive the feeling can be. This comparison gives Porter's point about the emergence of hatred in marriage an impact, a power, that it might not otherwise have. This is the primary reason for making such comparisons. A metaphor—or a simile or an analogy—can really drive a point home, like the best hammer in the toolroom.

The very last word in the essay is *ally*. This word, too, is most commonly used in the context of war. An ally is a nation, group, or individual who has joined with another to defeat an enemy or for some other common purpose. When Porter says, at the end, "Her hatred is part of it, the necessary enemy and ally," she is saying that the hatred need not be entirely destructive; it can be an ally too—it can be helpful.

The excellence of this essay lies in the surprising paradoxical idea that it presents: that mixed in with the young wife's deep love of her husband is hatred of him as well. A marriage counselor might have written an essay with exactly the same thesis, but it is unlikely that the marriage counselor's essay would have the power of Porter's. The source of that power is not a difference that is noticeable from word to word or from sentence to sentence; the power lies in Porter's occasional use of metaphors.

It is not until paragraph 6 that Porter's genius as a writer is revealed—in her metaphors. In this paragraph, Porter attempts to convey the effect of the wife's saying out loud for the first time, "I hate you!" Porter says, "It leaves a mark on that surface love had worn so smooth with its eternal caresses." Porter likens the effect of the wife's outburst to a mark that suddenly appears on a surface, perhaps the surface of a piece of fine wood, that has been lovingly smoothed—sanded. The sudden appearance of the mark means that all the effort expended on smoothing the surface has been wasted. With the metaphor of the marred surface, Porter has made the effect of that first "I hate you!" vivid and potent.

Porter goes on to make the point that the wife's outburst should not be a surprise, for hatred is "the unacknowledged presence in the house." This metaphor conveys in just six words the idea that the hatred within a happy marriage has been there all along but no one has paid it any attention. Such hatred is like "that faint smell of brimstone among the roses"—a smell, in other words, that no one would want to smell because the other smells are so good. Such hatred is like an "invisible tongue-tripper"; that is, it activates the tongue, causing the words "I hate you!" to leap out and make a silence-shattering explosion. Finally, such hatred is an "unkempt finger in every pie." With these five metaphors, Porter has made very real the inevitability and destructiveness of the hatred hidden within a loving marriage.

Other metaphors can be found throughout the essay, and they, too, do the job of intensifying. Metaphors (similes and analogies too, but especially metaphors) affect a reader in ways that literal language cannot. Metaphors take a reader by surprise, and the absence in them of literal truth makes the writer's point seem more true than it actually may be. Metaphors are lies of a sort, but they do make readers see and feel as literal statements cannot. Metaphors are a great tool of persuasion. Metaphors are a poet's bread and butter.

Writers should always be on the alert for metaphors. The most effective ones usually come as a result of concentration, of an intense effort by the writer to make himself see or feel. On the other hand, just saying to oneself, "I could use a metaphor here," and reaching for an easy comparison is not likely to produce a good result. Also, writers should remember this bit of advice given in Strunk and White's *The Elements of Style*. "Use figures of speech sparingly. . . . The reader needs time to catch his breath; he can't be expected to compare everything with something else. . . ."

LA CONQUISTADORA

1926

Rosalie Caden Evans was an American woman, born in Galveston,   *1*
Texas. She married a British subject, Harry Evans, who became owner of
several haciendas in Mexico during the Diaz regime. They lost their property
in the Madero revolution, and for several years lived in the United States and
in Europe. In 1917 Mr. Evans died while in Mexico, after an unsuccessful
attempt to regain his property under the Carranza administration. Mrs. Evans
returned to Mexico, and for more than six years she proved a tough enemy
to the successive revolutionary governments, holding her hacienda under
almost continuous fire. This contest required a great deal of attention from
three governments, Mexico, Great Britain, and the United States, and
furnished a ready bone of contention in the long-drawn argument between
Mexico and foreign powers respecting the famous Article 27 of the new
Mexican Constitution, which provides among other things that the large
landholdings of Mexico shall be repartitioned among the Indians, subject to
proper indemnification to the former owner.

H. A. C. Cummins, of the British legation, was expelled from Mexico
for his championship of Mrs. Evans, and a fair amount of trouble ensued
between Mexico and Great Britain about it. The case of Mrs. Evans was cited
in the United States as an argument against our recognition of the Obregón
government. An impressive volume of diplomatic correspondence was
exchanged between the three governments concerning the inflexible lady,
who held her ground, nevertheless, saying that she could be removed from
her holdings only as a prisoner or dead.

In August, 1924, the news came that Mrs. Evans had been shot from
ambush by a number of men while driving in a buckboard from the village
of San Martin to her hacienda, San Pedro Coxtocan.

Reading the letters Rosalie Evans wrote her sister, Mrs. Daisy Caden
Pettus, from Mexico, this adventure takes on all the colors of a lively
temperament; the story is lighted for us like a torch. The aim in publishing
the letters was to present Mrs. Evans to a presumably outraged Anglo-Saxon
world as a martyr to the sacred principles of private ownership of property:
to fix her as a symbol of devotion to a holy cause. "Some Americans," says
Mrs. Pettus in a foreward to the volume, "in ignorance of Mexican
conditions, have said the fight carried on by Mrs. Evans was unwise, if not
unworthy, in that it is charged that she was resisting the duly established laws
and principles of the Mexican people. This is very far from true."

It is true, however, that she opposed, and to her death, the attempts of   *5*
the Mexican people to establish those laws and principles which were the
foundation of their revolution, and on which their national future depends.
She cast her individual weight against the march of an enormous social
movement, and though her fight was gallant, brilliant and wholehearted,
admirable as a mere exhibition of daring, energy and spirit, still I cannot see

how she merits the title of martyr. She was out for blood, and she had a glorious time while the fight lasted.

Her letters are a swift-moving account of a life as full of thrills and action as any novel of adventure you may find. They are written at odd moments, dashed off in the midst of a dozen things all going at once: the episodes are struck off white-hot. The result is a collection of letters that could scarcely be equaled for speed, for clarity, for self-revelation, for wit and charm. We are shown the most fantastic blend of a woman: fanaticism, physical courage, avarice, mystical exaltation and witch-wife superstition; social poise and financial shrewdness, a timeless feminine coquetry tempered by that curious innocence which is the special gift of the American woman: all driven mercilessly by a tautness of the nerves, a deep-lying hysteria that urges her to self-hypnosis. Toward the last she had almost lost her natural reactions. Anger, fear, delight, hope—no more of these. She was a Will.

Mrs. Evans returned to Mexico to take up her husband's fight when he had wearied to death of it. Belief in private property had not yet become a religion. She was animated by sentiment for her dead husband. All feminine, she insisted that his shade still guarded and directed her. The demon that possessed her was by no means of so spiritual a nature as she fancied: she was ruled by a single-minded love of money and power. She came into Mexico at harvest time, and after a short, sharp battle she got hold of the ripened wheat on her main hacienda. This victory fired her, and was the beginning of the end. Shortly afterward the shade of her husband left her. "I stand alone."

No single glimmer of understanding of the causes of revolution or the rights of the people involved ever touched her mind. She loved Spaniards, the British, the Americans of the foreign colony. She thought the Indians made good servants, though occasionally they betrayed her. She writes with annoyance of Obregón's taking Mexico City and creating a disturbance when she was on the point of wresting from the Indians her second crop of wheat—"gold in color, gold in reality!" She is most lyrical, most poetic when she contemplates this gold which shall be hers, though all Mexico go to waste around her. Carranza's flight interested her merely because it menaced her chances of getting the only threshing machine in the Puebla Valley.

Of all the machinations, the crooked politics, the broken faiths, the orders and counterorders, the plots and counterplots that went on between literally thousands of people over this single holding, I have not time to tell. Mrs. Evans was passed from hand to hand, nobody wanted to be responsible for what must eventually happen to her. She pressed everybody into her service, from her maids to the high diplomats. Every man of any official note in Mexico, connected with the three governments, finally got into the business, and she shows them all up in turn.

The story of the double-dealing here revealed is not pretty, showing as it does some of our eminent diplomats engaged in passing the buck and gossiping behind each other's backs. But sooner or later they all advised her to listen to reason, accept 100,000 pesos for her land and give way. At least they perceived what she could not; that here was a national movement that must be reckoned with.

At first she would not. And later, she could not. She loved the romantic danger of her situation, she admired herself in the role of heroine. Her appetite for excitement increased; she confessed herself jaded, and sought greater danger.

Speaking of a safe conduct she obtained in order to go over her hacienda and inspect the crops, she says: "You see it means a chance of gaining 80,000 pesos besides the adventure." After each hairbreadth encounter with sullen Indians armed with rope and scythe, with troops bearing bared arms, she was flushed with a tense joy. Later, when she came to open war, she would ride into armed groups with her pistol drawn, singing *"Nous sommes les enfants de Gasconne!"* She cracked an Indian agrarian over the head with her riding whip during an altercation over the watercourse and patrolled the fields during harvest with a small army.

Her love of the drama was getting the upper hand of principle. If at first her cry was all for law and justice, later she refers to herself merrily as an outlaw, "You have no idea how naturally one takes to the greenwood!" She became a female conquistador—victory was her aim, and she was as unscrupulous in her methods as any other invader.

There is not a line in her letters to show that she had any grasp of the true inward situation, but her keen eye and ready wit missed no surface play of event. She maintained peaceable relations first with one, then another of the many groups of rebels. Inexplicably the situation would shift and change, her allies would vanish, leaving her mystified. She had all Mexico divided into two classes: the Good, who were helping her hold her property, and the Bad, who were trying to take it from her.

She could be self-possessed in the grand manner, and seemed to have second-sight in everything immediately concerning herself. She sat for three days and fed her pigeons while serious persons advised her to pay the 300 pesos ransom demanded for her majordomo, kidnapped to the hills. She refused. It was too much to pay for a majordomo, and she felt they would not shoot him anyhow. They did not. When he returned she sent him back with a present of $80 to the kidnappers.

At another crisis she played chess. After a brilliant encounter with some hint of gunfire, she came in and washed her hair. At times she studied astronomy, other times she read Marcus Aurelius or poetry. At all times she played the great lady. Her love for her horses, her dogs, her servants, her workers and allies was all of a piece, grounded in her sense of possession. They were hers; almost by virtue of that added grace she loved them, and she looked after them in the feudal manner.

There was something wild and strange in her, a hint of madness that touches genius; she lived in a half-burned ranch house with her dogs, near a haunted chapel, hourly expecting attack, and longed to join the coyotes in their weird dances outside her door. She foretold the manner of her own death, and related for sober fact the most hair-raising ghost story I have ever read:

> The last night I was there I had been in bed an hour perhaps and was growing drowsy when I heard some one crying at my window. The most gentle attenuated sobbing; the most pitiful sounds you ever heard. I never for a minute thought of the spirits, but called the girl to light the candle. She heard it too—but the strange part is, *I* said it was at the back window and *she* heard it at the front, and neither did *she* think of spirits. As she opened to see who was there, IT came in sobbing—and we looked at each other and closed the windows. Perhaps you think we were frightened or horrified? I can only answer for myself—it filled me with an intense pity. I only wanted to comfort it and I said to the girl: "If it would *only* be quiet." I then promised to have the mass said and invite the people, and it left, sobbing. And we, of course, both went to our beds to sleep dreamlessly till morning.

Revolution is not gentle, either for those who make it or those who oppose it. This story has its own value as a record of one life lived very fully and consciously. I think the life and death of Mrs. Evans were her own private adventures, most gladly sought and enviably carried through. As a personality, she is worth attention, being beautiful, daring and attractive. As a human being she was avaricious, with an extraordinary hardness of heart and ruthlessness of will; and she died in a grotesque cause.

Questions for Understanding

1. What is Porter saying about Mrs. Evans when she says that a part of the blend of which Mrs. Evans was made was "a timeless feminine coquetry"?
2. What is the main fault Porter finds with Mrs. Evans?
3. "Toward the last she had almost lost her natural reactions. Anger, fear, delight, hope—no more of these. She was a Will." Is the connotation here favorable or unfavorable? Why?
4. To what is Porter alluding when she says Mrs. Evans became a "female conquistadora"?
5. What is Porter's attitude toward the shooting of Mrs. Evans?

Suggestions for Writing

1. Was the kind of death Mrs. Evans met inevitable? Discuss.
2. Mrs. Evans for a while insisted that her husband's shade "guarded and directed her." Have you known anyone who believed that his or her behavior had supernatural origins? Describe the person and a significant action taken by that person which he or she said had a supernatural cause. Explain your reaction to the cause-and-effect relationship that was claimed.

3. Have you observed the use of coquetry to gain a particular end? Describe the situation and what the coquette desired. Describe the coquettish behavior. Explain your reaction to the behavior you observed.

4. "She had Mexico divided into two classes: the Good, who were helping her hold her property, and the Bad, who were trying to take it from her." For Mrs. Evans there was no in-between, no gray. Have you known a person whose judgments of other people were so clear-cut? Describe that person's general approach to problems and issues, and then focus on one particular issue. What were the consequences of the clear-cut judgments for him or her?

5. In summing up, Porter says of Mrs. Evans, "As a human being she was avaricious, with an extraordinary hardness of heart and ruthlessness of will." From what you have observed of similar persons, what has been the quality of the lives they have lived? If they could live their lives over, do you think they would live the same way? Describe and discuss.

Ralph Waldo Emerson

[1803–1882]

Although the Bible says, "The days of our years are threescore and ten," such longevity was rare until the middle of the twentieth century. Ralph Waldo Emerson lived seventy-nine years, but from an early age he was well aware of the fragility and uncertainty of human life and of life's inevitable pain. His father died when Emerson was eight, and he also lost a brother and a sister during his childhood. While in his twenties, he saw two of his younger brothers afflicted with severe mental illness. Of one he wrote, "There he lay— Edward the admired learned eloquent thriving boy—a maniac." Sixteen months after Emerson's marriage, his bride died. Within five years, he remarried, but then his first son died before the boy's sixth birthday. Emerson had cause enough for despair and pessimism, but he never allowed such life-deniers to get a firm clutch on him: "I am Defeated all the time," he said, "yet to Victory I am born."

Reading Emerson's essays is exhilarating. They are the work of a man who knew life—lots of the bad but also lots of the good. Upon finishing an Emerson essay, countless readers have felt their self-confidence boosted, and they have been inspired to set higher goals for themselves. If Emerson could cope with defeat, disappointment, and disillusionment, so could they. If bad times led Emerson to find challenges rather than excuses, so could they.

The essays reflect the life of a man who had had an unhappy, "ugly duckling" childhood. He was aware that his parents and teachers thought his brothers would be a source of greater pride than he. His adolescence was troubled, and as a young man, he was moody and solitary. At Harvard Emerson was only a mediocre student, because he did more of what he wanted to do than what was expected of a young man slated to become a teacher or minister. Although he attended Harvard Divinity School and followed nine generations of his family into the ministry, he disliked doing many of the things a minister was expected to do—such as visiting the sick, officiating at weddings and funerals, and repeating known "truths" from the pulpit. To Emerson's mind, nothing was settled; he wanted all questions open for discussion. Three-and-a-half years after he became pastor of the Second Unitarian Church of Boston, he resigned and bade farewell to the ministry.

During the nineteenth century, new theories were advanced in geology, biology, and astronomy—theories that tended to minimize the role played by God in creation. Emerson was greatly interested in these new theories and weighed them against the theological dogma he had been taught, but he remained firmly convinced that God "lent his hand" in the making of all things, although, over the years, his God became less like man and more the personification of Mind or Reason or Over-Soul. Through close observation of the ways of his own mind, Emerson became confident that, in a mysterious way, a greater Mind was working on his mind, as, for example, in dreams or in wide-awake sudden intuitions.

In 1841, Emerson published *Essays,* which contained "Self-Reliance" and eleven other pieces, including "Spiritual Laws," "Love," "Friendship," "Heroism," and "The Over-Soul." Many of the ideas found in these essays he had expressed earlier, both in his very extensive journal and in lectures. But according to the biographer Gay Wilson Allen, the familiar ideas that he incorporated into the essays were polished until they "glow[ed] with a brilliance found nowhere else in Emerson's writings, past or future." The essay was Emerson's natural medium, and the essays in this first collection sparkle with wit, ingenuity, paradox, surprising twists of language, and a first-hand knowledge of good and evil.

Emerson was a descendant of one of the founders of the town of Concord, Massachusetts. Emerson's father had lived in Concord as a child, in a house *his* father had built. But our Emerson was born in Boston, where his father was pastor of the First Unitarian Church, and, although he had been on numerous visits to Concord, he did not become a resident until 1835. Henry David Thoreau, the author of *Walden* (1854), was born in Concord in 1817, and he lived most of his life in the town or close by. Although Emerson was fourteen years older than Thoreau, when they became neighbors, the two men also became close friends. An entry in Emerson's journal testifies to the pleasure he found in the young Thoreau's company: "My good friend Henry Thoreau made this else solitary afternoon sunny with his simplicity & clear perception. How comic is simplicity in this doubledealing quacking world. Every thing that boy says makes merry with society though nothing can be graver than his meaning. . . ." A later entry suggests that, to Emerson, Thoreau had become a model of the truly self-reliant man. "My brave Henry here who is content to live now, & feels no shame in not studying any profession, for he does not postpone his life but lives already. . . ." Of course, by 1862, when Emerson wrote his comprehensive assessment of Thoreau, his enthusiasm for the man and his self-reliance had become somewhat tempered.

"Education" was written relatively late in Emerson's life and represents the culmination of his experience as a father, son, and student—and as an educator, preacher, lecturer, and reformer. Between 1821 and 1826, Emerson taught in city and country schools and, in the course of his life, served on many school boards, from the Concord School Committee to the Board of Overseers of Harvard College. Emerson first recorded his thoughts on education in a systematic way in "The American Scholar" address in 1837. For years afterward, he gave commencement addresses in which he dealt again and again with the question of what constitutes an ideal education.

EDUCATION

1864

A new degree of intellectual power seems cheap at any price. The use   *1*
of the world is that man may learn its laws. And the human race have wisely
signified their sense of this, by calling wealth, means,—Man being the end.
Language is always wise.

Therefore I praise New England because it is the country in the world
where is the freest expenditure for education. We have already taken, at
the planting of the Colonies (for aught I know for the first time in the
world), the initial step, which for its importance might have been resisted
as the most radical of revolutions, thus deciding at the start the destiny of
this country,—this, namely, that the poor man, whom the law does not
allow to take an ear of corn when starving, nor a pair of shoes for his
freezing feet, is allowed to put his hand into the pocket of the rich, and
say, You shall educate me, not as you will, but as I will: not alone in the
elements, but, by further provision, in the languages, in sciences, in the
useful and in elegant arts. The child shall be taken up by the State, and
taught, at the public cost, the rudiments of knowledge, and at last, the ripest
results of art and science.

Humanly speaking, the school, the college, society, make the difference
between men. All the fairy tales of Aladdin or the invisible Gyges or the
talisman that opens kings' palaces or the enchanted halls underground or in
the sea, are only fictions to indicate the one miracle of intellectual
enlargement. When a man stupid becomes a man inspired, when one and the
same man passes out of the torpid into the perceiving state, leaves the din of
trifles, the stupor of the senses, to enter into the quasi-omniscience of high
thought,—up and down, around, all limits disappear. No horizon shuts
down. He sees things in their causes, all facts in their connection.

One of the problems of history is the beginning of civilization. The
animals that accompany and serve man make no progress as races. Those
called domestic are capable of learning of man a few tricks of utility or
amusement, but they cannot communicate the skill to their race. Each
individual must be taught anew. The trained dog cannot train another dog.
And Man himself in many races retains almost the unteachableness of the
beast. For a thousand years the islands and forests of a great part of the world
have been filled with savages who made no steps of advance in art or skill
beyond the necessity of being fed and warmed. Certain nations, with a better
brain and usually in more temperate climates, have made such progress as to
compare with these as these compare with the bear and the wolf.

Victory over things is the office of man. Of course, until it is accom-   *5*
plished, it is the war and insult of things over him. His continual tendency, his
great danger, is to overlook the fact that the world is only his teacher, and the
nature of sun and moon, plant and animal only means of arousing his interior
activity. Enamoured of their beauty, comforted by their convenience, he

seeks them as ends, and fast loses sight of the fact that they have worse than no values, that they become noxious, when he becomes their slave.

This apparatus of wants and faculties, this craving body, whose organs ask all the elements and all the functions of Nature for their satisfaction, educate the wondrous creature which they satisfy with light, with heat, with water, with wood, with bread, with wool. The necessities imposed by this most irritable and all-related texture have taught Man hunting, pasturage, agriculture, commerce, weaving, joining, masonry, geometry, astronomy. Here is a world pierced and belted with natural laws, and fenced and planted with civil partitions and properties, which all put new restraints on the young inhabitant. He too must come into this magic circle of relations, and know health and sickness, the fear of injury, the desire of external good, the charm of riches, the charm of power. The household is a school of power. There, within the door, learn the tragi-comedy of human life. Here is the sincere thing, the wondrous composition for which day and night go round. In that routine are the sacred relations, the passions that bind and sever. Here is poverty and all the wisdom its hated necessities can teach, here labor drudges, here affections glow, here the secrets of character are told, the guards of man, the guards of woman, the compensations which, like angels of justice, pay every debt: the opium of custom, whereof all drink and many go mad. Here is Economy, and Glee, and Hospitality, and Ceremony, and Frankness, and Calamity, and Death, and Hope.

Every one has a trust-of-power,—every man, every boy a jurisdiction, whether it be over a cow or a rood of a potato-field, or a fleet of ships, or the laws of a state. And what activity the desire of power inspires! What toils it sustains! How it sharpens the perceptions and stores the memory with facts. Thus a man may well spend many years of life in trade. It is a constant teaching of the laws of matter and of mind. No dollar of property can be created without some direct communication with Nature, and of course some acquisition of knowledge and practical force. It is a constant contest with the active faculties of men, a study of the issues of one and another course of action, an accumulation of power, and, if the higher faculties of the individual be from time to time quickened, he will gain wisdom and virtue from his business.

As every wind draws music out of the Æolian harp, so doth every object in Nature draw music out of his mind. Is it not true that every landscape I behold, every friend I meet, every act I perform, every pain I suffer, leaves me a different being from that they found me? That poverty, love, authority, anger, sickness, sorrow, success, all work actively upon our being and unlock for us the concealed faculties of the mind? Whatever private or petty ends are frustrated, this end is always answered. Whatever the man does, or whatever befalls him, opens another chamber in his soul,—that is, he has got a new feeling, a new thought, a new organ. Do we not see how amazingly for this end man is fitted to the world?

What leads him to science? Why does he track in the midnight heaven a pure spark, a luminous patch wandering from age to age, but because he acquires thereby a majestic sense of power; learning that in his own constitution he can set the shining maze in order, and finding and carrying their law in his mind, can, as it were, see his simple idea realized up yonder in giddy distances and frightful periods of duration. If Newton come and first of men perceive that not alone certain bodies fall to the ground at a certain rate, but that all bodies in the Universe, the universe of bodies, fall always, and at one rate; that every atom in Nature draws to every other atom,—he extends the power of his mind not only over every cubic atom of his native planet, but he reports the condition of millions of worlds which his eye never saw. And what is the charm which every ore, every new plant, every new fact touching winds, clouds, ocean currents, the secrets of chemical composition and decomposition possess for Humboldt?° What but that much revolving of similar facts in his mind has shown him that always the mind contains in its transparent chambers the means of classifying the most refractory phenomena, of depriving them of all casual and chaotic aspect, and subordinating them to a bright reason of its own, and so giving to man a sort of property,—yea, the very highest property in every district and particle of the globe.

By the permanence of Nature, minds are trained alike, and made   10
intelligible to each other. In our condition are the roots of language and communication, and these instructions we never exhaust.

In some sort the end of life is that the man should take up the universe into himself, or out of that quarry leave nothing unrepresented. Yonder mountain must migrate into his mind. Yonder magnificent astronomy he is at last to import, fetching away moon, and planet, solstice, period, comet and binal star, by comprehending their relation and law. Instead of the timid stripling he was, he is to be the stalwart Archimedes, Pythagoras, Columbus, Newton, of the physic, metaphysic and ethics of the design of the world.

For truly the population of the globe has its origin in the aims which their existence is to serve; and so with every portion of them. The truth takes flesh in forms that can express it; and thus in history an idea always overhangs, like the moon, and rules the tide which rises simultaneously in all the souls of a generation.

Whilst thus the world exists for the mind; whilst thus the man is ever invited inward into shining realms of knowledge and power by the shows of the world, which interpret to him the infinitude of his own consciousness,—it becomes the office of a just education to awaken him to the knowledge of this fact.

We learn nothing rightly until we learn the symbolical character of life. Day creeps after day, each full of facts, dull, strange, despised things, that we cannot enough despise,—call heavy, prosaic and desert. The time we seek to kill: the attention it is elegant to divert from things around us. And presently the aroused intellect finds gold and gems in one of these

---

Humboldt: Wilhelm Freiherr von Humboldt (1767–1835), Prussian educator, statesman, and philologist.

scorned facts,—then finds that the day of facts is a rock of diamonds; that a fact is an Epiphany of God.

We have our theory of life, our religion, our philosophy: and the event   15
of each moment, the shower, the steamboat disaster, the passing of a beautiful face, the apoplexy of our neighbor, are all tests to try our theory, the approximate result we call truth, and reveal its defects. If I have renounced the search of truth, if I have come into the port of some pretending dogmatism, some new church or old church, some Schelling° or Cousin,° I have died to all use of these new events that are born out of prolific time into multitude of life every hour. I am as a bankrupt to whom brilliant opportunities offer in vain. He has just foreclosed his freedom, tied his hands, locked himself up and given the key to another to keep.

When I see the doors by which God enters into the mind; that there is no sot or fop, ruffian or pedant into whom thoughts do not enter by passages which the individual never left open, I can expect any revolution in character. "I have hope," said the great Leibnitz,° "that society may be reformed, when I see how much education may be reformed."

It is ominous, a presumption of crime, that this word Education has so cold, so hopeless a sound. A treatise on education, a convention for education, a lecture, a system, affects us with slight paralysis and a certain yawning of the jaws. We are not encouraged when the law touches it with its fingers. Education should be as broad as man. Whatever elements are in him that should foster and demonstrate. If he be dexterous, his tuition should make it appear; if he be capable of dividing men by the trenchant sword of his thought, education should unsheathe and sharpen it; if he is one to cement society by his all-reconciling affinities, oh! hasten their action! If he is jovial, if he is mercurial, if he is great-hearted, a cunning artificer, a strong commander, a potent ally, ingenious, useful, elegant, witty, prophet, diviner,—society has need of all these. The imagination must be addressed. Why always coast on the surface and never open the interior of Nature, nor by science, which is surface still, but by poetry? Is not the Vast an element of the mind? Yet what teaching, what book of this day appeals to the Vast?

Our culture has truckled to the times,—to the senses. It is not manworthy. If the vast and the spiritual are omitted, so are the practical and the moral. It does not make us brave or free. We teach boys to be such men as we are. We do not teach them to aspire to be all they can. We do not give them a training as if we believed in their noble nature. We scarce educate their bodies. We do not train the eye and the hand. We exercise their understandings to the apprehension and comparison of some facts, to a skill in numbers, in words; we aim to make accountants, attorneys, engineers; but not to make

---

Schelling: Friedrich Wilhelm Joseph von Schelling (1775–1854), German philosopher.

Cousin: Victor Cousin (1792–1867), French philosopher and educator, greatly influenced by Schelling.

Leibnitz: Gottfried Wilhelm Leibnitz (1646–1716), German philosopher, mathematician, and diplomat.

able, earnest, great-hearted men. The great object of Education should be commensurate with the object of life. It should be a moral one; to teach self-trust: to inspire the youthful man with an interest in himself; with a curiosity touching his own nature; to acquaint him with the resources of his mind, and to teach him that there is all his strength, and to inflame him with a piety towards the Grand Mind in which he lives. Thus would education conspire with the Divine Providence. A man is a little thing whilst he works by and for himself, but, when he gives voice to the rules of love and justice, is godlike, his word is current in all countries; and all men, though his enemies, are made his friends and obey it as their own.

In affirming that the moral nature of man is the predominant element and should therefore be mainly consulted in the arrangements of a school, I am very far from wishing that it should swallow up all the other instincts and faculties of man. It should be enthroned in his mind, but if it monopolize the man he is not yet sound, he does not yet know his wealth. He is in danger of becoming merely devout, and wearisome through the monotony of his thought. It is not less necessary that the intellectual and the active faculties should be nourished and matured. Let us apply to this subject the light of the same torch by which we have looked at all the phenomena of the time; the infinitude, namely, of every man. Everything teaches that.

One fact constitutes all my satisfaction, inspires all my trust, viz., this perpetual youth, which, as long as there is any good in us, we cannot get rid of. It is very certain that the coming age and the departing age seldom understand each other. The old man thinks the young man has no distinct purpose, for he could never get anything intelligible and earnest out of him. Perhaps the young man does not think it worth his while to explain himself to so hard and inapprehensive a confessor. Let him be led up with a long-sighted forbearance, and let not the sallies of his petulance or folly be checked with disgust or indignation or despair.

I call our system a system of despair, and I find all the correction, all the revolution that is needed and that the best spirits of this age promise, in one word, in Hope. Nature, when she sends a new mind into the world, fills it beforehand with a desire for that which she wishes it to know and do. Let us wait and see what is this new creation, of what new organ the great Spirit had need when it incarnated this new Will. A new Adam in the garden, he is to name all the beasts in the field, all the gods in the sky. And jealous provision seems to have been made in his constitution that you shall not invade and contaminate him with the worn weeds of your language and opinions. The charm of life is this variety of genius, these contrasts and flavors by which Heaven has modulated the identity of truth, and there is a perpetual hankering to violate this individuality, to warp his ways of thinking and behavior to resemble or reflect your thinking and behavior. A low self-love in the parent desires that his child should repeat his character and fortune; an expectation which the child, if justice is done him, will nobly disappoint. By working on the theory that this resemblance exists, we shall do what in us lies to defeat his proper promise and produce the ordinary and mediocre. I suffer whenever I see that common sight of a parent or senior imposing his opinion and way of thinking and being on a young soul to which they are totally unfit. Cannot we let people be themselves, and enjoy life in their own way? You are trying to make that man another *you*. One's enough.

Or we sacrifice the genius of the pupil, the unknown possibilities of his nature, to a neat and safe uniformity, as the Turks whitewash the costly mosaics of ancient art which the Greeks left on their temple walls. Rather let us have men whose manhood is only the continuation of their boyhood, natural characters still; such are able and fertile for heroic action; and not that sad spectacle with which we are too familiar, educated eyes in uneducated bodies.

I like boys, the masters of the playground and of the street,—boys, who have the same liberal ticket of admission to all shops, factories, armories, town-meetings, caucuses, mobs, target-shootings, as flies have: quite unsuspected, coming in as naturally as the janitor,—known to have no money in their pockets, and themselves not suspecting the value of this poverty; putting nobody on his guard, but seeing the inside of the show,—hearing all the asides. There are no secrets from them, they know everything that befalls in the fire-company, the merits of every engine and of every man at the brakes, how to work it, and are swift to try their hand at every part; so too the merits of every locomotive on the rails, and will coax the engineer to let them ride with him and pull the handles when it goes to the engine-house. They are there only for fun, and not knowing that they are at school, in the court-house, or the cattle-show, quite as much and more than they were, an hour ago, in the arithmetic class.

They know truth from counterfeit as quick as the chemist does. They detect weakness in your eye and behavior a week before you open your mouth, and have given you the benefit of their opinion quick as a wink. They make no mistakes, have no pedantry, but entire belief on experience. Their elections at baseball or cricket are founded on merit, and are right. They don't pass for swimmers until they can swim, nor for stroke-oar until they can row; and I desire to be saved from their contempt. If I can pass with them, I can manage well enough with their fathers.

Everybody delights in the energy with which boys deal and talk with   *25* each other; the mixture of fun and earnest, reproach and coaxing, love and wrath, with which the game is played;—the good-natured yet defiant independence of a leading boy's behavior in the school-yard. How we envy in later life the happy youths to whom their boisterous games and rough exercise furnish the precise element which frames and sets off their school and college tasks, and teaches them, when least they think it, the use and meaning of these. In their fun and extreme freak they hit on the topmost sense of Horace. The young giant, brown from his hunting-tramp, tells his story well, interlarded with lucky allusions to Homer, to Virgil, to college-songs, to Walter Scott; and Jove and Achilles, partridge and trout, opera and binomial theorem, Cæsar in Gaul, Sherman in Savannah, and hazing in Holworthy, dance through the narrative in merry confusion, yet the logic is good. If he can turn his books to such picturesque account in his fishing and hunting, it is easy to see how his reading and experience, as he has more of both, will interpenetrate each other. And every one desires that this pure vigor of action and wealth of narrative, cheered with so much humor and street rhetoric, should be carried into the habit of the young man, purged of its uproar and rudeness, but with all its vivacity entire. His hunting and campings-out have given him an indispensable base: I wish to add a taste for good company through his impatience of bad. That stormy genius of his needs a little direction to games, charades, verses of society, song, and a correspondence year by year with his wisest and best friends. Friendship is an order of nobility; from its revelations we come more worthily into nature. Society he must have or he is poor indeed; he gladly enters a school which forbids conceit, affectation, emphasis and dulness, and requires of each only the flower of his nature and experience; requires good will, beauty, wit and select information; teaches by practice the law of conversation, namely, to hear as well as to speak.

Meantime, if circumstances do not permit the high social advantages, solitude has also its lessons. The obscure youth learns there the practice instead of the literature of his virtues; and, because of the disturbing effect of passion and sense, which by a multitude of trifles impede the mind's eye from the quiet search of that fine horizon-line which truth keeps,—the way to knowledge and power has ever been an escape from too much engagement with affairs and possessions; a way, not through plenty and superfluity, but by denial and renunciation, into solitude and privation; and, the more is taken away, the more real and inevitable wealth of being is made known to us. The solitary knows the essence of the thought, the scholar in society only its fair face. There is no want of example of great men, great benefactors, who have been monks and hermits in habit. The bias of mind is sometimes irresistible in that direction. The man is, as it were, born deaf and dumb, and dedicated to a narrow and lonely life. Let him study the art of solitude, yield as gracefully as he can to his destiny. Why cannot he get the good of his doom, and if it is from eternity a settled fact that he and society shall be nothing to each other, why need he blush so, and make wry faces to keep up a freshman's seat in the fine world? Heaven often protects valuable souls charged with great secrets, great ideas, by long shutting them up with their own thoughts. And the most genial and amiable of men must alternate society with solitude, and learn its severe lessons.

There comes the period of the imagination to each, a later youth; the power of beauty, the power of books, of poetry. Culture makes his books realities to him, their characters more brilliant, more effective on his mind than his actual mates. Do not spare to put novels into the hands of young people as an occasional holiday and experiment; but, above all, good poetry in all kinds, epic, tragedy, lyric. If we can touch the imagination, we serve them, they will never forget it. Let him read Tom Brown at Rugby, read Tom Brown at Oxford,—better yet, read Hodson's Life—Hodson who took prisoner the king of Delhi. They teach the same truth,—a trust, against all appearances, against all privations, in your own worth, and not in tricks, plotting, or patronage.

I believe that our own experience instructs us that the secret of Education lies in respecting the pupil. It is not for you to choose what he shall know, what he shall do. It is chosen and foreordained, and he only holds the key to his own secret. By your tampering and thwarting and too much governing he may be hindered from his end and kept out of his own. Respect the child. Wait and see the new product of Nature. Nature loves analogies, but not repetitions. Respect the child. Be not too much his parent. Trespass not on his solitude.

But I hear the outcry which replies to this suggestion:—Would you verily throw up the reins of public and private discipline; would you leave the young child to the mad career of his own passions and whimsies, and call this anarchy a respect for the child's nature? I answer,—Respect the child, respect him to the end, but also respect yourself. Be the companion of his thought, the friend of his friendship, the lover of his virtue,—but no kinsman of his sin. Let him find you so true to yourself that you are the irreconcilable hater of his vice and the imperturbable slighter of his trifling.

The two points in a boy's training are, to keep his *naturel* and train off   30
all but that:—to keep his *naturel,* but stop off his uproar, fooling and horse-play;—keep his nature and arm it with knowledge in the very direction in which it points. Here are the two capital facts, Genius and Drill. The first is the inspiration in the well-born healthy child, the new perception he has of nature. Somewhat he sees in forms or hears in music or apprehends in mathematics, or believes practicable in mechanics or possible in political society, which no one else sees or hears or believes. This is the perpetual romance of new life, the invasion of God into the old dead world, when he sends into quiet houses a young soul with a thought which is not met, looking for something which is not there, but which ought to be there: the thought is dim but it is sure, and he casts about restless for means and masters to verify it; he makes wild attempts to explain himself and invoke the aid and consent of the bystanders. Baffled for want of language and methods to convey his meaning, not yet clear to himself, he conceives that though not in this house or town, yet in some other house or town is the wise master who can put him in possession of the rules and instruments to execute his will. Happy this child with a bias, with a thought which entrances him, leads him, now into deserts now into cities, the fool of an idea. Let him follow it in good and in evil report, in good or bad company; it will justify itself; it will lead him at last into the illustrious society of the lovers of truth.

In London, in a private company, I became acquainted with a gentleman, Sir Charles Fellowes,° who, being at Xanthus, in the Ægean Sea,

---

Sir Charles Fellowes: British archaeologist (1799–1860) who discovered the ruins of Xanthus, the ancient capital of Lycia, and thirteen other ancient cities.

had seen a Turk point with his staff to some carved work on the corner of a stone almost buried in the soil. Fellowes scraped away the dirt, was struck with the beauty of the sculptured ornaments, and, looking about him, observed more blocks and fragments like this. He returned to the spot, procured laborers and uncovered many blocks. He went back to England, bought a Greek grammar and learned the language; he read history and studied ancient art to explain his stones; he interested Gibson the sculptor; he invoked the assistance of the English Government; he called in the succor of Sir Humphry Davy to analyze the pigments; of experts in coins, of scholars and connoisseurs; and at last in his third visit brought home to England such statues and marble reliefs and such careful plans that he was able to reconstruct, in the British Museum, where it now stands, the perfect model of the Ionic trophy-monument, fifty years older than the Parthenon of Athens, and which had been destroyed by earthquakes, then by iconoclast Christians, then by savage Turks. But mark that in the task he had achieved an excellent education, and become associated with distinguished scholars whom he had interested in his pursuit; in short, had formed a college for himself; the enthusiast had found the master, the masters, whom he sought. Always genius seeks genius, desires nothing so much as to be a pupil and to find those who can lend it aid to perfect itself.

Nor are the two elements, enthusiasm and drill, incompatible. Accuracy is essential to beauty. The very definition of the intellect is Aristotle's: "that by which we know terms or boundaries." Give a boy accurate perceptions. Teach him the difference between the similar and the same. Make him call things by their right names. Pardon in him no blunder. Then he will give you solid satisfaction as long as he lives. It is better to teach the child arithmetic and Latin grammar than rhetoric or moral philosophy, because they require exactitude of performance; it is made certain that the lesson is mastered, and that power of performance is worth more than the knowledge. He can learn anything which is important to him now that the power to learn is secured: as mechanics say, when one has learned the use of tools, it is easy to work at a new craft.

Letter by letter, syllable by syllable, the child learns to read, and in good time can convey to all the domestic circle the sense of Shakespeare. By many steps each just as short, the stammering boy and the hesitating collegian, in the school debate, in college clubs, in mock court, comes at last to full secure, triumphant unfolding of his thought in the popular assembly, with a fulness of power that makes all the steps forgotten.

But this function of opening and feeding the human mind is not to be fulfilled by any mechanical or military method; is not to be trusted to any skill less large than Nature itself. You must not neglect the form, but you must secure the essentials. It is curious how perverse and intermeddling we are, and what vast pains and cost we incur to do wrong. Whilst we all know in our own experience and apply natural methods in our own business,—in education our common sense fails us, and we are continually trying costly machinery against nature, in patent schools and academies and in great colleges and universities.

The natural method forever confutes our experiments, and we must still   35 come back to it. The whole theory of the school is on the nurse's or mother's knee. The child is as hot to learn as the mother is to impart. There is mutual delight. The joy of our childhood in hearing beautiful stories from some skilful aunt who loves to tell them, must be repeated in youth. The boy wishes to learn to skate, to coast, to catch a fish in the brook, to hit a mark with a snowball or a stone; and a boy a little older is just as well pleased to teach him these sciences. Not less delightful is the mutual pleasure of teaching and learning the secret of algebra, or of chemistry, or of good reading and good recitation of poetry or of prose, or of chosen facts in history or in biography.

Nature provided for the communication of thought, by planting with it in the receiving mind a fury to impart it. 'T is so in every art, in every science. One burns to tell the new fact, the other burns to hear it. See how far a young doctor will ride or walk to witness a new surgical operation. I have seen a carriage-maker's shop emptied of all its workmen into the street, to scrutinize a new pattern from New York. So in literature, the young man who has taste for poetry, for fine images, for noble thoughts, is insatiable for this nourishment, and forgets all the world for the more learned friend,—who finds equal joy in dealing out his treasures.

Happy the natural college thus self-instituted around every natural teacher; the young men of Athens around Socrates; of Alexandria around Plotinus; of Paris around Abelard; of Germany around Fichte, or Niebuhr, or Goethe: in short the natural sphere of every leading mind. But the moment this is organized, difficulties begin. The college was to be the nurse and home of genius; but, though every young man is born with some determination in his nature, and is a potential genius; is at last to be one; it is, in the most, obstructed and delayed, and, whatever they may hereafter be, their senses are now opened in advance of their minds. They are more sensual than intellectual. Appetite and indolence they have, but no enthusiasm. These come in numbers to the college: few geniuses: and the teaching comes to be arranged for these many, and not for those few. Hence the instruction seems to require skilful tutors, of accurate and systematic mind, rather than ardent and inventive masters. Besides, the youth of genius are eccentric, won't drill, are irritable, uncertain, explosive, solitary, not men of the world, not good for every-day association. You have to work for large classes instead of individuals; you must lower your flag and reef your sails to wait for the dull sailors; you grow departmental, routinary, military almost with your discipline and college police. But what doth such a school to form a great and heroic character? What abiding Hope can it inspire? What Reformer will it nurse? What poet will it breed to sing to the human race? What discoverer of Nature's laws will it prompt to enrich us by disclosing in the mind the statute which all matter must obey? What fiery soul will it send out to warm a nation with his charity? What tranquil mind will it have fortified to walk with meekness in private and obscure duties, to wait and to suffer? Is it not manifest that our academic institutions should have a wider scope; that they should not be timid and keep the ruts of the last generation, but that wise men thinking for themselves and heartily seeking the good of mankind, and counting the cost of innovation, should dare to arouse the young to a just and heroic life; that the moral nature should be addressed in the school-room, and children should be treated as the high-born candidates of truth and virtue?

So to regard the young child, the young man, requires, no doubt, rare patience; a patience that nothing but faith in the remedial forces of the soul can give. You see his sensualism; you see his want of those tastes and perceptions which make the power and safety of your character. Very likely. But he has something else. If he has his own vice, he has its correlative virtue. Every mind should be allowed to make its own statement in action, and its balance will appear. In these judgments one needs that foresight which was attributed to an eminent reformer, of whom it was said "his patience could see in the bud of the aloe the blossom at the end of a hundred years." Alas for the cripple Practice when it seeks to come up with the bird Theory, which flies before it. Try your design on the best school. The scholars are of all ages and temperaments and capacities. It is difficult to class them, some are too young, some are slow, some perverse. Each requires so much consideration, that the morning hope of the teacher, of a day of love and progress, is often closed at evening by despair. Each single case, the more it is considered, shows more to be done; and the strict conditions of the hours, on one side, and the number of tasks, on the other. Whatever becomes of our method, the conditions stand fast,—six hours, and thirty, fifty, or a hundred and fifty pupils. Something must be done, and done speedily, and in this distress the wisest are tempted to adopt violent means, to proclaim martial law, corporal punishment, mechanical arrangement, bribes, spies, wrath, main strength and ignorance, in lieu of that wise genial providential influence they had hoped, and yet hope at some future day to adopt. Of course the devotion to details reacts injuriously on the teacher. He cannot indulge his genius, he cannot delight in personal relations with young friends, when his eye is always on the clock, and twenty classes are to be dealt with before the day is done. Besides, how can he please himself with genius, and foster modest virtue? A sure proportion of rogue and dunce finds its way into every school and requires a cruel share of time, and the gentle teacher, who wished to be a Providence to youth, is grown a martinet, sore with suspicions; knows as much vice as the judge of a police court, and his love of learning is lost in the routine of grammars and books of elements.

A rule is so easy that it does not need a man to apply it; an automaton, a machine, can be made to keep a school so. It facilitates labor and thought so much that there is always the temptation in large schools to omit the endless task of meeting the wants of each single mind, and to govern by steam. But it is at frightful cost. Our modes of Education aim to expedite, to save labor; to do for masses what cannot be done for masses, what must be done reverently, one by one: say rather, the whole world is needed for the tuition of each pupil. The advantages of this system of emulation and display are so prompt and obvious, it is such a time-saver, it is so energetic on slow and on bad natures, and is of so easy application, needing no sage or poet, but any tutor or schoolmaster in his first term can apply it,—that it is not strange that this calomel of culture should be a popular medicine. On the other hand, total abstinence from this drug, and the adoption of simple discipline and the following of nature, involves at once immense claims on the time, the thoughts, on the life of the teacher. It requires time, use, insight, event, all the great lessons and assistances of God; and only to think of using it implies character and profoundness; to enter on this course of discipline is to be good and great. It is precisely analogous to the difference between the use of corporal punishment and the methods of love. It is so easy to bestow on a bad boy a blow, overpower him, and get obedience without words, that in this world of hurry and distraction, who can wait for the returns of reason and the conquest of self; in the uncertainty too whether that will ever come? And yet the familiar observation of the universal compensations might suggest the fear that so summary a stop of a bad humor was more jeopardous than its continuance.

Now the correction of this quack practice is to import into Education   *40* the wisdom of life. Leave this military hurry and adopt the pace of Nature. Her secret is patience. Do you know how the naturalist learns all the secrets of the forest, of plants, of birds, of beasts, of reptiles, of fishes, of the rivers and the sea? When he goes into the woods the birds fly before him and he finds none; when he goes to the river-bank, the fish and the reptile swim away and leave him alone. His secret is patience; he sits down, and sits still; he is a statue; he is a log. These creatures have no value for their time, and he must put as low a rate on his. By dint of obstinate sitting still, reptile, fish, bird and beast, which all wish to return to their haunts, begin to return. He sits still; if they approach, he remains passive as the stone he sits upon. They lose their fear. They have curiosity too about him. By and by the curiosity masters the fear, and they come swimming, creeping and flying towards him; and as he is still immovable, they not only resume their haunts and their ordinary labors and manners, show themselves to him in their work-day trim, but also volunteer some degree of advances towards fellowship and good understanding with a biped who behaves so civilly and well. Can you not baffle the impatience and passion of the child by your tranquillity? Can you not wait for him, as Nature and Providence do? Can you not keep for his mind and ways, for his secret, the same curiosity you give to the squirrel, snake, rabbit, and the sheldrake and the deer? He has a secret; wonderful methods in him; he is,—every child,—a new style of man; give him time and opportunity. Talk of Columbus and Newton! I tell you the child just born in yonder hovel is the beginning of a revolution as great as theirs. But you must have the believing and prophetic eye. Have the self-command you wish to inspire. Your teaching and discipline must have the reserve and taciturnity of Nature. Teach them to hold their tongues by holding your own. Say little; do not snarl; do not chide; but govern by the eye. See what they need, and that the right thing is done.

I confess myself utterly at a loss in suggesting particular reforms in our ways of teaching. No discretion that can be lodged with a school-committee, with the overseers or visitors of an academy, of a college, can at all avail to reach these difficulties and perplexities, but they solve themselves when we leave institutions and address individuals. The will, the male power, organizes, imposes its own thought and wish on others, and makes that military eye which controls boys as it controls men; admirable in its results, a fortune to him who has it, and only dangerous when it leads the workman to overvalue and overuse it and precludes him from finer means. Sympathy, the female force,—which they must use who have not the first,—deficient in instant control and the breaking down of resistance, is more subtle and lasting and creative. I advise teachers to cherish mother-wit. I assume that you will keep the grammar, reading, writing and arithmetic in order; it is easy and of course you will. But smuggle in a little contraband wit, fancy, imagination, thought. If you have a taste which you have suppressed because it is not shared by those about you, tell them that. Set this law up, whatever becomes of the rules of the school: they must not whisper, much less talk; but if one of the young people says a wise thing, greet it, and let all the children clap their hands. They shall have no book but schoolbooks in the room; but if one has brought in a Plutarch or Shakespeare or Don Quixote or Goldsmith or any other good book, and understands what he reads, put him at once at the head of the class. Nobody shall be disorderly, or leave his desk without permission, but if a boy runs from his bench, or a girl, because the fire falls, or to check some injury that a little dastard is inflicting behind his desk on some helpless sufferer, take away the medal from the head of the class and give it on the instant to the brave rescuer. If a child happens to show that he knows any fact about astronomy, or plants, or birds, or rocks, or history, that interests him and you, hush all the classes and encourage him to tell it so that all may hear. Then you have made your school-room like the world. Of course you will insist on modesty in the children, and respect to their teachers, but if the boy stops you in your speech, cries out that you are wrong and sets you right, hug him!

To whatsoever upright mind, to whatsoever beating heart I speak, to you it is committed to educate men. By simple living, by an illimitable soul, you inspire, you correct, you instruct, you raise, you embellish all. By your own act you teach the beholder how to do the practicable. According to the depth from which you draw your life, such is the depth not only of your strenuous effort, but of your manners and presence.

The beautiful nature of the world has here blended your happiness with your power. Work straight on in absolute duty, and you lend an arm and an encouragement to all the youth of the universe. Consent yourself to be an organ of your highest thought, and lo! suddenly you put all men in your debt, and are the fountain of an energy that goes pulsing on with waves of benefit to the borders of society, to the circumference of things.

Questions for Understanding

1. Emerson urges parents to be no "kinsman" of a child's sin. He then says about child and parent, "Let him find you so true to yourself that you are the irreconcilable hater of his vice and imperturbable slighter of his trifling." What is the benefit to the child of such parental "hating" and "slighting"?
2. "Always genius seeks genius, desires nothing so much as to be a pupil and to find those who can lend it aid to perfect itself." With this statement Emerson sums up his point about the endeavors of Sir Charles Fellowes regarding the Ionic trophy-monument. In broader language, what is Emerson's point?
3. "Whilst we all know in our own experience and apply natural methods in our own business,—in education our common sense fails us, and we are continually trying costly machinery against nature. . . ." What does Emerson mean by "machinery" and "nature"?
4. Emerson complains that, in too many pupils, genius is "obstructed and delayed," and "appetite and indolence they have, but no enthusiasm." What is Emerson saying about most pupils?
5. Emerson speaks of "The will, the male power" and "Sympathy, the female force." Why does he believe the female force will be of greater benefit to the child?

Suggestions for Writing

1. Emerson says, "The household is a school of power," and in it are taught "Economy, and Glee, and Hospitality, and Ceremony, and Frankness, and Calamity, and Death, and Hope." What did the school that was your household teach you? Write an essay in which you discuss two or three of the lessons you took away from your household.
2. Emerson suggests that as we become aware of natural phenomena, the mind classifies them, "depriving them of all casual and chaotic aspect, and subordinating them to a bright reason of its own." Can you recall doing this in regard to some aspect of the natural world? Describe the phenomena that engaged your interest. Discuss the classification you imposed on them. Discuss the extent to which the order you imposed gave you "a sort of property" and a pride in ownership.
3. One of the most compelling passages in "Education" is the one in which Emerson asserts that we must not lock ourselves into fixed and unchanging beliefs. To do so is to die "to all use of these new events that are born out of prolific time into multitude of life every hour." When a person makes all experience fit a belief system, "he has just foreclosed his freedom, tied his hands, locked himself up and given the key to another to keep." Have you ever found yourself locked up this way? If so, describe the belief system you were committed to. Describe the events that made you aware you were locked up. Discuss the adjustments you made to your thinking about the nature of things.

4. Emerson calls the system of education of his day "a system of despair." Have you had a similar feeling about the system of education you have experienced? If so, describe the main characteristics of that system and explain what caused your despair. Discuss changes that realistically could be made that would take despair out of the system.

5. If you plan to be, or are, responsible for the education of a child, which of Emerson's assertions about education will you try to apply? Write an essay about your philosophy of education and indicate where you have been influenced by Emerson—or where you definitely reject what Emerson prescribes.

NUTS AND BOLTS 8: EXAMPLES

Good writers are well aware of the pleasure they've experienced in reading, and they want to give similar pleasure to those who read their work. Being lifted out of oneself and allowed to see things that may be very far away in time or space is a rich source of such pleasure. This effect is generally achieved through the use of images—words that trigger a sensory experience in the reader—hearing, smelling, tasting, touching, but most often seeing. One of the rewards of reading Emerson is the sense we get of his daily life, because he enables us to visualize certain persons, scenes, and situations. Giving the reader such experiences was not Emerson's purpose, however—at least not in the essays. His purpose was to influence how and what the reader *thinks*—to bring the reader closer to accepting *his* view of the world. He knew that if he could make the reader see what he was talking about, he would be more likely to accomplish his purpose.

Emerson fills his essays with ideas, which by their nature are abstractions, but he also provides many concrete examples to support those ideas. An idea cannot be seen or touched; it exists in words only. An idea usually does not trigger a sensory experience the way an image does. In the simplest case, images are produced by single-word nouns: *Knife, brick, bullet, lake, rose;* these are "concrete" words. "The truth," says Emerson in a somewhat different context, "takes flesh in forms that can express it." Such forms, therefore, exemplify the writer's truth. The more examples a writer uses, the more likely the writer is to convince a reader to accept his or her ideas.

Concrete examples (those that evoke a sensory image) are especially effective, but they are not suitable or logical for every idea. Effective examples can take other forms, such as facts, statistics, historical references, anecdotes, opinions—whatever helps explain or prove the particular truth being discussed. Any truth will be more readily believed if what expresses that truth can be pointed to; indeed, a good writer usually provides at least *three* examples. A good writer realizes that as soon as a good reader hears a statement that is questionable, that reader will want some examples. Good writers try to anticipate such demands. When they succeed in this, they give readers pleasure and convince them as well.

In paragraph 15, Emerson states his idea that one's theory of life is constantly being tested by the various events one experiences or witnesses in the course of a day. He then gives some concrete examples of such events: "the shower, the steamboat disaster, the passing of a beautiful face, the apoplexy of our neighbor. . . ."

In paragraph 22, Emerson, in arguing for education that is not the same for everyone, says that he likes to see men "whose manhood is only the continuation of their boyhood, natural characters still; such are able and fertile for heroic action; and not that sad spectacle with which we are too familiar, educated eyes in uneducated bodies." Okay, fine, Emerson! But what exactly do you mean? In the paragraph that follows, he tells us—with concrete examples. He wants to see men who as boys hung around "shops, factories, armories, town-meetings, caucuses, mobs, target shootings. . . ." With this list, he makes the reader see curious boys who are eager to find out what is going on. "There are no secrets from them, they know everything that befalls in the fire-company, the merits of every engine and of every man at the brakes, how to work it, and are swift to try their hand at every part; so too the merits of every locomotive on the rails, and will coax the engineer to let them ride with him and pull the handles when it goes to the engine-house." By the time we get to this point, we should have a pretty clear idea of the kind of boyhood Emerson's ideal men had. They were at school *everywhere*.

The word *education* usually triggers images of pupils and teachers. In proposing his revolutionary ideas about education, Emerson makes it clear that, although he favors dismantling the traditional classroom, he does not intend to send all teachers packing. "Happy the natural college," he says in paragraph 37, "thus self-instituted around every natural teacher. . . ." *Natural* and *self-instituted* are the key words. To explain, he offers a list of examples of natural teachers from ancient Athens through the nineteenth century.

In paragraph 30, Emerson asserts that there are two key elements of the kind of education he espouses: drilling the child in calling things by their right names and cultivating the child's "genius." Most of paragraph 30 is devoted to an explanation of what is meant by *genius*. But to Emerson that is not enough to clarify what he means, so he also gives an *extended example*. Admittedly, the story of Sir Charles Fellowes and the fragments of Xanthus is not the story of a child, but it nevertheless makes clear what Emerson means when he says, "Happy this child with a bias, with a thought which entrances him, leads him, now into deserts now into cities, the fool of an idea." By the time Emerson concludes his story of Fellowes and the Xanthus fragments, the reader is very likely to have been convinced: By following his own genius, Fellowes must have achieved an excellent education.

To the extent that the student writer can incorporate examples to explain or prove "big" statements—"truths," generalizations, major ideas—to that extent will the writing have greater power to convince and to give pleasure.

THOREAU

1862

Henry David Thoreau was the last male descendant of a French ancestor who came to this country from the Isle of Guernsey. His character exhibited occasional traits drawn from this blood, in singular combination with a very strong Saxon genius.

He was born in Concord, Massachusetts, on the 12th of July, 1817. He was graduated at Harvard College in 1837, but without any literary distinction. An iconoclast in literature, he seldom thanked colleges for their service to him, holding them in small esteem, whilst yet his debt to them was important. After leaving the University, he joined his brother in teaching a private school, which he soon renounced. His father was a manufacturer of lead-pencils, and Henry applied himself for a time to this craft, believing he could make a better pencil than was then in use. After completing his experiments, he exhibited his work to chemists and artists in Boston, and having obtained their certificates to its excellence and to its equality with the best London manufacture, he returned home contented. His friends congratulated him that he had now opened his way to fortune. But he replied that he should never make another pencil. "Why should I? I would not do again what I have done once." He resumed his endless walks and miscellaneous studies, making every day some new acquaintance with Nature, though as yet never speaking of zoölogy or botany, since, though very studious of natural facts, he was incurious of technical and textual science.

At this time, a strong, healthy youth, fresh from college, whilst all his companions were choosing their profession, or eager to begin some lucrative employment, it was inevitable that his thoughts should be exercised on the same question, and it required rare decision to refuse all the accustomed paths and keep his solitary freedom at the cost of disappointing the natural expectations of his family and friends: all the more difficult that he had a perfect probity, was exact in securing his own independence, and in holding every man to the like duty. But Thoreau never faltered. He was a born protestant. He declined to give up his large ambition of knowledge and action for any narrow craft or profession, aiming at a much more comprehensive calling, the art of living well. If he slighted and defied the opinions of others, it was only that he was more intent to reconcile his practice with his own belief. Never idle or self-indulgent, he preferred, when he wanted money, earning it by some piece of manual labor agreeable to him, as building a boat or a fence, planting, grafting, surveying or other short work, to any long engagements. With his hardy habits and few wants, his skill in wood-craft, and his powerful arithmetic, he was very competent to live in any part of the world. It would cost him less time to supply his wants than another. He was therefore secure of his leisure.

A natural skill for mensuration, growing out of his mathematical knowledge and his habit of ascertaining the measures and distances of objects which interested him, the size of trees, the depth and extent of ponds and rivers, the height of mountains and the air-line distance of his favorite summits,—this, and his intimate knowledge of the territory about Concord, made him drift into the profession of land-surveyor. It had the advantage for him that it led him continually into new and secluded grounds, and helped his studies of Nature. His accuracy and skill in this work were readily appreciated, and he found all the employment he wanted.

He could easily solve the problems of the surveyor, but he was daily beset with graver questions, which he manfully confronted. He interrogated every custom, and wished to settle all his practice on an ideal foundation. He was a protestant *à outrance,* and few lives contain so many renunciations. He was bred to no profession; he never married; he lived alone; he never went to church; he never voted; he refused to pay a tax to the State; he ate no flesh, he drank no wine, he never knew the use of tobacco; and, though a naturalist, he used neither trap nor gun. He chose, wisely no doubt for himself, to be the bachelor of thought and Nature. He had no talent for wealth, and knew how to be poor without the least hint of squalor or inelegance. Perhaps he fell into his way of living without forecasting it much, but approved it with later wisdom. "I am often reminded," he wrote in his journal, "that if I had bestowed on me the wealth of Crœsus° my aims must be still the same, and my means essentially the same." He had no temptations to fight against,—no appetites, no passions, no taste for elegant trifles. A fine house, dress, the manners and talk of highly cultivated people were all thrown away on him. He much preferred a good Indian, and considered these refinements as impediments to conversation, wishing to meet his companion on the simplest terms. He declined invitations to dinner-parties, because there each was in every one's way, and he could not meet the individuals to any purpose. "They make their pride," he said, "in making their dinner cost much; I make my pride in making my dinner cost little." When asked at table what dish he preferred, he answered, "The nearest." He did not like the taste of wine, and never had a vice in his life. He said,— "I have a faint recollection of pleasure derived from smoking dried lily-stems, before I was a man. I had commonly a supply of these. I have never smoked anything more noxious."

He chose to be rich by making his wants few, and supplying them himself. In his travels, he used the railroad only to get over so much country as was unimportant to the present purpose, walking hundreds of miles, avoiding taverns, buying a lodging in farmers' and fishermen's houses, as cheaper, and more agreeable to him, and because there he could better find the men and the information he wanted.

Crœsus: King of Lydia (?–c. 547 B.C.) in western Asia Minor; known for his great wealth.

There was somewhat military in his nature, not to be subdued, always manly and able, but rarely tender, as if he did not feel himself except in opposition. He wanted a fallacy to expose, a blunder to pillory, I may say required a little sense of victory, a roll of the drum, to call his powers into full exercise. It cost him nothing to say No; indeed he found it much easier than to say Yes. It seemed as if his first instinct on hearing a proposition was to controvert it, so impatient was he of the limitations of our daily thought. This habit, of course, is a little chilling to the social affections; and though the companion would in the end acquit him of any malice or untruth, yet it mars conversation. Hence, no equal companion stood in affectionate relations with one so pure and guileless. "I love Henry," said one of his friends, "but I cannot like him; and as for taking his arm, I should as soon think of taking the arm of an elm-tree."

Yet, hermit and stoic as he was, he was really fond of sympathy, and threw himself heartily and childlike into the company of young people whom he loved, and whom he delighted to entertain, as he only could, with the varied and endless anecdotes of his experiences by field and river: and he was always ready to lead a huckleberry-party or a search for chestnuts or grapes. Talking, one day, of a public discourse, Henry remarked that whatever succeeded with the audience was bad. I said, "Who would not like to write something which all can read, like Robinson Crusoe? and who does not see with regret that his page is not solid with a right materialistic treatment, which delights everybody?" Henry objected, of course, and vaunted the better lectures which reached only a few persons. But, at supper, a young girl, understanding that he was to lecture at the Lyceum, sharply asked him, "Whether his lecture would be a nice, interesting story, such as she wished to hear, or whether it was one of those old philosophical things that she did not care about." Henry turned to her, and bethought himself, and, I saw, was trying to believe that he had matter that might fit her and her brother, who were to sit up and go to the lecture, if it was a good one for them.

He was a speaker and actor of the truth, born such, and was ever running into dramatic situations from this cause. In any circumstance it interested all bystanders to know what part Henry would take, and what he would say; and he did not disappoint expectation, but used an original judgment on each emergency. In 1845 he built himself a small framed house on the shores of Walden Pond, and lived there two years alone, a life of labor and study. This action was quite native and fit for him. No one who knew him would tax him with affectation. He was more unlike his neighbors in his thought than in his action. As soon as he had exhausted the advantages of that solitude, he abandoned it. In 1847, not approving some uses to which the public expenditure was applied, he refused to pay his town tax, and was put in jail. A friend paid the tax for him, and he was released. The like annoyance was threatened the next year. But as his friends paid the tax, notwithstanding his protest, I believe he ceased to resist. No opposition or ridicule had any weight with him. He coldly and fully stated his opinion without affecting to believe that it was the opinion of the company. It was of no consequence if every one present held the opposite opinion. On one occasion he went to the University Library to procure some books. The librarian refused to lend them. Mr. Thoreau repaired to the President, who stated to him the rules and usages, which permitted the loan of books to resident graduates, to clergymen who were alumni, and to some others resident within a circle of ten miles' radius from the College. Mr. Thoreau explained to the President that the railroad had destroyed the old scale of distances,—that the library was useless, yes, and President and College useless, on the terms of his rules,— that the one benefit he owed to the College was its library,—that, at this moment, not only his want of books was imperative, but he wanted a large number of books, and assured him that he, Thoreau, and not the librarian, was the proper custodian of these. In short, the President found the petitioner so formidable, and the rules getting to look so ridiculous, that he ended by giving him a privilege which in his hands proved unlimited thereafter.

No truer American existed than Thoreau. His preference of his   10
country and condition was genuine, and his aversion from English and European manners and tastes almost reached contempt. He listened impatiently to news or *bonmots* gleaned from London circles; and though he tried to be civil, these anecdotes fatigued him. The men were all imitating each other, and on a small mould. Why can they not live as far apart as possible, and each be a man by himself? What he sought was the most energetic nature; and he wished to go to Oregon, not to London. "In every part of Great Britain," he wrote in his diary, "are discovered traces of the Romans, their funereal urns, their camps, their roads, their dwellings. But New England, at least, is not based on any Roman ruins. We have not to lay the foundations of our houses on the ashes of a former civilization."

But idealist as he was, standing for abolition of slavery, abolition of tariffs, almost for abolition of government, it is needless to say he found himself not only unrepresented in actual politics, but almost equally opposed to every class of reformers. Yet he paid the tribute of his uniform respect to the Anti-Slavery party. One man, whose personal acquaintance he had formed, he honored with exceptional regard. Before the first friendly word had been spoken for Captain John Brown,° he sent notices to most houses in Concord that he would speak in a public hall on the condition and character of John Brown, on Sunday evening, and invited all people to come. The Republican Committee, the Abolitionist Committee, sent him word that it was premature and not advisable. He replied,—"I did not send to you for advice, but to announce that I am to speak." The hall was filled at an early hour by people of all parties, and his earnest eulogy of the hero was heard by all respectfully, by many with a sympathy that surprised themselves.

Captain John Brown: An ardent abolitionist (1800–1859) who believed he was an instrument in the hand of God. He planned to liberate slaves and set up a stronghold to which they could flee. On October 16, 1859, he was hanged for his role in the attack on the U.S. arsenal at Harpers Ferry.

It was said of Plotinus° that he was ashamed of his body, and 'tis very likely he had good reason for it,—that his body was a bad servant, and he had not skill in dealing with the material world, as happens often to men of abstract intellect. But Mr. Thoreau was equipped with a most adapted and serviceable body. He was of short stature, firmly built, of light complexion, with strong, serious blue eyes, and a grave aspect,—his face covered in the late years with a becoming beard. His senses were acute, his frame well-knit and hardy, his hands strong and skilful in the use of tools. And there was a wonderful fitness of body and mind. He could pace sixteen rods more accurately than another man could measure them with rod and chain. He could find his path in the woods at night, he said, better by his feet than his eyes. He could estimate the measure of a tree very well by his eye; he could estimate the weight of a calf or a pig, like a dealer. From a box containing a bushel or more of loose pencils, he could take up with his hands fast enough just a dozen pencils at every grasp. He was a good swimmer, runner, skater, boatman, and would probably outwalk most countrymen in a day's journey. And the relation of body to mind was still finer than we have indicated. He said he wanted every stride his legs made. The length of his walk uniformly made the length of his writing. If shut up in the house he did not write at all.

He had a strong common sense, like that which Rose Flammock, the weaver's daughter in Scott's romance, commends in her father, as resembling a yardstick, which, whilst it measures dowlas and diaper, can equally well measure tapestry and cloth of gold. He had always a new resource. When I was planting forest trees, and had procured half a peck of acorns, he said that only a small portion of them would be sound, and proceeded to examine them and select the sound ones. But finding this took time, he said, "I think if you put them all into water the good ones will sink;" which experiment we tried with success. He could plan a garden or a house or a barn; would have been competent to lead a "Pacific Exploring Expedition;" could give judicious counsel in the gravest private or public affairs.

He lived for the day, not cumbered and mortified by his memory. If he brought you yesterday a new proposition, he would bring you to-day another not less revolutionary. A very industrious man, and setting, like all highly organized men, a high value on his time, he seemed the only man of leisure in town, always ready for any excursion that promised well, or for conversation prolonged into late hours. His trenchant sense was never stopped by his rules of daily prudence, but was always up to the new occasion. He liked and used the simplest food, yet, when some one urged a vegetable diet, Thoreau thought all diets a very small matter, saying that "the man who shoots the buffalo lives better than the man who boards at the Graham House." He said,—"You can sleep near the railroad, and never be disturbed: Nature knows very well what sounds are worth attending to, and has made up her mind not to hear the railroad-whistle. But things respect the devout

---

Plotinus: Roman philosopher (c. A.D. 205–270) who founded Neoplatonism.

mind, and a mental ecstasy was never interrupted." He noted what repeatedly befell him, that, after receiving from a distance a rare plant, he would presently find the same in his own haunts. And those pieces of luck which happen only to good players happened to him. One day, walking with a stranger, who inquired where Indian arrow-heads could be found, he replied, "Everywhere," and, stooping forward, picked one on the instant from the ground. At Mount Washington, in Tuckerman's Ravine, Thoreau had a bad fall, and sprained his foot. As he was in the act of getting up from his fall, he saw for the first time the leaves of the *Arnica mollis*.

His robust common sense, armed with stout hands, keen perceptions   15
and strong will, cannot yet account for the superiority which shone in his simple and hidden life. I must add the cardinal fact, that there was an excellent wisdom in him, proper to a rare class of men, which showed him the material world as a means and symbol. This discovery, which sometimes yields to poets a certain casual and interrupted light, serving for the ornament of their writing, was in him an unsleeping insight; and whatever faults or obstructions of temperament might cloud it, he was not disobedient to the heavenly vision. In his youth, he said, one day, "The other world is all my art; my pencils will draw no other; my jack-knife will cut nothing else; I do not use it as a means." This was the muse and genius that ruled his opinions, conversation, studies, work and course of life. This made him a searching judge of men. At first glance he measured his companion, and, though insensible to some fine traits of culture, could very well report his weight and calibre. And this made the impression of genius which his conversation sometimes gave.

He understood the matter in hand at a glance, and saw the limitations and poverty of those he talked with, so that nothing seemed concealed from such terrible eyes. I have repeatedly known young men of sensibility converted in a moment to the belief that this was the man they were in search of, the man of men, who could tell them all they should do. His own dealing with them was never affectionate, but superior, didactic, scorning their petty ways,—very slowly conceding, or not conceding at all, the promise of his society at their houses, or even at his own. "Would he not walk with them?" "He did not know. There was nothing so important to him as his walk; he had no walks to throw away on company." Visits were offered him from respectful parties, but he declined them. Admiring friends offered to carry him at their own cost to the Yellowstone River,—to the West Indies,—to South America. But though nothing could be more grave or considered than his refusals, they remind one, in quite new relations, of that fop Brummel's reply to the gentleman who offered him his carriage in a shower, "But where will *you* ride, then?"—and what accusing silences, and what searching and irresistible speeches, battering down all defences, his companions can remember!

Mr. Thoreau dedicated his genius with such entire love to the fields, hills and waters of his native town, that he made them known and interesting to all reading Americans, and to people over the sea. The river on whose banks he was born and died he knew from its springs to its confluence with the Merrimack. He had made summer and winter observations on it for many years, and at every hour of the day and night. The result of the recent survey of the Water Commissioners appointed by the State of Massachusetts he had reached by his private experiments, several years earlier. Every fact which occurs in the bed, on the banks or in the air over it; the fishes, and their spawning and nests, their manners, their food; the shad-flies which fill the air on a certain evening once a year, and which are snapped at by the fishes so ravenously that many of these die of repletion; the conical heaps of small stones on the river-shallows, the huge nests of small fishes, one of which will sometimes overfill a cart; the birds which frequent the stream, heron, duck, sheldrake, loon, osprey; the snake, muskrat, otter, woodchuck and fox, on the banks; the turtle, frog, hyla and cricket, which make the banks vocal,—were all known to him, and, as it were, townsmen and fellow creatures; so that he felt an absurdity or violence in any narrative of one of these by itself apart, and still more of its dimensions on an inch-rule, or in the exhibition of its skeleton, or the specimen of a squirrel or a bird in brandy. He liked to speak of the manners of the river, as itself a lawful creature, yet with exactness, and always to an observed fact. As he knew the river, so the ponds in this region.

One of the weapons he used, more important to him than microscope or alcohol-receiver to other investigators, was a whim which grew on him by indulgence, yet appeared in gravest statement, namely, of extolling his own town and neighborhood as the most favored centre for natural observation. He remarked that the Flora of Massachusetts embraced almost all the important plants of America,—most of the oaks, most of the willows, the best pines, the ash, the maple, the beech, the nuts. He returned Kane's Arctic Voyage to a friend of whom he had borrowed it, with the remark, that "Most of the phenomena noted might be observed in Concord." He seemed a little envious of the Pole, for the coincident sunrise and sunset, or five minutes' day after six months: a splendid fact, which Annursnuc had never afforded him. He found red snow in one of his walks, and told me that he expected to find yet the *Victoria regia* in Concord. He was the attorney of the indigenous plants, and owned to a preference of the weeds to the imported plants, as of the Indian to the civilized man, and noticed, with pleasure, that the willow bean-poles of his neighbor had grown more than his beans. "See these weeds," he said, "which have been hoed at by a million farmers all spring and summer, and yet have prevailed, and just now come out triumphant over all lanes, pastures, fields and gardens, such is their vigor. We have insulted them with low names, too,—as Pigweed, Wormwood, Chickweed, Shad-blossom." He says, "They have brave names, too,—Ambrosia, Stellaria, Amelanchier, Amaranth, etc."

I think his fancy for referring everything to the meridian of Concord did not grow out of any ignorance or depreciation of other longitudes or latitudes, but was rather a playful expression of his conviction of the indifference of all places, and that the best place for each is where he stands. He expressed it once in this wise: "I think nothing is to be hoped from you, if this bit of mould under your feet is not sweeter to you to eat than any other in this world, or in any world."

The other weapon with which he conquered all obstacles in science   *20* was patience. He knew how to sit immovable, a part of the rock he rested on, until the bird, the reptile, the fish, which had retired from him, should come back and resume its habits, nay, moved by curiosity, should come to him and watch him.

It was a pleasure and a privilege to walk with him. He knew the country like a fox or a bird, and passed through it as freely by paths of his own. He knew every track in the snow or on the ground, and what creature had taken this path before him. One must submit abjectly to such a guide, and the reward was great. Under his arm he carried an old music-book to press plants; in his pocket, his diary and pencil, a spy-glass for birds, microscope, jack-knife and twine. He wore a straw hat, stout shoes, strong gray trousers, to brave scrub-oaks and smilax, and to climb a tree for a hawk's or a squirrel's nest. He waded into the pool for the water-plants, and his strong legs were no insignificant part of his armor. On the day I speak of he looked for the Menyanthes, detected it across the wide pool, and, on examination of the florets, decided that it had been in flower five days. He drew out of his breast-pocket his diary, and read the names of all the plants that should bloom on this day, whereof he kept account as a banker when his notes fall due. The Cypripedium, not due till to-morrow. He thought that, if waked up from a trance, in this swamp, he could tell by the plants what time of the year it was within two days. The redstart was flying about, and presently the fine grosbeaks, whose brilliant scarlet "makes the rash gazer wipe his eye," and whose fine clear note Thoreau compared to that of a tanager which has got rid of its hoarseness. Presently he heard a note which he called that of the night-warbler, a bird he had never identified, had been in search of twelve years, which always, when he saw it, was in the act of diving down into a tree or bush, and which it was vain to seek; the only bird which sings indifferently by night and by day. I told him he must beware of finding and booking it, lest life should have nothing more to show him. He said, "What you seek in vain for, half your life, one day you come full upon, all the family at dinner. You seek it like a dream, and as soon as you find it you become its prey."

His interest in the flower or the bird lay very deep in his mind, was connected with Nature,—and the meaning of Nature was never attempted to be defined by him. He would not offer a memoir of his observations to the Natural History Society. "Why should I? To detach the description from its connections in my mind would make it no longer true or valuable to me: and they do not wish what belongs to it." His power of observation seemed to indicate additional senses. He saw as with microscope, heard as with ear-trumpet, and his memory was a photographic register of all he saw and heard. And yet none knew better than he that it is not the fact that imports, but the impression or effect of the fact on your mind. Every fact lay in glory in his mind, a type of the order and beauty of the whole.

His determination on Natural History was organic. He confessed that he sometimes felt like a hound or a panther, and, if born among Indians, would have been a fell hunter. But, restrained by his Massachusetts culture, he played out the game in this mild form of botany and ichthyology. His intimacy with animals suggested what Thomas Fuller records of Butler the apiologist, that "either he had told the bees things or the bees had told him." Snakes coiled round his legs; the fishes swam into his hand, and he took them out of the water; he pulled the woodchuck out of its hole by the tail, and took the foxes under his protection from the hunters. Our naturalist had perfect magnanimity; he had no secrets: he would carry you to the heron's haunt, or even to his most prized botanical swamp,—possibly knowing that you could never find it again, yet willing to take his risks.

No college ever offered him a diploma, or a professor's chair; no academy made him its corresponding secretary, its discoverer or even its member. Perhaps these learned bodies feared the satire of his presence. Yet so much knowledge of Nature's secret and genius few others possessed; none in a more large and religious synthesis. For not a particle of respect had he to the opinions of any man or body of men, but homage solely to the truth itself; and as he discovered everywhere among doctors some leaning of courtesy, it discredited them. He grew to be revered and admired by his townsmen, who had at first known him only as an oddity. The farmers who employed him as a surveyor soon discovered his rare accuracy and skill, his knowledge of their lands, of trees, of birds, of Indian remains and the like, which enabled him to tell every farmer more than he knew before of his own farm; so that he began to feel a little as if Mr. Thoreau had better rights in his land than he. They felt, too, the superiority of character which addressed all men with a native authority.

Indian relics abound in Concord,—arrow-heads, stone chisels, pestles   25 and fragments of pottery; and on the river-bank, large heaps of clam-shells and ashes mark spots which the savages frequented. These, and every circumstance touching the Indian, were important in his eyes. His visits to Maine were chiefly for love of the Indian. He had the satisfaction of seeing the manufacture of the bark canoe, as well as of trying his hand in its management on the rapids. He was inquisitive about the making of the stone arrow-head, and in his last days charged a youth setting out for the Rocky Mountains to find an Indian who could tell him that: "It was well worth a visit to California to learn it." Occasionally, a small party of Penobscot Indians would visit Concord, and pitch their tents for a few weeks in summer on the riverbank. He failed not to make acquaintance with the best of them; though he well knew that asking questions of Indians is like catechizing beavers and rabbits. In his last visit to Maine he had great satisfaction from Joseph Polis, an intelligent Indian of Oldtown, who was his guide for some weeks.

He was equally interested in every natural fact. The depth of his perception found likeness of law throughout Nature, and I know not any genius who so swiftly inferred universal law from the single fact. He was no pedant of a department. His eye was open to beauty, and his ear to music. He found these, not in rare conditions, but wheresoever he went. He thought the best of music was in single strains; and he found poetic suggestion in the humming of the telegraph-wire.

His poetry might be bad or good; he no doubt wanted a lyric facility and technical skill, but he had the source of poetry in his spiritual perception. He was a good reader and critic, and his judgment on poetry was to the ground of it. He could not be deceived as to the presence or absence of the poetic element in any composition, and his thirst for this made him negligent and perhaps scornful of superficial graces. He would pass by many delicate rhythms, but he would have detected every live stanza or line in a volume and knew very well where to find an equal poetic charm in prose. He was so enamoured of the spiritual beauty that he held all actual written poems in very light esteem in the comparison. He admired Æschylus and Pindar; but when some one was commending them, he said that Æschylus and the Greeks, in describing Apollo and Orpheus, had given no song, or no good one. "They ought not to have moved trees, but to have chanted to the gods such a hymn as would have sung all their old ideas out of their heads, and new ones in." His own verses are often rude and defective. The gold does not yet run pure, is drossy and crude. The thyme and marjoram are not yet honey. But if he want lyric fineness and technical merits, if he have not the poetic temperament, he never lacks the causal thought, showing that his genius was better than his talent. He knew the worth of the Imagination for the uplifting and consolation of human life, and liked to throw every thought into a symbol. The fact you tell is of no value, but only the impression. For this reason his presence was poetic, always piqued the curiosity to know more deeply the secrets of his mind. He had many reserves, an unwillingness to exhibit to profane eyes what was still sacred in his own, and knew well how to throw a poetic veil over his experience. All readers of Walden will remember his mythical record of his disappointments:—

"I long ago lost a hound, a bay horse and a turtle-dove, and am still on their trail. Many are the travellers I have spoken concerning them, describing their tracks, and what calls they answered to. I have met one or two who have heard the hound, and the tramp of the horse, and even seen the dove disappear behind a cloud; and they seemed as anxious to recover them as if they had lost them themselves."

His riddles were worth the reading, and I confide that if at any time I do not understand the expression, it is yet just. Such was the wealth of his truth that it was not worth his while to use words in vain. His poem entitled "Sympathy" reveals the tenderness under that triple steel of stoicism, and the intellectual subtility it could animate. His classic poem on "Smoke" suggests Simonides,° but is better than any poem of Simonides. His biography is in his

---

Simonides: Greek poet (556?–468?).

verses. His habitual thought makes all his poetry a hymn to the Cause of causes, the Spirit which vivifies and controls his own:—

"I hearing get, who had but ears,
And sight, who had but eyes before;
I moments live, who lived but years,
And truth discern, who knew but learning's lore."

And still more in these religious lines:—

"Now chiefly is my natal hour,
And only now my prime of life;
I will not doubt the love untold,
Which not my worth nor want have bought;
Which wooed me young, and wooes me old,
And to this evening hath me brought."

Whilst he used in his writings a certain petulance of remark in reference   30
to churches or churchmen, he was a person of a rare, tender and absolute religion, a person incapable of any profanation, by act or by thought. Of course, the same isolation which belonged to his original thinking and living detached him from the social religious forms. This is neither to be censured nor regretted. Aristotle long ago explained it, when he said, "One who surpasses his fellow citizens in virtue is no longer a part of the city. Their law is not for him, since he is a law to himself."

Thoreau was sincerity itself, and might fortify the convictions of prophets in the ethical laws by his holy living. It was an affirmative experience which refused to be set aside. A truth-speaker he, capable of the most deep and strict conversation; a physician to the wounds of any soul; a friend, knowing not only the secret of friendship, but almost worshipped by those few persons who resorted to him as their confessor and prophet, and knew the deep value of his mind and great heart. He thought that without religion or devotion of some kind nothing great was ever accomplished: and he thought that the bigoted sectarian had better bear this in mind.

His virtues, of course, sometimes ran into extremes. It was easy to trace to the inexorable demand on all for exact truth that austerity which made this willing hermit more solitary even than he wished. Himself of a perfect probity, he required not less of others. He had a disgust at crime, and no worldly success would cover it. He detected paltering as readily in dignified and prosperous persons as in beggars, and with equal scorn. Such dangerous frankness was in his dealing that his admirers called him "that terrible Thoreau," as if he spoke when silent, and was still present when he had departed. I think the severity of his ideal interfered to deprive him of a healthy sufficiency of human society.

The habit of a realist to find things the reverse of their appearance inclined him to put every statement in a paradox. A certain habit of antago-nism defaced his earlier writings,—a trick of rhetoric not quite outgrown in his later, of substituting for the obvious word and thought its diametrical opposite. He praised wild mountains and winter forests for their domestic air, in snow and ice he would find sultriness, and commended the wilderness for resembling Rome and Paris. "It was so dry, that you might call it wet."

The tendency to magnify the moment, to read all the laws of Nature in the one object or one combination under your eye, is of course comic to those who do not share the philosopher's perception of identity. To him there was no such thing as size. The pond was a small ocean; the Atlantic, a large Walden Pond. He referred every minute fact to cosmical laws. Though he meant to be just, he seemed haunted by a certain chronic assumption that the science of the day pretended completeness, and he had just found out that the *savans* had neglected to discriminate a particular botanical variety, had failed to describe the seeds or count the sepals. "That is to say," we replied, "the blockheads were not born in Concord; but who said they were? It was their unspeakable misfortune to be born in London, or Paris, or Rome; but, poor fellows, they did what they could, considering that they never saw Bateman's Pond, or Nine-Acre Corner, or Becky Stow's Swamp; besides, what were you sent into the world for, but to add this observation?"

Had his genius been only contemplative, he had been fitted to his life, but with his energy and practical ability he seemed born for great enterprise and for command; and I so much regret the loss of his rare powers of action, that I cannot help counting it a fault in him that he had no ambition. Wanting this, instead of engineering for all America, he was the captain of a huckleberry-party. Pounding beans is good to the end of pounding empires one of these days; but if, at the end of years, it is still only beans!

But these foibles, real or apparent, were fast vanishing in the incessant growth of a spirit so robust and wise and which effaced its defeats with new triumphs. His study of Nature was a perpetual ornament to him, and inspired his friends with curiosity to see the world through his eyes, and to hear his adventures. They possessed every kind of interest.

He had many elegancies of his own, whilst he scoffed at conventional elegance. Thus, he could not bear to hear the sound of his own steps, the grit of gravel; and therefore never willingly walked in the road, but in the grass, on mountains and in woods. His senses were acute, and he remarked that by night every dwelling-house gives out bad air, like a slaughter-house. He liked the pure fragrance of melilot. He honored certain plants with special regard, and, over all, the pond-lily,—then, the gentian, and the *Mikania scandens,* and "life-everlasting," and a bass-tree which he visited every year when it bloomed, in the middle of July. He thought the scent a more oracular inquisition than the sight,—more oracular and trustworthy. The scent, of course, reveals what is concealed from the other senses. By it he detected earthiness. He delighted in echoes, and said they were almost the only kind of kindred voices that he heard. He loved Nature so well, was so happy in her solitude, that he became very jealous of cities and the sad work which their refinements and artifices made with man and his dwelling. The axe was always destroying his forest. "Thank God," he said, "they cannot cut down the

35

clouds!" "All kinds of figures are drawn on the blue ground with this fibrous white paint."

I subjoin a few sentences taken from his unpublished manuscripts, not only as records of his thought and feeling, but for their power of description and literary excellence:—

"Some circumstantial evidence is very strong, as when you find a trout in the milk."

"The chub is a soft fish, and tastes like boiled brown paper salted."

"The youth gets together his materials to build a bridge to the moon, or, perchance, a palace or temple on the earth, and, at length the middle-aged man concludes to build a wood-shed with them."

"The locust z-ing."

"Devil's-needles zigzagging along the Nut-Meadow brook."

"Sugar is not so sweet to the palate as sound to the healthy ear."

"I put on some hemlock-boughs, and the rich salt crackling of their leaves was like mustard to the ear, the crackling of uncountable regiments. Dead trees love the fire."

"The bluebird carries the sky on his back."

"The tanager flies through the green foliage as if it would ignite the leaves."

"If I wish for a horse-hair for my compass-sight I must go to the stable; but the hair-bird, with her sharp eyes, goes to the road."

"Immortal water, alive even to the superficies."

"Fire is the most tolerable third party."

"Nature made ferns for pure leaves, to show what she could do in that line."

"No tree has so fair a bole and so handsome an instep as the beech."

"How did these beautiful rainbow-tints get into the shell of the fresh-water clam, buried in the mud at the bottom of our dark river?"

"Hard are the times when the infant's shoes are second-foot."

"We are strictly confined to our men to whom we give liberty."

"Nothing is so much to be feared as fear. Atheism may comparatively be popular with God himself."

"Of what significance the things you can forget? A little thought is sexton to all the world."

"How can we expect a harvest of thought who have not had a seed-time of character?"

"Only he can be trusted with gifts who can present a face of bronze to expectations."

"I ask to be melted. You can only ask of the metals that they be tender to the fire that melts them. To nought else can they be tender."

There is a flower known to botanists, one of the same genus with our summer plant called "Life-Everlasting," a *Gnaphalium* like that, which grows on the most inaccessible cliffs of the Tyrolese mountains, where the chamois dare hardly venture, and which the hunter, tempted by its beauty, and by his love (for it is immensely valued by the Swiss maidens), climbs the cliffs to gather, and is sometimes found dead at the foot, with the flower in his hand. It is called by botanists the *Gnaphalium leontopodium,* but by the Swiss *Edelweisse,* which signifies *Noble Purity.* Thoreau seemed to me living in the hope to gather this plant, which belonged to him of right. The scale on which his studies proceeded was so large as to require longevity, and we were the less prepared for his sudden disappearance. The country knows not yet, or in the least part, how great a son it has lost. It seems an injury that he should leave in the midst his broken task which none else can finish, a kind of indignity to so noble a soul that he should depart out of Nature before yet he has been really shown to his peers for what he is. But he, at least, is content. His soul was made for the noblest society; he had in a short life exhausted the capabilities of this world; wherever there is knowledge, wherever there is virtue, wherever there is beauty, he will find a home.

Questions for Understanding

1. What does Emerson mean when he says of Thoreau, "He was a born protestant"?
2. If, as Emerson says, Thoreau had "no appetites, no passions, no taste for elegant trifles," did Thoreau find much pleasure in life?
3. Why would Emerson say that he loved Henry Thoreau but could not like him?
4. Was there anything hypocritical in Thoreau's going to live at Walden Pond and then leaving "as soon as he had exhausted the advantages of that solitude"?
5. Emerson gives this testament to the power Thoreau could have over others: "I have repeatedly known young men of sensibility converted in a moment to the belief that this was the man they were in search of, the man of men, who could tell them all they should do." In other words, Emerson saw numerous young men ready to submit to Thoreau and let him guide their lives. What use did Thoreau make of this power?

Suggestions for Writing

1. "Never idle or self-indulgent, he preferred, when he wanted money, earning it by some piece of manual labor agreeable to him. . . ." Write an essay in which you discuss the pros and cons of Thoreau's way of providing. Refer to people you know who are good examples of Thoreau's way and to people for whom Thoreau's way would not be possible.
2. Thoreau wrote in his journal, "if I had bestowed on me the wealth of Crœsus, my aims must still be the same, and my means essentially the same." Write an essay in which you discuss whether this statement is to Thoreau's credit or discredit. Refer to persons you know who say they would not be affected by sudden wealth and also to persons whose aims and means would change drastically.
3. Thoreau refused to accept the decision of the University Librarian not to allow him to borrow books because technically he did not meet the

qualifications to be a borrower. Have you ever successfully fought a comparable decision? Describe the situation and explain what you did when you were denied what you wanted. Discuss the conclusions you came to as a result of that experience.

4. When Emerson says that "no truer American existed than Thoreau," he is referring to Thoreau's individualism and his contempt for men who eagerly picked up the latest fashions and fads from London, a city they regarded as the pace-setter in all things cultural. Among your contemporaries, who or what sets the trends? Among your contemporaries, are there any individualists—or only imitators? Among your contemporaries, are the nonconformists really conformists? Describe and discuss.

5. Emerson says of Thoreau that "with his energy and practical ability he seemed born for great enterprise and command." But, in the end, Emerson counts it a fault in Thoreau that he had no ambition: "instead of engineering for all America, he was the captain of a huckleberry-party." Are you acquainted with anyone about whom something similar might be said—that he or she has great energy and ability but is failing to make good use of them? Do you know anyone who could make a difference on important matters but who shows no inclination to venture beyond his own street or town? Describe such a person and his or her situation. What talents and abilities does the person have? What has the person accomplished? Discuss what you think are the causes of the person's reluctance to take on more.

SELF-RELIANCE

1838

I read the other day some verses written by an eminent painter which   *1*
were original and not conventional. The soul always hears an admonition in
such lines, let the subject be what it may. The sentiment they instil is of more
value than any thought they may contain. To believe your own thought, to
believe that what is true for you in your private heart is true for all men,—that
is genius. Speak your latent conviction, and it shall be the universal sense; for
the inmost in due time becomes the outmost, and our first thought is
rendered back to us by the trumpets of the Last Judgment. Familiar as the
voice of the mind is to each, the highest merit we ascribe to Moses, Plato and
Milton is that they set at naught books and traditions, and spoke not what
men, but what *they* thought. A man should learn to detect and watch that
gleam of light which flashes across his mind from within, more than the lustre
of the firmament of bards and sages. Yet he dismisses without notice his
thought, because it is his. In every work of genius we recognize our own
rejected thoughts; they come back to us with a certain alienated majesty.
Great works of art have no more affecting lesson for us than this. They teach
us to abide by our spontaneous impression with good-humored inflexibility
then most when the whole cry of voices is on the other side. Else to-morrow
a stranger will say with masterly good sense precisely what we have thought
and felt all the time, and we shall be forced to take with shame our own
opinion from another.

There is a time in every man's education when he arrives at the
conviction that envy is ignorance; that imitation is suicide; that he must take
himself for better, for worse, as his portion; that though the wide universe is
full of good, no kernel of nourishing corn can come to him but through his
toil bestowed on that plot of ground which is given to him to till. The power
which resides in him is new in nature, and none but he knows what that is
which he can do, nor does he know until he has tried. Not for nothing one
face, one character, one fact, makes much impression on him, and another
none. This sculpture in the memory is not without pre-established harmony.
The eye was placed where one ray should fall, that it might testify of that
particular ray. We but half express ourselves, and are ashamed of that divine
idea which each of us represents. It may be safely trusted as proportionate and
of good issues, so it be faithfully imparted, but God will not have his work
made manifest by cowards. A man is relieved and gay when he has put his
heart into his work and done his best; but what he has said or done otherwise
shall give him no peace. It is a deliverance which does not deliver. In the
attempt his genius deserts him; no muse befriends; no invention, no hope.

Trust thyself: every heart vibrates to that iron string. Accept the place
the divine providence has found for you, the society of your contemporaries,
the connection of events. Great men have always done so, and confided
themselves childlike to the genius of their age, betraying their perception that

the absolutely trustworthy was seated at their heart, working through their hands, predominating in all their being. And we are now men, and must accept in the highest mind the same transcendent destiny; and not minors and invalids in a protected corner, not cowards fleeing before a revolution, but guides, redeemers and benefactors, obeying the Almighty effort and advancing on Chaos and the Dark.

What pretty oracles nature yields us on this text in the face and behavior of children, babes, and even brutes! That divided and rebel mind, that distrust of a sentiment because our arithmetic has computed the strength and means opposed to our purpose, these have not. Their mind being whole, their eye is as yet unconquered, and when we look in their faces we are disconcerted. Infancy conforms to nobody; all conform to it; so that one babe commonly makes four or five out of the adults who prattle and play to it. So God has armed youth and puberty and manhood no less with its own piquancy and charm, and made it enviable and gracious and its claims not to be put by, if it will stand by itself. Do not think the youth has no force, because he cannot speak to you and me. Hark! in the next room his voice is sufficiently clear and emphatic. It seems he knows how to speak to his contemporaries. Bashful or bold then, he will know how to make us seniors very unnecessary.

The nonchalance of boys who are sure of a dinner, and would disdain as much as a lord to do or say aught to conciliate one, is the healthy attitude of human nature. A boy is in the parlor what the pit is in the playhouse; independent, irresponsible, looking out from his corner on such people and facts as pass by, he tries and sentences them on their merits, in the swift, summary way of boys, as good, bad, interesting, silly, eloquent, troublesome. He cumbers himself never about consequences, about interests; he gives an independent, genuine verdict. You must court him; he does not court you. But the man is as it were clapped into jail by his consciousness. As soon as he has once acted or spoken with *éclat* he is a committed person, watched by the sympathy or the hatred of hundreds, whose affections must now enter into his account. There is no Lethe for this. Ah, that he could pass again into his neutrality! Who can thus avoid all pledges and, having observed, observe again from the same unaffected, unbiased, unbribable, unaffrighted innocence,—must always be formidable. He would utter opinions on all passing affairs, which being seen to be not private but necessary, would sink like darts into the ear of men and put them in fear.

These are the voices which we hear in solitude, but they grow faint and inaudible as we enter into the world. Society everywhere is in conspiracy against the manhood of every one of its members. Society is a joint-stock company, in which the members agree, for the better securing of his bread to each shareholder, to surrender the liberty and culture of the eater. The virtue in most request is conformity. Self-reliance is its aversion. It loves not realities and creators, but names and customs.

Whoso would be a man, must be a nonconformist. He who would gather immortal palms must not be hindered by the name of goodness, but must explore if it be goodness. Nothing is at last sacred but the integrity of your own mind. Absolve you to yourself, and you shall have the suffrage of the world. I remember an answer which when quite young I was prompted to make to a valued adviser who was wont to importune me with the dear old doctrines of the church. On my saying, "What have I to do with the sacredness of traditions, if I live wholly from within?" my friend suggested,— "But these impulses may be from below, not from above." I replied, "They do not seem to me to be such; but if I am the Devil's child, I will live then from the Devil." No law can be sacred to me but that of my nature. Good and bad are but names very readily transferable to that or this; the only right is what is after my constitution; the only wrong what is against it. A man is to carry himself in the presence of all opposition as if every thing were titular and ephemeral but he. I am ashamed to think how easily we capitulate to badges and names, to large societies and dead institutions. Every decent and well-spoken individual affects and sways me more than is right. I ought to go upright and vital, and speak the rude truth in all ways. If malice and vanity wear the coat of philanthropy, shall that pass? If an angry bigot assumes this bountiful cause of Abolition, and comes to me with his last news from Barbadoes, why should I not say to him, 'Go love thy infant; love thy wood-chopper; be good-natured and modest; have that grace; and never varnish your hard, uncharitable ambition with this incredible tenderness for black folk a thousand miles off. Thy love afar is spite at home.' Rough and graceless would be such greeting, but truth is handsomer than the affectation of love. Your goodness must have some edge to it,—else it is none. The doctrine of hatred must be preached, as the counteraction of the doctrine of love, when that pules and whines. I shun father and mother and wife and brother when my genius calls me. I would write on the lintels of the door-post, *Whim.* I hope it is somewhat better than whim at last, but we cannot spend the day in explanation. Expect me not to show cause why I seek or why I exclude company. Then again, do not tell me, as a good man did to-day, of my obligation to put all poor men in good situations. Are they *my* poor? I tell thee, thou foolish philanthropist, that I grudge the dollar, the dime, the cent I give to such men as do not belong to me and to whom I do not belong. There is a class of persons to whom by all spiritual affinity I am bought and sold; for them I will go to prison if need be; but your miscellaneous popular charities; the education at college of fools; the building of meeting-houses to the vain end to which many now stand; alms to sots, and the thousand-fold Relief Societies;—though I confess with shame I sometimes succumb and give the dollar, it is a wicked dollar, which by and by I shall have the manhood to withhold.

Virtues are, in the popular estimate, rather the exception than the rule. There is the man *and* his virtues. Men do what is called a good action, as some piece of courage or charity, much as they would pay a fine in expiation of daily non-appearance on parade. Their works are done as an apology or extenuation of their living in the world,—as invalids and the insane pay a high board. Their virtues are penances. I do not wish to expiate, but to live. My life is for itself and not for a spectacle. I much prefer that it should be of a lower strain, so it be genuine and equal, than that it should be glittering and unsteady. I wish it to be sound and sweet, and not to need diet and bleeding. I ask primary evidence that you are a man, and refuse this appeal from the man to his actions. I know that for myself it makes no difference whether I do or forbear those actions which are reckoned excellent. I cannot consent to pay for a privilege where I have intrinsic right. Few and mean as my gifts may be, I actually am, and do not need for my own assurance or the assurance of my fellows any secondary testimony.

What I must do is all that concerns me, not what the people think. This rule, equally arduous in actual and in intellectual life, may serve for the whole distinction between greatness and meanness. It is the harder because you will always find those who think they know what is your duty better than you know it. It is easy in the world to live after the world's opinion; it is easy in solitude to live after our own; but the great man is he who in the midst of the crowd keeps with perfect sweetness the independence of solitude.

The objection to conforming to usages that have become dead to you   10
is that it scatters your force. It loses your time and blurs the impression of your character. If you maintain a dead church, contribute to a dead Bible-society, vote with a great party either for the government or against it, spread your table like base housekeepers,—under all these screens I have difficulty to detect the precise man you are: and of course so much force is withdrawn from your proper life. But do your work, and I shall know you. Do your work, and you shall reinforce yourself. A man must consider what a blind-man's-buff is this game of conformity. If I know your sect I anticipate your argument. I hear a preacher announce for his text and topic the expediency of one of the institutions of his church. Do I not know beforehand that not possibly can he say a new and spontaneous word? Do I not know that with all this ostentation of examining the grounds of the institution he will do no such thing? Do I not know that he is pledged to himself not to look but at one side, the permitted side, not as a man, but as a parish minister? He is a retained attorney, and these airs of the bench are the emptiest affectation. Well, most men have bound their eyes with one or another handkerchief, and attached themselves to some one of these communities of opinion. This conformity makes them not false in a few particulars, authors of a few lies, but false in all particulars. Their every truth is not quite true. Their two is not the real two, their four not the real four; so that every word they say chagrins us and we know not where to begin to set them right. Meantime nature is not slow to equip us in the prison-uniform of the party to which we adhere. We come to wear one cut of face and figure, and acquire by degrees the gentlest asinine expression. There is a mortifying experience in particular, which does not fail to wreak itself also in the general history; I mean "the foolish face of praise," the forced smile which we put on in company where we do not feel at ease, in answer to conversation which does not interest us. The muscles, not spontaneously moved but moved by a low usurping wilfulness, grow tight about the outline of the face, with the most disagreeable sensation.

For nonconformity the world whips you with its displeasure. And therefore a man must know how to estimate a sour face. The by-standers look askance on him in the public street or in the friend's parlor. If this aversion had its origin in contempt and resistance like his own he might well go home with a sad countenance; but the sour faces of the multitude, like their sweet faces, have no deep cause, but are put on and off as the wind blows and a newspaper directs. Yet is the discontent of the multitude more formidable than that of the senate and the college. It is easy enough for a firm man who knows the world to brook the rage of the cultivated classes. Their rage is decorous and prudent, for they are timid, as being very vulnerable themselves. But when to their feminine rage the indignation of the people is added, when the ignorant and the poor are aroused, when the unintelligent brute force that lies at the bottom of society is made to growl and mow, it needs the habit of magnanimity and religion to treat it godlike as a trifle of no concernment.

The other terror that scares us from self-trust is our consistency; a reverence for our past act or word because the eyes of others have no other data for computing our orbit than our past acts, and we are loth to disappoint them.

But why should you keep your head over your shoulder? Why drag about this corpse of your memory, lest you contradict somewhat you have stated in this or that public place? Suppose you should contradict yourself; what then? It seems to be a rule of wisdom never to rely on your memory alone, scarcely even in acts of pure memory, but to bring the past for judgment into the thousand-eyed present, and live ever in a new day. In your metaphysics you have denied personality to the Deity, yet when the devout motions of the soul come, yield to them heart and life, though they should clothe God with shape and color. Leave your theory, as Joseph his coat in the hand of the harlot, and flee.

A foolish consistency is the hobgoblin of little minds, adored by little statesmen and philosophers and divines. With consistency a great soul has simply nothing to do. He may as well concern himself with his shadow on the wall. Speak what you think now in hard words and to-morrow speak what to-morrow thinks in hard words again, though it contradict every thing you said to-day.—'Ah, so you shall be sure to be misunderstood.'—Is it so bad then to be misunderstood? Pythagoras was misunderstood, and Socrates, and Jesus, and Luther, and Copernicus, and Galileo, and Newton, and every pure and wise spirit that ever took flesh. To be great is to be misunderstood.

I suppose no man can violate his nature. All the sallies of his will are rounded in by the law of his being, as the inequalities of Andes and Himmaleh are insignificant in the curve of the sphere. Nor does it matter how you gauge and try him. A character is like an acrostic or Alexandrian stanza;—read it forward, backward, or across, it still spells the same thing. In this pleasing contrite wood-life which God allows me, let me record day by day my honest thought without prospect or retrospect, and, I cannot doubt, it will be found symmetrical, though I mean it not and see it not. My book should smell of pines and resound with the hum of insects. The swallow over my window should interweave that thread or straw he carries in his bill into my web also. We pass for what we are. Character teaches above our wills. Men imagine that they communicate their virtue or vice only by overt actions, and do not see that virtue or vice emit a breath every moment.

There will be an agreement in whatever variety of actions, so they be each honest and natural in their hour. For of one will, the actions will be harmonious, however unlike they seem. These varieties are lost sight of at a little distance, at a little height of thought. One tendency unites them all. The voyage of the best ship is a zigzag line of a hundred tacks. See the line from a sufficient distance, and it straightens itself to the average tendency. Your genuine action will explain itself and will explain your other genuine actions. Your conformity explains nothing. Act singly, and what you have already done singly will justify you now. Greatness appeals to the future. If I can be firm enough to-day to do right and scorn eyes, I must have done so much right before as to defend me now. Be it how it will, do right now. Always scorn appearances and you always may. The force of character is cumulative. All the foregone days of virtue work their health into this. What makes the majesty of the heroes of the senate and the field, which so fills the imagination? The consciousness of a train of great days and victories behind. They shed a united light on the advancing actor. He is attended as by a visible escort of angels. That is it which throws thunder into Chatham's° voice, and dignity into Washington's port, and America into Adam's eye. Honor is venerable to us because it is no ephemera. It is always ancient virtue. We worship it to-day because it is not of to-day. We love it and pay it homage because it is not a trap for our love and homage, but is self-dependent, self-derived, and therefore of an old immaculate pedigree, even if shown in a young person.

I hope in these days we have heard the last of conformity and consistency. Let the words be gazetted and ridiculous henceforward. Instead of the gong for dinner, let us hear a whistle from the Spartan fife. Let us never bow and apologize more. A great man is coming to eat at my house. I do not wish to please him; I wish that he should wish to please me. I will stand here for humanity, and though I would make it kind, I would make it true. Let us affront and reprimand the smooth mediocrity and squalid contentment of the times, and hurl in the face of custom and trade and office, the fact which is the upshot of all history, that there is a great responsible Thinker and Actor working wherever a man works; that a true man belongs to no other time or place, but is the centre of things. Where he is, there is nature. He measures you and all men and all events. Ordinarily, every body in society reminds us of somewhat else, or of some other person. Character, reality, reminds you of

---

Chatham's voice: William Pitt, first earl of Chatham (1708–1778). British statesman renowned for his integrity.

nothing else; it takes place of the whole creation. The man must be so much that he must make all circumstances indifferent. Every true man is a cause, a country, and an age; requires infinite spaces and numbers and time fully to accomplish his design;—and posterity seem to follow his steps as a train of clients. A man Cæsar is born, and for ages after we have a Roman Empire. Christ is born, and millions of minds so grow and cleave to his genius that he is confounded with virtue and the possible of man. An institution is the lengthened shadow of one man; as, Monachism, of the Hermit Antony; the Reformation, of Luther; Quakerism, of Fox; Methodism, of Wesley; Abolition, of Clarkson. Scipio, Milton called "the height of Rome;" and all history resolves itself very easily into the biography of a few stout and earnest persons.

Let a man then know his worth, and keep things under his feet. Let him not peep or steal, or skulk up and down with the air of a charity-boy, a bastard, or an interloper in the world which exists for him. But the man in the street, finding no worth in himself which corresponds to the force which built a tower or sculptured a marble god, feels poor when he looks on these. To him a palace, a statue, or a costly book have an alien and forbidding air, much like a gay equipage, and seem to say like that, "Who are you, Sir?" Yet they all are his, suitors for his notice, petitioners to his faculties that they will come out and take possession. The picture waits for my verdict; it is not to command me, but I am to settle its claims to praise. That popular fable of the sot who was picked up dead drunk in the street, carried to the duke's house, washed and dressed and laid in the duke's bed, and, on his waking, treated with all obsequious ceremony like the duke, and assured that he had been insane, owes its popularity to the fact that it symbolizes so well the state of man, who is in the world a sort of sot, but now and then wakes up, exercises his reason and finds himself a true prince.

Our reading is mendicant and sycophantic. In history our imagination plays us false. Kingdom and lordship, power and estate, are a gaudier vocabulary than private John and Edward in a small house and common day's work; but the things of life are the same to both; the sum total of both is the same. Why all this deference to Alfred and Scanderbeg and Gustavus? Suppose they were virtuous; did they wear out virtue? As great a stake depends on your private act to-day as followed their public and renowned steps. When private men shall act with original views, the lustre will be transferred from the actions of kings to those of gentlemen.

The world has been instructed by its kings, who have so magnetized the eyes of nations. It has been taught by this colossal symbol the mutual reverence that is due from man to man. The joyful loyalty with which men have everywhere suffered the king, the noble, or the great proprietor to walk among them by a law of his own, make his own scale of men and things and reverse theirs, pay for benefits not with money but with honor, and represent the law in his person, was the hieroglyphic by which they obscurely signified their consciousness of their own right and comeliness, the right of every man.

The magnetism which all original action exerts is explained when we inquire the reason of self-trust. Who is the Trustee? What is the aboriginal Self, on which a universal reliance may be grounded? What is the nature and power of that science-baffling star, without parallax, without calculable elements, which shoots a ray of beauty even into trivial and impure actions, if the least mark of independence appear? The inquiry leads us to that source, at once the essence of genius, of virtue, and of life, which we call Spontaneity or Instinct. We denote this primary wisdom as Intuition, whilst all later teachings are tuitions. In that deep force, the last fact behind which analysis cannot go, all things find their common origin. For the sense of being which in calm hours rises, we know not how, in the soul, is not diverse from things, from space, from light, from time, from man, but one with them and proceeds obviously from the same source whence their life and being also proceed. We first share the life by which things exist and afterwards see them as appearances in nature and forget that we have shared their cause. Here is the fountain of action and of thought. Here are the lungs of that inspiration which giveth man wisdom and which cannot be denied without impiety and atheism. We lie in the lap of immense intelligence, which makes us receivers of its truth and organs of its activity. When we discern justice, when we discern truth we do nothing of ourselves, but allow a passage to its beams. If we ask whence this comes, if we seek to pry into the soul that causes, all philosophy is at fault. Its presence or its absence is all we can affirm. Every man discriminates between the voluntary acts of his mind and his involuntary perceptions, and knows that to his involuntary perceptions a perfect faith is due. He may err in the expression of them, but he knows that these things are so, like day and night, not to be disputed. My wilful actions and acquisitions are but roving;—the idlest reverie, the faintest native emotion, command my curiosity and respect. Thoughtless people contradict as readily the statement of perceptions as of opinions, or rather much more readily; for they do not distinguish between perception and notion. They fancy that I choose to see this or that thing. But perception is not whimsical, but fatal. If I see a trait, my children will see it after me, and in course of time all mankind,—although it may chance that no one has seen it before me. For my perception of it is as much a fact as the sun.

The relations of the soul to the divine spirit are so pure that it is profane to seek to interpose helps. It must be that when God speaketh he should communicate, not one thing, but all things; should fill the world with his voice; should scatter forth light, nature, time, souls, from the centre of the present thought; and new date and new create the whole. Whenever a mind is simple and receives a divine wisdom, old things pass away,—means, teachers, texts, temples fall; it lives now, and absorbs past and future into the present hour. All things are made sacred by relation to it,—one as much as another. All things are dissolved to their centre by their cause, and in the universal miracle petty and particular miracles disappear. If therefore a man claims to know and speak of God and carries you backward to the phraseology of some old mouldered nation in another country, in another world, believe him not. Is the acorn better than the oak which is its fulness and completion? Is the parent better than the child into whom he has cast his ripened being? Whence then this worship of the past? The centuries are conspirators against the sanity and authority of the soul. Time and space are but physiological colors which the eye makes, but the soul is light: where it is, is day; where it was, is night; and history is an impertinence and an injury if it be any thing more than a cheerful apologue or parable of my being and becoming.

Man is timid and apologetic; he is no longer upright; he dares not say 'I think,' 'I am,' but quotes some saint or sage. He is ashamed before the blade of grass or the blowing rose. These roses under my window make no reference to former roses or to better ones; they are for what they are; they exist with God to-day. There is no time to them. There is simply the rose; it is perfect in every moment of its existence. Before a leaf-bud has burst, its whole life acts; in the full-blown flower there is no more; in the leafless root there is no less. Its nature is satisfied and it satisfies nature in all moments alike. But man postpones or remembers; he does not live in the present, but with reverted eye laments the past, or, heedless of the riches that surround him, stands on tiptoe to foresee the future. He cannot be happy and strong until he too lives with nature in the present, above time.

This should be plain enough. Yet see what strong intellects dare not yet hear God himself unless he speak the phraseology of I know not what David, or Jeremiah, or Paul. We shall not always set so great a price on a few texts, on a few lives. We are like children who repeat by rote the sentences of grandames and tutors, and, as they grow older, of the men of talents and character they chance to see,—painfully recollecting the exact words they spoke; afterwards, when they come into the point of view which those had who uttered these sayings, they understand them and are willing to let the words go; for at any time they can use words as good when occasion comes. If we live truly, we shall see truly. It is as easy for the strong man to be strong, as it is for the weak to be weak. When we have new perception, we shall gladly disburden the memory of its hoarded treasures as old rubbish. When a man lives with God, his voice shall be as sweet as the murmur of the brook and the rustle of the corn.

And now at last the highest truth on this subject remains unsaid; *25* probably cannot be said; for all that we say is the far-off remembering of the intuition. That thought by what I can now nearest approach to say it, is this. When good is near you, when you have life in yourself, it is not by any known or accustomed way; you shall not discern the footprints of any other; you shall not see the face of man; you shall not hear any name;—the way, the thought, the good, shall be wholly strange and new. It shall exclude example and experience. You take the way from man, not to man. All persons that ever existed are its forgotten ministers. Fear and hope are alike beneath it. There is somewhat low even in hope. In the hour of vision there is nothing that can be called gratitude, nor properly joy. The soul raised over passion beholds identity and eternal causation, perceives the self-existence of Truth and

Right, and calms itself with knowing that all things go well. Vast spaces of nature, the Atlantic Ocean, the South Sea; long intervals of time, years, centuries, are of no account. This which I think and feel underlay every former state of life and circumstances, as it does underlie my present, and what is called life and what is called death.

Life only avails, not the having lived. Power ceases in the instant of repose; it resides in the moment of transition from a past to a new state, in the shooting of the gulf, in the darting to an aim. This one fact the world hates; that the soul *becomes;* for that forever degrades the past, turns all riches to poverty, all reputation to a shame, confounds the saint with the rogue, shoves Jesus and Judas equally aside. Why then do we prate of self-reliance? Inasmuch as the soul is present there will be power not confident but agent. To talk of reliance is a poor external way of speaking. Speak rather of that which relies because it works and is. Who has more obedience than I masters me, though he should not raise his finger. Round him I must revolve by the gravitation of spirits. We fancy it rhetoric when we speak of eminent virtue. We do not yet see that virtue is Height, and that a man or a company of men, plastic and permeable to principles, by the law of nature must overpower and ride all cities, nations, kings, rich men, poets, who are not.

This is the ultimate fact which we so quickly reach on this, as on every topic, the resolution of all into the ever-blessed ONE. Self-existence is the attribute of the Supreme Cause, and it constitutes the measure of good by the degree in which it enters into all lower forms. All things real are so by so much virtue as they contain. Commerce, husbandry, hunting, whaling, war, eloquence, personal weight, are somewhat, and engage my respect as examples of its presence and impure action. I see the same law working in nature for conservation and growth. Power is, in nature, the essential measure of right. Nature suffers nothing to remain in her kingdoms which cannot help itself. The genesis and maturation of a planet, its poise and orbit, the bended tree recovering itself from the strong wind, the vital resources of every animal and vegetable, are demonstrations of the self-sufficing and therefore self-relying soul.

Thus all concentrates: let us not rove; let us sit at home with the cause. Let us stun and astonish the intruding rabble of men and books and institutions by a simple declaration of the divine fact. Bid the invaders take the shoes from off their feet, for God is here within. Let our simplicity judge them, and our docility to our own law demonstrate the poverty of nature and fortune beside our native riches.

But now we are a mob. Man does not stand in awe of man, nor is his genius admonished to stay at home, to put itself in communication with the internal ocean, but it goes abroad to beg a cup of water of the urns of other men. We must go alone. I like the silent church before the service begins, better than any preaching. How far off, how cool, how chaste the persons look, begirt each one with a precinct or sanctuary! So let us always sit. Why should we assume the faults of our friend, or wife, or father, or child, because they sit around our hearth, or are said to have the same blood? All men have my blood and I all men's. Not for that will I adopt their petulance or folly, even to the extent of being ashamed of it. But your isolation must not be mechanical, but spiritual, that is, must be elevation. At times the whole world seems to be in conspiracy to importune you with emphatic trifles. Friend, client, child, sickness, fear, want, charity, all knock at once at thy closet door and say,—'Come out unto us.' But keep thy state; come not into their confusion. The power men possess to annoy me I give them by a weak curiosity. No man can come near me but through my act. "What we love that we have, but by desire we bereave ourselves of the love."

If we cannot at once rise to the sanctities of obedience and faith, let us   *30*
at least resist our temptations; let us enter into the state of war and wake Thor and Woden, courage and constancy, in our Saxon breasts. This is to be done in our smooth times by speaking the truth. Check this lying hospitality and lying affection. Live no longer to the expectation of these deceived and deceiving people with whom we converse. Say to them, 'O father, O mother, O wife, O brother, O friend, I have lived with you after appearances hitherto. Henceforward I am the truth's. Be it known unto you that henceforward I obey no law less than the eternal law. I will have no covenants but proximities. I shall endeavor to nourish my parents, to support my family, to be the chaste husband of one wife,—but these relations I must fill after a new and unprecedented way. I appeal from your customs. I must be myself. I cannot break myself any longer for you, or you. If you can love me for what I am, we shall be the happier. If you cannot, I will still seek to deserve that you should. I will not hide my tastes or aversions. I will so trust that what is deep is holy, that I will do strongly before the sun and moon whatever inly rejoices me and the heart appoints. If you are noble, I will love you; if you are not, I will not hurt you and myself by hypocritical attentions. If you are true, but not in the same truth with me, cleave to your companions; I will seek my own. I do this not selfishly but humbly and truly. It is alike your interest, and mine, and all men's, however long we have dwelt in lies, to live in truth. Does this sound harsh to-day? You will soon love what is dictated by your nature as well as mine, and if we follow the truth it will bring us out safe at last.'—But so may you give these friends pain. Yes, but I cannot sell my liberty and my power, to save their sensibility. Besides, all persons have their moments of reason, when they look out into the region of absolute truth; then will they justify me and do the same thing.

The populace think that your rejection of popular standards is a rejection of all standard, and mere antinomianism; and the bold sensualist will use the name of philosophy to gild his crimes. But the law of consciousness abides. There are two confessionals, in one or the other of which we must be shriven. You may fulfil your round of duties by clearing yourself in the *direct,* or in the *reflex* way. Consider whether you have satisfied your relations to father, mother, cousin, neighbor, town, cat and dog—whether any of these can upbraid you. But I may also neglect this reflex standard and absolve me to myself. I have my own stern claims and perfect circle. It denies the name of duty to many offices that are called duties. But if I can discharge its debts it enables me to dispense with the popular code. If any one imagines that this law is lax, let him keep its commandment one day.

And truly it demands something godlike in him who has cast off the common motives of humanity and has ventured to trust himself for a taskmaster. High be his heart, faithful his will, clear his sight, that he may in good earnest be doctrine, society, law, to himself, that a simple purpose may be to him as strong as iron necessity is to others!

If any man consider the present aspects of what is called by distinction *society*, he will see the need of these ethics. The sinew and heart of man seem to be drawn out, and we are become timorous, desponding whimperers. We are afraid of truth, afraid of fortune, afraid of death, and afraid of each other. Our age yields no great and perfect persons. We want men and women who shall renovate life and our social state, but we see that most natures are insolvent, cannot satisfy their own wants, have an ambition out of all proportion to their practical force and do lean and beg day and night continually. Our housekeeping is mendicant, our arts, our occupations, our marriages, our religion we have not chosen, but society has chosen for us. We are parlor soldiers. We shun the rugged battle of fate, where strength is born.

If our young men miscarry in their first enterprises they lose all heart. If the young merchant fails, men say he is *ruined*. If the finest genius studies at one of our colleges and is not installed in an office within one year afterwards in the cities or suburbs of Boston or New York, it seems to his friends and to himself that he is right in being disheartened and in complaining the rest of his life. A sturdy lad from New Hampshire or Vermont, who in turn tries all the professions, who *teams it, farms it, peddles,* keeps a school, preaches, edits a newspaper, goes to Congress, buys a township, and so forth, in successive years, and always like a cat falls on his feet, is worth a hundred of these city dolls. He walks abreast with his days and feels no shame in not "studying a profession," for he does not postpone his life, but lives already. He has not one chance, but a hundred chances. Let a Stoic open the resources of man and tell men they are not leaning willows, but can and must detach themselves; that with the exercise of self-trust, new powers shall appear; that a man is the word made flesh, born to shed healing to the nations; that he should be ashamed of our compassion, and that the moment he acts from himself, tossing the laws, the books, idolatries and customs out of the window, we pity him no more but thank and revere him;—and that teacher shall restore the life of man to splendor and make his name dear to all history.

It is easy to see that a greater self-reliance must work a revolution in all the offices and relations of men; in their religion; in their education; in their pursuits; their modes of living; their association; in their property; in their speculative views.

1. In what prayers do men allow themselves! That which they call a holy office is not so much as brave and manly. Prayer looks abroad and asks for some foreign addition to come through some foreign virtue, and loses itself in endless mazes of natural and supernatural, and mediatorial and miraculous. Prayer that craves a particular commodity, anything less than all

good, is vicious. Prayer is the contemplation of the facts of life from the highest point of view. It is the soliloquy of a beholding and jubilant soul. It is the spirit of God pronouncing his works good. But prayer as a means to effect a private end is meanness and theft. It supposes dualism and not unity in nature and consciousness. As soon as the man is at one with God, he will not beg. He will then see prayer in all action. The prayer of the farmer kneeling in his field to weed it, the prayer of the rower kneeling with the stroke of his oar, are true prayers heard throughout nature, though for cheap ends. Caratach, in Fletcher's "Bonduca," when admonished to inquire the mind of the god Audate, replies,—

> His hidden meaning lies in our endeavors;
> Our valors are our best gods.

Another sort of false prayers are our regrets. Discontent is the want of self-reliance: it is infirmity of will. Regret calamities if you can thereby help the sufferer; if not, attend your own work and already the evil begins to be repaired. Our sympathy is just as base. We come to them who weep foolishly and sit down and cry for company, instead of imparting to them truth and health in rough electric shocks, putting them once more in communication with their own reason. The secret of fortune is joy in our hands. Welcome evermore to gods and men is the self-helping man. For him all doors are flung wide; him all tongues greet, all honors crown, all eyes follow with desire. Our love goes out to him and embraces him because he did not need it. We solicitously and apologetically caress and celebrate him because he held on his way and scorned our disapprobation. The gods love him because men hated him. "To the persevering mortal," said Zoroaster, "the blessed Immortals are swift."

As men's prayers are a disease of the will, so are their creeds a disease of the intellect. They say with those foolish Israelites, 'Let not God speak to us, lest we die. Speak thou, speak any man with us, and we will obey.' Everywhere I am hindered of meeting God in my brother, because he has shut his own temple doors and recites fables merely of his brother's, or his brother's brother's God. Every new mind is a new classification. If it prove a mind of uncommon activity and power, a Locke, a Lavoisier, a Hutton, a Bentham, a Fourier,° it imposes its classification on other men, and lo! a new system. In proportion to the depth of the thought, and so to the number of the objects it touches and brings within reach of the pupil, is his complacency. But chiefly is this apparent in creeds and churches, which are also

---

Locke: John Locke (1632–1704), an English philosopher.
Lavoisier: Antoine Laurent Lavoisier (1743–1797), a French chemist.
Hutton: James Hutton (1726–1797), a Scottish geologist.
Bentham: Jeremy Bentham (1748–1832), an English philosopher.
Fourier: Francois Fourier (1772–1837), a French socialist.

classifications of some powerful mind acting on the elemental thought of duty and man's relation to the Highest. Such is Calvinism, Quakerism, Sweden-borgism. The pupil takes the same delight in subordinating every thing to the new terminology as a girl who has just learned botany in seeing a new earth and new seasons thereby. It will happen for a time that the pupil will find his intellectual power has grown by the study of his master's mind. But in all unbalanced minds the classification is idolized, passes for the end and not for a speedily exhaustible means, so that the walls of the system blend to their eye in the remote horizon with the walls of the universe; the luminaries of heaven seem to them hung on the arch their master built. They cannot imagine how you aliens have any right to see,—how you can see; 'It must be somehow that you stole the light from us.' They do not yet perceive that light, unsystematic, indomitable, will break into any cabin, even into theirs. Let them chirp awhile and call it their own. If they are honest and do well, presently their neat new pinfold will be too strait and low, will crack, will lean, will rot and vanish, and the immortal light, all young and joyful, million-orbed, million-colored, will beam over the universe as on the first morning.

2. It is for want of self-culture that the superstition of Travelling, whose idols are Italy, England, Egypt, retains its fascination for all educated Americans. They who made England, Italy, or Greece venerable in the imagination, did so by sticking fast where they were, like an axis of the earth. In manly hours we feel that duty is our place. The soul is no traveller; the wise man stays at home, and when his necessities, his duties, on any occasion call him from his house, or into foreign lands, he is at home still and shall make men sensible by the expression of his countenance that he goes, the missionary of wisdom and virtue, and visits cities and men like a sovereign and not like an interloper or a valet.

I have no churlish objection to the circumnavigation of the globe for the purposes of art, of study, and benevolence, so that the man is first domesticated, or does not go abroad with the hope of finding somewhat greater than he knows. He who travels to be amused, or to get somewhat which he does not carry, travels away from himself, and grows old even in youth among old things. In Thebes, in Palmyra, his will and mind have become old and dilapidated as they. He carries ruins to ruins. 40

Travelling is a fool's paradise. Our first journeys discover to us the indifference of places. At home I dream that at Naples, at Rome, I can be intoxicated with beauty and lose my sadness. I pack my trunk, embrace my friends, embark on the sea and at last wake up in Naples, and there beside me is the stern fact, the sad self, unrelenting, identical, that I fled from. I seek the Vatican and the palaces. I affect to be intoxicated with sights and suggestions, but I am not intoxicated. My giant goes with me wherever I go.

3. But the rage of travelling is a symptom of a deeper unsoundness affecting the whole intellectual action. The intellect is vagabond, and our system of education fosters restlessness. Our minds travel when our bodies are forced to stay at home. We imitate; and what is imitation but the travelling of the mind? Our houses are built with foreign taste; our shelves are garnished

with foreign ornaments; our opinions, our tastes, our faculties, lean, and follow the Past and the Distant. The soul created the arts wherever they have flourished. It was in his own mind that the artist sought his model. It was an application of his own thought to the thing to be done and the conditions to be observed. And why need we copy the Doric or the Gothic model? Beauty, convenience, grandeur of thought and quaint expression are as near to us as to any, and if the American artist will study with hope and love the precise thing to be done by him, considering the climate, the soil, the length of the day, the wants of the people, the habit and form of the government, he will create a house in which all these will find themselves fitted, and taste and sentiment will be satisfied also.

Insist on yourself; never imitate. Your own gift you can present every moment with the cumulative force of a whole life's cultivation; but of the adopted talent of another you have only an extemporaneous half possession. That which each can do best, none but his Maker can teach him. No man yet knows what it is, nor can, till that person has exhibited it. Where is the master who could have taught Shakespeare? Where is the master who could have instructed Franklin, or Washington, or Bacon, or Newton? Every great man is a unique. The Scipionism of Scipio is precisely that part he could not borrow. Shakespeare will never be made by the study of Shakespeare. Do that which is assigned you, and you cannot hope too much or dare too much. There is at this moment for you an utterance brave and grand as that of the colossal chisel of Phidias, or trowel of the Egyptians, or the pen of Moses or Dante, but different from all these. Not possibly will the soul, all rich, all eloquent, with thousand-cloven tongue, deign to repeat itself; but if you can hear what these patriarchs say, surely you can reply to them in the same pitch of voice; for the ear and the tongue are two organs of one nature. Abide in the simple and noble regions of thy life, obey thy heart, and thou shalt reproduce the Foreworld again.

4. As our Religion, our Education, our Art look abroad, so does our spirit of society. All men plume themselves on the improvement of society, and no man improves.

Society never advances. It recedes as fast on one side as it gains on the other. It undergoes continual changes; it is barbarous, it is civilized, it is christianized, it is rich, it is scientific; but this change is not amelioration. For every thing that is given something is taken. Society acquires new arts and loses old instincts. What a contrast between the well-clad, reading, writing, thinking American, with a watch, a pencil and a bill of exchange in his pocket, and the naked New Zealander, whose property is a club, a spear, a mat and an undivided twentieth of a shed to sleep under! But compare the health of the two men and you shall see that the white man has lost his aboriginal strength. If the traveller tell us truly, strike the savage with a broad-axe and in a day or two the flesh shall unite and heal as if you struck the blow into soft pitch, and the same blow shall send the white to his grave.

The civilized man has built a coach, but has lost the use of his feet. He is supported on crutches, but lacks so much support of muscle. He has a fine

Geneva watch, but he fails of the skill to tell the hour by the sun. A Greenwich nautical almanac he has, and so being sure of the information when he wants it, the man in the street does not know a star in the sky. The solstice he does not observe; the equinox he knows as little; and the whole bright calendar of the year is without a dial in his mind. His note-books impair his memory; his libraries overload his wit; the insurance-office increases the number of accidents; and it may be a question whether machinery does not encumber; whether we have not lost by refinement some energy, by a Christianity, entrenched in establishments and forms, some vigor of wild virtue. For every Stoic was a Stoic; but in Christendom where is the Christian?

There is no more deviation in the moral standard than in the standard of height or bulk. No greater men are now than ever were. A singular equality may be observed between the great men of the first and of the last ages; nor can all the science, art, religion, and philosophy of the nineteenth century avail to educate greater men than Plutarch's heroes, three or four and twenty centuries ago. Not in time is the race progressive. Phocion, Socrates, Anaxagoras, Diogenes, are great men, but they leave no class. He who is really of their class will not be called by their name, but will be his own man, and in his turn the founder of a sect. The arts and inventions of each period are only its costume and do not invigorate men. The harm of the improved machinery may compensate its good. Hudson and Behring accomplished so much in their fishing-boats as to astonish Parry and Franklin, whose equipment exhausted the resources of science and art. Galileo, with an opera-glass, discovered a more splendid series of celestial phenomena than any one since. Columbus found the New World in an undecked boat. It is curious to see the periodical disuse and perishing of means and machinery which were introduced with loud laudation a few years or centuries before. The great genius returns to essential man. We reckoned the improvements of the art of war among the triumphs of science, and yet Napoleon conquered Europe by the bivouac, which consisted of falling back on naked valor and disencumbering it of all aids. The Emperor held it impossible to make a perfect army, says Las Cases, "without abolishing our arms, magazines, commissaries and carriages, until, in imitation of the Roman custom, the soldier should receive his supply of corn, grind it in his hand-mill and bake his bread himself."

Society is a wave. The wave moves onward, but the water of which it is composed does not. The same particle does not rise from the valley to the ridge. Its unity is only phenomenal. The persons who make up a nation to-day, next year die, and their experience dies with them.

And so the reliance on Property, including the reliance on governments which protect it, is the want of self-reliance. Men have looked away from themselves and at things so long that they have come to esteem the religious, learned and civil institutions as guards of property, and they deprecate assaults on these, because they feel them to be assaults on property. They measure their esteem of each other by what each has, and not by what each is. But a cultivated man becomes ashamed of his property, out of new respect for his nature. Especially he hates what he has if he see that it is accidental,—came to him by inheritance, or gift, or crime; then he feels that it is not having; it does not belong to him, has no root in him and merely lies there because no revolution or no robber takes it away. But that which a man is, does always by necessity acquire; and what the man acquires, is living property, which does not wait the beck of rulers, or mobs, or revolutions, or fire, or storm, or bankruptcies, but perpetually renews itself wherever the man breathes. "Thy lot or portion of life," said the Caliph Ali, "is seeking after thee; therefore be at rest from seeking after it." Our dependence on these foreign goods leads us to our slavish respect for numbers. The political parties meet in numerous conventions; the greater the concourse and with each new uproar of announcement, The delegation from Essex! The Democrats from New Hampshire! The Whigs of Maine! the young patriot feels himself stronger than before by a new thousand of eyes and arms. In like manner the reformers summon conventions and vote and resolve in multitude. Not so, O friends! will the God deign to enter and inhabit you, but by a method precisely the reverse. It is only as a man puts off all foreign support and stands alone that I see him to be strong and to prevail. He is weaker by every recruit to his banner. Is not a man better than a town? Ask nothing of men, and, in the endless mutation, thou only firm column must presently appear the upholder of all that surrounds thee. He who knows that power is inborn, that he is weak because he has looked for good out of him and elsewhere, and, so perceiving, throws himself unhesitatingly on his thought, instantly rights himself, stands in the erect position, commands his limbs, works miracles; just as a man who stands on his feet is stronger than a man who stands on his head.

So use all that is called Fortune. Most men gamble with her, and gain all, and lose all, as her wheel rolls. But do thou leave as unlawful these winnings, and deal with Cause and Effect, the chancellors of God. In the Will work and acquire, and thou hast chained the wheel of Chance, and shall sit hereafter out of fear from her rotations. A political victory, a rise of rents, the recovery of your sick or the return of your absent friend, or some other favorable event raises your spirits, and you think good days are preparing for you. Do not believe it. Nothing can bring you peace but yourself. Nothing can bring you peace but the triumph of principles.   *50*

Questions for Understanding

1. What does Emerson mean when he says, "A man should learn to detect and watch that gleam of light which flashes across his mind from within, more than the lustre of the firmament of bards and sages"?

2. Why does Emerson compare "the man" unfavorably with the boy? What does Emerson have in mind when he says, "the man is as it were clapped into jail by his consciousness"?

3. What does Emerson mean in saying, "He who would gather immortal palms must not be hindered by the name of goodness, but must explore if it be goodness"?

4. Why does Emerson seem to be so opposed to charitable and philanthropic acts?

5. Why does Emerson insist that "with consistency a great soul has simply nothing to do"? Is Emerson urging that we deliberately cultivate inconsistency?

Suggestions for Writing

1. Emerson says that a person must accept himself or herself for better or for worse, that a person must accept "that plot of ground which is given to him to till," "that divine idea which each of us represents." If people accept the lot that falls to them, then putting their hearts into their work and doing their best will bring satisfaction and joy. But Emerson recognizes that too often "we but half express ourselves, and are ashamed of that divine idea which each of us represents." Emerson shows great understanding of human nature here, because most people do struggle to find their true identity. Write an essay in which you describe your struggle to find the unique *you*. What are some of the issues and questions you had to confront?

2. "The objection to conforming to usages that have become dead to you is that it scatters your force. It loses your time and blurs the impression of your character." Are you aware of usages—customs—that you conform to and that "scatter your force"? Are you aware of customs that have an opposite effect on you, concentrating your force and providing opportunities for you to express your essential self? Write an essay in which you describe the ways in which you view customs.

3. Emerson urges that we not worry about whether we are consistent or contradictory in our speech and behavior. We cannot evolve and grow if we worry about being misunderstood. Can you recall times when you were misunderstood because your intellectual or spiritual growth made you look inconsistent? Describe where you were and where you arrived. Discuss the consequences of your journey.

4. Emerson asserts that "a true man belongs to no other time or place, but is the centre of things. . . . The man must be so much that he must make all circumstances indifferent." Later in the essay he says, "He cannot be happy and strong until he too lives with nature in the present, above time." That is, we must wholeheartedly accept the time and place in which we find ourselves; we must not scatter our force by wishing that the time, place, or circumstances were different. Do you agree or disagree? Do you know people who live in a way that is contrary to this principle? Write an essay in which you discuss the extent to which it is possible to live one's own unique life regardless of time, place, or circumstances.

5. Emerson: "Prayer that craves a particular commodity, anything less than all good, is vicious. Prayer is the contemplation of the facts of life from the

highest point of view. It is the soliloquy of a beholding and jubilant soul. It is the spirit of God pronouncing his works good. But prayer as a means to effect a private end is meanness and theft." Write an essay in which you discuss your experience with prayer. In what states of mind have you prayed? What were the purposes of your prayers? What was your state of mind after prayer? Has the nature of your prayers changed? How would Emerson assess your resort to prayer?

William Hazlitt

[1778–1830]

William Hazlitt was the son of an Irish Unitarian minister, a man who was thoroughly familiar with the free-thinkers of his day such as Benjamin Franklin and William Godwin. In the family home at Wem in Shropshire, words such as *liberty, truth, justice,* and *honor* were often used. Humankind, it was assumed, could be taught to value these concepts as much as they were in the Hazlitt household.

One of the great influences on Hazlitt was the poet Samuel Taylor Coleridge, whom Hazlitt came to know when Coleridge came to Shropshire to apply for the position of minister of the Unitarian church in Shrewsbury. The twenty-year-old Hazlitt heard Coleridge, who was unmistakably a radical at the time, give his sermon—and became a devotee. Before he left Shropshire, Coleridge invited Hazlitt to visit him in a few months at his home in Somerset. As Hazlitt later wrote in his essay "My First Acquaintance with Poets," the invitation had a sensational impact: "During these months the chill breath of winter gave me a welcoming; the vernal air was balm and inspiration to me. The golden sunsets, the silver star of evening, lighted me on my way to new hopes and prospects. *I was to visit Coleridge in the spring.*"

Hazlitt had a fine visit with Coleridge in Somerset, where he also met the great poet William Wordsworth, with whom Coleridge was collaborating at the time. Not long after the visit, however, Hazlitt embarked on a career as a portrait painter. It was a career that lasted ten years and that he finally abandoned when he became convinced that he would never be better than mediocre. When Hazlitt started painting, however, he was infatuated with the work of Rembrandt, Titian, and Raphael, and he loved the process of trying to duplicate nature on canvas. In his 1820 essay "On the Pleasure of Painting," he explained it this way: "There is a pleasure in painting which none but painters know. In writing, you have to contend with the world; in painting you have only to carry on a friendly strife with Nature. You sit down to your task, and are happy. From the moment that you take up the pencil, and look Nature in the face, you are at peace with your own heart. No angry passions rise to disturb the silent progress of the work, to shake the hand, or dim the brow. . . ."

In 1802, Hazlitt visited Paris, to which Napoleon had brought hundreds of masterpieces "liberated" by his troops from their aristocratic owners; they now hung in the Louvre for anyone to see. This egalitarian act was one of the reasons for Hazlitt's great enthusiasm for Napoleon. To Hazlitt, Napoleon had been the hope of the world, and when he finally was defeated at Waterloo in 1815, Hazlitt was devastated. Throughout his life, Hazlitt remained committed to the principles of the French Revolution, which, he believed, were embodied in the person of Napoleon. In the years after Waterloo, when, in the eyes of most of the English, Napoleon was just another self-aggrandizing tyrant who had been brought down, Hazlitt persisted in his admiration, eventually producing his four-volume *Life of Napoleon Buonaparte.*

Hazlitt's commitment to radical politics was one reason his friendships with Coleridge and Wordsworth foundered. More forbearing was another writer-friend, Charles Lamb, whose portrait Hazlitt painted in 1805 and who, despite provocations, remained a close friend from their first meeting through Hazlitt's fatal bout with stomach cancer. Hazlitt's life was stormy and filled with disappointments. He was opinionated. He had strong feelings. He wrote what he considered the truth. He had no use for compromise. "I am not in the ordinary acceptance of the term," he wrote, "*a good-natured man,* that is, many things annoy me besides what interferes with my own ease and interest. I hate a lie; a piece of injustice wounds me to the quick, though nothing but the report of it reaches me."

He would have preferred to write about metaphysics and stay away from personalities and contemporary issues, but his need for income forced him to write for newspapers. At first he wrote Parliamentary news and reviews of plays, but then he wrote personal essays and essays on topics drawn from English literature. He wrote about Shakespeare and characters in Shakespeare's plays. Like Emerson, he wrote an essay on Montaigne. When the sum of Hazlitt's accomplishments with the essay is considered, the assessment of one critic may not be far wrong: "He wrote as marvellously as any essayist who was not Montaigne."

In addition to the three reprinted here, Hazlitt's well-known essays include "The Fight," "My First Acquaintance with Poets," "On Gusto," "On Consistency of Opinion," "On Genius and Common Sense," "On the Ignorance of the Learned," "On Vulgarity and Affectation," "On Going on a Journey," "On the Pleasure of Painting," and "On Prejudice."

ON THE FEELING OF
IMMORTALITY IN YOUTH

1827

No young man believes he shall ever die. It was a saying of my brother's,   *1*
and a fine one. There is a feeling of Eternity in youth which makes us amends
for everything. To be young is to be as one of the Immortals. One half of time
indeed is spent—the other half remains in store for us with all its countless
treasures, for there is no line drawn, and we see no limit to our hopes and
wishes. We make the coming age our own—

The vast, the unbounded prospect lies before us.°

Death, old age, are words without a meaning, a dream, a fiction, with which we
have nothing to do. Others may have undergone, or may still undergo them—we
"bear a charmed life,"° which laughs to scorn all such idle fancies. As in setting
out on a delightful journey, we strain our eager sight forward,

Bidding the lovely scenes at distance hail,°

and see no end to prospect after prospect, new objects presenting themselves as
we advance, so in the outset of life we see no end to our desires nor to the
opportunities of gratifying them. We have as yet found no obstacle, no
disposition to flag, and it seems that we can go on so for ever. We look round in
a new world, full of life and motion, and ceaseless progress, and feel in ourselves
all the vigour and spirit to keep pace with it, and do not foresee from any present
signs how we shall be left behind in the race, decline into old age, and drop into
the grave. It is the simplicity and, as it were, abstractedness of our feelings in youth
that (so to speak) identifies us with Nature and (our experience being weak and
our passions strong) makes us fancy ourselves immortal like it. Our short-lived
connexion with being, we fondly flatter ourselves, is an indissoluble and lasting
union. As infants smile and sleep, we are rocked in the cradle of our desires, and
hushed into fancied security by the roar of the universe around us—we quaff the
cup of life with eager thirst without draining it, and joy and hope seem ever
mantling to the brim—objects press around us, filling the mind with their
magnitude and with the throng of desires that wait upon them, so that there is
no room for the thoughts of death. We are too much dazzled by the gorgeousness
and novelty of the bright waking dream about us to discern the dim shadow
lingering for us in the distance. Nor would the hold that life has taken of us permit
us to detach our thoughts that way, even if we could. We are too much absorbed

---

The vast . . . us.: Joseph Addison's *Cato* act 5, scene 1.
"bear a charmed life,": William Shakespeare, *Macbeth* act 5, scene 7.
Bidding . . . hail,: From William Collins, "The Passions."

in present objects and pursuits. While the spirit of youth remains unimpaired, ere "the wine of life is drunk,"° we are like people intoxicated or in a fever, who are hurried away by the violence of their own sensations: it is only as present objects begin to pall upon the sense, as we have been disappointed in our favourite pursuits, cut off from our closest ties, that we by degrees become weaned from the world, that passion loosens its hold upon futurity, and that we begin to contemplate as in a glass darkly the possibility of parting with it for good. Till then, the example of others has no effect upon us. Casualties we avoid; the slow approaches of age we play at *hide and seek* with. Like the foolish fat scullion in Sterne, who hears that Master Bobby° is dead, our only reflection is, "So am not I!" The idea of death, instead of staggering our confidence, only seems to strengthen and enhance our sense of the possession and enjoyment of life. Others may fall around us like leaves, or be mowed down by the scythe of Time like grass; these are but metaphors to the unreflecting, buoyant ears and overweening presumption of youth. It is not till we see the flowers of Love, Hope, and Joy withering around us, that we give up the flattering delusions that before led us on, and that the emptiness and dreariness of the prospect before us reconciles us hypothetically to the silence of the grave.

Life is indeed a strange gift, and its privileges are most mysterious. No wonder when it is first granted to us, that our gratitude, our admiration, and our delight should prevent us from reflecting on our own nothingness, or from thinking it will ever be recalled. Our first and strongest impressions are borrowed from the mighty scene that is opened to us, and we unconsciously transfer its durability as well as its splendour to ourselves. So newly found, we cannot think of parting with it yet, or at least put off that consideration *sine die.*° Like a rustic at a fair, we are full of amazement and rapture, and have no thought of going home, or that it will soon be night. We know our existence only by ourselves, and confound our knowledge with the objects of it. We and Nature are therefore one. Otherwise the illusion, the "feast of reason and the flow of soul,"° to which we are invited, is a mockery and a cruel insult. We do not go from a play till the last act is ended, and the lights are about to be extinguished. But the fairy face of Nature still shines on: shall we be called away before the curtain falls, or ere we have scarce had a glimpse of what is going on? Like children, our step-mother Nature holds us up to see the raree-show of the universe, and then, as if we were a burden to her to support, lets us fall down again. Yet what brave sublunary things does not this pageant present, like a ball or fête of the universe!

To see the golden sun, the azure sky, the outstretched ocean; to walk upon the green earth, and be lord of a thousand creatures; to look down

---

"the wine of life is drunk": William Shakespeare, *Macbeth* act 2, scene 3, line 96.
Master Bobby: A character in *Tristram Shandy,* by Laurence Stern (1713–1768).
sine die: Indefinitely.
"feast . . . soul": Alexander Pope, *Imitations of Horace* line 128.

yawning precipices or over distant sunny vales; to see the world spread out under one's feet on a map; to bring the stars near; to view the smallest insects through a microscope; to read history, and consider the revolutions of empire and the successions of generations; to hear the glory of Tyre, of Sidon, of Babylon, and of Susa,° and so say all these were before me and are now nothing; to say I exist in such a point of time, and in such a point of space; to be a spectator and a part of its ever-moving scene; to witness the change of season, of spring and autumn, of winter and summer; to feel hot and cold, pleasure and pain, beauty and deformity; right and wrong; to be sensible to the accidents of Nature; to consider the mighty world of eye and ear; to listen to the stock-dove's notes amid the forest deep; to journey over moor and mountain; to hear the midnight sainted choir; to visit lighted halls, or the cathedral's gloom, or sit in crowded theatres and see life itself mocked; to study the works of art and refine the sense of beauty to agony; to worship fame, and to dream of immortality; to look upon the Vatican, and to read Shakespeare; to gather up the wisdom of the ancients, and to pry into the future; to listen to the trump of war, the shout of victory; to question history as to the movements of the human heart; to seek for truth; to plead the cause of humanity; to overlook the world as if time and Nature poured their treasures at our feet—to be and to do all this, and then in a moment to be nothing—to have it all snatched from us as by a juggler's trick, or a phantasmagoria! There is something in this transition from all to nothing that shocks us and damps the enthusiasm of youth new flushed with hope and pleasure, and we cast the comfortless thought as far from us as we can. In the first enjoyment of the estate of life we discard the fear of debts and duns, and never think of the final payment of our great debt to Nature. Art we know is long; life, we flatter ourselves, should be so too. We see no end of the difficulties and delays we have to encounter: perfection is slow of attainment, and we must have time to accomplish it in. The fame of the great names we look up to is immortal: and shall not we who contemplate it imbibe a portion of ethereal fire, the *divinae particula aurae,*° which nothing can extinguish? A wrinkle in Rembrandt or in Nature takes whole days to resolve itself into its component parts, its softenings and its sharpnesses; we refine upon our perfections, and unfold the intricacies of Nature. What a prospect for the future! What a task have we not begun! And shall we be arrested in the middle of it? We do not count our time thus employed lost, or our pains thrown away; we do not flag or grow tired, but gain new vigour at our endless task. Shall Time, then, grudge us to finish what we have begun, and have formed a compact with Nature to do? Why not fill up the blank that is left us in this manner? I have looked for hours at a Rembrandt without being conscious of the flight of time, but with ever new wonder and delight, have thought that

---

Tyre . . . Susa: Old Middle-Eastern cities.
divinae particula aurae: A portion of the divine breath.

not only my own but another existence I could pass in the same manner. This rarefied, refined existence seemed to have no end, nor stint, nor principle of decay in it. The print would remain long after I who looked on it had become the prey of worms. The thing seems in itself out of all reason: health, strength, appetite are opposed to the idea of death, and we are not ready to credit it till we have found our illusions vanished, and our hopes grown cold. Objects in youth, from novelty, etc., are stamped upon the brain with such force and integrity that one thinks nothing can remove or obliterate them. They are riveted there, and appear to us as an element of our nature. It must be a mere violence that destroys them, not a natural decay. In the very strength of this persuasion we seem to enjoy an age by anticipation. We melt down years into a single moment of intense sympathy, and by anticipating the fruits defy the ravages of time. If, then, a single moment of our lives is worth years, shall we set any limits to its total value and extent? Again, does it not happen that so secure do we think ourselves of an indefinite period of existence, that at times, when left to ourselves, and impatient of novelty, we feel annoyed at what seems to us the slow and creeping progress of time, and argue that if it always moves at this tedious snail's pace it will never come to an end? How ready are we to sacrifice any space of time which separates us from a favourite object, little thinking that before long we shall find it move too fast.

For my part, I started in life with the French Revolution, and I have lived, alas! to see the end of it. But I did not foresee this result. My sun arose with the first dawn of liberty, and I did not think how soon both must set. The new impulse to ardour given to men's minds imparted a congenial warmth and glow to mine; we were strong to run a race together, and I little dreamed that long before mine was set, the sun of liberty would turn to blood, or set once more in the night of despotism. Since then, I confess, I have no longer felt myself young, for with that my hopes fell.

I have since turned my thoughts to gathering up some of the fragments ⁵ of my early recollections, and putting them into a form to which I might occasionally revert. The future was barred to my progress, and I turned for consolation and encouragement to the past. It is thus that, while we find our personal and substantial identity vanishing from us, we strive to gain a reflected and vicarious one in our thoughts: we do not like to perish wholly, and wish to bequeath our names, at least, to posterity. As long as we can make our cherished thoughts and nearest interests live in the minds of others, we do not appear to have retired altogether from the stage. We still occupy the breasts of others, and exert an influence and power over them, and it is only our bodies that are reduced to dust and powder. Our favourite speculations still find encouragement, and we make as great a figure in the eye of the world, or perhaps a greater than in our lifetime. The demands of our self-love are thus satisfied, and these are the most imperious and unremitting. Besides, if by our intellectual superiority we survive ourselves in this world, by our virtues and faith we may attain an interest in another, and a higher state of being, and may thus be recipients at the same time of men and of angels.

E'en from the tomb the voice of Nature cries,
E'en in our ashes live their wonted fires.°

As we grow old, our sense of the value of time becomes vivid. Nothing else, indeed, seems of any consequence. We can never cease wondering that that which has ever been should cease to be. We find many things remain the same: why then should there be change in us. This adds a convulsive grasp of whatever is, a sense of fallacious hollowness in all we see. Instead of the full, pulpy feeling of youth tasting existence and every object in it, all is flat and vapid,—a whited sepulchre, fair without but full of ravening and all uncleanness within. The world is a witch that puts us off with false shows and appearances. The simplicity of youth, the confiding expectation, the boundless raptures, are gone: we only think of getting out of it as well as we can, and without any great mischance or annoyance. The flush of illusion, even the complacent retrospect of past joys and hopes, is over; if we can slip out of life without indignity, can escape with little bodily infirmity, and frame our minds to the calm and respectable composure of *still-life* before we return to absolute nothingness, it is as much as we can expect. We do not die wholly at our deaths: we have mouldered away gradually long before. Faculty after faculty, interest after interest, attachment after attachment disappear: we are torn from ourselves while living, year after year sees us no longer the same, and death only consigns the last fragment of what we were to the grave. That we should wear out by slow stages, and dwindle at last into nothing, is not wonderful, when even in our prime our strongest impressions leave little trace but for the moment, and we are the creatures of petty circumstance. How little effect is made on us in our best days by the books we have read, the scenes we have witnessed, the sensations we have gone through! Think only of the feelings we experience in reading a fine romance (one of Sir Walter's,° for instance); what beauty, what sublimity, what interest, what heart-rending emotions! You would suppose the feelings you then experienced would last for ever, or subdue the mind to their own harmony and tone: while we are reading it seems as if nothing could ever put us out of our way, or trouble us:—the first splash of mud that we get on entering the street, the first twopence we are cheated out of, the feeling vanishes clean out of our minds, and we become the prey of petty and annoying circumstance. The mind soars to the lofty: it is at home in the grovelling, the disagreeable, and the little. And yet we wonder that age should be feeble and querulous,—that the freshness of youth should fade away. Both worlds would hardly satisfy the extravagance of our desires and of our presumption.

Questions for Understanding

1. Does Hazlitt believe that it is unnatural for young people to be unaware of "the dim shadow lingering for us in the distance"?

E'en from . . . wonted fires: From Thomas Gray, "Elegy Written in a Country Churchyard."
Sir Walter: Sir Walter Scott (1771–1832), Scottish poet and novelist.

2. What is it that brings on the awareness of death?
3. What is Hazlitt saying in the following sentence: "We know our existence only by ourselves, and confound our knowledge with the objects of it"?
4. What is Hazlitt suggesting with his use of the analogy of a person at a play?
5. What role did the French Revolution play in Hazlitt's life?

Suggestions for Writing

1. Judging by your own feelings and attitudes, and those you know are common to other young people, do you think Hazlitt is correct? Would you say that young people today feel immortal? Discuss how close Hazlitt has come to describing you and the young people you know.
2. Hazlitt says that a young person is like a hick at a fair, "full of amazement and rapture." To what extent is that description true of you? To what extent, in other words, do you respond to the world around you with amazement and rapture? Discuss.
3. To Hazlitt, youth is a time of continual joy, of an unbroken succession of pleasurable experiences, a time when it seems "as if time and nature poured their treasures at our feet." Youth, in Hazlitt's conception, is a time when a person's emotions range narrowly between intense pleasure and somewhat softer and milder pleasure. Have you lived through such a period? Have you gone through days and weeks when every experience and encounter was pleasurable to some degree? Have you gone through a period in your life that might be analogous to a baseball team's twenty-game winning streak? What was it like? Write an essay in which you describe what your "streak" was like, and analyze some aspect of it.
4. On the other hand, for some people youth may not be such an unmixed blessing, but rather a stage of life that is characterized by conflicting emotions. Can you take issue with Hazlitt's notion that youth is an unmixed blessing? Write an essay in which you describe and analyze your view of youth.
5. In youth, says Hazlitt, pleasurable objects "are stamped upon the brain with such force and integrity that one thinks nothing can remove or obliterate them." Yet in recent times teenage suicide has become an acute problem in America. How do the lives of potential young suicides differ from the youthful life Hazlitt describes? What differences seem critical in determining a young person's outlook? Write an essay in which you compare and contrast the two kinds of lives.

ON FAMILIAR STYLE

1821

It is not easy to write a familiar style. Many people mistake a familiar for   *1*
a vulgar style, and suppose that to write without affectation is to write at
random. On the contrary, there is nothing that requires more precision, and,
if I may so say, purity of expression, than the style I am speaking of. It utterly
rejects not only all unmeaning pomp, but all low, cant phrases, and loose,
unconnected, *slipshod* allusions. It is not to take the first word that offers, but
the best word in common use; it is not to throw words together in any
combinations we please, but to follow and avail ourselves of the true idiom
of the language. To write a genuine familiar or truly English style, is to write
as any one would speak in common conversation, who had a thorough
command and choice of words, or who could discourse with ease, force, and
perspicuity, setting aside all pedantic and oratorical flourishes. Or to give
another illustration, to write naturally is the same thing in regard to common
conversation, as to read naturally is in regard to common speech. It does not
follow that it is an easy thing to give the true accent and inflection to the
words you utter, because you do not attempt to rise above the level of
ordinary life and colloquial speaking. You do not assume indeed the
solemnity of the pulpit, or the tone of stage-declamation: neither are you at
liberty to gabble on at a venture, without emphasis or discretion, or to resort
to vulgar dialect or clownish pronunciation. You must steer a middle course.
You are tied down to a given and appropriate articulation, which is
determined by the habitual associations between sense and sound, and which
you can only hit by entering into the author's meaning, as you must find the
proper words and style to express yourself by fixing your thoughts on the
subject you have to write about. Any one may mouth out a passage with a
theatrical cadence, or get upon stilts to tell his thoughts: but to write or speak
with propriety and simplicity is a more difficult task. Thus it is easy to affect
a pompous style, to use a word twice as big as the thing you want to express:
it is not so easy to pitch upon the very word that exactly fits it. Out of eight
or ten words equally common, equally intelligible, with nearly equal
pretensions, it is a matter of some nicety and discrimination to pick out the
very one, the preferableness of which is scarcely perceptible, but decisive. The
reason why I object to Dr. Johnson's° style is, that there is no discrimination,
no selection, no variety in it. He uses none but 'tall, opaque words,' taken
from the 'first row of the rubric:'—words with the greatest number of
syllables, or Latin phrases with merely English terminations. If a fine style
depended on this sort of arbitrary pretension, it would be fair to judge
of an author's elegance by the measurement of his words, and the substitu-
tion of foreign circumlocutions (with no precise associations) for the

---

Dr. Johnson: Samuel Johnson (1709–1784), English lexicographer and writer.

mother-tongue.[1] How simple it is to be dignified without ease, to be pompous without meaning! Surely, it is but a mechanical rule for avoiding what is low to be always pedantic and affected. It is clear you cannot use a vulgar English word, if you never use a common English word at all. A fine tact is shown in adhering to those which are perfectly common, and yet never falling into any expressions which are debased by disgusting circumstances, or which owe their signification and point to technical or professional allusions. A truly natural or familiar style can never be quaint or vulgar, for this reason, that it is of universal force and applicability, and that quaintness and vulgarity arise out of the immediate connection of certain words with coarse and disagreeable, or with confined ideas. The last form what we understand by *cant* or *slang* phrases.—To give an example of what is not very clear in the general statement. I should say that the phrase *To cut with a knife,* or *To cut a piece of wood,* is perfectly free from vulgarity, because it is perfectly common: but to *cut an acquaintance* is not quite unexceptionable, because it is not perfectly common or intelligible, and has hardly yet escaped out of the limits of slang phraseology. I should hardly therefore use the word in this sense without putting it in italics as a license of expression, to be received *cum grano salis.*° All provincial or bye-phrases come under the same mark of reprobation—all such as the writer transfers to the page from his fireside or a particular *coterie,* or that he invents for his own sole use and convenience. I conceive that words are like money, not the worse for being common, but that it is the stamp of custom alone that gives them circulation or value. I am fastidious in this respect, and would almost as soon coin the currency of the realm as counterfeit the King's English. I never invented or gave a new and unauthorised meaning to any word but one single one (the term *impersonal* applied to feelings) and that was in an abstruse metaphysical discussion to express a very difficult distinction. I have been (I know) loudly accused of revelling in vulgarisms and broken English. I cannot speak to that point: but so far I plead guilty to the determined use of acknowledged idioms and common elliptical expressions. I am not sure that the critics in question know the one from the other, that is, can distinguish any medium between formal pedantry and the most barbarous solecism. As an author, I endeavour to employ plain words and popular modes of construction, as were I a chapman and dealer, I should common weights and measures.

The proper force of words lies not in the words themselves, but in their application. A word may be a fine-sounding word, of an unusual length, and very imposing from its learning and novelty, and yet in the connection in which it is introduced, may be quite pointless and irrelevant. It is not pomp

---

[1] I have heard of such a thing as an author, who makes it a rule never to admit a monosyllable into his vapid verse. Yet the charm and sweetness of Marlow's lines depended often on their being made up almost entirely of monosyllables.

cum grano salis: With a grain of salt.

or presentation, but the adaptation of the expression to the idea that clenches a writer's meaning:—as it is not the size or glossiness of the materials, but their being fitted each to its place, that gives strength to the arch; or as the pegs and nails are as necessary to the support of the building as the larger timbers, and more so than the mere shewy, unsubstantial ornaments. I hate any thing that occupies more space than it is worth. I hate to see a load of bandboxes go along the street, and I hate to see a parcel of big words without any thing in them. A person who does not deliberately dispose of all his thoughts alike in cumbrous draperies and flimsy disguises, may strike out twenty varieties of familiar every-day language, each coming somewhat nearer to the feeling he wants to convey, and at last not hit upon that particular and only one, which may be said to be identical with the exact impression in his mind. This would seem to shew that Mr. Cobbett° is hardly right in saying that the first word that occurs is always the best. It may be a very good one; and yet a better may present itself on reflection or from time to time. It should be suggested naturally, however, and spontaneously, from a fresh and lively conception of the subject. We seldom succeed by trying at improvement, or by merely substituting one word for another that we are not satisfied with, as we cannot recollect the name of a place or person by merely plaguing ourselves about it. We wander farther from the point by persisting in a wrong scent but it starts up accidentally in the memory when we least expected it, by touching some link in the chain of previous association.

There are those who hoard up and make a cautious display of nothing but rich and rare phraseology;—ancient medals, obscure coins, and Spanish pieces of eight. They are very curious to inspect; but I myself would neither offer nor take them in the course of exchange. A sprinkling of archaisms is not amiss; but a tissue of obsolete expressions is more fit *for keep than wear.* I do not say I would not use any phrase that had been brought into fashion before the middle or the end of the last century; but I should be shy of using any that had not been employed by any approved author during the whole of that time. Words, like clothes, get old-fashioned, or mean and ridiculous, when they have been for some time laid aside. Mr. Lamb° is the only imitator of old English style I can read with pleasure; and he is so thoroughly imbued with the spirit of his authors, that the idea of imitation is almost done away. There is an inward unction, a marrowy vein both in the thought and feeling, an intuition, deep and lively, of his subject, that carries off any quaintness or awkwardness arising from an antiquated style and dress. The matter is completely his own, though the manner is assumed. Perhaps his ideas are altogether so marked and individual, as to require their point and pungency to be neutralised by the affectation of a singular but traditional form of conveyance. Tricked out in the prevailing costume, they would probably

---

Mr. Cobbett: William Cobbett (1763–1835), English journalist and essayist.
Mr. Lamb: Charles Lamb (1775–1834), English essayist.

seem more startling and out of the way. The old English authors, Burton, Fuller, Coryate, Sir Thomas Brown,° are a kind of mediators between us and the more eccentric and whimsical modern, reconciling us to his peculiarities. I do not however know how far this is the case or not, till he condescends to write like one of us. I must confess that what I like best of his papers under the signature of Elia (still I do not presume, amidst such excellence, to decide what is most excellent) is the account of *Mrs Battle's Opinions on Whist,* which is also the most free from obsolete allusions and turns of expression—

'A well of native English undefiled.'

To those acquainted with his admired prototypes, these Essays of the ingenious and highly gifted author have the same sort of charm and relish, that Erasmus's° Colloquies or a fine piece of modern Latin have to the classical scholar. Certainly, I do not know any borrowed pencil that has more power or felicity of execution than the one of which I have here been speaking.

It is as easy to write a gaudy style without ideas, as it is to spread a pallet of shewy colours, or to smear in a flaunting transparency. 'What do you read,'—'Words, words, words.'—'What is the matter?'—'*Nothing,*' it might be answered. The florid style is the reverse of the familiar. The last is employed as an unvarnished medium to convey ideas; the first is resorted to as a spangled veil to conceal the want of them. When there is nothing to be set down but words, it costs little to have them fine. Look through the dictionary, and cull out a *florilegium,* rival the *tulippomania. Rouge* high enough, and never mind the natural complexion. The vulgar, who are not in the secret, will admire the look of preternatural health and vigour; and the fashionable, who regard only appearances, will be delighted with the imposition. Keep to your sounding generalities, your tinkling phrases, and all will be well. Swell out an unmeaning truism to a perfect tympany of style. A thought, a distinction is the rock on which all this brittle cargo of verbiage splits at once. Such writers have merely *verbal* imaginations, that retain nothing but words. Or their puny thoughts have dragon-wings, all green and gold. They soar far above the vulgar failing of the *Sermo humi obrepens*°—their most ordinary speech is never short of an hyperbole, splendid, imposing, vague, incomprehensible, magniloquent, a cento of sounding common-places. If some of us, whose 'ambition is more lowly,' pry a little too narrowly into nooks and corners to pick up a number of 'unconsidered trifles,' they never once direct their eyes or lift their hands to seize on any but the most gorgeous, tarnished, thread-bare patch-work set of phrases, the left-off finery of poetic extravagance, transmitted down through successive generations of barren pretenders. If they criticise actors and actresses, a huddled phantasmagoria of feathers, spangles, floods of light, and oceans of sound float before

---

Burton, Fuller, Coryate, Sir Thomas Brown: Seventeenth-century writers.

Erasmus: Desiderius Erasmus (1466?–1536), Dutch humanist and scholar.

Sermo humi obrepens: Literally, speech creeping on the ground.

their morbid sense, which they paint in the style of Ancient Pistol. Not a glimpse can you get of the merits or defects of the performers: they are hidden in a profusion of barbarous epithets and wilful rhodomontade. Our hypercritics are not thinking of these little fantoccini beings—

'That strut and fret their hour upon the stage'—°

but of tall phantoms of words, abstractions, *genera* and *species,* sweeping clauses, periods that unite the Poles, forced alliterations, astounding antitheses—

'And on their pens *Fustian* sits plumed.'°

If they describe kings and queens, it is an Eastern pageant. The Coronation at either House is nothing to it. We get at four repeated images—a curtain, a throne, a sceptre, and a foot-stool. These are with them the wardrobe of a lofty imagination; and they turn their servile strains to servile uses. Do we read a description of pictures? It is not a reflection of tones and hues which 'nature's own sweet and cunning hand laid on,'° but piles of precious stones, rubies, pearls, emeralds, Golconda's mines, and all the blazonry of art. Such persons are in fact besotted with words, and their brains are turned with the glittering, but empty and sterile phantoms of things. Personifications, capital letters, seas of sunbeams, visions of glory, shining inscriptions, the figures of a transparency, Britannia with her shield, or Hope leaning on an anchor, make up their stock in trade. They may be considered as *hieroglyphical* writers. Images stand out in their minds isolated and important merely in themselves, without any ground-work of feeling— there is no context in their imaginations. Words affect them in the same way, by the mere sound, that is, by their possible, not by their actual application to the subject in hand. They are fascinated by first appearances, and have no sense of consequences. Nothing more is meant by them than meets the ear: they understand or feel nothing more than meets their eye. The web and texture of the universe, and of the heart of man, is a mystery to them: they have no faculty that strikes a chord in unison with it. They cannot get beyond the daubings of fancy, the varnish of sentiment. Objects are not linked to feelings, words to things, but images revolve in splendid mockery, words represent themselves in their strange rhapsodies. The categories of such a mind are pride and ignorance—pride in outside show, to which they sacrifice every thing, and ignorance of the true worth and hidden structure both of words and things. With a sovereign contempt for what is familiar and natural, they are the slaves of vulgar affectation—of a routine of high-flown phrases. Scorning to imitate realities, they are unable to invent any thing, to strike out one original idea. They are not copyists of nature, it is true: but they are the poorest of all plagiarists, the plagiarists of words. All is far-fetched, dear-bought, artificial, oriental in subject

---

'*That strut . . . stage*'—: William Shakespeare, *Macbeth* act 5, scene 5, line 25.

'*And on . . . plumed.*': Probably from John Milton, *Paradise Lost* stanza 4, line 988.

'*nature's own . . . laid on,*': William Shakespeare, *Twelfth Night* act 1, scene 5, line 258.

and allusion: all is mechanical, conventional, vapid, formal, pedantic in style and execution. They startle and confound the understanding of the reader, by the remoteness and obscurity of their illustrations: they soothe the ear by the monotony of the same everlasting round of circuitous metaphors. They are the *mock-school* in poetry and prose. They flounder about between fustian in expression, and bathos in sentiment. They tantalise the fancy, but never reach the head nor touch the heart. Their Temple of Fame is like a shadowy structure raised by Dulness to Vanity, or like Cowper's description of the Empress of Russia's palace of ice, as 'worthless as in shew 'twas glittering'—

'It smiled, and it was cold!'°

Questions for Understanding

1. What does Hazlitt mean when he says that most people believe that "to write without affectation is to write at random"? Do you believe this is true today as well?
2. Hazlitt states that a genuine familiar style is the style of "common conversation." But he does not mean the conversational style of just anyone. Whose conversational style does he have in mind?
3. What word best describes Hazlitt's tone when he says, "How simple it is to be dignified without ease, to be pompous without meaning"?
4. Cant or slang phrases, Hazlitt says, are "confined ideas"; that is, they are phrases that are confined to a particular group. As an example, Hazlitt gives the phrase "cut an acquaintance." Has that phrase "escaped out of the limits of slang phraseology"? Is it used today more widely than it was in Hazlitt's time?
5. Of those who write in a gaudy style, Hazlitt says, "Such writers have merely *verbal* imaginations, that retain nothing but words." What does Hazlitt wish such writers had besides their verbal imaginations?

Suggestions for Writing

1. Hazlitt makes fun of the art and theater reviewers of his day. They are, he says, "besotted with words, and their brains are turned with the glittering, but empty and sterile phantoms of things." In other words, their reviews turn out to have little to do with what they have been looking at. Write a review of a film or TV drama, or give an account of a ball game. Make a special effort to avoid using words solely for their sound or look. Get "beyond the daubings of fancy, the varnish of sentiment."
2. Hazlitt has no use for what is "pedantic in style and execution." A pedant is someone who makes an excessive show of his or her learning, going well beyond what is appropriate to the circumstances. Some college professors get carried away and let themselves become pedants. Write an essay in which you describe such a professor. Make your examples of the person's

---

'It smiled . . . was cold!': William Cowper's *The Task* 5.173.

pedantry so numerous that your essay is, in effect, an extended definition of the word *pedant*.

3. Recall someone who frequently speaks in public—a member of the clergy, a candidate, an officeholder. Try to recall things the person has said. Make a point of listening very carefully the next time the person speaks. Assess the person's use of language. Is the style primarily that of a limited group, is it basically a sound, familiar style, or is it largely a gaudy style? Write an essay in which you analyze and discuss this person's use of language.

4. Pick out a chapter of a book—nonfiction or fiction—that you have read recently. Make it a chapter in which there is little or no dialogue, a chapter in which the writer is speaking in his or her own voice. Reread the chapter and assess the writer's use of language. Is it the specialized language of a particular group, is it basically a sound, familiar style, or does it tend to be a gaudy style? Write an essay in which you analyze and discuss the writer's use of language.

5. Pick out an essay you wrote earlier in the semester that contained language you suspect Hazlitt would object to if he could read your essay. Rewrite that essay in a sound, familiar style. Don't just make substitutions for earlier words and phrases but rewrite the essay in its entirety. To say what you really mean, you might discover that it's necessary to write a whole paragraph where previously you used just a few words. On the other hand, you might discover that to help the reader understand exactly what you mean deleting is in order, because you said things that are irrelevant and distracting.

NUTS AND BOLTS 9: UNFAMILIAR STYLE

The word *pedant,* from the Italian word *pedante,* entered the English language during the sixteenth century—about six hundred years after the word *teacher.* Words are assimilated into a language because they convey a quality that previously could not be conveyed very well; new words allow us to express ourselves more accurately. Sometimes words originate with a specialized group, and because they answer a need, they pass into the general language. Examples include many words first used by the military and words drawn from the jargon of computer experts. Sometimes the need is so limited that a word enters the language only to fall into disuse within a decade or two. The word *pedant,* however, has been useful for over four hundred years. This must mean that there continue to be pedants: that some writers' styles are pedantic, that some professors teach pedantically, that pedantry is not dead. In other words, some people still need to show off what they know—and students are among them.

Students who deliberately use flowery language are simply showing off. Their first priority is not to communicate effectively but to create the impression of an extensive vocabulary. Such students hope to be rewarded for using long and uncommon words, not for being interesting or convincing. The thesaurus is a magical book for them. They can enter the thesaurus with a common word and emerge with an impressive-sounding uncommon word, which then goes into their writing. They can also pick up the thesaurus to find a word that will save them from repeating a word they've already used. Neither approach is a wise use of the thesaurus. Words come into a language because they convey specific qualities. When they are chosen because they are long, uncommon, or simply different, they are being misused.

To become a good writer, a student should make frequent use of a college-level dictionary. A good dictionary informs the user of the specific qualities, or connotations, that a word has come to convey; a good dictionary reveals the differences among words. A thesaurus emphasizes similarities and gives the impression that words are interchangeable—for example, that there is nothing wrong in substituting *apprentice* or *novice* for *student* and that a professor might just as well be called a pedagogue or a pedant. The more a student resorts to a thesaurus, the more his or her style will become unfamiliar.

There *are* writers whose styles are unfamiliar, elaborate, and even convoluted and who are nevertheless highly regarded—by some readers. Even so, most writers, editors, and professors prefer Hazlitt's familiar style—straightforward, unadorned, practical. The reason, as Hazlitt says, is that the familiar style does not obscure. The unfamiliar—or gaudy—style does. It draws attention to the writer and clouds the meaning or message, if there is one.

Hazlitt says that to write in a genuine familiar style is "to write as any one would speak in common conversation. . . ." He goes on to qualify that statement: The common conversation he is describing is that of educated people who can "discourse with ease, force, and perspicuity, setting aside all pedantic and oratorical flourishes." This is conversation in which the parties are not driven by a need to impress but rather by a desire to explore a topic and to learn from each other. It is conversation in which the parties do a good deal of editing in their minds before they speak, screening words and structuring questions and statements. It is conversation in which clarity and coherence are valued.

In such conversation, there is no opportunity to consult a thesaurus or dictionary. You have to use the vocabulary that is familiar to you. The basic, active vocabulary you use in conversation is the stock from which you should draw in your writing. As you continue to do serious reading in college and afterward, however, your recognition vocabulary—the words you understand when you run across them—will increase, and inevitably some of these words will become part of your active vocabulary. Moreover, you will find yourself among intellectual peers whose own vocabularies are growing. This leads to a good rule of thumb: If a word is in common use among your peers, you can use the word in speaking and in writing without fear of seeming pretentious. Here's another good test for appropriateness: If you've seen a word in a publication on the level of *Time, Newsweek,* or the *New York Times,* the word is appropriate for use in conversation with your fellow students and other educated people—and also in your writing.

ON GOOD NATURE

1816

    Lord Shaftesbury° somewhere remarks, that a great many people pass   *1*
for very good-natured persons, for no other reason than because they care
about nobody but themselves; and, consequently, as nothing annoys them but
what touches their own interest, they never irritate themselves unnecessarily
about what does not concern them, and seem to be made of the very milk
of human kindness.

    Good-nature, or what is often considered as such, is the most selfish of
all the virtues: it is nine times out of ten mere indolence of disposition. A
good-natured man is, generally speaking, one who does not like to be put out
of his way; and as long as he can help it, that is, till the provocation comes
home to himself, he will not. He does not create fictitious uneasiness out of
the distresses of others; he does not fret and fume, and make himself
uncomfortable about things he cannot mend, and that no way concern him,
even if he could: but then there is no one who is more apt to be disconcerted
by what puts him to any personal inconvenience, however trifling; who is
more tenacious of his selfish indulgences, however unreasonable; or who
resents more violently any interruption of his ease and comforts, the very
trouble he is put to in resenting it being felt as an aggravation of the injury.
A person of this character feels no emotions of anger or detestation, if you tell
him of the devastation of a province, or the massacre of the inhabitants of a
town, or the enslaving of a people; but if his dinner is spoiled by a lump of
soot falling down the chimney, he is thrown into the utmost confusion, and
can hardly recover a decent command of his temper for the whole day. He
thinks nothing can go amiss, so long as he is at his ease, though a pain in his
little finger makes him so peevish and quarrelsome, that nobody can come
near him. Knavery and injustice in the abstract are things that by no means
ruffle his temper, or alter the serenity of his countenance, unless he is to be
the sufferer by them; nor is he ever betrayed into a passion in answering a
sophism, if he does not think it immediately directed against his own interest.

    On the contrary, we sometimes meet with persons who regularly heat
themselves in an argument, and get out of humour on every occasion, and
make themselves obnoxious to a whole company about nothing. This is not
because they are ill-tempered, but because they are in earnest. Good-nature
is a hypocrite: it tries to pass off its love of its own ease and indifference to
everything else for a particular softness and mildness of disposition. All people
get in a passion, and lose their temper, if you offer to strike them, or cheat
them of their money, that is, if you interfere with that which they are really
interested in. Tread on the heel of one of these good-natured persons, who

---

Lord Shaftesbury: Anthony Ashley Cooper, third earl of Shaftesbury (1671–1713), English
philosopher.

do not care if the whole world is in flames, and see how he will bear it. If the truth were known, the most disagreeable people are the most amiable. They are the only persons who feel an interest in what does not concern them. They have as much regard for others as they have for themselves. They have as many vexations and causes of complaint as there are in the world. They are general righters of wrongs, and redressers of grievances. They not only are annoyed by what they can help, by an act of inhumanity done in the next street, or in a neighbouring country by their own countrymen, they not only do not claim any share in the glory, and hate it the more, the more brilliant the success,—but a piece of injustice done three thousand years ago touches them to the quick. They have an unfortunate attachment to a set of abstract phrases, such as *liberty, truth, justice, humanity, honour,* which are continually abused by knaves, and misunderstood by fools, and they can hardly contain themselves for spleen. They have something to keep them in perpetual hot water. No sooner is one question set at rest than another rises up to perplex them. They wear themselves to the bone in the affairs of other people, to whom they can do no manner of service, to the neglect of their own business and pleasure. They tease themselves to death about the morality of the Turks, or the politics of the French. There are certain words that afflict their ears, and things that lacerate their souls, and remain a plague-spot there forever after. They have a fellow-feeling with all that has been done, said, or thought in the world. They have an interest in all science and in all art. They hate a lie as much as a wrong, for truth is the foundation of all justice. Truth is the first thing in their thoughts, then mankind, then their country, last themselves. They love excellence, and bow to fame, which is the shadow of it. Above all, they are anxious to see justice done to the dead, as the best encouragement to the living, and the lasting inheritance of future generations. They do not like to see a great principle undermined, or the fall of a great man. They would sooner forgive a blow in the face than a wanton attack on acknowledged reputation. The contempt in which the French hold Shakespeare is a serious evil to them; nor do they think the matter mended, when they hear an Englishman, who would be thought a profound one, say that Voltaire was a man without wit. They are vexed to see genius playing at Tom Fool, and honesty turned bawd. It gives them a cutting sensation to see a number of things which, as they are unpleasant to see, we shall not here repeat. In short, they have a passion for truth; they feel the same attachment to the idea of what is right, that a knave does to his interest, or that a good-natured man does to his ease; and they have as many sources of uneasiness as there are actual or supposed deviations from this standard in the sum of things, or as there is a possibility of folly and mischief in the world.

Principle is a passion for truth; an incorrigible attachment to a general proposition. Good-nature is humanity that costs nothing. No good-natured man was ever a martyr to a cause, in religion or politics. He has no idea of striving against the stream. He may become a good courtier and a loyal subject; and it is hard if he does not, for he has nothing to do in that case but to consult his ease, interest, and outward appearances. The Vicar of Bray was a good-natured man. What a pity he was but a vicar! A good-natured man is utterly unfit for any situation or office in life that requires integrity, fortitude, or generosity,—any sacrifice, except of opinion, or any exertion, but to please. A good-natured man will debauch his friend's mistress, if he has an opportunity; and betray his friend, sooner than share disgrace or danger with him. He will not forego the smallest gratification to save the whole world. He makes his own convenience the standard of right and wrong. He avoids the feeling of pain in himself, and shuts his eyes to the sufferings of others. He will put a malefactor or an innocent person (no matter which) to the rack, and only laugh at the uncouthness of the gestures, or wonder that he is so unmannerly as to cry out. There is no villainy to which he will not lend a helping hand with great coolness and cordiality, for he sees only the pleasant and profitable side of things. He will assent to a falsehood with a leer of complacency, and applaud any atrocity that comes recommended in the garb of authority. He will betray his country to please a Minister, and sign the death-warrant of thousands of wretches, rather than forfeit the congenial smile, the well-known squeeze of the hand. The shrieks of death, the torture of mangled limbs, the last groans of despair, are things that shock his smooth humanity too much ever to make an impression on it: his good-nature sympathizes only with the smile, the bow, the gracious salutation, the fawning answer: vice loses its sting, and corruption its poison, in the oily gentleness of his disposition. He will not hear of any thing wrong in Church or State. He will defend every abuse by which any thing is to be got, every dirty job, every act of every Minister. In an extreme case, a very good-natured man indeed may try to hang twelve honester men than himself to rise at the Bar, and forge the seal of the realm to continue his colleagues a week longer in office. He is a slave to the will of others, a coward to their prejudices, a tool of their vices. A good-natured man is no more fit to be trusted in public affairs, than a coward or a woman is to lead an army. Spleen is the soul of patriotism and of public good. Lord Castlereagh is a good-natured man, Lord Eldon is a good-natured man, Charles Fox was a good-natured man.° The last instance is the most decisive. The definition of a true patriot is *a good hater.*

A king, who is a good-natured man, is in a fair way of being a great   5
tyrant. A king ought to feel concern for all to whom his power extends: but a good-natured man cares only about himself. If he has a good appetite, eats and sleeps well, nothing in the universe besides can disturb him. The destruction of the lives or liberties of his subjects will not stop him in the least of his caprices, but will concoct well with his bile, and 'good digestion wait on appetite, and health on both.' He will send out his mandate to kill and destroy with the same indifference or satisfaction that he performs any natural

---

Lord Castlereagh: Robert Stewart, second viscount of Castlereagh (1769–1822).
Lord Eldon: John Scott, first earl of Eldon (1751–1838).
Charles Fox: Charles James Fox (1749–1806).

function of his body. The consequences are placed beyond the reach of his imagination, or would not affect him if they were not, for he is a fool, and good-natured. A good-natured man hates more than any one else whatever thwarts his will, or contradicts his prejudices; and if he has the power to prevent it, depend upon it, he will use it without remorse and without control.

There is a lower species of this character which is what is usually understood by a *well-meaning man*. A well-meaning man is one who often does a great deal of mischief without any kind of malice. He means no one any harm, if it is not for his interest. He is not a knave, nor perfectly honest. He does not easily resign a good place. Mr Vansittart° is a well-meaning man.

The Irish are a good-natured people; they have many virtues, but their virtues are those of the heart, not of the head. In their passions and affections they are sincere, but they are hypocrites in understanding. If they once begin to calculate the consequences, self-interest prevails. An Irishman who trusts to his principles, and a Scotchman who yields to his impulses, are equally dangerous. The Irish have wit, genius, eloquence, imagination, affections: but they want coherence of understanding, and consequently have no standard of thought or action. Their strength of mind does not keep pace with the warmth of their feelings, or the quickness of their conceptions. Their animal spirits run away with them: their reason is a jade. There is something crude, indigested, rash, and discordant, in almost all that they do or say. They have no system, no abstract ideas. They are 'everything by starts, and nothing long.' They are a wild people. They hate whatever imposes a law on their understandings, or a yoke on their wills. To betray the principles they are most bound by their own professions and the expectations of others to maintain, is with them a reclamation of their original rights, and to fly in the face of their benefactors and friends, an assertion of their natural freedom of will. They want consistency and good faith. They unite fierceness with levity. In the midst of their headlong impulses, they have an undercurrent of selfishness and cunning, which in the end gets the better of them. Their feelings, when no longer excited by novelty or opposition, grow cold and stagnant. Their blood, if not heated by passion, turns to poison. They have a rancour in their hatred of any object they have abandoned, proportioned to the attachment they have professed to it. Their zeal, converted against itself, is furious. The late Mr Burke° was an instance of an Irish patriot and philosopher. He abused metaphysics, because he could make nothing out of them, and turned his back upon liberty, when he found he could get nothing more by her.—See to the same purpose the winding up of the character of *Judy* in Miss Edgeworth's° *Castle Rackrent*.

Mr. Vansittart: Nicholas Vansittart, first baron Bexley (1766–1851), British statesman, best known for his twelve years as chancellor of the exchequer.

Mr. Burke: Edmund Burke (1729–1797), Irish statesman and writer.

Miss Edgeworth: Maria Edgeworth (1767–1849), English novelist.

Questions for Understanding

1. What does Hazlitt mean when he says good nature "is nine times out of ten mere indolence of disposition"?
2. What kinds of events does Hazlitt believe should elicit "anger or detestation"?
3. What does Hazlitt like so much about those people he considers "the most amiable," whom others consider disagreeable?
4. Does what Hazlitt says about good-natured people apply to people today who like to be seen as "cool" or "laid back"?
5. Why does Hazlitt disapprove of the Irish?

Suggestions for Writing

1. "Spleen is the soul of patriotism and of public good." Think of "spleen" as meaning the opposite of good natured. Hazlitt is saying it takes a *bad*-natured person to be a true patriot or real worker for the public good. In your experience, how much truth is there in this statement? Are good-natured or splenetic politicians usually more concerned for the public good? Give examples and discuss.
2. "A good-natured man hates more than any one else whatever thwarts his will, or contradicts his prejudices; and if he has the power to prevent it, depend upon it, he will use it without remorse and without control." Let's substitute "woman" for "man" in Hazlitt's statement. Can you think of a woman to whom the statement applies? Describe and discuss.
3. Hazlitt says that a good-natured king is probably a great tyrant. For a king, let's substitute a person who has a lot of authority and who gives the appearance of being good natured. Do you know such a person? Describe the organization or place that the person controls, manages, or supervises. Describe the image that the person wishes to project. Discuss the person's tyrannical actions that belie the image.
4. In the 1980s and 1990s in the United States, the word *cool* has taken on some of the meaning that Hazlitt gave to *good-natured* in 1816. Just as Hazlitt's good-natured person strove to appear soft and mild, a cool person strives to appear calm, unaffected, uninvolved—not about to be carried away with enthusiasm for anything. Do you know someone who wants to be perceived as cool? What is important to that person? Is the person basically harmless, or does that person, in living the image, have an impact on others that is damaging to society? Describe and discuss.
5. Is Hazlitt's indictment of the Irish based on nothing more than an ethnic stereotype? Are the characteristics Hazlitt attributes to the Irish likely to be found in some people but unlikely to be typical of a whole nationality? Discuss.

Charles Lamb

[1775–1834]

Charles Lamb was born in London, the seventh and last child of Elizabeth and John Lamb, who worked as a servant for a barrister. Only two of Charles's siblings lived to adulthood: John, twelve years older than Charles, and Mary, ten years older. London was Lamb's home base throughout his life. He was never attracted by the back-to-nature movement of contemporaries such as the poets Wordsworth and Coleridge. Lamb met Coleridge when they were students at the private school (Christ's Hospital) that Lamb attended on a scholarship. At sixteen, however, Lamb had to go to work, and his formal schooling ended.

Lamb spent thirty-three years working as a clerk, first for about six months at South-Sea House and then until his retirement at East India House. Both places were headquarters for government-chartered companies that carried on trade with Asia. One day in the fall of 1796, a little more than four years after he began working at East India House, Lamb returned from work to find his household in chaos. His sister Mary, who worked at home as a seamstress, had been in a fury with her apprentice, and when her mother intervened to protect the apprentice, Mary stabbed her mother to death. "I date from the day of horrors," Lamb later wrote Coleridge.

In Lamb's time, a person like Mary, who was known to suffer from mental illness, usually would be committed to a public insane asylum and taken off the family's hands. But Charles, ignoring the urgings of his brother, did not allow it. He assumed full responsibility for Mary, even though he knew there would be future occasions when she would slip into psychosis. Having similar tastes and interests, Charles and his sister shared a great deal during the long periods when Mary was well. They went to plays and exhibitions together, hosted "evenings" at home for friends, and traveled together. *Tales from Shakespeare* (1807), retellings of the plays, was a work on which the two collaborated; they also collaborated on children's stories and poetry. Whenever Mary's symptoms returned, however, Charles had to take her to an asylum until the worst had passed.

Between 1800 and 1820, Lamb wrote poetry, reviews, fiction, drama, and some essays. Although little of the work of this period is memorable, *The Works of Charles Lamb* was published in 1818 in two volumes. In 1820, Lamb began to write for a new publication called *London Magazine*. During the short time Lamb was employed at South-Sea House, he got to know a clerk there who professed an interest in becoming a writer, and a friendship developed between Lamb and Elia (pronounced to rhyme with *desire*). Because the South-Sea House was the subject of his first essay for *London Magazine,* and because his brother worked there, Lamb thought it advisable not to attach his own name to the essay. He indulged a whim and chose the name of Elia. About a year later, when Lamb dropped by South-Sea House to tell Elia about the use of his name, he learned that Elia had died eleven months earlier. Although he regretted the real Elia's death, Lamb was now free to elaborate on a fictional Elia in future essays.

The essays for which Lamb is best known were first published in *London Magazine* between August 1820 and August 1825. "The Two Races of Men" was published in December 1820, "Imperfect Sympathies" in August 1821, and "The Praise of Chimney-Sweepers" in May 1822. Other well-loved essays that were first published in *London Magazine* during this period are "Christ's Hospital Five and Thirty Years Ago," "Mrs. Battle's Opinions on Whist," "Mackery End," "Dream Children," "A Dissertation upon Roast Pig," "Poor Relations," "The Superannuated Man," and "Old China."

Although essays are usually works of nonfiction, Lamb was not at all reluctant to employ fiction in his essays. Thus readers must not take it for granted that the "I" of the essays stands for the real Charles Lamb or that others mentioned represent real people. In walking the streets of London, in his place of employment, and in socializing, Lamb came to know hundreds of people, and in his writing he could not resist making up characters who were composites.

Despite his burdens, Charles Lamb loved his life. He especially loved living in one of the world's great cities and observing the great variety of its human specimens. He loved walking about, whether by day or night. He loved the noises and the smells. He loved observing tradesmen at their work. He loved seeing customers haggle with shopkeepers. He loved the central markets, printers' shops, stalls of old books, coffee houses, the theaters. One of the great pleasures of reading Lamb's essays is sharing with him all the bustle and detail of London life.

An important influence in Lamb's essays is Montaigne, about whom he wrote: "Montaigne is an immense treasure-house of observation, anticipating all the discoveries of succeeding essayists. You cannot dip into him without being struck by the aphorism, that there is nothing new under the sun."

THE PRAISE OF CHIMNEY-SWEEPERS

1822

I like to meet a sweep, understand me, not a grown sweeper—old   *1*
chimney-sweepers are by no means attractive—but one of those tender
novices, blooming through their first nigritude, the maternal washings not
quite effaced from the cheek—such as come forth with the dawn, or
somewhat earlier, with their little professional notes sounding like the
peep-peep of a young sparrow; or liker to the matin lark should I pronounce
them, in their aërial ascents not seldom anticipating the sunrise?

I have a kindly yearning toward these dim specks—poor blots—
innocent blacknesses.

I reverence the young Africans of our own growth—these almost clergy
imps, who sport their cloth without assumption: and from their little pulpits
(the tops of chimneys), in the nipping air of a December morning, preach a
lesson of patience to mankind.

When a child, what a mysterious pleasure it was to witness their
operation! To see a chit no bigger than one's self, enter, one knew not by what
process, into what seemed the *fauces Averni* °—to pursue him in imagination,
as he went sounding on through so many dark stifling caverns, horrid shades!
to shudder with the idea that "now, surely he must be lost forever!"—to
revive at hearing his feeble shout of discovered daylight—and then (O fullness
of delight!) running out of doors, to come just in time to see the sable
phenomenon emerge in safety, the brandished weapon of his art victorious
like some flag waver over a conquered citadel! I seem to remember having
been told that a bad sweep was once left in a stack with his brush, to indicate
which way the wind blew. It was an awful spectacle, certainly, not much
unlike the old stage direction in Macbeth, where the "Apparition of a child
crowned, with a tree in his hand, rises."

Reader, if thou meetest one of these small gentry in thy early rambles,   *5*
it is good to give him a penny—it is better to give him two-pence. If it be
starving weather, and to the proper troubles of his hard occupation a pair of
kibed heels (no unusual accompaniment) be superadded, the demand on thy
humanity will surely rise to a tester.

There is a composition, the ground work of which I have understood
to be the sweet wood yclept sassafras. This wood boiled down to a kind of tea,
and tempered with an infusion of milk and sugar, hath to some tastes a
delicacy beyond the China luxury. I know not how thy palate may relish it;
for myself, with every deference to the judicious Mr. Read, who hath time
out of mind kept open a shop (the only one he avers in London) for the
vending of this "wholesome and pleasant beverage," on the south side of Fleet

---

fauces Averni: The jaws of hell.

Street, as thou approachest Bridge Street—*the only Salopian house°*—I have never yet adventured to dip my own particular lip in a basin of his commended ingredients—a cautious premonition to the olfactories constantly whispering to me, that my stomach must infallibly, with all due courtesy, decline it. Yet I have seen palates, otherwise not uninstructed in dietetical elegancies, sup it up with avidity.

I know not by what particular conformation of the organ it happens, but I have always found that this composition is surprisingly gratifying to the palate of a young chimney-sweeper—whether the oily particles (sassafras is slightly oleaginous) do attenuate and soften the fuliginous concretions, which are sometimes found (in dissections) to adhere to the roof of the mouth in these unfledged practitioners; or whether Nature, sensible that she had mingled too much of bitter wood in the lot of these raw victims, caused to grow out of the earth her sassafras for a sweet lenitive—but so it is, that no possible taste or odor to the senses of a young chimney-sweeper can convey a delicate excitement comparable to this mixture. Being penniless, they will yet hang their black heads over the ascending steam, to gratify one sense if possible, seemingly no less pleased than those domestic animals, cats, when they purr over a new-found sprig of valerian. There is something more in these sympathies than philosophy can inculcate.

Now albeit Mr. Read boasteth, not without reason, that his is the *only Salopian house;* yet be it known to thee, reader—if thou art one who keepest what are called good hours, thou art haply ignorant of the fact—he hath a race of industrious imitators, who from stalls, and under open sky, dispense the same savory mess to humbler customers, at that dead time of the dawn, when (as extremes meet) the rake, reeling home from his midnight cups, and the hard-handed artisan leaving his bed to resume the premature labors of the day, jostle, not unfrequently to the manifest disconcerting of the former, for the honors of the pavement. It is the time when, in summer, between the expired and the not yet relumined kitchen-fires, the kennels of our fair metropolis give forth their least satisfactory odors. The rake, who wisheth to dissipate his o'ernight vapors in more grateful coffee, curses the ungenial fume, as he passeth; but the artisan stops to taste, and blesses the fragrant breakfast.

This is *saloop,* the precocious herb-woman's darling, the delight of the early gardener, who transports his smoking cabbages by break of day from Hammersmith to Covent Garden's famed piazzas, the delight, and oh! I fear, too often the envy, of the unpennied sweep. Him shouldst thou haply encounter, with his dim visage pendent over the grateful steam, regale him with a sumptuous basin (it will cost thee but three-halfpennies) and a slice of delicate bread and butter (an added halfpenny); so may thy culinary fires, eased of the o'ercharged secretions from thy worse-placed hospitalities, curl up a lighter volume to the welkin; so may the descending soot never taint thy costly well-ingredienced soups, nor the odious cry, quick-reaching from

---

the only Salopian house: Salop is the former name of Shropshire, a county in western England.

street to street, of the *fired chimney*, invite the rattling engines from ten adjacent parishes, to disturb for a casual scintillation thy peace and pocket!

I am by nature extremely susceptible of street affronts; the jeers and   *10* taunts of the populace; the low-brėd triumph they display over the casual trip, or splashed stocking, of a gentleman. Yet can I endure the jocularity of a young sweep with something more than forgiveness. In the last winter but one, pacing along Cheapside with my accustomed precipitation when I walk westward, a treacherous slide brought me upon my back in an instant. I scrambled up with pain and shame enough—yet outwardly trying to face it down, as if nothing had happened—when the roguish grin of one of these young wits encountered me. There he stood, pointing me out with his dusky finger to the mob, and to a poor woman (I suppose his mother) in particular, till the tears for the exquisiteness of the fun (so he thought it) worked themselves out at the corners of his poor red eyes, red from many a previous weeping, and soot-inflamed, yet twinkling through all with such a joy, snatched out of desolation, that Hogarth°—but Hogarth has got him already (how could he miss him?) in the March to Finchley, grinning at the pieman—there he stood, as he stands in the picture, irremovable, as if the jest was to last forever—with such a maximum of glee, and minimum of mischief, in his mirth—for the grin of a genuine sweep hath absolutely no malice in it—that I could have been content, if the honor of a gentleman might endure it, to have remained his butt and his mockery till midnight.

I am by theory obdurate to the seductiveness of what are called a fine set of teeth. Every pair of rosy lips (the ladies must pardon me) is the casket presumably holding such jewels; but, methinks, they should take leave to "air" them as frugally as possible. The fine lady, or fine gentleman, who show me their teeth, show me bones. Yet must I confess, that from the mouth of a true sweep a display (even to ostentation) of those white and shiny ossifications, strikes me as an agreeable anomaly in manners, and an allowable piece of foppery. It is, as when

A sable cloud
Turns forth her silver lining on the night.°

It is like some remnant of gentry not quite extinct; a badge of better days; a hint of nobility; and, doubtless, under the obscuring darkness and double night of their forlorn disguisement, oftentimes lurketh good blood, and gentle conditions, derived from lost ancestry, and a lapsed pedigree. The premature apprenticements of these tender victims give but too much encouragement, I fear, to clandestine and almost infantile abductions; the seeds of civility and true courtesy, so often discernible in these young grafts (not otherwise to be accounted for) plainly hint at some forced adoptions; many noble Rachels

---

Hogarth: William Hogarth (1697–1764), English painter and engraver.
A sable . . . on the night: From John Milton's *Comus*.

mourning for their children, even in our days, countenance the fact; the tales of fairy-spiriting may shadow a lamentable verity, and the recovery of the young Montagu° be but a solitary instance of good fortune out of many irreparable and hopeless *defiliations*.

In one of the state-beds at Arundel Castle,° a few years since, under a ducal canopy (that seat of the Howards is an object of curiosity to visitors, chiefly for its beds, in which the late duke was especially a connoisseur) encircled with curtains of the delicatest crimson, with starry coronets inwoven, folded between a pair of sheets whiter and softer than the lap where Venus lulled Ascanius°—was discovered by chance, after all methods of search had failed, at noonday, fast asleep, a lost chimney-sweeper. The little creature, having somehow confounded his passage among the intricacies of those lordly chimneys, by some unknown aperture had alighted upon this magnificent chamber; and, tired with his tedious explorations, was unable to resist the delicious invitement to repose, which he there saw exhibited; so creeping between the sheets very quietly, laid his black head upon the pillow, and slept like a young Howard.

Such is the account given to the visitors at the Castle. But I cannot help seeming to perceive a confirmation of what I had just hinted at in this story. A high instinct was at work in the case, or I am mistaken. Is it probable that a poor child of that description, with whatever weariness he might be visited, would have ventured, under such a penalty as he would be taught to expect, to uncover the sheets of a duke's bed, and deliberately to lay himself down between them, when the rug, or the carpet, presented an obvious couch, still far above his pretensions—is this probable, I would ask, if the great power of nature, which I contend for, had not been manifested within him, prompting to the adventure? Doubtless this young nobleman (for such my mind misgives me that he must be) was allured by some memory, not amounting to full consciousness, of his condition in infancy, when he was used to be lapped by his mother, or his nurse, in just such sheets as he there found, into which he was now but creeping back as into his proper *incunabula*° and resting-place. By no other theory than by this sentiment of a pre-existent state (as I may call it), can I explain a deed so venturous, and indeed, upon any other system, so indecorous, in this tender but unseasonable sleeper.

My pleasant friend Jem White was so impressed with a belief of metamorphoses like this frequently taking place, that in some sort to reverse the wrongs of fortune in these poor changelings, he instituted an annual feast of chimney-sweepers, at which it was his pleasure to officiate as host and waiter. It was a solemn supper held in Smithfield, upon the yearly return of

---

Montagu: Edward Wortley Montagu (1713–1776), who ran away from Westminster School several times, once becoming a chimney-sweeper.

Arundel Castle: Seat of the dukes of Norfolk, one of whom was Charles Howard.

Ascanius: In Virgil's *Aeneid,* Ascanius is the son of Aeneas and Creusa.

incunabula: Earliest home, or cradle.

the fair of St. Bartholomew. Cards were issued a week before to the master-sweeps in and about the metropolis, confining the invitation to their younger fry. Now and then an elderly stripling would get in among us, and be good-naturedly winked at; but our main body were infantry. One unfortunate wight, indeed, who, relying upon his dusky suit, had intruded himself into our party, but by tokens was providentially discovered in time to be no chimney-sweeper (all is not soot which looks so), was quoited out of the presence with universal indignation, as not having on the wedding garment; but in general the greatest harmony prevailed. The place chosen was a convenient spot among the pens, at the north side of the fair, not so far distant as to be impervious to the agreeable hubbub of that vanity, but remote enough not to be obvious to the interruption of every gaping spectator in it. The guests assembled about seven. In those little temporary parlors three tables were spread with napery, not so fine as substantial, and at every board a comely hostess presided with her pan of hissing sausages. The nostrils of the young rogues dilated at the savor. James White, as head waiter, had charge of the first table; and myself, with our trusty companion Bigod, ordinarily ministered to the other two. There was clambering and jostling, you may be sure, who should get at the first table, for Rochester in his maddest days could not have done the humors of the scene with more spirit than my friend. After some general expression of thanks for the honor the company had done him, his inaugural ceremony was to clasp the greasy waist of old dame Ursula (the fattest of the three), that stood frying and fretting, half-blessing, half-cursing "the gentleman," and imprint upon her chaste lips a tender salute, whereat the universal host would set up a shout that tore the concave, while hundreds of grinning teeth startled the night with their brightness. O it was a pleasure to see the sable younkers lick in the unctuous meat, with *his* more unctuous sayings; how he would fit the tit-bits to the puny mouths, reserving the lengthier links for the seniors; how he would intercept a morsel even in the jaws of some young desperado, declaring it "must to the pan again to be browned, for it was not fit for a gentleman's eating;" how he would recommend this slice of white bread, or that piece of kissing-crust, to a tender juvenile, advising them all to have a care of cracking their teeth, which were their best patrimony; how genteelly he would deal about the small ale, as if it were wine, naming the brewer, and protesting, if it were not good, he should lose their custom; with a special recommendation to wipe the lip before drinking. Then we had our toasts—"the King," "the Cloth," which, whether they understood or not, was equally diverting and flattering; and for a crowning sentiment, which never failed, "May the Brush supersede the Laurel!" All these, and fifty other fancies, which were rather felt than comprehended by his guests, would he utter, standing upon tables, and prefacing every sentiment with a "Gentlemen, give me leave to propose so and so," which was a prodigious comfort to those young orphans; every now and then stuffing into his mouth (for it did not do to be squeamish on these occasions) indiscriminate pieces of those reeking sausages, which pleased them mightily, and was the savoriest part, you may believe, of the entertainment.

> Golden lads and lasses must,
> As chimney-sweepers, come to dust.°

James White is extinct, and with him these suppers have long ceased.   15
He carried away with him half the fun of the world when he died—of my world at least. His old clients look for him among the pens; and, missing him, reproach the altered feast of St. Bartholomew, and the glory of Smithfield departed forever.

Questions for Understanding

1. What is the basis of the analogy between chimney-sweepers and clergymen?
2. What is the speaker's attitude toward the sweep who witnessed his fall on a winter's morning in Cheapside?
3. What conclusion does the speaker come to as a result of observing among sweeps "those white and shiny ossifications"?
4. What is the speaker's explanation for the presence of the sweep in the duke's bed at Arundel Castle?
5. Jem White, we are told, staged the annual feast of chimney-sweepers "to reverse the wrongs of fortune in these poor changelings." What does that mean? How were the sweeps wronged?

Suggestions for Writing

1. Lamb apparently knew what London streets were like at the "dead time of dawn," when sweeps were about, and the rake heading home and the artisan leaving home might jostle "for the honors of the pavement." Have you ever been out on city streets as dawn came? What activity was there? Have you been up and about anywhere else at dawn? Write an essay in which you describe what was to be seen at that hour and discuss what is special about dawn in that particular place.
2. Young boys—say, about age ten—were pressed into service as sweeps because they were small and could get into chimneys. Lamb felt toward them "a kindly yearning" and "a mysterious pleasure." Have you had similar feelings toward a child who has taken on a responsibility seemingly beyond his or her years? Write an essay in which you describe the child, explain the situation, and discuss the conclusion you came to as a result of what you observed.
3. Lamb suggests that sweeps must be *changelings.* They seem made of such good stuff that they must have been born into noble families and then stolen away, ordinary babies left in their places. Have you known a child who so far

---

"Golden lads . . . to dust": William Shakespeare, *Cymbeline* act 4, scene 2, lines 262–263.

exceeded his or her parents and other close relatives in ability, talent, and manners that you wondered whether there had been some kind of mix-up? Write an essay in which you describe the child and point out how the child differed from its parents. What conclusions can you draw about the workings of heredity?

4. Jem White's annual feast for the sweeps is something like the end-of-the-season banquet given for high school and college athletic teams—a way of showing affection and appreciation. Jem White certainly took great pleasure in putting on his feast. How have the banquets you've attended worked out? Were they occasions dominated by feelings of mutual affection and appreciation—or did they take on a different character? Write an essay in which you narrate, describe, and draw a conclusion.

5. Most of the states in the United States have child-labor laws intended to protect children from unscrupulous people who might put them to work too young. Is it ever too early for a child to begin to work? Would early involvement with work foster habits that would be beneficial to the child throughout his or her life? Or would working—at, say, age ten—lead to exploitation by employers and engender bitterness in the child? Write an essay in which you discuss the issue of the age at which children should be allowed to work for pay outside the family.

IMPERFECT SYMPATHIES

1821

> *I am of a constitution so general, that it consorts and sympathiseth with all things: I have no antipathy, or rather idiosyncrasy in anything. Those natural repugnancies do not touch me, nor do I behold with prejudice the French, Italian, Spaniard, or Dutch.*

RELIGIO MEDICI°

That the author of the Religio Medici mounted upon the airy stilts of   *1*
abstraction, conversant about notional and conjectural essences; in whose categories of Being the possible took the upper hand of the actual; should have overlooked the impertinent individualities of such poor concretions as mankind, is not much to be admired. It is rather to be wondered at, that in the genus of animals he should have condescended to distinguish that species at all. For myself—earth-bound and fettered to the scene of my activities,— "Standing on earth, not rapt above the sky,"° I confess that I do feel the differences of mankind, national or individual, to an unhealthy excess. I can look with no indifferent eye upon things or persons. Whatever is, is to me a matter of taste or distaste; or when once it becomes indifferent, it begins to be disrelishing. I am, in plainer words, a bundle of prejudices—made up of likings and dislikings—the veriest thrall to sympathies, apathies, antipathies. In a certain sense, I hope it may be said of me that I am a lover of my species. I can feel for all indifferently, but I cannot feel towards all equally. The more purely-English word that expresses sympathy, will better explain my meaning. I can be a friend to a worthy man, who upon another account cannot be my mate or *fellow*. I cannot *like* all people alike. [I would be understood as confining myself to the subject of imperfect sympathies. To nations or classes of men there can be no direct antipathy. There may be individuals born and constellated so opposite to another individual nature, that the same sphere cannot hold them. I have met with my moral antipodes, and can believe the story of two persons meeting (who never saw one another before in their lives) and instantly fighting.

—We by proof find there should be
"Twixt man and man such an antipathy,
That though he can show no just reason why
For any former wrong or injury,
Can neither find a blemish in his fame,

Religio Medici: In English *A Doctor's Religion,* by Sir Thomas Browne (1605–1682), physician and writer.

"Standing . . . sky": John Milton, *Paradise Lost* stanza 7, line 23.

> Nor aught in face or feature justly blame,
> Can challenge or accuse him of no evil,
> Yet notwithstanding hates him as a devil.

The lines are from old Heywood's "Hierarchie of Angels," and he subjoins a curious story in confirmation, of a Spaniard who attempted to assassinate a king Ferdinand of Spain, and being put to the rack could give no other reason for the deed but an inveterate antipathy which he had taken to the first sight of the king.

> ———The cause which to that act compell'd him
> Was, he ne'er loved him since he first beheld him.°]

I have been trying all my life to like Scotchmen, and am obliged to desist from the experiment in despair. They cannot like me—and in truth, I never knew one of that nation who attempted to do it. There is something more plain and ingenuous in their mode of proceeding. We know one another at first sight. There is an order of imperfect intellects (under which mine must be content to rank) which in its constitution is essentially anti-Caledonian. The owners of the sort of faculties I allude to, have minds rather suggestive than comprehensive. They have no pretences to much clearness or precision in their ideas, or in their manner of expressing them. Their intellectual wardrobe (to confess fairly) has few whole pieces in it. They are content with fragments and scattered pieces of Truth. She presents no full front to them— a feature or side-face at the most. Hints and glimpses, germs and crude essays at a system, is the utmost they pretend to. They beat up a little game peradventure—and leave it to knottier heads, more robust constitutions, to run it down. The light that lights them is not steady and polar, but mutable and shifting; waxing, and again waning. Their conversation is accordingly. They will throw out a random word in or out of season, and be content to let it pass for what it is worth. They cannot speak always as if they were upon their oath—but must be understood, speaking or writing, with some abatement. They seldom wait to mature a proposition, but e'en bring it to market in the green ear. They delight to impart their defective discoveries as they arise, without waiting for their full development. They are no systematizers, and would but err more by attempting it. Their minds, as I said before, are suggestive merely. The brain of a true Caledonian (if I am not mistaken) is constituted upon quite a different plan. His Minerva is born in panoply. You are never admitted to see his ideas in their growth—if, indeed, they do grow, and are not rather put together upon principles of clock-work. You never catch his mind in an undress. He never hints or suggests anything, but unlades his stock of ideas in perfect order and completeness. He brings his total wealth into company, and gravely unpacks it. His riches are always about him. He never stoops to catch a glittering something in your presence

---

"I would be . . . beheld him": What appears between the brackets here was in a footnote in Lamb's original text.

to share it with you, before he quite knows whether it be true touch or not. You cannot cry *halves* to anything that he finds. He does not find, but bring. You never witness his first apprehension of a thing. His understanding is always at its meridian—you never see the first dawn, the early streaks.—He has no falterings of self-suspicion. Surmises, guesses, misgivings, half-intuitions, semi-consciousness, partial illuminations, dim instincts, embryo conceptions, have no place in his brain or vocabulary. The twilight of dubiety never falls upon him. Is he orthodox—he has no doubts. Is he an infidel—he has none either. Between the affirmative and the negative there is no border-land with him. You cannot hover with him upon the confines of truth, or wander in the maze of a probable argument. He always keeps the path. You cannot make excursions with him—for he sets you right. His taste never fluctuates. His morality never abates. He cannot compromise, or understand middle actions. There can be but a right and a wrong. His conversation is as a book. His affirmations have the sanctity of an oath. You must speak upon the square with him. He stops a metaphor like a suspected person in an enemy's country. "A healthy book!"—said one of his countrymen to me, who had ventured to give that appellation to John Buncle.°—"Did I catch rightly what you said? I have heard of a man in health, and of a healthy state of body, but I do not see how that epithet can be properly applied to a book." Above all, you must beware of indirect expressions before a Caledonian. Clap an extinguisher upon your irony, if you are unhappily blest with a vein of it. Remember you are upon your oath. I have a print of a graceful female after Leonardo da Vinci, which I was showing off to Mr. ✴✴✴✴ After he had examined it minutely, I ventured to ask him how he liked MY BEAUTY (a foolish name it goes by among my friends)—when he very gravely assured me, that "he had considerable respect for my character and talents" (so he was pleased to say), "but had not given himself much thought about the degree of my personal pretensions." The misconception staggered me, but did not seem much to disconcert him.— Persons of this nation are particularly fond of affirming a truth—which nobody doubts. They do not so properly affirm, as annunciate it. They do indeed appear to have such a love of truth (as if, like virtue, it were valuable for itself) that all truth becomes equally valuable, whether the proposition that contains it be new or old, disputed, or such as impossible to become a subject of disputation. I was present not long since at a party of North Britons, where a son of Burns° was expected; and happened to drop a silly expression (in my South British way), that I wished it were the father instead of the son—when four of them started up at once to inform me, that "that was impossible, because he was dead." An impracticable wish, it seems, was

John Buncle: A character in *The Life of John Buncle, Esq.,* by Thomas Amory, published in two parts in 1756 and 1757.
Burns: Robert Burns (1759–1796), Scottish poet.
Swift: Jonathan Swift (1667–1745), English satirist, born in Ireland.

more than they could conceive. Swift° has hit off this part of their character, namely their love of truth, in his biting way, but with an illiberality that necessarily confines the passage to the margin. [There are some people who think they sufficiently acquit themselves, and entertain their company, with relating facts of no consequence, not at all out of the road of such common incidents as happen every day; and this I have observed more frequently among the Scots than any other nation, who are very careful not to omit the minutest circumstances of time or place; which kind of discourse, if it were not a little relieved by the uncouth terms and phrases, as well as accent and gesture, peculiar to that country, would be hardly tolerable.— *Hints toward an Essay on Conversation.*]° The tediousness of these people is certainly provoking. I wonder if they ever tire one another!—In my early life I had a passionate fondness for the poetry of Burns. I have sometimes foolishly hoped to ingratiate myself with his countrymen by expressing it. But I have always found that a true Scot resents your admiration of his compatriot even more than he would your contempt of him. The latter he imputes to your "imperfect acquaintance with many of the words which he uses": and the same objection makes it a presumption in you to suppose that you can admire him.—Thomson° they seem to have forgotten. Smollett° they have neither forgotten nor forgiven for his delineations of Rory and his companion, upon their first introduction to our metropolis.— Speak of Smollett as a great genius, and they will retort upon you Hume's° History compared with *his* Continuation of it. What if the historian had continued Humphrey Clinker?°

I have, in the abstract, no disrespect for Jews. They are a piece of stubborn antiquity, compared with which Stonehenge is in its nonage. They date beyond the pyramids. But I should not care to be in habits of familiar intercourse with any of that nation. I confess that I have not the nerves to enter their synagogues. Old prejudices cling about me. I cannot shake off the story of Hugh of Lincoln.° Centuries of injury, contempt, and hate, on the one side,—of cloaked revenge, dissimulation, and hate, on the other, between our and their fathers, must and ought to affect the blood of the children. I cannot believe it can run clear and kindly yet, or that a few fine words, such as candour, liberality, the light of a nineteenth century, can close up the breaches of so deadly a disunion. A Hebrew is nowhere congenial to me. He

---

There are some . . . on Conversation.: Bracketed text is footnoted in Lamb's original text.

Thomson: James Thomson (1700–1748), a Scottish poet.

Smollett: Tobias Smollett (1721–1771), a Scottish novelist, who wrote *Roderick Random,* whose title character has the nickname Rory.

Hume: David Hume (1711–1776), Scottish philosopher, who, in addition to his philosophical works wrote *History of England* (1752–1764).

Humphrey Clinker: Tobias George Smollet's novel about a coach tour through Britain.

Hugh of Lincoln: A little Christian boy in Chaucer's "The Prioress' Tale" whose throat is slit by Jews.

is least distasteful on Change°—for the mercantile spirit levels all distinctions, as all are beauties in the dark. I boldly confess that I do not relish the approximation of Jew and Christian, which has become so fashionable. The reciprocal endearments have, to me, something hypocritical and unnatural in them. I do not like to see the Church and Synagogue kissing and congeeing in awkward postures of an affected civility. If *they* are converted, why do they not come over to us altogether? Why keep a form of separation, when the life of it is fled? If they can sit with us at table, why do they keck° at our cookery? I do not understand these half convertites. Jews christianizing—Christians judaizing—puzzle me. I like fish or flesh. A moderate Jew is a more confounding piece of anomaly than a wet Quaker.° The spirit of the synagogue is essentially separative. B—would have been more in keeping if he had abided by the faith of his forefathers. There is a fine scorn in his face, which nature meant to be of—Christians. The Hebrew spirit is strong in him, in spite of his proselytism. He cannot conquer the Shibboleth.° How it breaks out, when he sings, "The Children of Israel passed through the Red Sea!" The auditors, for the moment, are as Egyptians to him, and he rides over our necks in triumph. There is no mistaking him. *B*——has a strong expression of sense in his countenance, and it is confirmed by his singing. The foundation of his vocal excellence is sense. He sings with understanding, as Kemble° delivered dialogue. He would sing the Commandments, and give an appropriate character to each prohibition. His nation, in general, have not over-sensible countenances. How should they?—but you seldom see a silly expression among them.—Gain, and the pursuit of gain, sharpen a man's visage. I never heard of an idiot being born among them.—Some admire the Jewish female-physiognomy. I admire it—but with trembling. Jael° had those full dark inscrutable eyes.

In the Negro countenance you will often meet with strong traits of ⁵ benignity. I have felt yearnings of tenderness towards some of these faces—or rather masks—that have looked out kindly upon one in casual encounters in the streets and highways. I love what Fuller° beautifully calls—these "images of God cut in ebony." But I should not like to associate with them, to share my meals and my good nights with them—because they are black.

I love Quaker ways, and Quaker worship. I venerate the Quaker principles. It does me good for the rest of the day when I meet any of their people in my path. When I am ruffled or disturbed by any occurrence, the

---

change: Stock exchange.

keck: To make a vomiting sound.

a wet Quaker: A Quaker who drinks.

Shibboleth: A kind of password.

Kemble: J. P. Kemble (1757–1823), a prominent actor of tragedies.

Jael: In Judges 4–5, the heroine Jael pretends to provide safety for her people's enemy Sisera but murders him while he sleeps.

Fuller: Thomas Fuller (1608–1661), a Cavalier preacher and writer.

sight, or quiet voice of a Quaker, acts upon me as a ventilator, lightening the air, and taking of a load from the bosom. But I cannot like the Quakers (as Desdemona would say) "to live with them."° I am all over sophisticated—with humours, fancies,° craving hourly sympathy. I must have books, pictures, theatres, chit-chat, scandal, jokes, ambiguities, and a thousand whimwhams, which their simpler taste can do without. I should starve at their primitive banquet. My appetites are too high for the salads which (according to Evelyn°) Eve dressed for the angel; my gusto too excited "To sit a guest with Daniel at his pulse."°

The indirect answers which Quakers are often found to return to a question put to them may be explained, I think, without the vulgar assumption, that they are more given to evasion and equivocating than other people. They naturally look to their words more carefully, and are more cautious of committing themselves, upon their veracity. A Quaker is by law exempted from taking an oath. The custom of resorting to an oath in extreme cases, sanctified as it is by all religious antiquity, is apt (it must be confessed) to introduce into the laxer sort of minds the notion of two kinds of truth—the one applicable to the solemn affairs of justice, and the other to the common proceedings of daily intercourse. As truth bound upon the conscience by an oath can be but truth, so in the common affirmations of the shop and the marketplace a latitude is expected and conceded upon questions wanting this solemn covenant. Something less than truth satisfies. It is common to hear a person say, "You do not expect me to speak as if I were upon my oath." Hence a great deal of incorrectness and inadvertency, short of falsehood, creeps into ordinary conversation; and a kind of secondary or laic-truth is tolerated, where clergy-truth—oath-truth, by the nature of the circumstances, is not required. A Quaker knows none of this distinction. His simple affirmation being received upon the most sacred occasions, without any further test, stamps a value upon the words which he is to use upon the most indifferent topics of life. He looks to them, naturally, with more severity. You can have of him no more than his word. He knows, if he is caught tripping in a casual expression, he forfeits, for himself at least, his claim to the invidious exemption. He knows that his syllables are weighed—and how far a consciousness of this particular watchfulness, exerted against a person, has a tendency to produce indirect answers, and a diverting of the question by honest means, might be illustrated, and the practice justified by a more sacred example than is proper to be adduced upon this occasion. The admirable presence of mind, which is notorious in Quakers upon all contingencies, might be traced to this imposed self-watchfulness—if it did not seem rather an humble and secular scion of that old stock of religious constancy, which

---

"to live with them": William Shakespeare, *Othello* act 1, scene 3, line 249.
fancies: Whims.
Evelyn: John Evelyn (1620–1706), an English diarist.
pulse: A kind of porridge.

never bent or faltered, in the Primitive Friends, or gave way to the winds of persecution, to the violence of judge or accuser, under trials and racking examinations. "You will never be the wiser, if I sit here answering your questions till midnight," said one of those upright Justicers to Penn,° who had been putting law-cases with a puzzling subtlety. "Thereafter as the answers may be," retorted the Quaker. The astonishing composure of this people is sometimes ludicrously displayed in lighter instances.—I was travelling in a stage-coach with three male Quakers, buttoned up in the straitest nonconformity of their sect. We stopped to bait° at Andover, where a meal, partly tea apparatus, partly supper was set before us. My friends confined themselves to the tea-table. I in my way took supper. When the landlady brought in the bill, the eldest of my companions discovered that she had charged for both meals. This was resisted. Mine hostess was very clamorous and positive. Some mild arguments were used on the part of the Quakers, for which the heated mind of the good lady seemed by no means a fit recipient.

The guard came in with his usual peremptory notice. The Quakers pulled out their money and formally tendered it—so much for the tea—I, in humble imitation, tendering mine—for the supper I had taken. She would not relax in her demand. So they all three put up their silver, as did myself, and marched out of the room, the eldest and gravest going first, with myself closing up the rear, who thought I could not do better than follow the example of such grave and warrantable personages. We got in. The steps went up. The coach drove off.

The murmurs of mine hostess, not very indistinctly or ambiguously pronounced, became after a time inaudible—and now my conscience, which the whimsical scene had for a while suspended, beginning to give me some twitches, I waited, in the hope that some justification would be offered by these serious persons for the serious injustice of their conduct. To my great surprise not a syllable was dropped on the subject. They sat as mute as at a meeting. At length, the eldest of them broke silence, by inquiring of his next neighbor, "Hath thee heard how indigos go at the India House?" and the question acted as a soporific on my moral feeling as far as Exeter.

Questions for Understanding

1. What is Lamb's objection to what is said in the passage he quotes from Thomas Browne's *Religio Medici?*
2. What is it about the Scots that Lamb laments when he says, "surmises, guesses, misgivings, half-intuitions, semi-consciousness, partial illuminations, dim instincts, embryo conceptions, have no place in his brain or vocabulary"?

Penn: William Penn (1644–1718), English Quaker who established the colony that became the state of Pennsylvania.

to bait: to feed horses and passengers.

3. In the London that Lamb knew, Jews freely engaged in the city's commerce. What is the basis of Lamb's prejudice against the Jews he met?

4. Quakers also freely engaged in the city's commerce, but Lamb says he cannot like Quakers. Why not?

5. In his first paragraph, Lamb says, "I confess that I do feel the differences of mankind, national or individual, to an unhealthy excess." In your judgment, does Lamb go to an unhealthy excess in taking note of differences and reacting to them?

Suggestions for Writing

1. Lamb thinks that Thomas Browne is fooling himself when he says he has no antipathies and does not "behold with prejudice the French, Italian, Spaniard, or Dutch." According to Lamb, Browne has "overlooked the impertinent individualities of such poor concretions as mankind." Lamb means that to be an individual is to have prejudices and to respond differently to different types of people. Is Browne's assertion believable? Do you believe it was possible for Browne, living in seventeenth-century England, to arrive at adulthood without prejudices? Or do you go along with Lamb? Write an essay in which you discuss the extent to which it is possible to become an adult without harboring certain ethnic and racial prejudices.

2. Write an essay in which you compare and contrast your reactions to members of two different ethnic groups.

3. Are you aware of having "imperfect sympathies" in regard to some other particular area of your life? Are you aware of disliking people whom you are expected to like or at least sympathize with? To what extent do you conceal your feelings? To what extent do you allow yourself to be frank? Describe and discuss.

4. Lamb says, "I have been trying all my life to like Scotchmen, and am obliged to desist from the experiment in despair." Have you had a similar experience? Describe and discuss.

5. What we call *multiculturalism* strives to make a world in which there are no "natural repugnancies" toward any ethnic or racial group. Are the proponents of multiculturalism succeeding? Discuss how and why.

THE TWO RACES OF MEN

1820

The human species, according to the best theory I can form of it,   *1*
composed of two distinct races, *the men who borrow, and the men who lend.* To
these two original diversities may be reduced all those impertinent classifications of Gothic and Celtic tribes, white men, black men, red men. All the
dwellers upon earth, "Parthians, and Medes, and Elamites,"° flock hither, and
do naturally fall in with one or other of these primary distinctions. The
infinite superiority of the former, which I chose to designate as the *great race,*
is discernible in their figure, port, and a certain instinctive sovereignty. The
latter are born degraded. "He shall serve his brethren."° There is something
in the air of one of this cast, lean and suspicious; contrasting with the open,
trusting, generous manners of the other.

Observe who have been the greatest borrowers of all ages—Alcibiades,°
Falstaff,° Sir Richard Steele,° our late incomparable Brinsley,° what a family
likeness in all four!°

What a careless, even deportment hath your borrower! what rosy gills!
what a beautiful reliance on Providence doth he manifest, taking no more
thought than lilies! What contempt for money, accounting it (yours and mine
especially) no better than dross! What a liberal confounding of those pedantic
distinctions of *meum* and *tuum!* or rather, what a noble simplification of
language (beyond Tooke°), resolving these supposed opposites into one clear,
intelligible pronoun adjective! What near approaches doth he make to the
primitive *community,* to the extent of one half of the principle at least.

He is the true taxer who "calleth all the world up to be taxed;" and the
distance is as vast between him and *one of us,* as subsisted between the
Augustan Majesty and the poorest obolary Jew that paid it tribute-pittance at
Jerusalem! His exactions, too, have such a cheerful, voluntary air! So far
removed from your sour parochial or state-gatherers, those ink-born varlets,
who carry their want of welcome in their faces! He cometh to you with a
smile, and troubleth you with no receipt; confining himself to no set season.

"Parthians, and Medes, and Elamites,": From Acts 2:9.

"He shall serve his brethren.": From Genesis 9:25.

Alcibiades: An Athenian politician and general (450?–404 B.C.).

Falstaff: The jovial but unscrupulous knight in Shakespeare's *Henry IV,* Part 1 and 2, and *The
Merry Wives of Windsor.*

Sir Richard Steele: An English essayist, dramatist, and politician, born in Ireland (1672–1729).

Brinsley: Probably refers to Richard Brinsley Sheridan (1751–1816), playwright, politician,
and orator, renowned for his wit, charm, drinking, womanizing—and, apparently, borrowing.

beyond Tooke: A pun on the surname of John Horne Tooke (1736–1812), an English politician
and philologist.

Every day is his Candlemas, or his feast of Holy Michael.° He applieth the *lene tormentum*° of a pleasant look to your purse, which to that gentle warmth expands her silken leaves as naturally as the cloak of the traveler, for which sun and wind contended! He is the true Propontic° which never ebbeth! The sea which taketh handsomely at each man's hand. In vain the victim, whom he delighteth to honor, struggles with destiny; he is in the net. Lend therefore cheerfully, O man ordained to lend, that thou lose not in the end, with thy worldly penny, the reversion promised. Combine not preposterously in thine own person the penalties of Lazarus and of Dives!°—but, when thou seest the proper authority coming, meet it smilingly, as it were half way. Come, a handsome sacrifice! See how light *he* makes of it! Strain not courtesies with a noble enemy.

Reflections like the foregoing were forced upon my mind by the death   5 of my old friend Ralph Bigod, Esq., who parted this life on Wednesday evening—dying, as he had lived, without much trouble. He boasted himself a descendant from mighty ancestors of that name, who heretofore held ducal dignities in this realm. In his actions and sentiments he belied not the stock to which he pretended. Early in life he found himself invested with ample revenues; which, with that noble disinterestedness which I have noticed as inherent in men of the *great race,* he took almost immediate measures entirely to dissipate and bring to nothing; for there is something revolting in the idea of a king holding a private purse; and the thoughts of Bigod were all regal. Thus furnished, by the very act of disfurnishment, getting rid of the cumbersome luggage of riches, more apt (as one sings)

> To slacken virtue, and abate her edge,
> Than prompt her to do aught may merit praise,°

he set forth, like some Alexander, upon his great enterprise, "borrowing and to borrow."

In his periegesis, or triumphant progress throughout this island, it has been calculated that he laid a tithe part of the inhabitants under contribution. I reject this estimate as greatly exaggerated; but having had the honor of accompanying my friend, divers times, in his perambulations about this vast city, I own I was greatly struck at first with the prodigious number of faces we met, who claimed a sort of respectful acquaintance with us. He was one day so obliging as to explain the phenomenon. It seems, these were his tributaries; feeders of his exchequer; gentlemen, his good friends (as he was pleased to express himself), to whom he had occasionally been beholden for a loan. Their multitudes did no way

---

Every day . . . Holy Michael: These are British quarter days, days regarded as beginning the quarters of the year, days on which quarterly payments frequently are due.

lene tormentum: Gentle stimulus.

Propontic: The Sea of Marmora.

the penalties of Lazarus and of Dives: From Proverbs 19:17; Luke 16:20–31.

To slacken . . . praise: John Milton, *Paradise Regained* stanza 2, lines 455–456.

disconcert him. He rather took a pride in numbering them; and, with Comus, seemed pleased to be "stocked with so fair a herd."°

With such sources, it was a wonder how he contrived to keep his treasury always empty. He did it by force of an aphorism, which he had often in his mouth, that "money kept longer than three days stinks." So he made use of it while it was fresh. A good part he drank away (for he was an excellent toss-pot), some he gave away, the rest he threw away, literally tossing and hurling it violently from him—as boys do burrs, or as if it had been infectious—into ponds, or ditches, or deep holes, inscrutable cavities of the earth; or he would bury it (where he would never seek it again) by a river's side under some bank, which (he would facetiously observe) paid no interest—but out away from him it must go peremptorily, as Hagar's offspring into the wilderness, while it was sweet. He never missed it. The streams were perennial which fed his fisc. When new supplies became necessary, the first person that had the felicity to fall in with him, friend or stranger, was sure to contribute to the deficiency. For Bigod had an *undeniable* way with him. He had a cheerful, open exterior, a quick, jovial eye, a bald forehead, just touched with gray *(cana fides).*° He anticipated no excuse, and found none. And, waiving for a while my theory as to the *great race,* I would put it to the most untheorizing reader, who may at times have disposable coin in his pocket, whether it is not more repugnant to the kindliness of his nature to refuse such a one as I am describing, than to say *no* to a poor petitionary rogue (your bastard borrower), who, by his mumping visnomy, tells you that he expects nothing better; and, therefore, whose preconceived notions and expectations you do in reality so much less shock in the refusal.

When I think of this man; his fiery glow of heart; his swell of feeling; how magnificent, how *ideal* he was; how great at the midnight hour; and when I compare with him the companions with whom I have associated since, I grudge the saving of a few idle ducats, and think that I am fallen into the society of *lenders,* and *little men.*

To one like Elia, whose treasures are rather cased in leather covers than closed in iron coffers, there is a class of alienators more formidable than that which I have touched upon; I mean your *borrowers of books*—those mutilators of collections, spoilers of the symmetry of shelves, and creators of odd volumes. There is Comberbatch,° matchless in his depredations!

That foul gap in the bottom shelf facing you, like a great eye-tooth   10
knocked out (you are now with me in my little back study in Bloomsbury, reader), with the huge Switzer-like tomes on each side (like the Guildhall giants, in their reformed posture, guardant of nothing) once held the tallest of my folios, *Opera Bonaventuræ,* choice and massy divinity, to which its two supporters (school divinity also, but of a lesser caliber, Bellarmine, and Holy

---

"*with Comus . . . herd.*": John Milton, *Comus* line 152.

cana fides: The hoary honor.

Comberbatch: Samuel Taylor Coleridge, who had enlisted in the army under the name of Silas Titus Comberback.

Thomas), showed but as dwarfs, itself an Ascapart!° *that* Comberbatch abstracted upon the faith of a theory he holds, which is more easy, I confess, for me to suffer by than to refute, namely, that "the title to property in a book (my Bonaventure, for instance) is in exact ratio to the claimant's powers of understanding and appreciating the same." Should he go on acting upon this theory, which of our shelves is safe?

The slight vacuum in the left-hand case, two shelves from the ceiling, scarcely distinguishable but by the quick eye of a loser, was whilom the commodious resting-place of Browne° on Urn Burial. C. will hardly allege that he knows more about that treatise than I do, who introduced it to him, and was indeed the first (of the moderns) to discover its beauties, but so have I known a foolish lover to praise his mistress in the presence of a rival more qualified to carry her off than himself. Just below, Dodsley's dramas want their fourth volume, where Vittoria Corombona is! The remainder nine are as distasteful as Priam's° refuse sons, when the Fates *borrowed* Hector. Here stood the Anatomy of Melancholy, in sober state. There loitered the Complete Angler, quiet as in life, by some stream side. In younger nook, John Buncle, a widower-volume, with "eyes closed," mourns his ravished mate.

One justice I must do my friend, that if he sometimes, like the sea, sweeps away a treasure, at another time, sea-like, he throws up as rich an equivalent to match it. I have a small under-collection of this nature (my friend's gatherings in his various calls), picked up, he has forgotten at what odd places, and deposited with as little memory at mine. I take in these orphans, the twice-deserted. These proselytes of the gate are welcome as the true Hebrews. There they stand in conjunction—natives, and naturalized. The latter seem as little disposed to inquire out their true lineage as I am. I charge no warehouse-room for these deodands,° nor shall ever put myself to the ungentlemanly trouble of advertising a sale of them to pay expenses.

To lose a volume to C. carries some sense and meaning in it. You are sure that he will make one hearty meal on your viands, if he can give no account of the platter after it. But what moved thee, wayward, spiteful K., to be so importunate to carry off with thee, in spite of tears and adjurations to thee to forbear, the Letters of that princely woman, the thrice noble Margaret Newcastle—knowing at the time, and knowing that I knew also, thou most assuredly wouldst never turn over one leaf of the illustrious folio: what but the mere spirit of contradiction, and childish love of getting the better of thy friend? Then, worst cut of all! to transport it with thee to the Gallican land—

Ascapart: A giant in *Polyolbion,* by Michael Drayton (1563–1631).

Browne: Sir Thomas Browne (1605–1682).

Priam: In Homer's *Iliad,* King Priam of Troy begs from Achilles the body of Hector, the most beloved son of the fifty born him, nine of whom were still living.

deodands: Personal articles.

Unworthy land to harbor such a sweetness,
A virtue in which all ennobling thoughts dwelt,
Pure thoughts, kind thoughts, high thoughts, her sex's wonder!°

Hadst thou not thy play-books, and books of jests and fancies, about thee, to keep
thee merry, even as thou keepest all companies with thy quips and mirthful tales?
Child of the Green-Room, it was unkindly done of thee. Thy wife, too, that part
French, better-part Englishwoman! that *she* could fix upon no other treatise to
bear away, in kindly token of remembering us, than the works of Fulke Greville,
Lord Brook—of which no Frenchman, nor woman of France, Italy or England,
was ever by nature constituted to comprehend a tittle! *Was there not Zimmerman
on Solitude?*

Reader, if haply thou art blessed with a moderate collection, be shy of
showing it; or if thy heart overfloweth to lend them, lend thy books; but let
it be to such a one as S. T. C.; he will return them (generally anticipating the
time appointed) with usury; enriched with annotations, tripling their value.
I have had experience. Many are these precious MSS. of his (in *matter*
oftentimes, and almost in *quantity* not unfrequently, vying with the originals),
in no very clerkly hand; legible in my Daniel; in old Burton; in Sir Thomas
Browne; and those abstruser cogitations of the Greville, now, alas! wandering
in Pagan lands. I counsel thee, shut not thy heart, nor thy library, against
S. T. C.

Questions for Understanding

1. What is it about the appearance of borrowers that leads Lamb to speak of their
   "infinite superiority"?
2. What are the differences in manner between the borrower as "true taxer" and
   the typical tax collector?
3. How should the lender behave when confronted by the borrower?
4. In dissipating the "ample revenues" that he had early in life, Bigod did so with
   "noble disinterestedness." What does that last phrase suggest about Bigod's
   dissipation?
5. What compensation does Comberbatch sometimes offer for the books he
   takes away?

Suggestions for Writing

1. Consider an experience you have had with a friend who borrowed something
   from you. Describe what happened to the friendship from the moment the
   request to borrow was made. Discuss the lesson that can be drawn from the
   experience.

"Unworthy . . . sex's wonder!": Scholars think Lamb himself wrote these lines.

2. Consider the experiences you have had with several people who asked to borrow from you. Write an essay in which you describe and discuss types of borrowers.
3. In Shakespeare's *Hamlet,* Polonius advises his son, "Neither a borrower, nor a lender be." Discuss the problems one may bring on by refusing to be a lender.
4. Polonius goes on to explain why his son should not be a borrower by saying, "borrowing dulls the edge of husbandry"—that is, the ability to be productive. Write an essay in which you discuss your own experiences as a borrower. To what extent did borrowing make you less productive? To what extent did borrowing make you more productive?
5. Borrowing is the engine of modern capitalist economies. Write an essay in which you discuss the desirability of having an economy dependent on borrowing.

NUTS AND BOLTS 10: WRITING FOCUSED DESCRIPTION

A well-written descriptive paragraph is a pleasure to read. Such a paragraph effectively reports what has been experienced by the imagination or senses, and succeeds in making the reader a participant. Effective description is a basic requirement of good writing—but it takes more than finely honed senses. It requires the use of considerable intellect to select from among abundant impressions and to construct with those selected a paragraph that is orderly and focused.

One of the principles of good descriptive writing is to focus on only one thing at a time. Whether it be an object, a place, an animal, a person, or whatever, the focus should not stray. That sounds obvious, but when lots of words, images, and sensory impressions flow into our heads, we make associations, and it is not uncommon for such associations to find their way into our paragraphs and shift the focus. When it is done consciously and deliberately, moving the focus back and forth from one thing to another is a very effective technique. The description is enhanced by showing how the subject is both similar to and different from something within the same general class—rugby and football, St. Louis and New Orleans, Caesar and Alexander. Comparing and contrasting within a single paragraph takes skill and experience. If you can write such paragraphs successfully, great! But here the objective is to provide some tips for keeping the focus on the one thing you've decided to describe.

If you're describing one thing, that one thing should be the grammatical subject of most of the sentences in your paragraph. To be more precise, let's make that *clauses* instead of sentences, because many sentences have more than one clause, and each clause has its own subject word. If your focus strays, that straying will be revealed in the number of different subjects your clauses have. From sentence to sentence, the grammatical subjects should, for the most part, point to the subject you've decided to focus on.

Once the subject of the paragraph has been named, a pronoun usually takes the place of the naming noun. If your focus remains steady and you continue to describe the same thing, the same pronoun will be used several times. If the pronoun changes, that may mean your focus has shifted to something else. If the same pronoun is used several times as a grammatical subject, the focus is likely to be clear and distinct throughout the paragraph.

Let us consider several paragraphs in the first half of Charles Lamb's "The Two Races of Men." Lamb lets us know in his first paragraph that, of the two races into which he has divided humanity, he will focus on the superior race, the borrowers. He then proceeds to talk about borrowers generally, and in paragraph 4 he injects humor by likening the borrower to a grandiose tax collector. Notice that in the first half of the paragraph, before Lamb decides to shift the focus to the tax collector's victims, four sentences begin with *he*. The focus is on the tax collector, and repeating that pronoun, especially by using it as the first word of sentences, helps keep the focus there.

Then, in Paragraph 5, Lamb brings in a specific borrower, his fictitious friend Ralph Bigod (as in "By God!"). In this paragraph of five sentences, four have *he* as the grammatical subject of the first clause: "*He* boasted himself . . ."; "*he* belied not the stock . . ."; "*he* found himself . . ."; *he* set forth. . . ." Lamb's purpose in this paragraph is to portray Bigod as a member of a "mighty" aristocratic family—and as careless in his spending habits as such aristocrats often were. Through the repetition of *he,* Lamb maintains his focus and preserves the unity of his subject, neither consciously shifting nor unknowingly sliding.

The development of Paragraph 6 is somewhat different. While Lamb here portrays Bigod as a conquering Alexander, a second character enters the essay: the author as a companion who has accompanied Bigod in his "perambulations." Lamb does this so that Bigod will seem more believable. We meet someone who has seen him in operation and can testify to the "multitudes" who were "feeders of his exchequer."

Having let us know how Bigod came by his funds, Lamb in Paragraph 7 tells us "how *he* contrived to keep his treasury always empty." Five of the sentences that follow begin with *he* and tell us what Bigod did or felt. Among them is the marvelous fantasy of the fourth sentence, which contains four independent clauses, each with *he* as its grammatical subject: "A good part *he* drank away . . ."; "some *he* gave away, the rest *he* threw away . . ." "or *he* would bury it. . . ."

As a writer, try to remember the sharp focus that we've seen here in Lamb. Once you begin to look for it, you will see it in the descriptive passages of other skillful writers. An effective technique for keeping your focus clear is to repeat the pronoun that takes the place of the word that names your subject. If, in reading over what you've written, you find more than one recurring pronoun, check carefully to be sure your focus has not shifted.

CONFESSIONS OF A DRUNKARD°

1813

Dehortations from the use of strong liquors have been the favorite topic   *1*
of sober declaimers in all ages, and have been received with abundance of
applause by water-drinking critics. But with the patient himself, the man that
is to be cured, unfortunately their sound has seldom prevailed. Yet the evil is
acknowledged, the remedy simple. Abstain. No force can oblige a man to
raise the glass to his head against his will. 'Tis as easy as not to steal, not to tell
lies.

Alas! the hand to pilfer, and the tongues to bear false witness, have no
constitutional tendency. These are actions indifferent to them. At the first
instance of the reformed will, they can be brought off with a murmur. The
itching finger is but a figure in speech, and the tongue of the liar can with the
same natural delight give forth useful truths with which it has been
accustomed to scatter their pernicious contraries. But when a man has
commenced sot——

O pause, thou sturdy moralist, thou person of stout nerves and a strong
head, whose liver is happily untouched, and ere thy gorge riseth at the *name*
which I had written, first learn what the *thing* is; how much of compassion,
how much of human allowance, thou mayest virtuously mingle with thy
disapprobation. Trample not on the ruins of a man. Exact not, under so
terrible a penalty as infamy, a resuscitation from a state of death almost as real
as that from which Lazarus rose not but by a miracle.

Begin a reformation, and custom will make it easy. But what if the
beginning be dreadful, the first steps not like climbing a mountain but going
through fire? what if the whole system must undergo a change violent as that
which we conceive of the mutation of form in some insects? what if a process
comparable to flaying alive be to be gone through? is the weakness that sinks
under such struggles to be confounded with the pertinacity which clings to
other vices, which have induced no constitutional necessity, no engagement
of the whole victim, body and soul?

I have known one in that state, when he has tried to abstain but for one   *5*
evening,—though the poisonous potion had long ceased to bring back its
first enchantments, though he was sure it would rather deepen his gloom than
brighten it,—in the violence of the struggle, and the necessity he had felt of
getting rid of the present sensation at any rate. I have known him to scream
out, to cry aloud, for the anguish and pain of the strife within him.

Confessions of a Drunkard: This essay was published anonymously in 1813. In 1822, it was
reprinted in *London Magazine* as an essay of Elia, to which Lamb added a lengthy note. In the
note, Lamb explains that "Confessions" is not about Elia but is "a compound extracted out
of his long observations of the effects of drinking upon all the world about him; and this
accumulated mass of misery he hath centered (as the custom is with judicious essayists) in a
single figure."

Why should I hesitate to declare that the man of whom I speak is myself? I have no puling apology to make to mankind. I see them in one way or another deviating from the pure reason. It is to my own nature alone I am accountable for the woe that I have brought upon it.

I believe that there are constitutions, robust heads and iron insides, whom scarce any excesses can hurt; whom brandy (I have seen them drink it like wine), at all events whom wine, taken in ever so plentiful a measure, can do no worse injury to than just to muddle their faculties, perhaps never very pellucid. On them this discourse is wasted. They would but laugh at a weak brother, who, trying his strength with them, and coming off foiled from the contest, would fain persuade them that such agonistic exercises are dangerous. It is to a very different description of person I speak. It is to the weak—the nervous; to those who feel the want of some artificial aid to raise their spirits in society to what is no more than the ordinary pitch of all around them without it. This is the secret of our drinking. Such must fly the convivial board in the first instance, if they do not mean to sell themselves for their term of life.

Twelve years ago I had completed my six-and-twentieth year. I had lived from the period of leaving school to that time pretty much in solitude. My companions were chiefly books, or at most one or two living ones of my own book-loving and sober stamp. I rose early, went to bed betimes, and the faculties which God had given me, I have reason to think, did not rust in me unused.

About that time I fell in with some companions of a different order. They were men of boisterous spirits, sitters up a-nights, disputants, drunken; yet seemed to have something noble about them. We dealt about the wit, or what passes for it after midnight, jovially. Of the quality called fancy I certainly possessed a larger share than my companions. Encouraged by their applause, I set up for a professed joker! I, who of all men am least fitted for such an occupation, having, in addition to the greatest difficulty which I experience at all times of finding words to express my meaning, a natural nervous impediment in my speech!

Reader, if you are gifted with nerves like mine, aspire to any character but that of a wit. When you find a tickling relish upon your tongue disposing you to that sort of conversation, especially if you find a preternatural flow of ideas setting in upon you at the first sight of a bottle and fresh glasses, avoid giving way to it as you would fly your greatest destruction. If you cannot crush the power of fancy, or that within you which you mistake for such, divert it, give it some other play. Write an essay, pen a character or description, but not as I do now, with tears trickling down your cheeks.

To be an object of compassion to friends, of derision to foes; to be suspected by strangers, stared at by fools; to be esteemed dull when you cannot be witty; to be applauded for witty when you know that you have been dull; to be called upon for the extemporaneous exercise of that faculty which no premeditation can give; to be spurred on to efforts which end in contempt; to be set on to provoke mirth which procures the procurer hatred;

to give pleasure and be paid with squinting malice; to swallow draughts of life-destroying wine which are to be distilled into airy breath to tickle vain auditors; to mortgage miserable morrows for nights of madness; to waste whole seas of time upon those who pay it back in little inconsiderate drops of grudging applause, are the wages of buffoonery and death.

Time, which has a sure stroke at dissolving all connections which have no solider fastenings than this liquid cement, more kind to me than my own taste or penetration, at length opened my eyes to the supposed qualities of my first friends. No trace of them is left but in the vices which they introduced, and the habits they infixed. In them my friends survive still and exercise ample retribution for any supposed infidelity that I may have been guilty of toward them.

My next more immediate companions were and are persons of such intrinsic and felt worth, that though accidentally their acquaintance has proved pernicious to me, I do not know that if the thing were to do over again, I should have the courage to eschew the mischief at the price of forfeiting the benefit. I came to them reeking from the steams of my late overheated notions of companionship; and the slightest fuel which they unconsciously afforded, was sufficient to feed my old fires into a propensity.

They were no drinkers; but, one from professional habit, and another from a custom derived from his father, smoked tobacco. The devil could not have devised a more subtle trap to re-take a backsliding penitent. The transition, from gulping down draughts of liquid fire to puffing out innocuous blasts of dry smoke, was so like cheating him. But he is too hard for us when we hope to commute. He beats us at barter; and when we think to set off a new failing against an old infirmity, 'tis odds but he puts the trick upon us of two for one. That (comparatively) white devil of tobacco brought with him in the end seven worse than himself.

It were impertinent to carry the reader through all the processes by   15
which, from smoking at first with malt liquor, I took my degrees through thin wines, through stronger wine and water, through small punch to those juggling compositions, which under the name of mixed liquors, slur a great deal of brandy or other poison under less and less water continually, until they come next to none, and so to none at all. But it is hateful to disclose the secrets of my Tartarus.

I should repel my readers, from a mere incapacity of believing me, were I to tell them what tobacco has been to me, the drudging service which I have paid, the slavery which I have vowed to it. How, when I have resolved to quit it, a feeling as of ingratitude has started up; how it has put on personal claims and made the demands of a friend upon me. How the reading of it casually in a book, as where Adams° takes his whiff in the chimney-corner of some inn in Joseph Andrews, or Piscator in the Complete Angler° breaks his fast

---

Adams: Parson Adams, a character in the novel *Joseph Andrews,* by Henry Fielding (1707–1754).

Piscator in the Complete Angler: A pipe is Piscator's breakfast in *The Complete Angler,* by Izaak Walton (1593–1683).

upon a morning pipe in that delicate room *Piscatoribus Sacrum,* has in a moment broken down the resistance of weeks. How a pipe was ever in my midnight path before me, till the vision forced me to realize it; how then its ascending vapors curled, its fragrance lulled, and the thousand delicious ministerings conversant about it, employing every faculty, extracted the sense of pain. How from illuminating it came to darken, from a quick solace it turned to a negative relief, thence to a restlessness and dissatisfaction, thence to a positive misery. How, even now, when the whole secret stands confessed in all its dreadful truth before me, I feel myself linked to it beyond the power of revocation. Bone of my bone—

Persons not accustomed to examine the motives of their actions, to reckon up the countless nails that rivet the chains of habit, or perhaps being bound by none so obdurate as those I have confessed to, may recoil from this as from an overcharged picture. But what short of such a bondage is it, which in spite of protesting friends, a weeping wife and a reprobating world, chains down many a poor fellow, of no original indisposition to goodness, to his pipe and his pot?

I have seen a print after Correggio,° in which three female figures are ministering to a man who sits fast bound at the root of a tree. Sensuality is soothing him, Evil Habit is nailing him to a branch, and Repugnance at the same instant of time is applying a snake to his side. In his face is feeble delight, the recollection of past rather than perception of present pleasures, languid enjoyment of evil with utter imbecility to good, a Sybaritic effeminacy, a submission to bondage, the springs of the will gone down like a broken clock, the sin and the suffering co-instantaneous, or the latter forerunning the former, remorse preceding action—all this represented in one point of time. When I saw this, I admired the wonderful skill of the painter. But when I went away, I wept, because I thought of my own condition.

Of *that* there is no hope that it should ever change. The waters have gone over me. But out of the black depths, could I be heard, I would cry out to all those who have but set a foot in the perilous flood. Could the youth, to whom the flavor of his first wine is delicious as the opening scenes of life or the entering upon some newly-discovered paradise, look into my desolation, and be made to understand what a dreary thing it is when a man shall feel himself going down a precipice with open eyes and a passive will, to see his destruction and have no power to stop it, and yet to feel it all the way emanating from himself; to perceive all goodness emptied out of him, and yet not to be able to forget a time when it was otherwise; to bear about the piteous spectacle of his own self-ruin: could he see my fevered eye, feverish with last night's drinking, and feverishly looking for this night's repetition of the folly; could he feel the body of the death out of which I cry hourly with feebler and feebler outcry to be delivered, it were enough to

---

a print after Corregio: "Vice: An Allegory," by the Italian painter Antonio Allegri da Corregio (1494–1534).

make him dash the sparkling beverage to the earth in all the pride of its mantling temptation; to make him clasp his teeth,

> —and not undo 'em
> To suffer WET DAMNATION to run thro 'em.°

Yea, but (methinks I hear somebody object) if sobriety be that fine thing 20
you would have us to understand, if the comforts of a cool brain are to be preferred to that state of heated excitement which you describe and deplore, what hinders in your instance that you do not return to those habits from which you would induce others never to swerve? if the blessing be worth preserving, is it not worth recovering?

Recovering!—O if a wish could transport me back to those days of youth, when a draught from the next clear spring could slake any heats which summer suns and youthful exercise had power to stir up in the blood, how gladly would I return to thee, pure element, the drink of children and of child-like holy hermit! In my dreams I can sometimes fancy thy cool refreshment purling over my burning tongue. But my waking stomach rejects it. That which refreshes innocence only makes me sick and faint.

But is there no middle way between total abstinence and the excess which kills you? For your sake, reader, and that you may never attain to my experience, with pain I must utter the dreadful truth, that there is none—none that I can find. In my stage of habit (I speak not of habits less confirmed—for some of them I believe the advice to be most prudential), in the stage which I have reached, to stop short of that measure which is sufficient to draw on torpor and sleep, the benumbing apoplectic sleep of the drunkard, is to have taken none at all. The pain of the self-denial is all one. And what that is, I had rather the reader should believe on my credit, than know from his own trial. He will come to know it, whenever he shall arrive in that state in which, paradoxical as it may appear, *reason shall only visit him through intoxication;* for it is a fearful truth, that the intellectual faculties by repeating acts of intemperance may be driven from their orderly sphere of action, their clear daylight ministries, until they shall be brought at last to depend, for the faint manifestation of their departing energies, upon the returning periods of the fatal madness to which they owe their devastation. The drinking man is never less himself than during his sober intervals. Evil is so far his good.[1]

Behold me, then, in the robust period of life, reduced to imbecility and decay. Hear me count my gains, and the profits which I have derived from the midnight cup.

—and not . . . thro 'em: Cyril Tourneur (1580?–1626), *Revenger's Tragedy* act 3, scene 5.
[1] When poor M——painted his last picture with a pencil on one trembling hand, and a glass of brandy and water in the other, his fingers owed the comparative steadiness with which they were enabled to go through their task in an imperfect manner, to a temporary firmness derived from a repetition of practices, the general effect of which had shaken both them and him so terribly.

Twelve years ago I was possessed of a healthy frame of mind and body. I was never strong, but I think my constitution (for a weak one) was as happily exempt from the tendency to any malady as it was possible to be. I scarce knew what it was to ail anything. Now, except when I am losing myself in a sea of drink, I am never free from those uneasy sensations in head and stomach, which are so much worse to bear than any definite pains or aches.

At that time I was seldom in bed after six in the morning, summer and winter. I awoke refreshed, and seldom without some merry thoughts in my head, or some piece of a song to welcome the new-born day. Now, the first feeling which besets me, after stretching out the hours of recumbence to their last possible extent, is a forecast of the wearisome day that lies before me, with a secret wish that I could have lain on still, or never awaked.

Life itself, my waking life, has much of the confusion, the trouble, and obscure perplexity, of an ill dream. In the day time I stumble upon dark mountains.

Business, which, though never very particularly adapted to my nature, yet as something of necessity to be gone through, and therefore best undertaken with cheerfulness, I used to enter upon with some degree of alacrity, now wearies, affrights, perplexes me. I fancy all sorts of discourage-ments, and am ready to give up an occupation which gives me bread, from a harassing conceit of incapacity. The slightest commission given me by a friend, or any small duty which I have to perform for myself, as giving orders to a tradesman, etc., haunts me as a labor impossible to be got through. So much the springs of action are broken.

The same cowardice attends me in all my intercourse with mankind. I dare not promise that a friend's honor, or his cause, would be safe in my keeping, if I were put to the expense of any manly resolution in defending it. So much the springs of moral action are deadened within me.

My favorite occupations in times past now cease to entertain. I can do nothing readily. Application for ever so short a time kills me. This poor abstract of my condition was penned at long intervals; with scarcely an attempt at connection of thought, which is now difficult to me.

The noble passages which formerly delighted me in history or poetic fiction now only draw a few tears, allied to dotage. My broken and dispirited nature seems to sink before anything great and admirable.

I perpetually catch myself in tears, for any cause, or none. It is inexpressible how much this infirmity adds to a sense of shame, and a general feeling of deterioration.

These are some of the instances, concerning which I can say with truth, that it was not always so with me.

Shall I lift up the veil of my weakness any further? or is this disclosure sufficient?

I am a poor nameless egotist, who have no vanity to consult by these Confessions. I know not whether I shall be laughted at, or heard seriously. Such as they are, I commend them to the reader's attention, if he finds his own case any way touched. I have told him what I am come to. Let him stop in time.

Questions for Understanding

1. What is the tone in the first two paragraphs?
2. What is tone in the third and fourth paragraphs?
3. What is the connection between drinking and wit?
4. Is the speaker pleased that he is able to substitute tobacco for alcohol?
5. Does the speaker argue that, despite nightly bouts of drinking, his daytime performance was unaffected?

Suggestions for Writing

1. Is the consumption of alcohol a "constitutional necessity," as the speaker in this essay implies? That is, is alcoholism a disease more than it is a failure of will? Write an essay in which you thoroughly discuss this issue.
2. The speaker says it is the weak and nervous whom he is addressing; those who "scarce any excesses can hurt" don't need his advice. But the weak and nervous, when they find themselves in the midst of a spirited, boisterous bunch, need some "artificial aid" to raise their spirits to the level of the people around them. On the basis of your own observations of drunkards, to what extent do you agree with this? Write an essay in which you discuss the likelihood that partying will make a drunkard of a certain type of person.
3. Write an essay in which you discuss the question of whether it is possible for a group of people to have a good time together on a Saturday night without consuming alcohol. How much does the gender of those present matter?
4. The speaker implies that drinking buddies really have nothing to hold them together beyond the "liquid cement." How true would you say this is? Write an essay in which you discuss the role of alcohol in a real friendship.
5. At one time in the United States, alcohol seemed so destructive to family life that women's groups and religious groups were successful in getting passed a Constitutional amendment prohibiting "the manufacture, sale, or transportation of intoxicating liquors." The 18th Amendment—the Prohibition Amendment—became law in 1919; in 1933 it was repealed. Write an essay in which you discuss whether it is generally beneficial or harmful to try to prevent self-destructive behavior through the enactment of laws.

Francis Bacon

[1561–1626]

Nowadays, when the heart is removed from the body of a young crash victim, packed in ice, and rushed to a hospital where a person with a failing heart waits hopefully, cardiologists have a pretty good idea of what will happen after the diseased heart is replaced with the healthy one. They know, because records have been kept, because statistics have been compiled, and because a great deal of experimentation was done before the first transplant operation was performed on a human being. What we call "the scientific method" has been employed not only in developing transplants and other surgical procedures, but also in a multitude of other forms of medical treatment. In fact, virtually all advances in technology—for example, the designing of more and more efficient refrigerators, air conditioners, and automobiles—have depended on the use of the scientific method. Francis Bacon's writings in the early seventeenth century mark the beginning of the widespread use of the scientific method in the modern world. Before Bacon, there was only sporadic interest in establishing facts about the physical world; there was greater interest in the world of metaphysics, whose components could not even be seen, let alone measured.

Bacon thought of the printing press, the navigator's compass, and gunpowder as examples of the kinds of inventions the human mind was capable of contriving. However, with the notable exceptions of Copernicus and Galileo, thinkers of his own time had little interest in carrying out experiments that could yield greater mastery over nature. Bacon, in fact, thought that no significant progress had been made in "natural philosophy" since the ancient Greeks.

In *The Great Instauration* (1620), Bacon asserts that he has taken it upon himself to oppose the habits of mind of the past. He despised the thinkers of the Middle Ages known as the Schoolmen, whose endless disputations never bore fruit in verifiable knowledge. He also opposed the habits of mind of many of his Renaissance contemporaries who were infatuated with the writing and thinking of the recently rediscovered ancient Greeks. Unfortunately, it was the Greeks' eloquence that most impressed them, and, as a result, in their own writings they cultivated eloquence for its own sake. As Bacon put it, they "hunt after words more than matter." To his despair, Bacon concluded that what most philosophers sought in knowledge was "a couch whereon to rest a searching and restless spirit" instead of "a rich storehouse for the glory of the Creator and the relief of man's estate."

In the preface to *The Interpretation of Nature* (1603), Bacon wrote the following: "For myself I found that I was fitted for nothing so well as the study of truth, as having a mind nimble and versatile enough to catch the resemblances of things . . . and at the same time steady enough to fix and distinguish their subtler differences; as being gifted by nature with desire to seek, patience to doubt, fondness to meditate, slowness to assert, readiness to reconsider, carefulness to dispose and set in order; and as being a man that neither affects what is new nor admires what is old, and hates every kind of imposture. So I thought my mind had a kind of familiarity with truth." It was this cast of mind that made Bacon one of the founders of modern science. Although he himself never worked as a scientist, his writings provided much of the rationale and inspiration for those who did.

Bacon is the father of the essay in English. He knew of the essay writing in France of Montaigne, who was twenty-eight years his senior, but he was not influenced by Montaigne. Bacon's cast of mind was dramatically different. He was determined to contribute to the "relief of man's estate" by discovering the truth about beliefs, emotions, motivations, and manners. In his essays, as in his other writings, he bent his analytical power to that purpose, most often by examining closely the subtle differences among things that seemed alike. Thus, unlike Montaigne's essays, Bacon's are strictly pragmatic. So, too, is his stripped-down style. In the typical essay, Bacon focuses on a particular subject and the parts into which it can be divided. He remains objective and is reluctant to use as examples experiences from his most interesting life (during which he knew the disfavor of Queen Elizabeth, and enjoyed both the highest advancement and removal from office in disgrace by King James). With rare exceptions, Bacon excludes whatever is not directly relevant to his subject.

In Bacon's first collection, published in 1597, there were only ten essays. With a few changes, this collection was printed again in 1606. In 1612, an edition of forty essays was published, including nine of the original ten. In 1625, under the title *Essays or Counsels Civil and Moral,* the final collection of fifty-eight essays appeared. Bacon's other well-known works are *The Advancement of Learning* (1605) and *The New Organon* (1620).

OF ENVY

1625

There be none of the affections which have been noted to fascinate or   *1*
bewitch, but love and envy. They both have vehement wishes; they frame
themselves readily into imaginations and suggestions; and they come easily
into the eye, especially upon the presence of the objects; which are the points
that conduce to fascination, if any such thing there be. We see likewise the
scripture calleth envy an *evil eye;* and the astrologers call the evil influence of
the stars *evil aspects;* so that still there seemeth to be acknowledged, in the act
of envy, an ejaculation or irradiation of the eye. Nay some have been so
curious as to note, that the times when the stroke or percussion of an envious
eye doth most hurt, are when the party envied is beheld in glory or triumph;
for that sets an edge upon envy: and besides, at such times the spirits of the
person envied do come forth most into the outward parts, and so meet the
blow.

But leaving these curiosities, (though not unworthy to be thought on
in fit place,) we will handle, what persons are apt to envy others; what persons
are most subject to be envied themselves; and what is the difference between
public and private envy.

A man that hath no virtue in himself, ever envieth virtue in others. For
men's minds will either feed upon their own good or upon others' evil; and
who wanteth the one will prey upon the other; and whoso is out of hope to
attain to another's virtue, will seek to come at even hand by depressing
another's fortune.

A man that is busy and inquisitive is commonly envious. For to know
much of other men's matters cannot be because all that ado may concern his
own estate; therefore it must needs be that he taketh a kind of play-pleasure
in looking upon the fortunes of others. Neither can he that mindeth but his
own business find much matter for envy. For envy is a gadding passion, and
walketh the streets, and doth not keep home: *Non est curiosus, quin idem sit
malevolus.°*

Men of noble birth are noted to be envious towards new men when   *5*
they rise. For the distance is altered; and it is like a deceit of the eye, that when
others come on they think themselves go back.

Deformed persons, and eunuchs, and old men, and bastards, are
envious. For he that cannot possibly mend his own case will do what he can
to impair another's; except these defects light upon a very brave and heroical
nature, which thinketh to make his natural wants part of his honour; in that
it should be said, that an eunuch, or a lame man, did such great matters;

Non est . . . malevolus: There is no curious man but has some malevolence to quicken his
curiosity.

affecting the honour of a miracle; as it was in Narses the eunuch, and Agesilaus and Tamberlanes, that were lame men.

The same is the case of men that rise after calamities and misfortunes. For they are as men fallen out with the times; and think other men's harms a redemption of their own suffering.

They that desire to excel in too many matters, out of levity and vain glory, are ever envious. For they cannot want work; it being impossible but many in some one of those things should surpass them. Which was the character of Adrian the Emperor; that mortally envied poets and painters and artificers, in works wherein he had a vein to excel.

Lastly, near kinsfolks, and fellows in office, and those that have been bred together, are more apt to envy their equals when they are raised. For it doth upbraid unto them their own fortunes, and pointeth at them, and cometh oftener into their remembrance, and incurreth likewise more into the note of others; and envy ever redoubleth from speech and fame. Cain's envy was the more vile and malignant towards his brother Abel, because when his sacrifice was better accepted there was no body to look on. Thus much for those that are apt to envy.

Concerning those that are more or less subject to envy: First, persons of eminent virtue, when they are advanced, are less envied. For their fortune seemeth but due unto them: and no man envieth the payment of a debt, but rewards and liberality rather. Again, envy is ever joined with the comparing of a man's self; and where there is no comparison, no envy; and therefore kings are not envied but by kings. Nevertheless it is to be noted that unworthy persons are most envied at their first coming in, and afterwards overcome it better; whereas contrariwise, persons of worth and merit are most envied when their fortune continueth long. For by that time, though their virtue be the same, yet it hath not the same lustre; for fresh men grow up that darken it.

Persons of noble blood are less envied in their rising. For it seemeth but right done to their birth. Besides, there seemeth not much added to their fortune; and envy is as the sunbeams, that beat hotter upon a bank or steep rising ground, than upon a flat. And for the same reason those that are advanced by degrees are less envied than those that are advanced suddenly and *per saltum.*°

Those that have joined with their honour great travels, cares, or perils, are less subject to envy. For men think that they earn their honours hardly, and pity them sometimes; and pity ever healeth envy. Wherefore you shall observe that the more deep and sober sort of politic persons, in their greatness, are ever bemoaning themselves, what a life they lead; chanting a *quanta patimur.*° Not that they feel it so, but only to abate the edge of envy. But this is to be understood of business that is laid upon men, and not such

10

---

per saltum: By a leap.
quanta patimur: How we suffer!

as they call unto themselves. For nothing increaseth envy more than an unnecessary and ambitious engrossing of business. And nothing doth extinguish envy more than for a great person to preserve all other inferior officers in their full rights and pre-eminences of their places. For by that means there be so many screens between him and envy.

Above all, those are most subject to envy, which carry the greatness of their fortunes in an insolent and proud manner; being never well but while they are shewing how great they are, either by outward pomp, or by triumphing over all opposition or competition: whereas wise men will rather do sacrifice to envy, in suffering themselves sometimes of purpose to be crossed and overborne in things that do not much concern them. Notwithstanding so much is true, that the carriage of greatness in a plain and open manner (so it be without arrogancy and vain glory) doth draw less envy than if it be in a more crafty and cunning fashion. For in that course a man doth but disavow fortune; and seemeth to be conscious of his own want in worth; and doth but teach others to envy him.

Lastly, to conclude this part; as we said in the beginning that the act of envy had somewhat in it of witchcraft, so there is no other cure of envy but the cure of witchcraft; and that is, to remove the *lot*° (as they call it) and to lay it upon another. For which purpose, the wiser sort of great persons bring in ever upon the stage somebody upon whom to derive the envy that would come upon themselves; sometimes upon ministers and servants; sometimes upon colleagues and associates; and the like; and for that turn there are never wanting some persons of violent and undertaking natures, who, so they may have power and business, will take it at any cost.

Now, to speak of public envy. There is yet some good in public envy, whereas in private there is none. For public envy is as an ostracism, that eclipseth men when they grow too great. And therefore it is a bridle also to great ones, to keep them within bounds.

This envy, being in the Latin word *invidia*, goeth in the modern languages by the name of *discontentment;* of which we shall speak in handling Sedition. It is a disease in a state like to infection. For as infection spreadeth upon that which is sound, and tainteth it; so when envy is gotten once into a state, it traduceth even the best actions thereof, and turneth them into an ill odour. And therefore there is little won by intermingling of plausible actions. For that doth argue but a weakness and fear of envy, which hurteth so much the more; as it is likewise usual in infections; which if you fear them you call them upon you.

This public envy seemeth to beat chiefly upon principal officers or ministers, rather than upon kings and estates themselves. But this is a sure rule, that if the envy upon the minister be great, when the cause of it in him is small; or if the envy be general in a manner upon all the ministers of an estate; then the envy (though hidden) is truly upon the state itself. And so much of public

the lot: The spell.

envy or discontentment, and the difference thereof from private envy, which was handled in the first place.

We will add this in general, touching the affection of envy; that of all other affections it is the most importune and continual. For of other affections there is occasion given but now and then; and therefore it was well said, *Invidia festos dies non agit:*° for it is ever working upon some or other. And it is also noted that love and envy do make a man pine, which other affections do not, because they are not so continual. It is also the vilest affection, and the most depraved; for which cause it is the proper attribute of the devil, who is called *The envious man, that soweth tares amongst the wheat by night;* as it always cometh to pass, that envy worketh subtilly, and in the dark; and to the prejudice of good things, such as is the wheat.

Questions for Understanding

1. What do envy and love have in common?
2. When is envy likely to be most pronounced?
3. How does a person without virtue think about a person known for being virtuous?
4. What does Bacon mean when he says that "envy is a gadding passion, and walketh the streets, and doth not keep home"?
5. What is the best way for a talented and highly regarded person to avoid being the object of envy?

Suggestions for Writing

1. Consider two people you know who seem to have been equally successful in life. Which one arouses more envy in you? Write an essay in which you describe both people and discuss the reasons for the different degrees of envy you feel.
2. Consider two popular entertainers or two stars in the same sport. Which of the two arouses more envy in you? Write an essay in which you describe both people and discuss the reasons for the different degrees of envy you feel.
3. Consider your parents or two other close relatives. Write an essay in which you compare and contrast the roles that envy plays in their lives. Of whom is each most envious? What are the causes of their envy? Does their envy cause them to behave badly?
4. Bacon says envy is "the vilest emotion and the most depraved." Do you agree? If so, write an essay in which you thoroughly explain why it is vile and degrading to envy.
5. Is envy necessarily vile and degrading? Can any benefits accrue to the individual and to society as a result of a person's feelings of envy? If you think so, write an essay in which you thoroughly explain those benefits.

Invidia . . . non agit: Envy keeps no holidays.

NUTS AND BOLTS 11: ANALYZING

In 430 B.C., the Athenian statesman Pericles gave a speech in which he analyzed the way of life of his city. The purpose of his speech, the famous funeral oration reported by Thucydides, was to convince his listeners that democracy was worth defending against Athens's militaristic enemy, Sparta. Among other things, Pericles said on this occasion that "the great impediment to action is not discussion but the want of that knowledge which is gained by discussion preparatory to action." Pericles believed that discussion leads to knowledge and that knowledge points to courses of action. Discussion often takes the form of analysis, and analysis produces new knowledge.

Usually, when we analyze we are trying to understand something better, whether it be ourselves, our enemies, an idea like democracy, a plan, the possible effects of implementing the plan, the emotions or conditions that led to the formulation of the plan—whatever. In the strictest sense, to analyze is to divide something into its component parts. When we analyze, we take apart. We do that to identify the parts and to discover the relationships among them. Pericles analyzed the uniqueness of Athenian life. The President of the United States gives state-of-the-union addresses in which he analyzes the condition of the country. After the touchdown, the TV analyst "dissects" the play to show what key players did to make it work. The coach constructed the play and taught his players how to coordinate their roles, but the analyst takes the play apart so that viewers can understand what happened. An automobile mechanic stands before a class and holds up some disassembled parts—a carburetor, a spark plug, a piston; he explains how, together, they make an engine run. In an essay, a literary critic analyzes a poem, pointing out how each stanza contributes to making the poem interesting and enjoyable.

Like Pericles, Francis Bacon believed in the value of knowledge, the dissemination of which could benefit all humanity. To Bacon, the people of his own time believed much that was in error ("false knowledge") because too much of the discourse among the learned consisted of mere speculation instead of productive analysis. When analysis *was* used, it dealt only with things that existed in the imagination, not with observable phenomena. Bacon had no use for discussion that produced little more than pedantic restatements of the ideas of past thinkers. He preferred statements made on the basis of accurate observation, which alone could lead to the formulation of verifiable laws of nature.

Essays or Counsels Civil and Moral (1625) is the fourth and fullest collection of Bacon's essays. The essays treat fifty-eight subjects, which, Bacon believed, worldly people (those interested in improving themselves and their societies) should know about. Indeed, almost any of Bacon's subjects would be a good choice for an essay writer today because the subjects continue to be relevant to individual lives and important for society. A writing instructor need look no further than Bacon's fifty-eight essays for a very good list of subjects for students to write on.

Typically, Bacon divides the general subject into parts and tells what his observations have led him to conclude about each part. Look, for example, at how he proceeds in "Of Envy." In the first paragraph, he establishes the importance of the subject. In the second paragraph, he explains how he divides the subject: He will talk about those who are likely to envy, those who are likely to be envied, and the difference between public and private envy. His final paragraph is a summary statement on the subject of envy. In this essay, the division is pure and simple. If there is such an emotion as envy, then there must be those who envy and those who are envied; the enviers may either keep the feeling to themselves, which is private envy, or let others know what they feel, which is making their envy public.

An outline of the essay might look like this:

Thesis: Envy is a fascinating emotion.

I.   Certain kinds of persons are most likely to envy.

    A.   A person without virtue is likely to envy virtuous people.

    B.   A person who is curious about the affairs of others is likely to be envious.

    C.   A person of noble birth is likely to envy people on the rise.

    D.   People with disabilities are likely to envy those without disabilities.

    E.   People who have suffered misfortunes are likely to envy those who have not and wish them harm.

    F.   People who are involved in many activities are likely to envy those who surpass them in any one activity.

    G.   People who know many others on their own social level are likely to envy those among them who advance.

II. Certain kinds of people are more or less likely to be envied.

    A.   People of eminent virtue are less envied when they are advanced, because their advance seems their due.

    B.   People of noble blood are less envied when they rise, because their rise seems their due.

    C.   Adventurous people are less envied, because their rise seems earned.

    D.   People of affairs who complain about how much is asked of them are likely to arouse envy.

    E.   People who have been very fortunate but who are insolent and proud are most likely to be envied.

III. Public envy is preferable to private envy.

    A.   Public envy is an indicator of discontent, which can act as a bridle upon great men.

    B.   Envy that is kept private produces nothing good.

Summary: Envy is the most persistent and vile of emotions.

What Bacon does here is to break down envy into components that he knows something about and that he thinks are interesting. Almost every human has envied, and as a high-ranking official, Bacon undoubtedly observed envious as well as envied persons—and experienced both roles himself. There is no one "right" way to divide a subject. Bacon calls envy "the vilest affection and the most depraved," whereas another writer might think of envy as both beneficial and harmful—possibly more beneficial than harmful. Still another writer might choose to analyze envy in terms of its causes and effects.

In the essay "Of Friendship," Bacon's division is again quite simple. He discusses four benefits of friendship: It allows "the ease and discharge of the fulness and swellings of the heart," it is healthful for the understanding, it is a source of good counsel, and it provides someone who is able to take one's place in various matters. Whereas Bacon chose not to address any other aspect of friendship, another writer might discuss the hurts a friend can cause, the beginnings and endings of friendships, or the degrees of friendship.

Anything we know or have experienced may be a suitable subject for analysis, but the analysis will not engage readers unless what the analyst says is both believable and interesting. The analysis won't be believable if it lacks balance or seems illogical. If the writer offers parts of the whole that are not clearly separate and distinct, and if the parts are not approximately equal in importance, then the analysis will seem illogical—and readers will be unlikely to accept it. For example, there would be nothing wrong with analyzing a typical major-league baseball team. The writer might logically choose to break down a team into the starters and the backups, but it would be illogical for the writer to devote most of the analysis to the role of a backup—say, a utility infielder. That would cost the writer credibility, because readers familiar with baseball would know that, however interesting a utility infielder might be, he is not a major player on a baseball team.

A good analysis is interesting. It provides insight. It makes readers aware of a truth or truths they were not aware of before. On the other hand, mechanically subdividing a subject and describing the parts in a way that adds no new insight is a pointless exercise, offering readers little or no return on the investment of their time.

In the essays presented here, which aspects of Bacon's subjects are fresh and insightful, and which are self-evident and uninteresting?

OF FRIENDSHIP

1612

It had been hard for him that spake it° to have put more truth and   *1*
untruth together in few words, than in that speech, *Whosoever is delighted in
solitude is either a wild beast or a god.* For it is most true that a natural and secret
hatred and aversation towards society in any man, hath somewhat of the
savage beast; but it is most untrue that it should have any character at all of the
divine nature; except it proceed, not out of a pleasure in solitude, but out of
a love and desire to sequester a man's self for a higher conversation: such as
is found to have been falsely and feignedly in some of the heathen; as
Epimenides the Candian,° Numa the Roman,° Empedocles the Sicilian,°
and Apollonius of Tyana,° and truly and really in divers of the ancient
hermits and holy fathers of the church. But little do men perceive what
solitude is, and how far it extendeth. For a crowd is not company; and faces
are but a gallery of pictures; and talk but a tinkling cymbal, where there is no
love. The Latin adage meeteth with it a little: *Magna civitas, magna solitudo;*°
because in a great town friends are scattered; so that there is not that
fellowship, for the most part, which is in less neighbourhoods. But we may
go further, and affirm most truly that it is a mere and miserable solitude to
want true friends; without which the world is but a wilderness; and even in
this sense also of solitude, whosoever in the frame of his nature and affections
is unfit for friendship, he taketh it of the beast, and not from humanity.

A principal fruit of friendship is the ease and discharge of the fulness and
swellings of the heart, which passions of all kinds do cause and induce. We
know diseases of stoppings and suffocations are the most dangerous in the
body; and it is not much otherwise in the mind; you may take sarza to open
the liver, steel to open the spleen, flower of sulphur for the lungs, castoreum
for the brain; but no receipt openeth the heart, but a true friend; to whom
you may impart griefs, joys, fears, hopes, suspicions, counsels, and whatsoever lieth upon the heart to oppress it, in a kind of civil shrift or confession.

It is a strange thing to observe how high a rate great kings and monarchs
do set upon this fruit of friendship whereof we speak: so great, as they
purchase it many times at the hazard of their own safety and greatness. For

---

him that spake it: Aristotle, *Politics,* 1.1.

Epimenides the Candian: A philosopher-poet of Crete who is said to have slept fifty-seven years
in a cave.

Numa the Roman: The legendary king of Rome who retired to a cave from time to time to
receive counsel from a nymph.

Empedocles the Sicilian: A philosopher who is said to have thrown himself into the crater of
Sicily's volcanic Mt. Etna.

Apollonius of Tyana: A philosopher of the first century A.D. to whom were ascribed many
wonders.

Magna civitas, magna solitudo: A great town is a great solitude.

princes, in regard of the distance of their fortune from that of their subjects and servants, cannot gather this fruit, except (to make themselves capable thereof) they raise some persons to be as it were companions and almost equals to themselves, which many times sorteth to inconvenience. The modern languages give unto such persons the name of favourites, or privadoes; as if it were matter of grace, or conversation. But the Roman name attaineth the true use and cause thereof, naming them *participes curarum;*° for it is that which tieth the knot. And we see plainly that this hath been done, not by weak and passionate princes only, but by the wisest and most politic that ever reigned; who have oftentimes joined to themselves some of their servants; whom both themselves have called friends, and allowed others likewise to call them in the same manner; using the word which is received between private men.

L. Sylla, when he commanded Rome, raised Pompey (after surnamed the Great) to that height, that Pompey vaunted himself for Sylla's over-match. For when he had carried the consulship for a friend of his, against the pursuit of Sylla, and that Sylla did a little resent thereat, and began to speak great, Pompey turned upon him again, and in effect bade him be quiet; *for that more men adored the sun rising than the sun setting.* With Julius Cæsar, Decimus Brutus had obtained that interest, as he set him down in his testament for heir in remainder after his nephew. And this was the man that had power with him to draw him forth to his death. For when Cæsar would have discharged the senate, in regard of some ill presages, and specially a dream of Calpurnia; this man lifted him gently by the arm out of his chair, telling him he hoped he would not dismiss the senate till his wife had dreamt a better dream. And it seemeth his favour was so great, as Antonius, in a letter which is recited *verbatim* in one of Cicero's Philippics, calleth him *venefica, witch;* as if he had enchanted Cæsar. Augustus raised Agrippa (though of mean birth) to that height, as when he consulted with Mæcenas about the marriage of his daughter Julia, Mæcenas took the liberty to tell him, *that he must either marry his daughter to Agrippa, or take away his life: there was no third way, he had made him so great.* With Tiberius Cæsar, Sejanus had ascended to that height, as they two were termed and reckoned as a pair of friends. Tiberius in a letter to him saith, *hæc pro amicitiâ nostrâ non occultavi;*° and the whole senate dedicated an altar to Friendship, as to a goddess, in respect of the great dearness of friendship between them two. The like or more was between Septimius Severus and Plautianus. For he forced his eldest son to marry the daughter of Plautianus; and would often maintain Plautianus in doing affronts to his son; and did write also in a letter to the senate, by these words: *I love the man so well, as I wish he may over-live me.* Now if these princes had been as a Trajan or a Marcus Aurelius, a man might have thought that this had proceeded of an abundant goodness of nature; but being men so wise, of such strength and

---

participes curarum: Sharers of cares.

hæc . . . occultavi: These things, as our friendship required, I have not concealed from you.

severity of mind, and so extreme lovers of themselves, as all these were, it proveth most plainly that they found their own felicity (though as great as ever happened to mortal men) but as an half piece, except they mought have a friend to make it entire; and yet, which is more, they were princes that had wives, sons, nephews; and yet all these could not supply the comfort of friendship.

It is not to be forgotten what Comineus° observeth of his first master, 5 Duke Charles the Hardy; namely, that he would communicate his secrets with none; and least of all, those secrets which troubled him most. Whereupon he goeth on and saith that towards his latter time *that closeness did impair and a little perish his understanding.* Surely Comineus mought have made the same judgment also, if it had pleased him, of his second master Lewis the Eleventh, whose closeness was indeed his tormentor. The parable of Pythagoras is dark, but true; *Cor ne edito; Eat not the heart.* Certainly, if a man would give it a hard phrase, those that want friends to open themselves unto are cannibals of their own hearts. But one thing is most admirable (wherewith I will conclude this first fruit of friendship), which is, that this communicating of a man's self to his friend works two contrary effects; for it redoubleth joys, and cutteth griefs in halfs. For there is no man that imparteth his joys to his friend, but he joyeth the more: and no man that imparteth his griefs to his friend, but he grieveth the less. So that it is in truth of operation upon a man's mind, of like virtue as the alchymists use to attribute to their stone for man's body; that it worketh all contrary effects, but still to the good and benefit of nature. But yet without praying in aid of alchymists, there is a manifest image of this in the ordinary course of nature. For in bodies, union strengtheneth and cherisheth any natural action; and on the other side weakeneth and dulleth any violent impression: and even so it is of minds.

The second fruit of friendship is healthful and sovereign for the understanding, as the first is for the affections. For friendship maketh indeed a fair day in the affections, from storm and tempests; but it maketh daylight in the understanding, out of darkness and confusion of thoughts. Neither is this to be understood only of faithful counsel, which a man receiveth from his friend; but before you come to that, certain it is that whosoever hath his mind fraught with many thoughts, his wits and understanding do clarify and break up, in the communicating and discoursing with another; he tosseth his thoughts more easily; he marshalleth them more orderly; he seeth how they look when they are turned into words: finally, he waxeth wiser than himself; and that more by an hour's discourse than by a day's meditation. It was well said by Themistocles° to the king of Persia, *That speech was like cloth of Arras, opened and put abroad; whereby the imagery doth appear in figure; whereas in thoughts they lie but as in packs.* Neither is this second fruit of friendship, in opening the understanding, restrained only to such friends as are able to give a man

---

Comineus: Phillipe de Comines (c.1447–c.1511), a French courtier, diplomat, and historian.
Themistocles: Athenian statesman and naval commander, (c.525–c.460 B.C.).

counsel; (they indeed are best;) but even without that, a man learneth of himself, and bringeth his own thoughts to light, and whetteth his wits as against a stone, which itself cuts not. In a word, a man were better relate himself to a statua or picture, than to suffer his thoughts to pass in smother.

Add now, to make this second fruit of friendship complete, that other point which lieth more open and falleth within vulgar observation; which is faithful counsel from a friend. Heraclitus° saith well in one of his enigmas, *Dry light is ever the best*. And certain it is, that the light that a man receiveth by counsel from another, is drier and purer than that which cometh from his own understanding and judgment; which is ever infused and drenched in his affections and customs. So as there is as much difference between the counsel that a friend giveth, and that a man giveth himself, as there is between the counsel of a friend and of a flatterer. For there is no such flatterer as is a man's self; and there is no such remedy against flattery of a man's self, as the liberty of a friend. Counsel is of two sorts; the one concerning manners, the other concerning business. For the first, the best preservative to keep the mind in health is the faithful admonition of a friend. The calling of a man's self to a strict account is a medicine, sometime, too piercing and corrosive. Reading good books of morality is a little flat and dead. Observing our faults in others is sometimes improper for our case. But the best receipt (best, I say, to work, and best to take) is the admonition of a friend. It is a strange thing to behold what gross errors and extreme absurdities many (especially of the greater sort) do commit, for want of a friend to tell them of them; to the great damage both of their fame and fortune: for, as St. James saith, they are as men *that look sometimes into a glass, and presently forget their own shape and favour.* As for business, a man may think, if he will, that two eyes see no more than one; or that a gamester seeth always more than a looker-on; or that a man in anger is as wise as he that hath said over the four and twenty letters; or that a musket may be shot off as well upon the arm as upon a rest; and such other fond and high imaginations, to think himself all in all. But when all is done, the help of good counsel is that which setteth business straight. And if any man think that he will take counsel, but it shall be by pieces; asking counsel in one business of one man, and in another business of another man; it is well, (that is to say, better perhaps than if he asked none at all;) but he runneth two dangers; one, that he shall not be faithfully counselled; for it is a rare thing, except it be from a perfect and entire friend, to have counsel given, but such as shall be bowed and crooked to some ends which he hath that giveth it. The other, that he shall have counsel given, hurtful and unsafe, (though with good meaning,) and mixed partly of mischief and partly of remedy; even as if you would call a physician that is thought good for the cure of the disease you complain of, but is unacquainted with your body; and therefore may put you in way for a present cure, but overthroweth your health in some other kind; and so cure the disease and kill the patient. But a friend that

---

Heraclitus: A philosopher of Epheseus, (c.525–c.475 B.C.).

is wholly acquainted with a man's estate will beware, by furthering any present business, how he dasheth upon other inconvenience. And therefore rest not upon scattered counsels; they will rather distract and mislead, than settle and direct.

After these two noble fruits of friendship, (peace in the affections, and support of the judgment,) followeth the last fruit; which is like the pomegranate, full of many kernels; I mean aid and bearing a part in all actions and occasions. Here the best way to represent to life the manifold use of friendship, is to cast and see how many things there are which a man cannot do himself; and then it will appear that it was a sparing speech of the ancients, to say, *that a friend is another himself;* for that a friend is far more than himself. Men have their time, and die many times in desire of some things which they principally take to heart; the bestowing of a child, the finishing of a work, or the like. If a man have a true friend, he may rest almost secure that the care of those things will continue after him. So that a man hath, as it were, two lives in his desires. A man hath a body, and that body is confined to a place; but where friendship is, all offices of life are as it were granted to him and his deputy. For he may exercise them by his friend. How many things are there which a man cannot, with any face or comeliness, say or do himself? A man can scarce allege his own merits with modesty, much less extol them; a man cannot sometimes brook to supplicate or beg; and a number of the like. But all these things are graceful in a friend's mouth, which are blushing in a man's own. So again, a man's person hath many proper relations which he cannot put off. A man cannot speak to his son but as a father; to his wife but as a husband; to his enemy but upon terms: whereas a friend may speak as the case requires, and not as it sorteth with the person. But to enumerate these things were endless; I have given the rule, where a man cannot fitly play his own part; if he have not a friend, he may quit the stage.

Questions for Understanding

1. What, to Bacon, is the great benefit of friendship to the affections?
2. In paragraph 4, what is the point Bacon makes by citing the examples of Sylla, Julius Caesar, Augustus, Tiberius Caesar, and Septimius Severus?
3. What does Bacon assert is the great benefit to the mind of an hour's discourse with a friend?
4. Why is Bacon opposed to "asking counsel in one business of one man, and in another business of another man"?
5. What is the benefit of friendship that is like the pomegranate—"full of many kernels"?

Suggestions for Writing

1. Friendship, Bacon says, doubles joy and halves grief. Write an essay in which you describe and discuss a friendship that bears out the basic truth of Bacon's assertion.

2. Bacon says that having a friend provides you with opportunities to discourse freely and that, in so doing, you gain a better understanding of things: "it maketh daylight in the understanding, out of darkness and confusion of thoughts." Write an essay in which you discuss two occasions when a friend helped you understand a problem better than you could by yourself.

3. Bacon says, "There is no such flatterer as a man's self." Write an essay in which you discuss two instances in which you flattered your understanding and as a result brought harm upon yourself.

4. Focus on one of your parents' friendships. Write an essay in which you discuss the extent to which that friendship illustrates Bacon's assertion that "a friend is another in himself."

5. Write an essay in which you discuss the obstacles to friendships that bear the kind of fruit Bacon values.

OF LOVE

1612

The stage is more beholding to Love, than the life of man. For as to the   *1*
stage, love is ever matter of comedies, and now and then of tragedies; but in
life it doth much mischief; sometimes like a syren, sometimes like a fury. You
may observe, that amongst all the great and worthy persons (whereof the
memory remaineth, either ancient or recent,) there is not one that hath been
transported to the mad degree of love: which shews that great spirits and great
business do keep out this weak passion. You must except nevertheless Marcus
Antonius, the half partner of the empire of Rome, and Appius Claudius, the
decemvir and lawgiver; whereof the former was indeed a voluptuous man,
and inordinate; but the latter was an austere and wise man: and therefore it
seems (though rarely) that love can find entrance not only into an open heart,
but also into a heart well fortified, if watch be not well kept. It is a poor saying
of Epicurus,° *Satis magnum alter alteri theatrum sumus:*° as if man, made for the
contemplation of heaven and all noble objects, should do nothing but kneel
before a little idol, and make himself a subject, though not of the mouth (as
beasts are), yet of the eye; which was given him for higher purposes. It is a
strange thing to note the excess of this passion, and how it braves the nature
and value of things, by this; that the speaking in a perpetual hyperbole is
comely in nothing but in love. Neither is it merely in the phrase; for whereas
it hath been well said that the arch-flatterer, with whom all the petty flatterers
have intelligence, is a man's self; certainly the lover is more. For there was
never proud man thought so absurdly well of himself as the lover doth of the
person loved; and therefore it was well said, *That it is impossible to love and to
be wise.* Neither doth this weakness appear to others only, and not to the party
loved; but to the loved most of all, except the love be reciproque. For it is a
true rule, that love is ever rewarded either with the reciproque or with an
inward and secret contempt. By how much the more men ought to beware
of this passion, which loseth not only other things, but itself. As for the other
losses, the poet's relation doth well figure them; That he that preferred
Helena, quitted the gifts of Juno and Pallas.° For whosoever esteemeth too
much of amorous affection quitteth both riches and wisdom. This passion
hath his floods in the very times of weakness; which are great prosperity and
great adversity; though this latter hath been less observed: both which times
kindle love, and make it more fervent, and therefore shew it to be the child
of folly. They do best, who if they cannot admit love, yet make it keep quarter;
and sever it wholly from their serious affairs and actions of life; for if it check

---

Epicurus: An Athenian philosopher, (c.342–270 B.C.).

satis . . . sumus: Each of us is to the other a sufficiently large theater.

he that preferred . . . Pallas: Paris, the Trojan prince, preferred Helen and her beauty to Juno and
her power and to Pallas Athene and her wisdom.

once with business, it troubleth men's fortunes, and maketh men that they can no ways be true to their own ends. I know not how, but martial men are given to love: I think it is but as they are given to wine; for perils commonly ask to be paid in pleasures. There is in man's nature a secret inclination and motion towards love of others, which if it be not spent upon some one or a few, doth naturally spread itself towards many, and maketh men become humane and charitable; as it is seen sometime in friars. Nuptial love maketh mankind; friendly love perfecteth it; but wanton love corrupteth and embaseth it.

Questions for Understanding

1. What is Bacon referring to when he says that love "doth much mischief; sometimes like a syren, sometimes like a fury"?
2. Which organ of the body brings on the mischief of love to men?
3. What does Bacon mean when he says that one of the characteristics of love is "speaking in a perpetual hyperbole"?
4. Why does Bacon believe it is impossible to love and to be wise?
5. Why, according to Bacon, are military men particularly given to love?

Suggestions for Writing

1. Bacon says that one is most vulnerable to love in times of great prosperity or great adversity. Do you agree? If so, write an essay in which you analyze what it is about each condition that makes one vulnerable to love at such times.
2. Do you agree with Bacon that love is a "weak passion" and "the child of folly"? If so, write an essay in which you demonstrate why love is folly and the product of weakness.
3. Is love ever the product of wisdom and strength, contrary to Bacon's opinion? Write an essay in which you show the ways in which falling in love can signify wisdom and strength.
4. Bacon warns that love should be severed wholly from men's "serious affairs and actions of life." In the early months of his presidency, Bill Clinton gave his wife, Hillary Rodham Clinton, a major role in formulating his administration's proposals for health-care reform. Write an essay in which you discuss whether President Clinton acted wisely or foolishly in giving such a responsibility to his wife.
5. Bacon clearly believes that it is not possible to be in love and exercise good judgment. To Bacon, love "braves the nature and value of things"—in other words, it leads the mind to distort, to make things other than what they really are. Do you agree? If so, write an essay in which you discuss the distortions that took place in your mind during a period when you were in love.

OF STUDIES

1597°

Studies serve for delight, for ornament, and for ability.° Their chief use   *1*
for delight, is in privateness and retiring;° for ornament, is in discourse; and
for ability, is in the judgement and disposition of business. For expert men°
can execute, and perhaps judge of particulars, one by one; but the general
counsels, and the plots and marshalling of affairs come best from those that
are learned. To spend too much time in studies is sloth; to use them too much
for ornament is affectation; to make judgement wholly by their rules is the
humour of a scholar. They perfect nature, and are perfected by experience,
for natural abilities are like natural plants that need proyning° by study; and
studies themselves do give forth directions too much at large, except they be
bounded in by experience. Crafty° men condemn studies, simple men
admire them, and wise men use them; for they teach not their own use; but
that is a wisdom without them and above them, won by observation. Read
not to contradict and confute; nor to believe and take for granted; nor to find
talk and discourse; but to weigh and consider. Some books are to be tasted,
others to be swallowed, and some few to be chewed and digested: that is,
some books are to be read only in parts; others to be read, but not curiously;°
and some few to be read wholly and with diligence and attention. Some
books also may be read by deputy, and extracts made of them by others, but
that would be only in the less important arguments, and the meaner° sort of
books; else distilled books are like common distilled waters, flashy° things.
Reading maketh a full man; conference a ready man; and writing an exact
man. And therefore, if a man write little, he had need have a great memory;
if he confer little, he had need have a present wit;° and if he read little, he had
need have much cunning, to seem to know that he doth not. Histories make
men wise, poets witty, the mathematics subtle, natural philosophy deep,
moral grave, logic and rhetoric able to contend. *Abeunt studia in mores.*° Nay,

---

1597: The first version of this essay was printed in 1597. The version here is about twice as
long and was published in the 1625 *Essays.*

ability: Providing knowledge needed for intelligent decision-making.

retiring: Being by oneself.

expert men: Men who are good at what they do because of their experience rather than their
learning.

proying: Pruning; shaping to improve.

Crafty: Those who are interested only in achieving their ends without regard for means.

curiously: With much intensity.

meaner: More common.

flashy: Without taste or spirit.

a present wit: A sharp mind.

Abeunt studia in mores: Studies go to make up a man's character (Ovid, *Heroides,* 15.83).

there is no stond° or impediment in the wit but may be wrought out by fit studies, like as diseases of the body may have appropriate exercises. Bowling is good for the stone and reins;° shooting° for the lungs and breast; gentle walking for the stomach; riding for the head; and the like. So if a man's wit be wandering, let him study the mathematics; for in demonstrations, if his wit be called away never so little, he must begin again. If his wit be not apt to distinguish or find differences, let him study the Schoolmen,° for they are *cymini sectores.*° If he be not apt to beat over matters,° and to call up one thing to prove and illustrate another, let him study the lawyers' cases. So every defect of the mind may have a special receipt.°

Questions for Understanding

1. According to Bacon, what is the difference in ability between "expert men" and learned men?
2. How might studies be used for "ornament"?
3. What does Bacon mean when he says that the proper use of reading is "to weigh and consider"?
4. What are the different abilities that reading, conferring, and writing give a person?
5. Why does Bacon recommend that those who have a problem making distinctions study the Schoolmen?

Suggestions for Writing

1. "Studies serve for delight, for ornament, and for ability." Consider what you are gaining from your studies. Are you gaining in delight, ornament, and ability? If not those, what? Write an essay in which you discuss, at approximately equal length, three benefits you are gaining from your education.
2. "Reading maketh a full man; conference a ready man; and writing an exact man." Assess your education thus far, and consider the extent to which you have become knowledgeable from reading, quick-witted from training in speaking, and exact from your writing. Write an essay in which you describe your present curriculum and discuss the changes you would make in it so that you might become full, ready, and exact.

---

stond: Obstacle.

Bowling is good . . . reins: Bowling helps prevent the growth of stones in the gallbladder and kidneys.

shooting: Archery.

the Schoolmen: Medieval theologians who wrote philosophy.

cymini sectores: Hair-splitters.

beat over matters: To study thoroughly.

receipt: Its particular method of improvement.

3. "There is no stond or impediment in the wit but may be wrought out by fit studies. . . ." Have you been aware of a gap in your knowledge or some limitation in your mental ability that has led you to make a special effort to overcome the handicap? If so, describe what you considered a handicap, and discuss what you did to try to overcome it.

4. Bacon believes that the study of mathematics can have a real benefit for certain people: "If a man's wit be wandering, let him study the mathematics; for in demonstrations, if his wit be called away never so little, he must begin again." Consider your own experience with math. To what extent has the study of mathematics helped you to concentrate? What other benefits did you gain from math? Did the study of mathematics have any negative effects on you? Write an essay in which you describe and discuss the role math has played in your life.

5. In "Of Studies," Bacon conceives of study as involving three basic activities: reading, speaking, and writing. He does not think of education as involving any career-oriented training. Do you believe that career-oriented courses should be part of an undergraduate college curriculum? Write an essay in which you describe and discuss your ideas of the optimal balance between the kind of education Bacon speaks of and career-oriented training.

Michel de Montaigne

[1533–1592]

Montaigne had the good fortune to be able to do what a lot of people would like to do: He retired at an early age and devoted himself to his favorite pastimes. At thirty-five he inherited his father's substantial estate; three years later he gave up worldly affairs for a life of reflection and writing. Although events in the outside world did not allow him to live in nearly as uninvolved a manner as he would have liked, whenever an emergency or a stint of public duty was over, he returned to his estate, near the city of Bordeaux in southwestern France, and resumed his retired life.

By the age of thirty-eight, Montaigne had learned a great deal about the world through both firsthand experience and a remarkable education. At his father's insistence, he heard and spoke only Latin until he was six years old; his native tongue was his second language. This early proficiency in Latin enabled Montaigne to read the great writers of ancient Rome, especially Ovid, Virgil, Horace, and Seneca. Through them he was able to enjoy a vicarious participation in the life and culture of Rome and to a lesser extent the life and culture of the Greeks, upon which so much of Roman culture was based. Throughout his life, Montaigne found wisdom and compelling examples of life's vicissitudes in the writings of the ancients.

Montaigne went away to school at the age of seven. At thirteen he undertook the study of law. At twenty-one he began a thirteen-year career as an official in the courts of Bordeaux. He did not particularly care for his legal work, and he made numerous trips to Paris and to the king's court in hopes of being offered a position that he could enjoy more. The best experience that came out of these years in Bordeaux was the "perfect friendship" with his fellow lawyer Etienne de La Boétie. Also in Bordeaux, Montaigne met the daughter of another colleague, and the two were married in 1565. She gave birth to six children, but only one lived beyond infancy. As the essay "Of Friendship" clearly reveals, Montaigne valued the five-year friendship with Boétie much more than his relationship with his wife.

In 1571, on his thirty-eighth birthday, Montaigne returned home and put an inscription on the wall of a little study next to his library. The inscription stated that he had "long grown weary of the servitude of the court and of public employments" and that he intended to spend his remaining years at his ancestral retreat, which he had consecrated to his freedom, tranquility, and leisure. He did not pass his remaining years exactly that way, however. He was forced to travel to seek a cure for the kidney stones from which he suffered greatly and which had killed his father; he and his family left the estate for a while to escape the plague; and in various ways he was drawn into the civil warfare between the dominant Catholics and the Protestants seeking toleration. He also served for four years as mayor of Bordeaux, a position he had not sought but to which he was elected anyway.

On March 1, 1580, Montaigne wrote a brief preface to the two books of his essays that were about to be printed. In this preface he speaks of his "domestic and private" objective. He has written the essays, he says, for "the private convenience of my relatives and friends, so that when they have lost me (as soon they must), they may recover here some features of my habits and temperament, and by this means keep the knowledge they have had of me more complete and alive." Although it is true that the essays reveal a great deal about Michel de Montaigne, their scope is not so limited. Reflecting the breadth of his speculations and his wide range of experiences, the essays offer many insights into the human condition in general.

Montaigne took little on faith. "I am free to give myself up to doubt and uncertainty," he says in one essay—and he did. In studying the way his own mind worked, he was discovering how most minds work. He found, for example, that some of the mind's functions are of "a lowly order." He found that the mind can give its full attention to only one thing at a time—and that it sees this one thing "not according to the nature of the thing but in accordance with itself"; each human mind shapes things according to its own peculiar conceptions. Still, generally agreed-upon values must be recognized by everyone: "Our good and our evil depend only on ourselves." Fortune, he insisted, has no power over our moral nature.

In thinking about his own and others' minds without reverting to dogma or conventional wisdom, Montaigne made trials, attempts, ventures of discovery. He made *essais*—essays—and in doing so, he invented the form. Since Montaigne, the essay as a literary genre has undergone many variations, including Bacon's only a generation later. But Montaigne is generally accepted as the father of the form, and he has had a great influence on many later essayists. Emerson, Hazlitt, and E. B. White have explicitly acknowledged Montaigne's influence.

It is characteristic of Montaigne the essayist that his "trials" never really ended. He kept revising. Even after an essay was published, he changed phrasing and wrote additions in the margins, sometimes contradicting what he had written earlier. Unless readers are aware that Montaigne hardly ever finished examining a subject, reading the essays can be quite puzzling.

In *The Complete Essays of Montaigne* (Stanford University Press, 1958), Donald M. Frame, the translator and editor, uses superscript letters to keep the reader informed of the different strata within each of the essays. Though these letters can be distracting, it is extremely instructive to see Montaigne's creative process at work. Anyone who wishes to read more of Montaigne should know that Frame's translations of Montaigne's French are more formal than, and not as lively as, those of J. M. Cohen in his edition of selected essays, published in paperback by Penguin Books.

OF LIARS

1580°

^AThere is no man who has less business talking about memory.° For I
recognize almost no trace of it in me, and I do not think there is another one
in the world so monstrously deficient. All my other faculties are low and
common; but in this one I think I am singular and very rare, and thereby
worthy of gaining a name and reputation.

^BBesides the natural inconvenience that I suffer by this—^Cfor certainly,
in view of its necessity, Plato is right to call memory a great and powerful
goddess—^Bif in my part of the country they want to say that a man has no
sense, they say he has no memory. And when I complain of the defectiveness
of mine, they argue with me and do not believe me, as if I were accusing
myself of witlessness. They see no distinction between memory and
understanding. This makes me look a lot worse than I am.

But they do me wrong. For rather the opposite is seen by experience:
that excellent memories are prone to be joined to feeble judgments. They do
me wrong also in this, I who know how to do nothing so well as be a friend:
that by the very words they use to denounce my malady they also make me
look ungrateful. They blame my feelings for my want of memory, and of a
natural lack they make a lack of conscience. "He has forgotten," they say, "this
request or that promise. He does not remember his friends. He did not
remember to say, or do, or be silent about such and such a thing, for my sake."
Certainly I may easily forget; but careless about the charge with which my
friend has entrusted me, that I am not. Let them be content with my infirmity,
without making it into a sort of malice, and a malice so alien to my nature.

I have some consolation. First, because ^Cit is an evil that has shown me
the way to correct a worse evil which would easily have developed in me—to
wit, ambition; for lack of memory is intolerable in anyone who is involved
in public negotiations. Because, as several similar examples of nature's
processes demonstrate, nature has tended to strengthen other faculties in me
in proportion as my memory has grown weaker; and I might easily rest my
mind and judgment and let them grow languid following on others' traces,
as everyone does, without exercising their own strength, if other men's
discoveries and opinions were always present to me by virtue of my memory.
^BMy speech is the briefer for it. For the magazine of memory is apt to be
better furnished with matter than that of invention. ^C(If my memory had
stood me in good stead, I would have deafened all my friends with babble; for

---

1580: The year the essay was first published.

^A*There . . . memory:* The use of the superscript letters A, B, and C follows the method
employed by Professor Donald M. Frame in his edition of *The Complete Essays,* Stanford
University Press, 1958. A designates material published before Montaigne's edition of 1588;
B designates material published in 1588; C designates material published after 1588. All
translations into English are Professor Frame's.

topics arouse the faculty, such as it is, that I have of handling and treating them, warming up my arguments and leading them on.) ^BThis is a pity.° I see it confirmed by the example of some of my close friends: to the extent that memory supplies them with the thing as present and entire, they push their narrative so far back and load it with such pointless circumstances, that if the story is good they smother its goodness; if it is not, you are left cursing either the felicity of their memory or the infelicity of their judgment. ^CAnd it is a difficult thing to close a train of speech and cut it short once you are under way. There is nothing in which the strength of a horse is better recognized than in making a full sharp stop. Even among people who speak to the point I see some who want to break off their run and cannot. While they are looking for the point at which to halt their steps, they go on fiddle-faddling and dragging along like men fainting from weakness. Old men especially are dangerous, whose memory of things past remains, but who have lost the memory of their repetitions. I have seen some very amusing stories become very boring in the mouth of one nobleman, everyone present having been sated with them a hundred times.

^BMy second consolation is that I remember injuries received less, as that ancient said; ^CI should need a prompter, like Darius, who, so as not to forget the harm he had received from the Athenians, had a page come every time he sat down to table and sing three times in his ear: "Sire, remember the Athenians." ^BAnd the places and books that I revisit always smile at me with a fresh newness.

^AIt is not unreasonably said that anyone who does not feel sufficiently strong in memory should not meddle with lying. I know very well that the grammarians make this distinction between telling a lie and lying: that telling a lie means saying something false but which we have taken for true; and that lying—as defined in Latin, from which our French is taken—implies going against our conscience, and thus applies only to those who say what is contrary to what they know: those of whom I am speaking. Now liars either invent everything out of whole cloth, or else disguise and alter something fundamentally true. When they disguise and change a story, if you put them back onto it often enough they find it hard not to get tangled up. For since the thing as it is has become lodged first in the memory and has imprinted itself there by way of consciousness and knowledge, it is difficult for it not to present itself to the imagination, dislodging the falsehood, which cannot have so firm and secure a foothold. Likewise, the circumstances that were learned first, slipping into the mind every moment, tend to weaken the memory of the false or corrupted parts that have been added. In what liars invent completely, inasmuch as there is no contrary impression which clashes with the falsehood, they seem to have the less reason to fear making a mistake. Nevertheless even this, since it is an empty thing without a grip, is prone to escape any but a very strong memory.

_5_

This is a pity: That is, it is a pity that we remember more quickly than we are able to think.

^BI have often seen the proof of this, and amusingly, at the expense of those who make a profession of fashioning their words only to suit the affairs they are negotiating and to please the great to whom they are speaking. For these circumstances, to which they are willing to enslave their honor and their conscience, being subject to many changes, their words must vary accordingly. Whence it happens that they describe the same thing as now gray, now yellow; to one man one way, to another another. And if by chance these men compare notes on such contrary reports, what becomes of this fine art? Let alone the fact that so often they imprudently entangle themselves; for what memory could suffice them to remember all the many different shapes into which they have cast the same subject? I have seen many in my time envy someone's reputation for this fine sort of prudence, who do not see that if the reputation is there, the effect cannot be.

^CIn truth lying is an accursed vice. We are men, and hold together, only by our word. If we recognized the horror and the gravity of lying, we would persecute it with fire more justly than other crimes. I find that people ordinarily fool around chastising harmless faults in children very inappropriately, and torment them for thoughtless actions that leave neither imprint nor consequences. Only lying, and a little below it obstinacy, seem to me to be the actions whose birth and progress one should combat insistently. They grow with the child. And once the tongue has been put on this wrong track, it cannot be called back without amazing difficulty. Whence it happens that we see otherwise honest men subject to this vice and enslaved by it. I have a fine lad of a tailor whom I have never heard speak a single truth, not even one that is right there ready to serve his advantage.

If falsehood, like truth, had only one face, we would be in better shape. For we would take as certain the opposite of what the liar said. But the reverse of truth has a hundred thousand shapes and a limitless field. The Pythagoreans make out the good to be certain and finite, evil infinite and uncertain. A thousand paths miss the target, one goes to it.

Truly I am not sure that I could bring myself to ward off even an evident   *10* and extreme danger by a shameless and solemn lie. An ancient Church Father [Saint Augustine] says that we are better off in the company of a dog we know than in that of a man whose language we do not know. *So that to man a foreigner is not like a man* [Pliny]. And how much less sociable is false speech than silence.

^AKing Francis I boasted that he had trapped by this means° Francesco Taverna, ambassador of Francesco Sforza, duke of Milan, a man very famous for skill in talking. This man had been dispatched to present his master's excuses to His Majesty about a matter of great consequence, which was this.

"trapped by this means . . .": That is, by providing every chance for the liar to entangle himself in his lies.

The king, in order to maintain some intelligence service in Italy, from which he had lately been driven out, and especially in the duchy of Milan, had decided to keep one of his own gentlemen near the duke, an ambassador in effect but in appearance a private person, who pretended to be there for his personal affairs; inasmuch as the duke, who had grown increasingly dependent on the Emperor (especially at that time, when he was negotiating a marriage with his niece, daughter of the king of Denmark, now dowager of Lorraine), could not openly deal or confer with us without great damage to himself. For this commission a Milanese gentleman named Merveille, equerry to the king, was found suitable. Dispatched with secret credentials and instructions as ambassador, and with other letters of recommendation to the duke regarding his personal affairs for mask and show, this man stayed so long with the duke that some inkling of it came to the Emperor, who, so we think, brought about what followed after: which was that on the pretext of some murder, the duke goes and has his head cut off one fine night, with his trial completed in two days. Sir Francesco, having come ready with a long counterfeit account of this affair—for the king had addressed himself, to demand satisfaction, to all the princes of Christendom and to the duke himself—was heard during the morning's business. After he had established as the basis of his case, and prepared to that end, several plausible explanations of the fact that his master had never taken our man for anything but a private gentleman and subject of his own, who had come to do business at Milan and had never lived there in any other guise; denying even having known that he was in the service of the king's household or known to him, so far was he from taking him for an ambassador—the king in his turn, pressing him with various objections and questions and attacking him from all sides, finally cornered him on the matter of the execution performed by night, and as it were by stealth. To which the poor man, embarrassed, answered, to play the honest man, that out of respect for His Majesty, the duke would have been very reluctant to have such an execution performed by day. Anyone may imagine how he was picked up for having contradicted himself so clumsily, and that before such a nose as that of King Francis.

Pope Julius II sent an ambassador to the king of England to incite him against the French king. When the ambassador had had his audience, and the king of England had dwelt in his reply on the difficulties he found in making the preparations that would be needed to combat so powerful a king, and stated some of the reasons for those difficulties, the ambassador inappropriately replied that he for his part had also considered them and indeed had mentioned them to the Pope. From this speech, so far removed from his mission, which was to urge him headlong into war, the king of England got the first inkling of what he later actually found out, that this ambassador in his private intent leaned toward the side of France. And when the man's master had been informed of this, the man's goods were confiscated and he barely avoided losing his life.

Questions for Understanding

1. Why are Montaigne's friends and neighbors unable to see the distinction between memory and understanding?
2. What does Montaigne mean when he says, "Excellent memories are prone to be joined to feeble judgments"?
3. What does Montaigne say are the consolations—or compensations—for a bad memory?
4. How seriously does Montaigne take lying?
5. What does Montaigne mean when he says that the reverse of truth "has a hundred thousand shapes and a limitless field"?

Suggestions for Writing

1. Montaigne says, that although his memory is bad, his understanding is good. Students sometimes say the same thing after an exam—that they understand the material but the exam tested only their memories. Are such student protests justified? To what extent should a college examination test a student's memory? Write an essay in which you discuss these questions and any others that may occur to you on the general subject of education and memory.
2. Montaigne says that one disadvantage of a good memory is that in conversation one can easily become a bore, loading up stories with "pointless circumstances." Compare and contrast two people you know who clearly have good memories; one who uses this memory to his or her benefit and credit and one who does not.
3. Montaigne says that a problem liars face is that they get tangled up; that is, they don't remember exactly what they invented. Can you recall a situation in which a liar got tangled up? What was the truth and what was the lie? What immediate consequences did the liar suffer as a result of revealing himself or herself to be a liar? Were there any long-range consequences? Describe and discuss.
4. Montaigne says that, once a young person finds it easy to lie, lying "cannot be called back without amazing difficulty." However, some people who have gone through their youth telling lies easily do have an "awakening" and purge themselves of the tendency to solve problems by lying. Have you, or has someone you know, gone through such a turnabout? Write an essay in which you explain what caused the turnabout and describe the difference between before and after it.
5. Is cheating on an exam or turning in a paper that is not your own work significantly different from lying? Should such acts of dishonesty be regarded with "the horror and the gravity of lying"? Describe and discuss.

NUTS AND BOLTS 12: REVISING

When Montaigne published his first two books of essays in 1580, he added a preface in which he writes that he has "had no thought of serving either you or my own glory. . . . If I had written to seek the world's favor, I should have bedecked myself better, and should present myself in a studied posture. I want to be seen here in my simple, natural, ordinary fashion, without straining or artifice. . . ." These remarks imply that Montaigne wrote the essays rather casually, more concerned with getting his thoughts down on paper than with using his skills to be as persuasive as possible.

Montaigne's approach is that of the informal essayist. He does not "bedeck" his writing; he has made no effort, he says, to polish his essays, which he might have done by resorting to the artifices of rhetoric. Nor has he assumed a consistent and "studied posture." In addition, he goes on to say, "I am myself the matter of my book." Bacon's essays, on the other hand, are good examples of the formal essay; their voice and subject are impersonal and serious. Furthermore, Bacon hoped that what he wrote would be useful and would be taken by the reader as advice, or "counsels." Montaigne gave the name *Essais* to his collection of short prose discussions because that word suggests he was only making attempts, trying out, proceeding tentatively. He was not offering counsels.

Montaigne, however, was not content to leave his essays in their "simple, natural, ordinary" state. Even after their publication, he revised them. It is probably not far from the truth to say that in 1580 Montaigne put his first drafts into print. When he reread them later, he saw ways in which they could be improved. What writing instructors tell students seems to have held true for Montaigne also! In focusing intensely and getting the first draft down, a writer is likely to overlook some details or arguments that could strengthen the piece. Therefore, when Montaigne went back to his first versions, he enriched the original concepts with further thoughts, recollections, examples, and quotations. In a first draft, it is not unusual to fail to include all that one could, and it is natural to assume that what one does include is both true and comprehensive, even though that might not be altogether the case. Reviewing a first draft, even an hour after writing it, can make one aware of important matters that were overlooked.

Are the first versions of Montaigne's and Bacon's essays, then, of little value? Are students' first drafts of little value? Not necessarily. Sometimes first drafts have considerable merit. An essay (or any work of an artist or craftsperson) in its "simple, natural, ordinary" state can be more appealing than the same thing worked over, dressed up, and consciously filled out. In its simplicity and economy, a first draft can have greater impact than a longer, more heavily laden piece. Just as a poem of only four lines can be more effective than a poem of four stanzas of four lines each, one paragraph can have more impact than four or five. Sometimes less is more. Most of the time, however, more really *is* more.

Let us look at what Montaigne did in the writing of "Of Liars." Thanks to the scholarship of Professor Donald M. Frame, we have a text of this essay that enables us to trace its evolution from the first to the final version. In the first version, Montaigne went directly from paragraph 1 to paragraph 6. He quickly moves from acknowledging his own bad memory to explaining how a bad memory complicates lying. The first sentence in paragraph 6 makes the connection: "It is not unreasonably said that anyone who does not feel sufficiently strong in memory should not meddle in lying." Then he defines lying and analyzes how liars lie, concluding the paragraph with the statement that effective lying requires a very strong memory. Montaigne next gives two examples of how a faulty memory and discovery as a liar can be costly. In the original version of "Of Liars," we have an introductory paragraph, a paragraph of definition and analysis, and two paragraphs containing examples of the main point. A pretty effective essay of approximately eight hundred words!

What does Montaigne do in his subsequent revisions? First, he interrupts the direct linking of memory with lying by explaining that, in his neighborhood, a person with a bad memory is regarded as a person with no sense. In another paragraph, he asserts that people with good memories often have poor judgment and that his forgetfulness often leads to misunderstandings. In the lengthy paragraph 4 and the brief paragraph 5, he discusses, with examples, the consolations of having a bad memory. Paragraph 6 is left as originally written but is followed by an added paragraph in which Montaigne elaborates further on how those who lie are betrayed by faulty memories.

Paragraphs 8, 9, and 10 were added still later, and indeed they form a separate section of the essay. In these paragraphs, Montaigne passes judgment on those who engage in lying by calling it "an accursed vice" that, unfortunately, has many faces. Montaigne doubts that he could bring himself to lie, even in extreme danger. Because Montaigne's position here is so passionate and unequivocal, this is perhaps the most powerful passage in the entire essay—and it was not present in the first two versions.

The original four paragraphs offer an interesting exploration of the relationship between memory and lying and by themselves constitute a valuable piece of writing. Yet the final revised version is much more interesting. The difference between the first version and the last is like the difference between a good student essay written in class and one written outside class that has gone through several revisions.

It is important to know the difference between revising and editing. Editing usually involves correcting, deleting, and finding more accurate and concise wording. In editing, one also may add material, especially material unintentionally omitted. In revising, on the other hand, one generally adds the product of further thinking and research. It's very unlikely that everything of interest and importance can be grasped the first time through, but if a writer remains focused on the subject, the chances are good that more material of interest or importance will be generated. Continuing to focus on the subject may also make one aware of better ways to arrange the material. In an in-class writing assignment, one can only edit. In doing a writing assignment outside class for which at least a week has been given, one should revise as well as edit.

ON THE POWER OF THE IMAGINATION

1580°

^A*A strong imagination creates the event,* say the scholars. I am one of those   *1*
who are very much influenced by the imagination. ^CEveryone feels its
impact, but some are overthrown by it. Its impression on me is piercing. And
my art is to escape it, not to resist it. I would live solely in the presence of gay,
healthy people. The sight of other people's anguish causes very real anguish
to me, and my feelings have often usurped the feelings of others. A continual
cougher irritates my lungs and throat. I visit less willingly the sick toward
whom duty directs me than those toward whom I am less attentive and
concerned. I catch the disease that I study, and lodge it in me. I do not find
it strange that imagination brings fevers and death to those who give it a free
hand and encourage it.

Simon Thomas was a great doctor in his time. I remember that one day,
when he met me at the house of a rich old consumptive with whom he was
discussing ways to cure his illness, he told him that one of these would be to
give me occasion to enjoy his company; and that by fixing his eyes on the
freshness of my face and his thoughts on the blitheness and overflowing vigor
of my youth, and filling all his senses with my flourishing condition, he might
improve his constitution. But he forgot to say that mine might get worse at
the same time.

^AGallus Vibius strained his mind so hard to understand the essence and
impulses of insanity that he dragged his judgment off its seat and never could
get it back again, and he could boast of having become mad through wisdom.
There are some who through fear anticipate the hand of the executioner. And
one man who was being unbound to have his pardon read him dropped stone
dead on the scaffold, struck down by his mere imagination. We drip with
sweat, we tremble, we turn pale and turn red at the blows of our imagination;
reclining in our feather beds we feel our bodies agitated by their impact,
sometimes to the point of expiring. And boiling youth, fast asleep, grows so
hot in the harness that in dreams it satisfies its amorous desires:

> So that as though it were an actual affair,
> They pour out mighty streams, and stain the clothes they wear.
>
> —LUCRETIUS

And although it is nothing new to see horns grow overnight on someone who
did not have them when he went to bed, nevertheless what happened to Cippus,
king of Italy, is memorable; having been in the daytime a very excited spectator
at a bullfight and having all night in his dreams had horns on his head, he grew

---

1580: The year the essay was first published.

actual horns on his forehead by the power of his imagination. Passion gave the son of Croesus° the voice that nature had refused him. And Antiochus took fever from the beauty of Stratonice too vividly imprinted in his soul. Pliny says he saw Lucius Cossitius changed from a woman into a man on his wedding day. Pontanus and others report similar metamorphoses as having happened in Italy in these later ages. And through his and his mother's vehement desire,

> Iphis the man fulfilled vows made when he was a girl.
>
> —OVID

^BPassing through Vitry-le-François, I might have seen a man whom the bishop of Soissons had named Germain at confirmation, but whom all the inhabitants of that place had seen and known as a girl named Marie until the age of twenty-two. He was now heavily bearded, and old, and not married. Straining himself in some way in jumping, he says, his masculine organs came forth; and among the girls there a song is still current by which they warn each other not to take big strides for fear of becoming boys, like Marie Germain. It is not so great a marvel that this sort of accident is frequently met with. For if the imagination has power in such things, it is so continually and vigorously fixed on this subject that in order not to have to relapse so often into the same thought and sharpness of desire, it is better off if once and for all it incorporates this masculine member in girls.

^ASome attribute to the power of imagination the scars of King Dagobert° and of Saint Francis.° It is said that thereby bodies are sometimes removed from their places. And Celsus° tells of a priest who used to fly with his soul into such ecstasy that his body would remain a long time without breath and without sensation. ^CSaint Augustine names another who whenever he heard lamentable and plaintive cries would suddenly go into a trance and get so carried away that it was no use to shake him and shout at him, to pinch him and burn him, until he had come to; then he would say that he had heard voices, but as if coming from afar, and he would notice his burns and bruises. And that this was no feigned resistance to his senses was shown by the fact that while in this state he had neither pulse nor breath.

^AIt is probable that the principal credit of miracles, visions, enchantments, and such extraordinary occurrences comes from the power of imagination, acting principally upon the minds of the common people, which are softer. Their belief has been so strongly seized that they think they see what they do not see.

Croesus: King of Lydia, (560–c.546 B.C.) His son, according to Herodotus, had been unable to speak from birth but found his voice when he saw his father in peril.

King Dagobert: A Frankish king, (c.612–c.639), whose scars were said to be caused by the fear of gangrene.

Saint Francis: Had wounds that were said to be the stigmata.

Celsus: A second-century Roman philosopher.

I am still of this opinion, that those comical inhibitions° by which our society is so fettered that people talk of nothing else are for the most part the effects of apprehension and fear. For I know by experience that one man, whom I can answer for as for myself, on whom there could fall no suspicion whatever of impotence and just as little of being enchanted, having heard a friend of his tell the story of an extraordinary impotence into which he had fallen at the moment when he needed it least, and finding himself in a similar situation, was all at once so struck in his imagination by the horror of this story that he incurred the same fate. ^CAnd from then on he was subject to relapse, for the ugly memory of his mishap checked him and tyrannized him. He found some remedy for this fancy by another fancy: which was that by admitting this weakness and speaking about it in advance, he relieved the tension of his soul, for when the trouble had been presented as one to be expected, his sense of responsibility diminished and weighed upon him less. When he had a chance of his own choosing, with his mind unembroiled and relaxed and his body in good shape, to have his bodily powers first tested, then seized and taken by surprise, with the other party's full knowledge of his problem, he was completely cured in this respect. A man is never after incapable, unless from genuine impotence, with a woman with whom he has once been capable.

^AThis mishap is to be feared only in enterprises where our soul is immoderately tense with desire and respect, and especially if the opportunity is unexpected and pressing; there is no way of recovering from this trouble. I know one man who found it helpful to bring to it a body that had already begun to be sated elsewhere, ^Cso as to lull his frenzied ardor, and who with age finds himself less impotent through being less potent. And I know another who was helped when a friend assured him that he was supplied with a counterbattery of enchantments that were certain to save him. I had better tell how this happened.

A count, a member of a very distinguished family, with whom I was quite intimate, upon getting married to a beautiful lady who had been courted by a man who was present at the wedding feast, had his friends very worried and especially an old lady, a relative of his, who was presiding at the wedding and holding it at her house. She was fearful of these sorceries, and gave me to understand this. I asked her to rely on me. I had by chance in my coffers a certain little flat piece of gold on which were engraved some celestial figures, to protect against sunstroke and take away a headache by placing it precisely on the suture of the skull; and, to keep it there, it was sewed to a ribbon intended to be tied under the chin: a kindred fancy to the one we are speaking of. Jacques Peletier had given me this singular present. I thought of making some use of it, and said to the count that he might incur the same fate as others, there being men present who would like to bring this about; but that he should boldly go to bed and I would do him a friendly turn and would

---

inhibitions: Temporary sexual impotence in men.

not, if he needed it, spare a miracle which was in my power, provided that he promised me on his honor to keep it most faithfully secret; he was only to make a given signal to me, when they came to bring him the midnight meal, if things had gone badly with him. He had had his soul and his ears so battered that he did find himself fettered by the trouble of his imagination, and gave me his signal. I told him then that he should get up on the pretext of chasing us out, and playfully take the bathrobe that I had on (we were very close in height) and put it on him until he had carried out my prescription, which was this: when we had left, he should withdraw to pass water, say certain prayers three times and go through certain motions; each of these three times he should tie the ribbon I was putting in his hand around him and very carefully lay the medal that was attached to it on his kidneys, with the figure in such and such a position; this done, having tied this ribbon firmly so that it could neither come untied nor slip from its place, he should return to his business with complete assurance and not forget to spread my robe over his bed so that it should cover them both. These monkey tricks are the main part of the business, our mind being unable to get free of the idea that such strange means must come from some abstruse science. Their inanity gives them weight and reverence. All in all, it is certain that the characters on my medal proved themselves more venereal than solar, more useful for action than for prevention. It was a sudden and curious whim that led me to do such a thing, which was alien to my nature. I am an enemy of subtle and dissimulated acts and hate trickery in myself, not only for sport but also for someone's profit. If the action is not vicious, the road to it is.

Amasis, king of Egypt, married Laodice, a very beautiful Greek girl; [10] and he, who showed himself a gay companion everywhere else, fell short when it came to enjoying her, and threatened to kill her, thinking it was some sort of sorcery. As is usual in matters of fancy, she referred him to religion; and having made his vows and promises to Venus, he found himself divinely restored from the first night after his oblations and sacrifices.

Now women are wrong to greet us with those threatening, quarrelsome, and coy countenances, which put out our fires even as they light them. The daughter-in-law of Pythagoras used to say that the woman who goes to bed with a man should put off her modesty with her skirt and put it on again with her petticoat. ^AThe soul of the assailant,° when troubled with many various alarms, is easily discouraged; and when imagination has once made a man suffer this shame—and it does so only at the first encounters, inasmuch as these are more boiling and violent, and also because in this first intimacy a man is much more afraid of failing—have begun badly, he gets from this accident a feverishness and vexation which lasts into subsequent occasions.

^CMarried people, whose time is all their own, should neither press their undertaking nor even attempt it if they are not ready; it is better to fail

---

the assailant: The would-be lover.

unbecomingly to handsel the nuptial couch,° which is full of agitation and feverishness, and wait for some other more private and less tense opportunity, than to fall into perpetual misery for having been stunned and made desperate by a first refusal. Before taking possession, the patient should try himself out and offer himself, lightly, by sallies at different times, without priding himself and obstinately insisting on convincing himself definitively. Those who know that their members° are naturally obedient, let them take care only to counteract the tricks of their fancies.

People are right to notice the unruly liberty of this member, obtruding so importunately when we have no use for it, and failing so importunately when we have the most use for it, and struggling for mastery so imperiously with our will, refusing with so much pride and obstinacy our solicitations, both mental and manual.

If, however, in the matter of his rebellion being blamed and used as proof to condemn him, he had paid me to plead his cause, I should perhaps place our other members, his fellows, under suspicion of having framed this trumped-up charge out of sheer envy of the importance and pleasure of the use of him, and of having armed everyone against him by a conspiracy, malignantly charging him alone with their common fault. For I ask you to think whether there is a single one of the parts of our body that does not often refuse its function to our will and exercise it against our will. They each have passions of their own which rouse them and put them to sleep without our leave. How many times do the forced movements of our face bear witness to the thoughts that we were holding secret, and betray us to those present. The same cause that animates this member also animates, without our knowledge, the heart, the lungs, and the pulse; the sight of a pleasing object spreading in us imperceptibly the flame of a feverish emotion. Are there only these muscles and these veins that stand up and lie down without the consent, not only of our will, but even of our thoughts? We do not command our hair to stand on end or our skin to shiver with desire or fear. The hand often moves itself to where we do not send it. The tongue is paralyzed, and the voice congealed, at their own time. Even when, having nothing to put in to fry, we should like to forbid it, the appetite for eating and drinking does not fail to stir the parts that are subject to it, no more nor less than that other appetite; and it likewise abandons us inopportunely when it sees fit. The organs that serve to discharge the stomach have their own dilatations and compressions, beyond and against our plans, just like those that are destined to discharge the kidneys. To vindicate the omnipotence of our will, Saint Augustine alleges that he knew a man who commanded his behind to produce as many farts as he wanted, and his commentator Vives goes him one better with another example of his own time, of farts arranged to suit the tone of verses pronounced to their accompaniment; but all this does not really argue any

---

to hansel the nuptial couch: To begin sexual relations in marriage.

members: "Member" is a euphemism for penis, and a word that lends itself to puns.

pure obedience in this organ; for is there any that is ordinarily more indiscreet or tumultuous? Besides, I know one so turbulent and unruly, that for forty years it has kept its master farting with a constant and unremitting wind and compulsion, and is thus taking him to his death.°

But as for our will, on behalf of whose rights, we set forth this   15
complaint, how much more plausibly may we charge it with rebellion and sedition for its disorderliness and disobedience! Does it always will what we would will it to will? Doesn't it often will what we forbid it to will, and that to our evident disadvantage? Is it any more amenable than our other parts to the decisions of our reason?

To conclude, I would say this in defense of the honorable member whom I represent: May it please the court to take into consideration that in this matter, although my client's case is inseparably and indistinguishably linked with that of an accessory, nevertheless he alone has been brought to trial; and that the arguments and charges against him are such as cannot—in view of the status of the parties—be in any manner pertinent or relevant to the aforesaid accessory.° Whereby is revealed his accusers' manifest animosity and disrespect for law. However that may be, Nature will meanwhile go her way, protesting that the lawyers and judges quarrel and pass sentence in vain. Indeed, she would have done no more than is right if she had endowed with some particular privilege this member, author of the sole immortal work of mortals. Wherefore to Socrates generation is a divine act; and love, a desire for immortality and itself an immortal daemon.°

^APerhaps it is by this effect of the imagination that one man here gets rid of the scrofula° which his companion carries back to Spain. This effect is the reason why, in such matters, it is customary to demand that the mind be prepared. Why do the doctors work on the credulity of their patient beforehand with so many false promises of a cure, if not so that the effect of the imagination may make up for the imposture of their decoction? They know that one of the masters of the trade left them this in writing, that there have been men for whom the mere sight of medicine did the job.

. . . *to his death:* Here the 1595 edition adds: "And would God I knew only from the history books how many times our stomach, by refusing one single fart, brings us to the gates of a very anguished death; and that the Emperor who gave us the liberty to fart anywhere had given us the power to." Suetonius reports that the Emperor Claudius had contemplated such a decree as this.

. . . *to the aforesaid accessory:* Here the 1595 edition adds: "for it is indeed in the nature of my client to solicit inopportunely at times, but never to refuse; and to solicit wordlessly and silently at that."

an immortal daemon: An immortal spirit.

scrofula: Scrofula, or king's evil, was supposed to be curable by the touch of the kings of France. In Montaigne's time great numbers of Spaniards came to France for this purpose.

And this whole caprice° has just come to hand apropos of the story than an apothecary, a servant of my late father, used to tell me, a simple man and Swiss, of a nation little addicted to vanity and lying. He had long known a merchant at Toulouse, sickly and subject to the stone, who often needed enemas, and ordered various kinds from his doctors according to the circumstances of his illness. Once they were brought to him, nothing was omitted of the accustomed formalities; often he tested them by hand to make sure they were not too hot. There he was, lying on his stomach, and all the motions were gone through—except that no injection was made. After this ceremony, the apothecary having retired and the patient being accommodated as if he had really taken the enema, he felt the same effect from it as those who do take them. And if the doctor did not find its operation sufficient, he would give him two or three more, of the same sort. My witness swears that when to save the expense (for he paid for them as if he had taken them) this sick man's wife sometimes tried to have just warm water used, the effect revealed the fraud; and having found that kind useless, they were obliged to return to the first method.

A woman, thinking she had swallowed a pin with her bread, was screaming in agony as though she had an unbearable pain in her throat, where she thought she felt it stuck; but because externally there was neither swelling nor alteration, a smart man, judging that it was only a fancy and notion derived from some bit of bread that had scratched her as it went down, made her vomit, and, on the sly, tossed a crooked pin into what she threw up. The woman, thinking she had thrown it up, felt herself suddenly relieved of her pain. I know that one gentleman, having entertained a goodly company at his house, three or four days later boasted, as a sort of joke (for there was nothing in it), that he had made them eat cat in a pie; at which one lady in the party was so horrified that she fell into a violent stomach disorder and fever, and it was impossible to save her. Even animals are subject like ourselves to the power of imagination. Witness dogs, who let themselves die out of grief for the loss of their masters. We also see them yap and twitch in their dreams, and horses whinny and writhe.

But all this may be attributed to the narrow seam between the soul and   *20* body, through which the experience of the one is communicated to the other. Sometimes, however, one's imagination acts not only against one's own body, but against someone else's. And just as the body passes on its sickness to its neighbor, as is seen in the plague, the pox, and soreness of the eyes, which are transmitted from one body to the other—

> By looking at sore eyes, eyes become sore:
> From body into body ills pass o'er
>
>   —OVID

And this whole caprice: Montaigne is referring to the trick he played upon his friend with the medal.

—likewise the imagination, when vehemently stirred, launches darts that can injure an external object. The ancients maintained that certain women of Scythia, when animated and enraged against anyone, would kill him with their mere glance. Tortoises and ostriches hatch their eggs just by looking at them, a sign that their sight has some ejaculative virtue. And as for sorcerers, they are said to have baleful and harmful eyes:

> Some evil eye bewitched my tender lambs.
>
> —VIRGIL

To me, magicians are poor authorities. Nevertheless, we know by experience that women transmit marks of their fancies to the bodies of the children they carry in their womb; witness the one who gave birth to the Moor.° And there was presented to Charles, king of Bohemia and Emperor, a girl from near Pisa, all hairy and bristly, who her mother said had been thus conceived because of a picture of Saint John the Baptist hanging by her bed.

With animals it is the same: witness Jacob's sheep, and the partridges and hares that the snow turns white in the mountains. Recently at my house a cat was seen watching a bird on a treetop, and, after they had locked gazes for some time, the bird let itself fall as if dead between the cat's paws, either intoxicated by its own imagination or drawn by some attracting power of the cat. Those who like falconry have heard the story of the falconer who, setting his gaze obstinately upon a kite in the air, wagered that by the sole power of his gaze he would bring it down, and did. At least, so they say—for I refer the stories that I borrow to the conscience of those from whom I take them. ^BThe reflections are my own, and depend on the proofs of reason, not of experience; everyone can add his own examples to them; and he who has none, let him not fail to believe that there are plenty, in view of the number and variety of occurrences. ^CIf I do not apply them well, let another apply them for me.

So in the study that I am making of our behavior and motives, fabulous testimonies, provided they are possible, serve like true ones. Whether they have happened or no, in Paris or Rome, to John or Peter, they exemplify, at all events, some human potentiality, and thus their telling imparts useful information to me. I see it and profit from it just as well in shadow as in substance. And of the different readings that histories often give, I take for my use the one that is most rare and memorable. There are authors whose end is to tell what has hapened. Mine, if I could attain it, would be to talk about what can happen. The schools are justly permitted to suppose similitudes when they have none at hand. I do not do so, however, and in that respect I surpass all historical fidelity, being scrupulous to the point of superstition. In

---

the one who gave birth to the Moor: Saint Jerome tells the story of a woman who gave birth to a black child and was thereupon accused of adultery. She was absolved when Hippocrates explained that she had a picture of a dark man hanging by her bed.

the examples that I bring in here of what I have heard, done, or said, I have forbidden myself to dare to alter even the slightest and most inconsequential circumstances. My conscience does not falsify one iota; my knowledge, I don't know.

In this connection, I sometimes fall to thinking whether it befits a theologian, a philosopher, and such people of exquisite and exact conscience and prudence, to write history. How can they stake their fidelity on the fidelity of an ordinary person? How be responsible for the thoughts of persons unknown and give their conjectures as coin of the realm? Of complicated actions that happen in their presence they would refuse to give testimony if placed under oath by a judge; and they know no man so intimately that they would undertake to answer fully for his intentions. I consider it less hazardous to write of things past than present, inasmuch as the writer has only to give an account of a borrowed truth.

Some urge me to write the events of my time, believing that I see them   25 with a view less distorted by passion than another man's, and from closer, because of the access that fortune has given me to the heads of different parties. What they forget is that even for all the glory of Sallust,° I would not take the trouble, being a sworn enemy of obligation, assiduity, perseverance; and that there is nothing so contrary to my style as an extended narration. I cut myself off so often for lack of breath; I have neither composition nor development that is worth anything; I am more ignorant than a child of the phrases and terms that serve for the commonest things. And so I have chosen to say what I know how to say, accommodating the matter to my power. If I took a subject that would lead me along, I might not be able to measure up to it; and with my freedom being so very free, I might publish judgments which, even according to my own opinion and to reason, would be illegitimate and punishable. Plutarch might well say to us, concerning his accomplishments in this line, that the credit belongs to others if his examples are wholly and everywhere true; but that their being useful to posterity, and presented with a luster which lights our way to virtue, that is his work. There is no danger—as there is in a medicinal drug—in an old story being this way or that.

Questions for Understanding

1. What treatment did Simon Thomas prescribe for the rich old consumptive?
2. To what extent do you believe the power of imagination was able to bring about sex changes in the cases referred to by Montaigne?
3. Explain, in your own words, the following assertion of Montaigne's: "These monkey tricks are the main part of the business, our mind being unable to get

---

Sallust: (86 B.C.–c.34 B.C.) Roman historian and political leader.

free of the idea that such strange means must come from some abstruse science."

4. In asserting that there is a "narrow seam between the soul and body," Montaigne takes a position that is quite modern. But does he take a modern position when he suggests that "the plague, the pox, and soreness of the eyes" are transmitted through the imagination?

5. In the last four paragraphs of the essay, Montaigne says that he has provided some "fabulous testimonies." (What exactly does *fabulous* mean here?) He has done so, he says, because "their telling imparts useful information" that helps him fulfill his purpose of talking about what can happen. How would you explain what did happen in Montaigne's story of the cat and the bird that fell dead between the cat's paws?

Suggestions for Writing

1. Montaigne begins his discussion of the power of the imagination by telling about the effects of healthy and sick people on each other. Have you had any interesting experiences as a participant in such a relationship? If so, write an essay in which you discuss the role the imagination played in the course of the relationship.

2. Montaigne tells the story of Marie Germain, who went from male to female to male. In recent times, sexual identity has been frankly discussed in the media, and people have become more open about unorthodox situations. Have you encountered an interesting case? If so, write an essay in which you discuss the role the imagination seems to have played in determining the person's sexual identity and roles.

3. Montaigne writes, "It is probable that the credit of miracles, visions, enchantments, and such extraordinary occurrences comes from the power of imagination. . . ." Do you agree, or do you think there are other causes of such extraordinary occurrences? Discuss.

4. Montaigne says that the human will is very sneaky, inclined to be rebellious and disobedient. "Is it any more amenable," he asks, "than our other parts to the decisions of our reason?" Write an essay in which you discuss some strange encounters you have had with your will.

5. Write an essay in which you discuss the most interesting case you know of that concerns the mind's effects on the body.

OF FRIENDSHIP

1580°

^AAs I was considering the way a painter I employ went about his work,   *1*
I had a mind to imitate him. He chooses the best spot, the middle of each wall,
to put a picture labored over with all his skill, and the empty space all around
it he fills with grotesques, which are fantastic paintings whose only charm lies
in their variety and strangeness. And what are these things of mine, in truth,
but grotesques and monstrous bodies, pieced together of divers members,
without definite shape, having no order, sequence, or proportion other than
accidental?°

A lovely woman tapers off into a fish.

—HORACE

I do indeed go along with my painter in this second point, but I fall short
in the first and better part; for my ability does not go far enough for me to
dare to undertake a rich, polished picture, formed according to art. It has
occurred to me to borrow one from Etienne de La Boétie, which will do
honor to all the rest of this work. It is a discourse to which he gave the name
La Servitude Volontaire; but those who did not know this have since very
fitly rebaptized it *Le Contre Un.*° He wrote it by way of essay in his early
youth, in honor of liberty against tyrants. It has long been circulating in the
hands of men of understanding, not without great and well-merited
commendation; for it is a fine thing, and as full as can be. Still, it is far from
being the best he could do; and if at the more mature age when I knew him,
he had adopted a plan such as mine, of putting his ideas in writing, we should
see many rare things which would bring us very close to the glory of
antiquity; for particularly in the matter of natural gifts, I know no one who
can be compared with him. But nothing of his has remained except this
treatise—and that by chance, and I think he never saw it after it left his
hands—and some observations on that Edict of January,° made famous by
our civil wars, which will perhaps yet find their place elsewhere. That was all
I could recover of what he left—^CI, to whom in his will, with such loving
recommendation, with death in his throat, he bequeathed his library and

---

1580: The year in which the essay was first published.

And what . . . accidental: Montaigne is referring to his essays.

It has occurred . . . Le Contre Un: Montaigne is saying that he would have liked to include an
essay by Boétie in his own collection. He would have included the work that was originally
called "Voluntary Servitude" but which has been changed to "Against One Man." The
Huguenots included it in a collection of pamphlets they put out in 1576. But Montaigne
believes the essay has been misused by people of "evil intent," and so he has decided not to
include it in his own collection.

Edict of January: The Edict of January, 1571, granted the Huguenots freedom of public worship.

his papers—^Aexcept for the little volume of his works which I have had published.

And yet I am particularly obliged to this work, since it served as the medium of our first acquaintance. For it was shown to me long before I had seen him, and gave me my first knowledge of his name, thus starting on its way this friendship which together we fostered, as long as God willed, so entire and so perfect that certainly you will hardly read of the like, and among men of today you see no trace of it in practice. So many coincidences are needed to build up such a friendship that it is a lot if fortune can do it once in three centuries.

There is nothing to which nature seems to have inclined us more than to society.° ^CAnd Aristotle says that good legislators have had more care for friendship than for justice. ^ANow the ultimate point in the perfection of society is this. For ^Cin general, all associations that are forged and nourished by pleasure or profit, by public or private needs, are the less beautiful and noble, and the less friendships, in so far as they mix into friendship another cause and object and reward than friendship itself. Nor do the four ancient types—natural, social, hospitable, erotic—come up to real friendship, either separately or together.

^AFrom children toward fathers, it is rather respect. Friendship feeds on   5
communication, which cannot exist between them because of their too great inequality, and might perhaps interfere with the duties of nature. For neither can all the secret thoughts of fathers be communicated to children, lest this beget an unbecoming intimacy, nor could the admonitions and corrections, which are one of the chief duties of friendship, be administered by children to fathers. There have been nations where by custom the children killed their fathers, and others where the fathers killed their children, to avoid the interference that they can sometimes cause each other; and by nature the one depends on the destruction of the other. There have been philosophers who disdained this natural tie, witness ^CAristippus:° ^Awhen pressed about the affection he owed his children for having come out of him, he began to spit, saying that that had come out of him just as well, and that we also bred lice and worms. And that other, whom Plutarch wanted to reconcile with his brother, said: "I don't think any more of him for having come out of the same hole."

Truly the name of brother is a beautiful name and full of affection, and for that reason he and I made our alliance a brotherhood. But that confusion of ownership, the dividing, and the fact that the richness of one is the poverty of the other, wonderfully softens and loosens the solder of brotherhood. Since brothers have to guide their careers along the same path and at the same rate, it is inevitable that they often jostle and clash with each other. Further-

---

to society: Socializing.

Aristippus: Aristippus (c.435–c.360 B.C.): Greek philosopher who founded hedonism and linked virtue to pleasure.

more, why should the harmony and kinship which begets these true and perfect friendships be found in them? Father and son may be of entirely different dispositions, and brothers also. He is my son, he is my kinsman, but he is an unsociable man, a knave, or a fool. And then, the more they are friendships which law and natural obligation impose on us, the less of our choice and free will there is in them. And our free will has no product more properly its own than affection and friendship. Not that I have not experienced all the friendship that can exist in that situation, having had the best father that ever was, and the most indulgent, even in his extreme old age, and being of a family famous and exemplary, from father to son, in this matter of brotherly concord:

> ^BKnown to others
> For fatherly affection toward my brothers.
>
> —HORACE

^ATo compare this brotherly affection with affection for women, even though it is the result of our choice—it cannot be done; nor can we put the love of women in the same category. Its ardor, I confess—

> Of us that goddess is not unaware
> Who blends a bitter sweetness with her care
>
> —CATULLUS

—is more active, more scorching, and more intense. But it is an impetuous and fickle flame, undulating and variable, a fever flame, subject to fits and lulls, that holds us only by one corner. In friendship it is a general and universal warmth, moderate and even, besides, a constant and settled warmth, all gentleness and smoothness, with nothing bitter and stinging about it. What is more, in love there is nothing but a frantic desire for what flees from us:

> Just as a huntsman will pursue a hare
> O'er hill and dale, in weather cold or fair;
> The captured hare is worthless in his sight;
> He only hastens after things in flight.
>
> —ARIOSTO

As soon as it enters the boundaries of friendship, that is to say harmony of wills, it grows faint and languid. Enjoyment destroys it, as having a fleshly end, subject to satiety. Friendship, on the contrary, is enjoyed according as it is desired; it is bred, nourished, and increased only in enjoyment, since it is spiritual, and the soul grows refined by practice. During the reign of this perfect friendship those fleeting affections once found a place in me, not to speak of my friend, who confesses only too many of them in these verses. Thus these two passions within me came to be known to each other, but to be compared, never; the first keeping its course in proud and lofty flight, and disdainfully watching the other making its way far, far beneath it.

As for marriage, for one thing it is a bargain to which only the entrance is free—its continuance being constrained and forced, depending otherwise than on our will—and a bargain ordinarily made for other ends. For another, there supervene a thousand foreign tangles to unravel, enough to break the thread and trouble the course of a lively affection; whereas in friendship there are no dealings or business except with itself. Besides, to tell the truth, the ordinary capacity of women is inadequate for that communion and fellowship which is the nurse of this sacred bond; nor does their soul seem firm enough to endure the strain of so tight and durable a knot. And indeed, but for that, if such a relationship, free and voluntary, could be built up, in which not only would the souls have this complete enjoyment, but the bodies would also share in the alliance, ^Cso that the entire man would be engaged, ^Ait is certain that the resulting friendship would be fuller and more complete. But this sex in no instance has yet succeeded in attaining it, ^Cand by the common agreement of the ancient schools is excluded from it.

^AAnd that other, licentious Greek love° is justly abhorred by our morality. ^CSince it involved, moreover, according to their practice, such a necessary disparity in age and such a difference in the lovers' functions, it did not correspond closely enough with the perfect union and harmony that we require here: *For what is this love of friendship? Why does no one love either an ugly youth, or a handsome old man?* [Cicero.] For even the picture the Academy° paints of it will not contradict me, I think, if I say this on the subject: that this first frenzy which the son of Venus inspired in the lover's heart at the sight of the flower of tender youth, in which they allow all the insolent and passionate acts that immoderate ardor can produce, was simply founded on external beauty, the false image of corporeal generation. For it could not be founded on the spirit, the signs of which were still hidden, which was only at its birth and before the age of budding. If this frenzy seized a base heart, the means of his courtship were riches, presents, favor in advancement to dignities, and other such base merchandise, which were generally condemned. If it fell on a nobler heart, the means were also noble: philosophical instruction, precepts to revere religion, obey the laws, die for the good of the country; examples of valor, prudence, justice; the lover studying to make himself acceptable by the grace and beauty of his soul, that of his body being long since faded, and hoping by this mental fellowship to establish a firmer and more lasting pact.

When this courtship attained its effect in due season (for whereas they do not require of the lover that he use leisure and discretion in his enterprise, they strictly require it of the loved one, because he had to judge an inner beauty, difficult to know and hidden from discovery), then there was born in the loved one the desire of spiritual conception through the medium of spiritual beauty. This was the main thing here, and corporeal beauty

10

Greek love: Love between two men.

Academy: In Plato's *Symposium,* the Academy refers to the Platonic school of philosophy, which had its origins in the public grove in Athens where Plato taught.

accidental and secondary; quite the opposite of the lover. For this reason they prefer the loved one, and prove that the gods also prefer him, and strongly rebuke the poet Aeschylus for having, in the love of Achilles and Patroclus, given the lover's part to Achilles, who was in the first beardless bloom of his youth, and the handsomest of all the Greeks.

After this general communion was established, the stronger and worthier part of it exercising its functions and predominating, they say that there resulted from it fruits very useful personally and to the public; that it constituted the strength of the countries which accepted the practice, and the principal defense of equity and liberty: witness the salutary loves of Harmodius and Aristogeiton. Therefore they call it sacred and divine. And, by their reckoning, only the violence of tyrants and the cowardice of the common people are hostile to it. In short, all that can be said in favor of the Academy is that this was a love ending in friendship; which corresponds pretty well to the Stoic definition of love: *Love is the attempt to form a friendship inspired by beauty* [Cicero].

I return to my description of a more equitable and more equable kind of friendship. *Only those are to be judged friendships in which the characters have been strengthened and matured by age* [Cicero].

^AFor the rest, what we ordinarily call friends and friendships are nothing but acquaintanceships and familiarities formed by some chance or convenience, by means of which our souls are bound to each other. In the friendship I speak of, our souls mingle and blend with each other so completely that they efface the seam that joined them, and cannot find it again. If you press me to tell why I loved him, I feel that this cannot be expressed, ^Cexcept by answering: Because it was he, because it was I.

^ABeyond all my understanding, beyond what I can say about this in particular, there was I know not what inexplicable and fateful force that was the mediator of this union. ^CWe sought each other before we met because of the reports we heard of each other, which had more effect on our affection than such reports would reasonably have; I think it was by some ordinance from heaven. We embraced each other by our names. And at our first meeting, which by chance came at a great feast and gathering in the city, we found ourselves so taken with each other, so well acquainted, so bound together, that from that time on nothing was so close to us as each other. He wrote an excellent Latin satire, which is published, in which he excuses and explains the precipitancy of our mutual understanding, so promptly grown to its perfection. Having so little time to last, and having begun so late, for we were both grown men, and he a few years older than I, it could not lose time and conform to the pattern of mild and regular friendships, which need so many precautions in the form of long preliminary association. Our friendship has no other model than itself, and can be compared only with itself. ^AIt is not one special consideration, nor two, nor three, nor four, nor a thousand: it is I know not what quintessence of all this mixture, which, having seized my whole will, led it to plunge and lose itself in his; ^Cwhich, having seized his whole will, led it to plunge and lose itself in mine, with equal hunger,

equal rivalry. ^AI say lose, in truth, for neither of us reserved anything for himself, nor was anything either his or mine.

When Laelius, in the presence of the Roman consuls—who, after comdemning Tiberius Gracchus,° prosecuted all those who had been in his confidence—came to ask Caius Blossius, who was Gracchus' best friend, how much he would have been willing to do for him, he answered: "Everything." "What, everything?" pursued Laelius. "And what if he had commanded you to set fire to our temples?" "He would never have commanded me to do that," replied Blossius. "But what if he had?" Laelius insisted. "I would have obeyed," he replied. If he was such a perfect friend to Gracchus as the histories say, he did not need to offend the consuls by this last bold confession, and he should not have abandoned the assurance he had of Gracchus' will. But nevertheless, those who charge that this answer is seditious do not fully understand this mystery, and fail to assume first what is true, that he had Gracchus' will up his sleeve, both by power over him and by knowledge of him. ^CThey were friends more than citizens, friends more than friends or enemies of their country or friends of ambition and disturbance. Having committed themselves absolutely to each other, they held absolutely the reins of each other's inclination; and if you assume that this team was guided by the strength and leadership of reason, as indeed it is quite impossible to harness it without that, Blossius' answer is as it should have been. If their actions went astray, they were by my measure neither friends to each other, nor friends to themselves.

For that matter, ^Athis answer has no better ring than would mine if someone questioned me in this fashion: "If your will commanded you to kill your daughter, would you kill her?" and I said yes. For that does not bear witness to any consent to do so, because I have no doubt at all about my will, and just as little about that of such a friend. It is not in the power of all the arguments in the world to dislodge me from the certainty I have of the intentions and judgments of my friend. Not one of his actions could be presented to me, whatever appearance it might have, that I could not immediately find the motive for it. Our souls pulled together in such unison, they regarded each other with such ardent affection, and with a like affection revealed themselves to each other to the very depths of our hearts, that not only did I know his soul as well as mine, but I should certainly have trusted myself to him more readily than to myself.

Let not these other, common friendships be placed in this rank. I have as much knowledge of them as another, and of the most perfect of their type, ^Bbut I advise you not to confuse the rules of the two; you would make a mistake. You must walk in those other friendships bridle in hand, with prudence and precaution; the knot is not so well tied that there is no cause to mistrust it. "Love him," Chilo used to say, "as if you are to hate him some day; hate him as if you are to love him." This precept, which is so abominable

---

Tiberius Gracchus: (163–133 B.C.) Roman political reformer.

in this sovereign and masterful friendship, is healthy in the practice of ordinary ^Cand customary ^Bfriendships, ^Cin regard to which we must use the remark that Aristotle often repeated: "O my friends, there is no friend."

^AIn this noble relationship, services and benefits, on which other friendships feed, do not even deserve to be taken into account; the reason for this is the complete fusion of our wills. For just as the friendship I feel for myself receives no increase from the help I give myself in time of need, whatever the Stoics say, and as I feel no gratitude to myself for the service I do myself; so the union of such friends, being truly perfect, makes them lose the sense of such duties, and hate and banish from between them these words of separation and distinction: benefit, obligation, gratitude, request, thanks, and the like. Everything actually being in common between them—wills, thoughts, judgments, goods, wives, children, honor, and life—^Cand their relationship being that of one soul in two bodies, according to Aristotle's very apt definition, ^Athey can neither lend nor give anything to each other. That is why the lawmakers, to honor marriage with some imaginary resemblance to this divine union, forbid gifts between husband and wife, wishing thus to imply that everything should belong to each of them and that they have nothing to divide and split up between them.

If, in the friendship I speak of, one could give to the other, it would be the one who received the benefit who would oblige his friend. For, each of them seeking above all things to benefit the other, the one who provides the matter and the occasion is the liberal one, giving his friend the satisfaction of doing for him what he most wants to do. ^CWhen the philosopher Diogenes was short of money, he used to say that he asked it back of his friends, not that he asked for it. ^AAnd to show how this works in practice, I will tell you an ancient example that is singular.

Eudamidas of Corinth had two friends, Charixenus, a Sicyonian, and Aretheus, a Corinthian. When he came to die, he being poor and his two friends rich, he made his will thus: "I leave this to Aretheus, to feed my mother and support her in her old age; this to Charixenus, to see my daughter married and give her the biggest dowry he can; and in case one of them should chance to die, I substitute the survivor in his place." Those who first saw this will laughed at it; but his heirs, having been informed of it, accepted it with singular satisfaction. And when one of them, Charixenus, died five days later, and the place of substitute was opened to Aretheus, he supported the mother with great care, and of five talents he had in his estate, he gave two and a half to his only daughter for her marriage, and two and a half for the marriage of the daughter of Eudamidas, holding their weddings on the same day.

This example is quite complete except for one circumstance, which is the plurality of friends. For this perfect friendship I speak of is indivisible: each one gives himself so wholly to his friend that he has nothing left to distribute elsewhere; on the contrary, he is sorry that he is not double, triple, or quadruple, and that he has not several souls and several wills, to confer them all on this one subject. Common friendships can be divided up: one may love in one man his beauty, in another his easygoing ways, in another liberality, in one paternal love, in another brotherly love, and so forth; but this friendship that possesses the soul and rules it with absolute sovereignty cannot possibly be double. ^CIf two called for help at the same time, which one would you run to? If they demanded conflicting services of you, how would you arrange it? If one confided to your silence a thing that would be useful for the other to know, how would you extricate yourself? A single dominant friendship dissolves all other obligations. The secret I have sworn to reveal to no other man, I can impart without perjury to the one who is not another man: he is myself. It is a great enough miracle to be doubled, and those who talk of tripling themselves do not realize the loftiness of the thing: nothing is extreme that can be matched. And he who supposes that of two men I love one just as much as the other, and that they love each other and me just as much as I love them, multiplies into a fraternity the most singular and unified of all things, of which even a single one is the rarest thing in the world to find.

^AThe rest of this story fits in very well with what I was saying, for Eudamidas bestows upon his friends the kindness and favor of using them for his need. He leaves them heirs to this liberality of his, which consists of putting into their hands a chance to do him good. And without doubt the strength of friendship is shown much more richly in his action than in that of Aretheus.

In short, these are actions inconceivable to anyone who has not tasted friendship, ^Cand which make me honor wonderfully the answer of that young soldier to Cyrus, who asked him for how much he would sell a horse with which he had just won the prize in a race, and whether he would exchange him for a kingdom: "No indeed, Sire, but I would most willingly let him go to gain a friend, if I found a man worthy of such an alliance." That was not badly spoken, "if I found one"; for it is easy to find men fit for a superficial acquaintance. But for this kind, in which we act from the very bottom of our hearts, which holds nothing back, truly it is necessary that all the springs of action be perfectly clean and true.

In the relationships which bind us only by one small part, we need look out only for the imperfections that particularly concern that part. The religion of my doctor or my lawyer cannot matter. That consideration has nothing in common with the functions of the friendship they owe me. And in the domestic relationship between me and those who serve me, I have the same attitude. I scarcely inquire of a lackey whether he is chaste; I try to find out whether he is diligent. And I am not as much afraid of a gambling mule driver as of a weak one, or of a profane cook as of an ignorant one. I do not make it my business to tell the world what it should do—enough others do that—but what I do in it.

That is my practice: do as you see fit.

—TERENCE

For the familiarity of the table I look for wit, not prudence; for the bed, beauty before goodness; in conversation, competence, even without uprightness. Likewise in other matters.

^AJust as the man who was found astride a stick, playing with his   25
children, asked the man who surprised him thus to say nothing about it until he was a father himself, in the belief that the passion which would then be born in his soul would make him an equitable judge of such an act, so I should like to talk to people who have experienced what I tell. But knowing how far from common usage and how rare such a friendship is, I do not expect to find any good judge of it. For the very discourses that antiquity has left us on this subject seem to me weak compared with the feeling I have. And in this particular the facts surpass even the precepts of philosophy:

> Nothing shall I, while sane, compare with a dear friend.
>
> —HORACE

The ancient Menander declared that man happy who had been able to meet even the shadow of a friend. He was certainly right to say so, especially if he spoke from experience. For in truth, if I compare all the rest of my life—though by the grace of God I have spent it pleasantly, comfortably, and, except for the loss of such a friend, free from any grievous affliction, and full of tranquility of mind, having accepted my natural and original advantages without seeking other ones—if I compare it all, I say, with the four years which were granted me to enjoy the sweet company and society of that man, it is nothing but smoke, nothing but dark and dreary night. Since the day I lost him,

> Which I shall ever recall with pain,
> Ever with reverence—thus, Gods, did you ordain—
>
> —VIRGIL

I only drag on a weary life. And the very pleasures that come my way, instead of consoling me, redouble my grief for his loss. We went halves in everything; it seems to me that I am robbing him of his share,

> Nor may I rightly taste of pleasures here alone,
> —So I resolved—when he who shared my life is gone.
>
> —TERENCE

I was already so formed and accustomed to being a second self everywhere that only half of me seems to be alive now.

> ^BSince an untimely blow has snatched away
> Part of my soul, when then do I delay,
> I the remaining part, less dear than he,
> And not entire surviving? The same day
> Brought ruin equally to him and me.
>
> —HORACE

^AThere is no action or thought in which I do not miss him, as indeed he would have missed me. For just as he surpassed me infinitely in every other ability and virtue, so he did in the duty of friendship.

> Why should I be ashamed or exercise control
> Mourning so dear a soul?
>
> —HORACE

> Brother, your death has left me sad and lone;
> Since you departed all our joys have gone,
> Which while you lived your sweet affection fed;
> My pleasures all lie shattered, with you dead.
> Our soul is buried, mine with yours entwined;
> And since then I have banished from my mind
> My studies, and my spirit's dearest joys.
> Shall I ne'er speak to you, or hear your voice?
> Or see your face, more dear than life to me?
> At least I'll love you to eternity.
>
> —CATULLUS

But let us listen a while to this boy of sixteen.

Because I have found that this work has since been brought to light, and with evil intent, by those who seek to disturb and change the state of our government without worrying whether they will improve it, and because they have mixed his work up with some of their own concoctions, I have changed my mind about putting it in here. And so that the memory of the author may not be damaged in the eyes of those who could not know his opinions and actions at close hand, I beg to advise them that this subject was treated by him in his boyhood, only by way of an exercise, as a common theme hashed over in a thousand places in books. I have no doubt that he believed what he wrote, for he was so conscientious as not to lie even in jest. And I know further that if he had had the choice, he would rather have been born in Venice than in Sarlat, and with reason. But he had another maxim sovereignly imprinted in his soul, to obey and submit most religiously to the laws under which he was born. There never was a better citizen, or one more devoted to the tranquility of his country, or more hostile to the commotions and innovations of his time. He would much rather have used his ability to suppress them than to give them material that would excite them further. His mind was molded in the pattern of other ages than this.

Now, in exchange for this serious work, I shall substitute another, 30 produced in that same season of his life, gayer and more lusty.

Questions for Understanding

1. Does Montaigne believe that if one seeks a great friendship one will ultimately find it?

2. According to Montaigne, what factors inhibit friendship between fathers and sons?

3. According to Montaigne, what factors inhibit friendship between men and women?

4. Once Montaigne and Etienne de la Boétie met, how long did it take for the relationship to deepen?

5. Montaigne says about Etienne de La Boétie, "It is not in the power of all the arguments in the world to dislodge me from the certainty I have of the intentions and judgments of my friend." Does Montaigne intend this statement to be taken completely literally?

Suggestions for Writing

1. Montaigne writes: "All associations that are forged and nourished by pleasure or profit, by public or private needs, are the less beautiful and noble, and the less friendships, in so far as they mix into friendship another cause and object and reward than friendship itself." Have you had a friendship that would lead you to disagree with Montaigne? What role did pleasure or profit or public or private needs play in the friendship? Did the friendship itself reduce the other factors to a point where they became inconsequential? Write an essay in which you demonstrate that the factors Montaigne mentions need not retard a friendship.

2. Montaigne says that "admonitions and corrections . . . are one of the chief duties of friendship." Do you agree? Have they been an important component of a friendship in which you have been involved? Write an essay in which you discuss the role of admonitions and corrections in a friendship you have had.

3. According to Montaigne, no friendship between a man and a woman can compare with true friendship between two men. Have you been involved in a "mixed friendship" that you think disproves Montaigne on this point? After reviewing the reasons Montaigne gives for his attitude toward mixed friendships, write an essay in which you demonstrate that a mixed friendship can be a true friendship.

4. For a brief, summary definition of friendship, Montaigne quotes Cicero: "Only those are to be judged friendships in which the characters have been strengthened and matured by age." Have you observed a relationship in which that has occurred? That is, have you observed a relationship that has made both participants better people? Write an essay in which you describe the participants before and after the relationship, and discuss the causes of their improvement.

5. Montaigne says about himself and his friend Etienne de La Boétie, "We sought each other before we met because of the reports we heard of each other. . . ." Have you ever done something similar? Were your experiences with the other person what the reports had led you to believe they would be? Were the reports wrong? Write an essay in which you discuss the extent to which you can believe what you hear about someone before you have met the person.

Acknowledgments

PHOTO CREDITS

TEXT CREDITS

Index of Authors and Titles